This book, a gift from an anonymous donor, honors your outstanding service to our Jewish communities as a Co-Chair of the Commission for Social Responsibility.

Robin Robbins

2017-2019

Carry the Light

Jewish Meaning in a World of Choice

David Ellenson. Courtesty Hebrew Union College–
Jewish Institute of Religion

UNIVERSITY OF NEBRASKA PRESS | LINCOLN

JPS דור דור
SCHOLAR ודורשיו
OF DISTINCTION
SERIES

Jewish Meaning in a World of Choice

Studies in Tradition and Modernity

David Ellenson

THE JEWISH PUBLICATION SOCIETY | PHILADELPHIA

© 2014 by David Ellenson
Acknowledgments for the use of copyrighted material appear on pages 333–35, which constitute an
extension of the copyright page.

Library of Congress Cataloging-in-Publication Data
Ellenson, David Harry, 1947–, author.
Jewish meaning in a world of choice: studies in
tradition and modernity / David Ellenson.
pages   cm.
—(JPS scholar of distinction series)
Includes bibliographical references.
ISBN 978-0-8276-1214-3 (cloth: alk. paper)
ISBN 978-0-8276-1183-2 (epub)
ISBN 978-0-8276-1184-9 (mobi)
ISBN 978-0-8276-1182-5 (pdf).
1. Judaism—United States—21st century.
2. Reform Judaism. 3. Orthodox Judaism—
Relations—Nontraditional Jews.
I. Title.

BM205.E58 2014
296.3'80973—dc23
2014019694

Set in Minion Pro by L. Auten.
Designed by A. Shahan.

The Jewish Publication Society
expresses its gratitude for the generosity
of the sponsors of this book:

In honor and memory of our parents

JOYCE AND IRVING GOLDMAN

and

RUTH AND LOUIS ISRAELOW

May their love of Judaism and learning
that inspired us to sponsor this publication
by our beloved teacher and friend

DAVID ELLENSON

be continued by our children and future
generations of our family.

Dorian Goldman and Marvin Israelow

To my teachers and my students
In the words of *Kaddish D'rabbanan*,
May God bestow blessing upon you

Contents

Preface

In 1973, when I sat in "Introduction to Modern Jewish Thought" at HUC-JIR as a second-year rabbinical student, I heard my teacher and rabbi Eugene Borowitz observe that the central problem of modern Jewish thought is that of articulating how to be simultaneously Jewish and modern in a western world of seemingly endless possibilities. His unadorned and direct statement of the problem struck me as clear and profound. In that moment, he gave me an intellectual-theological framework for analyzing the "intellectual arrangements" different Jewish thinkers and movements have advanced over the past two hundred years in their attempts to affirm Jewish meaning in a world where being Jewish is no longer required. My entire scholarly and intellectual project has been informed by my attempts to understand how different Jewish individuals and groups have responded to this challenge. All the essays in this volume center on a description and examination of the multivalent push and pull between Jewish tradition and Western culture.

A number of the essays I have chosen for inclusion in this volume are strictly *wissenschaftlich*, i.e., academic. In these articles, I strive to examine and embed the materials I explore within scholarly frameworks as dispassionately and as neutrally as humanly possible. Other essays employ historical and textual data and place that data within sociological or philosophical-theological frameworks that allow for partisan positions to emerge. These essays argue unashamedly for and celebrate an inclusive Jewish community that affirms gender equality, a lenient approach to conversion, the embrace of GLBTQ persons as equals, and a strong Israel that is faithful to the democratic and Jewish values that informed the founders of the Jewish state. As these partisan essays surely demonstrate, my interests and commitments have directed the objects and topics of my scholarly efforts. By presenting representative essays from my first years as a professor in the late 1970s through more recent articles I have written during these last years when I have served as president of HUC-JIR, I have striven to demonstrate the consistency of my intellectual-religious interests throughout my lifetime as well as the dialectical interplay between both sides of my being—the dispassionate academic as well as the committed Jew.

The forces that have animated my work cannot be understood without recourse to my family and my past as a Jewish boy growing up in the South during the 1950s and 1960s and the multilayered world I experienced. Everything in my world talked about difference and exclusion. My grandparents all emigrated from eastern Europe to the United States in the early 1900s. My maternal grandparents settled in Cambridge, Massachusetts, while my paternal grandparents improbably came to Newport News, Virginia. My parents, Rosalind Stern and Samuel Ellenson, met at Harvard Hillel in 1945, immediately after World War II, and they married in 1946. A year later, I was born, and six months after my birth, my father, a degree from Harvard Law School in hand, returned with my mother and me to Newport News, where he began to practice law.

Newport News and its sister city of Hampton were then small southern towns that were overwhelmingly Protestant. The politics of race was a central issue in the Virginia of my boyhood, and there was strict segregation in the schools and in all public facilities, along with ubiquitous signs separating "white" from "colored" people in all these venues. While the landmark 1954 *Brown v. Topeka* decision in which the U.S. Supreme Court reversed *Plessey v. Ferguson* (1896) and held that the doctrine of "separate, but equal" was unconstitutional, Virginia senator Harry Flood Byrd of Winchester—the dominant political voice in Virginia during those years—nevertheless formulated a policy of "massive resistance" to integration that guided the political direction of the commonwealth during those years.

Of course, there was resistance to Byrd as well. I still have strong remembrances of students from Hampton Institute (now Hampton University) engaging in nonviolent protests and marches to desegregate public restaurants, even as a former governor of Virginia, in a particularly obscene comment, stated that "integration was akin to mixing vanilla ice cream with coal dust. It ruined the ice cream and rendered the coal dust useless." I still cringe as I recall his words, and I remember shamefully that at one point during this period Prince Edward County in Virginia closed all its public schools rather than allow integration. It may have been the one place in the English-speaking world that had, for a short time, the disgraceful distinction of having no public school system.

At the same time, I have a vivid memory of how my parents felt about all this and the attitudes they conveyed to me as a young boy over supper at the dining room table, where events of the day were discussed. They were enthusiastic supporters of Governor Lindsay Almond of Roanoke, who, after his election in 1958, abandoned the policy of "massive resistance" that his political mentor, Senator Byrd, had promulgated. Instead, Almond stated that Virginia would obey the law of the land as dictated by the Supreme Court. Regarded as a "traitor" by his own class, Almond was a hero in my home, and he remains for me a shining model of political and moral courage. When I wrote about this in an earlier writing, my friend Professor Stephen Whitfield of Brandeis sent me an enlarged copy of a *Time* magazine cover graced by a picture of Governor Almond. It remains at the center of my office today.

During this period of my boyhood, my father took me to a segregationist rally being held in the southern countryside of Virginia. He was uncharacteristically silent as we drove to the rally. He said only that he wanted me to see firsthand and up close how "evil" appeared. My father made no other comment, either at the rally or as we drove home. However, he surely succeeded in his aim. More than half a century later, the memory of that ugly event remains at the very core of my being.

As I relate this story and describe this period, I would not want to convey the impression that my parents were outspoken political activists or that our existence as Jews was anything but comfortable on every visible level. To this day, I cannot fully capture how very much I love the South and the Peninsula. The approximately 2,000 Jews located on the Peninsula lived peacefully and prosperously among more than 150,000 gentiles. My father and one uncle enjoyed successful law practices. Another uncle had a roofing business while yet another was director of public works for the city. My entire extended family lived in the same pleasant neighborhood, and my childhood and adolescence were filled with family gatherings and events at which aunts, uncles, and cousins were present. Every Saturday night I would spend the night with my grandmother.

In 1962 I served as a page in the Virginia State Senate, and two years later in 1964 I was a page to the Virginia Delegation at the Democratic National Convention in Atlantic City. At Newport News High School I was elected president of the student body—I believe I was the first Jew ever to attain that position. I enrolled the next year at the College of William and Mary. In so doing, I followed my father, my uncle, and several cousins and preceded my younger brother. I assumed during that period that I would become an attorney, practice law with my father and uncle, and enter Virginia politics. I was and remain at some very deep level of my being a Virginian.

However, I was also a Jew, and that was "the rub." I never felt I fully belonged. My being a Jew in a Christian world made me an outsider and different from the time I was a small boy, an observer, even as I was an eager participant in the larger world. It left me feeling alienated, even as I was overwhelmingly social and active.

There was an extremely strong Jewish religious and communal life there, and this ingrained a strong feeling of Jewish identity—*yiddishkeit*—in me. My family belonged to the Orthodox *shul* that had a *mehitza* (ritual barrier separating men from women in prayer), and I loved learning Hebrew and the skills to lead every variety of Orthodox services. My father served as president of our synagogue, and my mother was extremely active in our Jewish Federation and Hadassah, as well as the National Council of Jewish Women. The celebration and observance of the Sabbath and Jewish holidays were at the very center of our family life, and nothing was impressed upon me more by both my parents than the miracle and importance of the State of Israel and a love for and responsibility to the entire Jewish people.

The influence of my mother was more pronounced than that of anyone. She was a wonderful Hebraist, and I still have a *siddur* (prayer book) she was awarded as a child, with the inscription in *maskilic* Hebrew, "*Nitnah l'tovah stern, peras rishon l'hitstayenutah bi-sefat ʻever*—Given to Tovah Stern, first prize for her distinction in Hebrew." My mother had attended Hebrew College in Boston, read Hebrew texts with me in an Ashkenazic accent, and regaled me with story after story of her cousin who had fought with the Haganah to secure the independence of the Jewish state. She would remind me that eight days after I was born (November 21, 1947), the United Nations voted to partition Palestine, and she would describe how the streets in her neighborhood in Cambridge erupted with joy when Israeli independence was declared in May 1948. When I was a teenager, she was appointed as director of social services for the city of Hampton,

Virginia. At her interview, she was asked how, as the wife of "a prominent attorney," she possibly could head an agency when a majority of its clients were of a different race and a different socioeconomic class. She replied, "You must not be aware. I am a Jew, and we are told every day to remember that we were slaves to Pharaoh in Egypt. We are commanded to remember the heart of the stranger, because we were strangers in the land of Egypt." My mother inculcated a love for Israel, a commitment to Jewish values, and a concern for the welfare of the less fortunate in the deepest recesses of my heart. She was completely committed to *Kelal Yisra-el*, and when one of my rabbis wanted me to be active only in the Orthodox National Conference of Synagogue Youth (NCSY), she protested strongly and insisted that I also be engaged in AZA (B'nai B'rith Youth), which brought together teenagers from across the denominational spectrum in our small Jewish community. I was also keenly aware that while my younger brother and I were assigned central roles in the liturgical rites of our synagogue, such roles were completely denied to my mother (who was not bothered by this) and my sister (who was hurt profoundly by this exclusion).

In sum, the fabric of my identity was fraught with tensions. The inequities and evils I witnessed as a child and as a teenager in matters of race and gender and the sense of being an outsider as a Jew to the gentile culture in which I was raised all left a permanent mark on me.

It was at William and Mary that I began to acquire the tools I would need to direct my life and answer the questions that lay in my heart. I was fortunate in my junior year to enroll in a course that Professor Ed Crapol taught on "The History of American Foreign Policy." At that point, I was an indifferent student. However, Professor Crapol, newly arrived from his graduate work at the University of Wisconsin under the direction of William Appleman Williams, changed all that. His lectures were filled with content, and he delivered them with excitement and passion. I still recall with the joy that is always associated with great learning and discovery how he applied the "frontier thesis" of Frederick Jackson Turner as a framework for understanding the course of American foreign policy from its origins during the early Federalist period up to the modern day. Ed Crapol modeled the relevance and excitement and the moral dimensions of what an academic life could and ought to be, and I would not have entered the Academy if it were not for him.

The other teacher I recall is Professor James Livingston. He came to William and Mary during my senior year to inaugurate the Department of Religion. It was he who taught me the works of Soren Kierkegaard, Martin Buber, Paul Tillich, and others. It was he who pointed out to me how many of the persons who were the great moral voices of that day—Abraham Joshua Heschel, Reinhold Niebuhr, Martin Luther King—possessed religious educations and commitments. Like Dr. Crapol, Professor Livingston displayed a complete mastery over the materials he presented in a soft yet comparably passionate way. He made me convinced that there was no field in the world I would rather pursue than that of religious studies. In his class, while reading *The Shaking of the Foundations* by Paul Tillich, I came across the following paragraph:

> The name of this infinite and inexhaustible depth and ground of all being is *God*. That depth is what God means. And if that word has not much meaning for you, translate it, and speak of the depths of your life, of the source of your being, of your ultimate concern, of what you take seriously without any reservation.

These words addressed my soul. Beset by conflicts over my identity as an Orthodox Jewish boy raised in Tidewater Virginia, Tillich prodded me to recognize who I was in the depths of my being. He awakened a nascent recognition in me that I was above all a Jew. While I was surely uncertain about the nature of my faith in God, I had no doubt that it was Judaism— its texts and traditions—and the Jewish people that constituted the core of who I was as a person, my "ultimate concerns" that I took "seriously without any reservation." Tillich's words began in earnest my lifetime quest to articulate why that was so and the pursuit of explaining why my religious and cultural traditions as a Jew were so significant to me in a world where Jewish meaning could not be taken for granted and where myriad choices and options challenged my commitments and identity as Jew.

I enrolled soon thereafter in the Religious Studies Department of the University of Virginia, where I received an MA degree under the tutelage of Alan Lettofsky. A rabbinic graduate of the Jewish Theological Seminary who went on to work for his doctorate at Yale University, Alan was the consummate pedagogue and mentor. He guided my nascent interests in Jewish studies with rigor and compassion. He was both demanding and understanding. It remains one of the signal blessings of my life that I had such a teacher at this point in my career, and I will always be grateful for the nurture and direction he provided. He advised me to enroll in a seminar on "The Sociology of Religion" taught by David Little. There, for the first time, I read the works of Durkheim and Weber, where I was provided the beginnings of a vocabulary that would allow me to frame and illuminate my concerns. It was also equally clear to me that I had so much more to learn if I was to explore seriously the nature of what it was to be a Jew in the modern world.

This led me to move to Israel for two years. The first year I lived on Kibbutz Mishmar Haemek in the Jezreel Valley—where I worked in the fields and advanced my spoken Hebrew. The second year I enrolled in the rabbinical program at Hebrew Union College in Jerusalem. While I seriously considered remaining in Israel and making *aliyah* at the end of that year, I decided to return to the United States, where for the next four years I would pursue rabbinical ordination at HUC-JIR in New York and doctoral studies in religion at Columbia University. I loved the College-Institute and was particularly influenced by Lawrence Hoffman. I immediately recognized him as a kindred spirit, and I marveled at his ability to use sociological and philosophical paradigms to illuminate Jewish texts and derive Jewish meanings and understandings. He genuinely inspired me. At the same time, I had the pleasure of studying Jewish intellectual history with Arthur Hertzberg and sociology of religion with Gillian Lindt and Joseph Blau at Columbia.

The precise character of my work was shaped by two men. Toward the end of my formal graduate education in 1976 and 1977, I came under the tutelage of Fritz Bamberger of HUC-JIR, and also Jacob Katz of Hebrew University, who was then at Columbia as a visiting professor. Dr. Bamberger was a German refugee scholar who was the embodiment of *Bildung*. Cultured and erudite, he possessed an unsurpassed knowledge of modern Jewish intellectual history. I flourished in my relationship with him as I wrote my rabbinical thesis on Esriel Hildesheimer under his guidance. He commented to me that my treatment of Hildesheimer derived from an overarching intellectual perspective of tension. He identified this perspective as quintessentially "American." I had described Hildesheimer as possessing a "hyphenated identity" in which the German and Jewish elements of his identity did not fit together perfectly. Dr. Bamberger maintained that I was not necessarily incorrect in my portrait of Rabbi Hildesheimer. However, he also assured me that Hildeseimer would not have viewed himself as I viewed him. That is, Dr. Bamberger—despite the dislocation he himself experienced as a German Jew during the 1930s—was convinced that a nineteenth-century acculturated Jew like Hildesheimer was the product of a German Jewish symbiosis that would have caused him to experience his life as a seamless whole. He told me that it took an American Jew like me, who had read Mordecai Kaplan, to understand Hildesheimer's life as I had. To this day, I still have my doubts about what Dr. Bamberger said. Nevertheless, his comments did make me aware that the hermeneutic of tension I have employed in all my work is embedded in a narrative that emerged from my own childhood experiences as a Jewish boy in Virginia.

My decision to employ this hermeneutic to illuminate the course of the modern Jewish experience in the West was reinforced by my study at the same time with Jacob Katz, who was surely the preeminent historian-sociologist of modern Judaism. Professor Katz provided me with the content and, even more important, the methodology that would guide and inform my work for decades to come. In his seminar on "Judaism in the Nineteenth Century," Professor Katz pointed out that Germany was the crucible in which modern Judaism was born. It was here that the conflict between an inherited Jewish tradition and a highly acculturated Jewish community first played itself out. Katz himself explored the diverse ways Jews emerged from the ghetto from the 1770s on. He contended that what was noteworthy was not that countless Jews ultimately assimilated in light of an open society in which Jews were culturally, politically, and ultimately socially and economically integrated. Rather, what he viewed as remarkable was that Judaism did not atrophy and die in the wake of these changes. Instead, Jews reconfigured their identity and observance in different ways, and the study of how they did this—the intellectual arrangements and observance patterns they created—was to become the subject of my own work. Indeed, it is a primary reason that I wrote my dissertation on Rabbi Hildesheimer, an Orthodox Jew completely committed to Jewish tradition who received a doctorate from a German university and who was completely comfortable in Western culture. A study of his life would indicate precisely how Jewish religious tradition could be and was adapted to the demands of the time and place in which he lived. In so doing, I could hold up a mirror to my own being and provide a case study of how Judaism could be adapted to the modern world.

Professor Katz also provided me with the insight that German Judaism was of special significance for an understanding of modern Judaism. Jews in Germany did not simply acculturate into the mores of the larger society as Jews in France or England had. By an appeal to a history of prior evolution and change, these German Jews provided an ideological platform that could be exported to other Jewish communities. They provided a rationale for religious reform and the emergence of Jewish religious movements that could challenge the hegemony of rabbinic Judaism and its notion of an unchanging and eternal Jewish law. Professor Katz hammered this point home in his seminar and provided countless examples drawn from his vast knowledge of Talmud and Jewish law, Western languages, Jewish and European history, and sociology to demonstrate his position. The transition of German Judaism from the medieval to the modern world grips my attention to this day.

However, it was his seminar on "The Uses of Halakha in the Writing of Jewish History" that had the greatest impact on the direction of my work. Professor Katz dissected the halakhic writings of great eighteenth- and nineteenth-century rabbinic decisors and taught us how this approach could be employed in the writing of history. It was an aesthetic delight to see this man—educated as a youth in Hungarian *yeshivot* and later trained as a sociologist at the University of Frankfurt—at work in this way, a genius at work in his laboratory. Dr. Katz said over and over again that we could assume that all the men whose work we investigated knew the Talmudic and rabbinic sources we read as well as we did! Thus if we found a "mistake" or "misreading" by one of these rabbis, Professor Katz said we should pay a great deal of attention to it because something of significance was undoubtedly happening. In order to uncover the reason for the "misreading," it was crucial to have a knowledge of history and sociology—the personal biography as well as the context in which the decisor lived—to successfully dig out nuggets of meaning from the texts we were mining. In addition, Professor Katz stated that what was important about a Talmudic precedent for a ruling was not that something was cited, but rather why the writer chose a particular precedent and not another to justify his ruling. After all, he observed, almost always there was a precedent cited. The historical significance of this choice could only be determined in light of economic, social, biographical, or political factors. Finally, Professor Katz pointed out to us that in looking at this legal material and attempting to define its historical import and meaning, the "ideal type" methodology of Max Weber could be invaluable. In this methodology, an analytical construct not found "empirically anywhere in reality" was employed to isolate elements of social reality to explain their significance and importance. Professor Katz himself used this method in his famed *Exclusiveness and Tolerance* as well as *Tradition and Crisis*. In both works, he was able to illuminate the transition of European Judaism and its culture and institutions from the relatively closed world of the Middle Ages to the much more expansive horizons of the modern period. He urged us to employ this model in our own work.

I am proud to say that in all these ways my own work follows in the path of Professor Katz. My life, my interests, and my education prior to my coming to Columbia prepared me for the lessons he taught. In the years subsequent to Columbia, my decision to center so many of my investigations on responsa literature and modern Jewish prayer books—with their diachronic elements that draw on the past and their synchronic elements that testify to contemporaneous influences—reflects the impress of his influence and method. My decision to employ his model to study rabbinic responsa and prayer book compositions in western Europe, North America, and my beloved Israel reflects my deepest personal commitments to Judaism and the State of Israel as well as scholarship as means to illuminate an understanding of life for myself, my Jewish community, and others in the larger world. In this sense, I hope my own work is at least a pale reflection of his immense shadow and influence.

The protagonist of South African author J. M. Coetzee's novel *Elizabeth Costello* states, after receiving an award for her literary work:

We all know, if we are being realistic, that it is only a matter of time before the books which you honour, and with whose genesis I have had something to do, will cease to be read and eventually cease to be remembered. And properly so. There must be some limit to the burden of remembering that we impose on our children and grandchildren. They have a world of their own, of which we should be less and less part.

As a Jew, I cannot agree with the fictional Costello. I cannot forget the books of my Jewish past, nor do I want to. Instead, I hope that my children and my students and their descendants will know of God and be students of Torah. This book is one attempt—my attempt—to place myself, as a Jew born in America and connected deeply both to Israel and the larger world that shaped me in late twentieth-century America, in that chain.

Rabbi Leo Baeck provides me with a language for that aspiration. The last duly elected leader of the Jewish community in Germany during the dark years of the Holocaust, Rabbi Baeck saved the life of my teacher Fritz Bamberger by securing a teaching position for him in Chicago. I feel connected to him in the deepest recesses of my soul. In his *This People Israel*, first published in 1948, three years after his release from Thereisenstadt, where three of his own sisters perished, Rabbi Baeck wrote:

> Every generation by choosing its way, its present way, at the same time chooses an essential part of the future, the way of its children. Perhaps the children will turn from the eternal way, but in this, too, they will be determined by the direction of their parents. The responsibility to those who follow after us is included in the responsibility to ourselves. The way of the children, whether accepting or rejecting the direction, emanates from our way. Ways bind, wind, and wander. When a man forms his life, he begins to create community. He is not only born into community as if by fate, but he has now been called to the task of molding it.

My own Jewish way has wandered. Surely the ways of my own children and grandchildren and also my students will wander as well. Nevertheless, they and I are also bound, and my way, just as theirs, emanates from those who lived before us. I have tried—through my researches and through my work as a teacher and as president of the College-Institute—to honor the way I have inherited even as I have struggled to mold a direction for a way that reflects who I am. This volume gives expression to that vision and to the Jewish enterprise that has animated my life.

New York City
July 30, 2013
23 Av 5773

Acknowledgments

I am honored to have this book included in the prestigious Scholars of Distinction series. Some of the leading teachers and scholars of our era have been included in this series, and all were my teachers—either in person or through their writings. I am humbled to now be among this pantheon, and I am grateful to the Jewish Publication Society and the University of Nebraska Press for the decision to include a collection of my work in this series. I would also like to express my gratitude to Ann Baker of the University of Nebraska Press and Elaine Otto, whose diligent and careful efforts helped assure the quality of this book.

I am very grateful to Rabbi Barry Schwartz and Carol Hupping. They were enthusiastic supporters of this project from the outset, and it has been the greatest pleasure to work with them in the preparation of this volume. I would also thank Hila Ratzabi. Her editing skill and close attention to detail in preparing these articles were outstanding. I am appreciative of all her efforts.

My deepest gratitude goes to Nicole Vandestienne. She serves as my assistant, and her care and support for this book and for me has gone far beyond the call of duty. It is a source of great pleasure to work with her.

My appreciation also goes to Elisheva Urbas, who has helped me with many of my books and writings—and she did so again with this volume. She is a friend as well as a consummate editor. Elisheva played a crucial role in guiding my selection of the essays included in this book, as well as with its organizational structure and the preface. I am fortunate to have such a talented, skilled, brilliant, and gracious friend.

Finally, I cannot express fully the gratitude I feel for Dorian Goldman and Marvin Israelow. In the daily prayers of the Jewish people, God is thanked for Divine goodness in daily renewing the work of creation. One of the great miracles of life is that it is always possible to develop deep and close relationships, and this has been true of the friendship that has developed between Dorian and Marvin and my wife, Jackie, and me over the last decade. We count them as the closest of friends. I am grateful that the *Shechinah* is so often present when we are together. Their generous subvention has made the publication of this book possible. For this—and for their love and care—I thank them.

ONE

Shaping Jewish Life in an Open Society

1

A Response by Modern Orthodoxy to Jewish Religious Pluralism

The Case of Esriel Hildesheimer

The Jewish community of Western and Central Europe experienced profound economic, social, and political transformations during the latter part of the eighteenth century and throughout the nineteenth. Prior to this era, the Jewish community in Europe had largely adhered to the cultural values and norms of rabbinic teachings.[1] As the structure of medieval Judaism began to collapse in the late eighteenth century, new Jewish responses to the changed character of the modern world emerged. Indeed, the birth of Reform, Conservative, Zionist, and modern Orthodox movements throughout the nineteenth century testify to the birth of a Jewish pluralism. For the Reform and Conservative movements, the advent of religious pluralism within Judaism posed no real problem. As Charles Liebman has succinctly stated: "While Conservative and Reform see themselves as legitimate heirs to the Jewish tradition, neither claims to be its exclusive bearer." On the other hand, Liebman observes: "Orthodoxy perceives itself as the only legitimate bearer of the Jewish tradition." Consequently, it is fair to say: "Since neither the Reform, nor the Conservative lays claim to exclusive doctrinal 'truth,' they are free to cooperate with one another, with Orthodoxy, and even with secular Jewish groups. . . . The doctrines of Orthodoxy, on the other hand, . . . are by definition beyond compromise or even the appearance of compromise."[2]

What type of relationship Orthodox Jewry will maintain with heterodox Jewish groups has been the subject of discussion since the rise of Haskalah and Reform until the present.[3] There is a broad spectrum of opinion ranging from cooperation to no cooperation with non-Orthodox Jewry. This paper will concern itself with one particular response to this problem: the attitude of Rabbi Esriel Hildesheimer (1820–99) of Germany, the founder of the Berlin Rabbinerseminar in 1873 and one of the great leaders of Orthodox Jewry in Germany during the last century. Hildesheimer's stance concerning the relationship between Orthodox and non-Orthodox religious institutions, as well as his position with respect to Orthodox involvement in non-Orthodox charitable and civic organizations, will be analyzed. In addition, Hildesheimer's position will be contrasted with Samson Raphael Hirsch's views.

I.

Esriel Hildesheimer was born in Halberstadt, Germany, in 1820, the son of a distinguished rabbinical family. As a boy, he attended Hasharat Tsvi, in Halberstadt, the first Orthodox Jewish school in Germany to include a program of secular studies in its curriculum.[4] At the age of seventeen, he enrolled in the yeshiva of Jacob Ettlinger (1798–1871) of Altona and while there was permitted to attend the lectures on philosophy which Isaac Bernays, the rabbi of Hamburg, delivered on Saturday afternoons.[5] Both Ettlinger and Bernays encouraged their outstanding students, such as Hildesheimer, to engage in secular studies.[6]

Moreover, Ettlinger and Bernays fought actively against the advances of Reform. Meir Hildesheimer, Esriel's great-grandson, writes:

> Rabbi Ettlinger did not enclose himself within the four ells of Halakhah, but waged a stormy war against the Reform Movement and for this purpose founded the weekly journal, "The Faithful Guardian of Zion." The Hakham Bernays also fought aggressively against the Reformers. The example of these two . . . men taught him [Esriel Hildesheimer] that a rabbi in Israel is obligated to take an active part in improving the religious situation [of Jewry].[7]

Exposed to and made conscious of Reform during his days in Altona, Hildesheimer himself spoke of the growing dominance of Reform and of the sorrow and consternation this caused him: "The lawless who denied Torah were dominant everywhere, . . . and those who feared God cowered before these enemies and despisers of religion. . . . Such a time of distress had never been visited upon Israel previously."[8]

Following the examples set by his teachers Ettlinger and Bernays, Hildesheimer felt compelled to take up the cudgels against Reform and wage an active fight against it. At the urging of his rabbis, Hildesheimer went to Berlin in 1843. There he attended the University and majored in the study of Semitic languages two years. Transferring to the University of Halle in 1846, he received a PhD degree for a dissertation entitled, "The Correct Way to Interpret Scripture." Hildesheimer became one of the few, perhaps the only, Orthodox rabbi in Germany up to that time to receive a secular doctorate. Armed with this degree, and thus capable of elevating "the estimation of our party" in the eyes of the public,[9] Hildesheimer felt himself capable of doing battle with those groups which had deviated from normative Judaism.

Hildesheimer returned to Halberstadt in 1847 and became secretary of the community. Reform came to Halberstadt in that year, and Ludwig Philippson (1811–89), the editor of the *Allgemeine Zeitung des Judentums*, began to campaign on its behalf in the pages of his journal. When Philippson convened a meeting of all the Jewish communities in Saxony on October 22, 1847, in the town of Magdeburg, for the purpose of adopting a reformed prayer book, Hildesheimer wrote a pamphlet entitled *The Necessity of Protest against the Actions of the Reformers* and circulated it among all the delegates who had attended the Magdeburg Conference.[10] In addition, Hildesheimer employed the Leipzig periodical *Der Orient* to defend Orthodoxy. Writing on November 20, 1847, Hildesheimer described the feelings motivating his involvement in this dispute.

> When I began to fight with Philippson and his lawless peers . . . I was very bitter that no one else seemed to be upset over the situation, that no great man stood up in order to overturn these licentious persons who disrupted the vineyard of the Lord of Hosts. . . . Finally, when I saw that no one acted, I felt that this was no time to refrain from expressing my thoughts on account of embarrassment or humility.[11]

As a result, Hildesheimer not only attacked Philippson and Reform in journal articles but when eight members of the community wished to secede from the general community in 1848 on grounds of religious conscience, Hildesheimer, in conjunction with the rabbi of the community, issued a legal responsum forbidding these Reformers to withdraw and threatening them with loss of all communal rights (e.g., burial) if they did.[12] Secession was thus prevented and the unity of the community maintained.

Hildesheimer's refusal to compromise on religious issues and his unwillingness to cooperate with non-Orthodox Jewish institutions on matters of religion is underscored by his attitude toward the Jewish Theological Seminary in Breslau, which was under the direction of Zacherias Frankel, the "father" of "positive-historical" Judaism. When the community of Trier asked Hildesheimer whether it would be permissible to select a Breslau graduate as rabbi of the community, Hildesheimer replied negatively, stating that if a Breslau graduate were selected, then observant Jews should secede from the community. Moreover, Hildesheimer held that religious unity between traditional graduates of the Breslau Seminary and the graduates of his own school was impossible because the Breslau Seminary was not totally committed "to the words of the Sages and their customs."[13] Indeed, one of the major reasons why Hildesheimer established a rabbinical school was so "the Children of Israel in Germany will no longer need to request rabbis from the Seminary in Breslau."[14]

Inasmuch as Hildesheimer believed that the fundamental assumption of Judaism was that "the Oral Law was given us from the mouth of the Almighty without any intermediary," he could not refrain from condemning Frankel for his work on the development of the Oral Law. While Hildesheimer respected Frankel's learning, he branded his religious views as heretical and considered his seminary an unfit place to train for the rabbinate. Moreover, Hildesheimer's hatred of the religious views of Heinrich Graetz, the famed nineteenth-century Jewish historian and faculty member at the Breslau Seminary, meant that Hildesheimer could "never give his approval" to the Breslau Seminary and could never cooperate with it concerning religious matters.[15] Graetz earned Hildesheimer's enmity because he claimed that Isaiah 52 was written by a second Isaiah who lived during the time of Ezra. Moreover, Graetz stated that the "servant of the Lord" passages referred not to a personal messiah who would arise from the House of David but to the people Israel. Hildesheimer responded by writing an article that set forth as a basic belief of the Jewish faith the coming of a personal messiah as referred to in that Isaiah passage. To deny this belief, Hildesheimer stated, was akin to denying God's revelation at Sinai.[16]

Given his religious beliefs, it was no surprise that Hildesheimer commented negatively on the propriety of Graetz's teaching in a rabbinical seminary:

Graetz teaches one class there [the Breslau Seminary] in Talmud. What a mockery under the guise of being Judaism. It is an unprecedented disgrace. Anyone who witnesses this needs to overcome a feeling of genuine grief. One sees innocent children being led there to the slaughter, one after another, and they are reduced to a lower level than that of common sinners in Israel. They are made into hypocrites, Jesuits, and heretics just like Graetz, who, as I know from a reliable source, waves the *lulav* in his hands on *Sukkot* as if he were a Hasidic rebbe.

It is therefore not surprising that Hildesheimer upbraided a classmate from his Berlin schooldays for teaching at Breslau, for he boasted: "For a long time I have had the merit of dissuading youth from going to Breslau to study, for they can only be transformed there into hypocrites and worse."[17]

Finally, to the *Hochschule für die Wissenschaft des Judentums*, the Reform rabbinical seminary established by Abraham Geiger in 1872, Hildesheimer applied the words, "Raze it, raze it to its very foundation."[18] Hildesheimer's fierce opposition to the notion of religious pluralism in modern Judaism is reflected in his condemnation of both the moderate and extreme reformers. Hildesheimer wrote: "How little is the difference between these reformers [the Breslau people] who do their work with silk gloves on their hands and the Reformer Geiger who strikes with a sledgehammer."[19] Though Hildesheimer recognized distinctions between Frankel and Geiger, both, in Hildesheimer's judgment, practiced and taught an inauthentic Judaism, a Judaism which, because of contemporary conditions, had to be tolerated, but which could not be seen as legitimate. Moreover, even to cooperate with these other branches of Judaism on religious matters was, according to Hildesheimer, unthinkable, for to do so might lead the unsuspecting into thinking that Orthodoxy sanctioned non-Orthodox varieties of Judaism. Consequently, under Hildesheimer's direction, the Orthodox rabbis in Germany, in 1897, seceded from the General Union of Rabbis in Germany to form the Union of Torah-Faithful Rabbis.[20] And in 1883, when a group of non-Orthodox rabbis issued a circular to counteract the charge that Judaism promulgated an internal and external morality, Hildesheimer argued that Orthodox rabbis should not sign it, for to do so would have implied that non-Orthodox rabbis could legitimately speak for Judaism. Instead, Hildesheimer offered another memorandum for Orthodox rabbis to sign.[21]

Hildesheimer's opposition to religious pluralism within Judaism was clearly evidenced by his support of Samson Raphael Hirsch over the issue of Orthodox secession from the general Jewish community in the Germany of the 1870s. As the struggle between the Reform and Orthodox continued throughout nineteenth-century Germany, the discord between them escalated. The Orthodox, soon outnumbered in most large communities by followers of Geiger or Frankel, felt that their religious needs could not be achieved so long as they remained a minority within general Jewish communities. Religious pluralism, however, was not sanctioned in Germany: all Jews were required by law to pay a tax to the Jewish community regardless of their personal religious beliefs. Indeed, the Prussian Jew Law of 1847 raised each Jewish community to the "status of a public body" and required each Jew "to become a member of the community of his place of domicile."[22] The only way to escape this obligation was to convert to Christianity, an alternative unpalatable to most Jews.[23]

In 1873, however, the Prussian Parliament promulgated a bill "Concerning Secession from the State Church," which granted to every Christian the right to secede from the State Church without thereby severing connection with Christianity.[24] The passage of this law granted an excellent opportunity for modifying the Prussian Jew Law of 1847. As Salo Baron notes:

> Eduard Lasker, the Jewish leader of the then powerful National Liberal Party, suggested on March 19, 1873, that, in accordance with the general principle of equality of all citizens, the government also be asked to submit a bill on the right of secession from the Jewish community. When a conservative deputy . . . objected that the Jewish community would thereby lose a precious privilege safeguarding its unity Lasker argued that this prerogative, based upon the denial of the liberty of conscience, was a *privilegium odiosum* and that the Jewish community itself should concur in its removal. The government promised to prepare a bill in due course.[25]

Lasker's proposal provoked great controversy within the Jewish community itself. Non-Orthodox Jews and representatives of both the Hochschule and the Breslau Seminary opposed it, claiming it would lead to the destruction of the Jewish community.[26] On the other hand, political liberals and certain Orthodox Jews, notably Samson Raphael Hirsch, labored long and hard on its behalf.

Hirsch himself appears to have been the major catalyst behind Lasker's proposal. Taking advantage of the Christian Kulturkampf and the dominant general trend that favored religious freedom, Hirsch wrote a pamphlet, *The Principle of Freedom of Conscience*, arguing that compulsion could not bring a religious community into existence. Only a sense of shared religious duty could do that. Hirsch concluded:

> The divergence between the religious beliefs of Reform and Orthodoxy is so profound that when an individual publicly secedes he is only giving formal expression to convictions which had long since matured and become perfectly clear to himself. All the institutions and establishments in the care of a community are religious in nature, and they are . . . intimately bound up with the religious law.[27]

Hirsch viewed Judaism solely in religious terms.[28] Consequently, it was logical for him to serve as the catalyst for the bill and urge its passage. When, on July 27, 1876, the Lasker Bill was passed, the lion's share of the credit for its success was attributed to Hirsch. The bill stated:

> Every Jew is entitled, without severing his religious affiliation, to secede, on account of his religious scruples, from the particular community to which he belongs by virtue of a law, custom, or administrative regulation.[29]

Throughout this struggle Hildesheimer supported Hirsch and urged passage of this law. To the Prussian Chamber of Deputies in 1875 he wrote:

> The gulf between the adherents of traditional Judaism and its religious opponents is at least as deep and wide as in any other religious faith; in fact, it is larger than in most and much bigger than what is permitted by law.[30]

Hildesheimer, like Hirsch, believed that compromise involving issues of religious principles was impossible. No less than Hirsch, Hildesheimer denied the validity of religious pluralism in modern Judaism, and in light of his other stances vis-à-vis non-Orthodox Judaism, it is not surprising that he supported Hirsch in this struggle, which wracked German Jewry.

II.

Nevertheless, it would be a mistake to view Hildesheimer purely as a religious sectarian opposed to religious pluralism. For as Isaac Unna has pointed out, Hildesheimer believed that "Jews of various nations were organs of the body of one nation."[31] Hildesheimer reflected this conviction early in his life, when as a student in Berlin he wrote to his fiancée, Henriette Hirsch, sister of the wealthy metal firm owner, Joseph Hirsch:

> The life of a religious Jew is never an autonomous one. [Judaism is] not a personal matter, closed or individual. In his thoughts, and in his feelings of joy as well as pain, the Jew finds himself connected with the rest of his people.[32]

Hildesheimer had a strong notion of *Kelal Yisra-el*, the community of Israel. Alone among nineteenth-century German rabbis, he argued for the reinstitution of Jewish courts and on behalf the superiority of Jewish civil law.[33] Moreover, even though he did advocate secession from the general Jewish community on matters of religious dispute, Hildesheimer "never considered secession the ideal; on the contrary, as far as possible, he maintained unity for the idea of *Kelal*, the feeling of solidarity with all Israel."[34] This is borne out by correspondence between Hirsch and Hildesheimer on the issue of secession.

S. R. Hirsch, in a letter dated July 6, 1876, assured Hildesheimer that Orthodox Jews would not exploit the secession law. Secession, Hirsch stated, would take place only in rare communities and would occur only on account of substantive religious issues.[35] This letter indicates that Hildesheimer only reluctantly accepted the notion of secession, and Hirsch's obvious attempts to alleviate Hildesheimer's anxieties shows that Hirsch was much more enthusiastic about the new law than Hildesheimer. In addition, Hildesheimer was disturbed over the opposition to the law expressed by Selig Baer Bamberger, the "Wuerzburger Rav." Bamberger felt secession from the general Jewish community by Orthodox Jews was legitimate only in the most extreme instances, and he and Hirsch disputed publicly over the issue in an exchange of open letters.[36] While Hildesheimer agreed with Hirsch, he nevertheless wrote: "This sad matter has distracted me from my work many hours, and it has caused me many sleepless nights in which I have shed many tears."[37]

Hildesheimer refused to comment publicly on the dispute between Bamberger and Hirsch for fear that no beneficial result could be derived from public comment. Moreover, while he acknowledged that Hirsch had "restored the traditional Judaism of our day to its place of prestige,"[38] in a letter to Hirsch he said:

> I do dissent from several passages [in your open letter] directed against Bamberger, which appear to me to be too strong. They make it even less likely for a bridge to be built from your congregation to those who are "secessionists."[39]

Hildesheimer's obvious ambivalence toward secession and its attendant division of the Jewish community indicates that he was not the sectarian that Hirsch was. His greater sense of Jewish solidarity is reflected in several other actions he took. While Hirsch wrote, "An Orthodox Jew must not consider joining a B'nai B'rith group, for it threatens traditional Judaism," Hildesheimer became an active participant in the Berlin lodge.[40] Another incident is even more telling. Hirsch noted that Hildesheimer delivered an address at a meeting of the Berlin chapter of the Alliance Israélite Universelle, a Paris-based Jewish educational and charitable organization. Non-Orthodox Jews, including graduates of the Breslau Seminary, were members of the group, and its Paris head, Adolph Cremieux, was not only non-Orthodox but permitted his wife to have their children baptized.[41] As a result, Hirsch wrote:

> I have absolutely no connection with the Alliance, . . . I fail to see how a man imbued with proper Jewish thought can attach himself to a group founded for the sake of a Jewish task, when its founder and administration are completely removed from genuine religious Judaism. . . . Indeed, it is very painful for me to see an honored name like Dr. Hildesheimer united with the Alliance and the men of the Breslau Seminary.[42]

Hirsch concluded by stating that this was not the way of the pious men of old who dwelt in Jerusalem and separated themselves absolutely from the rest of the community for the sake of preserving Judaism.

Hildesheimer disagreed. Replying to Hirsch, Hildesheimer stated that an article published by the famed Eastern Europe Orthodox rabbi and proto-Zionist Zvi Hirsch Kalisher (1795–1874) on behalf of the Alliance and its charitable activities persuaded him to join. Citing the charitable activities of the Alliance, Hildesheimer wrote, "I feel myself obligated to promote the unity of various Jewish communities." Hildesheimer informed Hirsch that their common opponents delighted in Orthodox isolation, for when groups performed positive functions, these opponents were able to claim that the Orthodox were negative and isolationist. Cremieux was not, in Hildesheimer's view, a fit representative of Judaism. Nonetheless, Jews were still obligated to join the Alliance because they promoted positive functions.[43]

Hildesheimer's moderate approach to the problem of Orthodox cooperation with the non-Orthodox Jewish world is further illustrated when he received a Rabbi Ungerleider who had come to discuss plans for a rabbinical union between Orthodox and non-Orthodox rabbis in Germany. Hirsch charged that Hildesheimer had committed "an offense against the holiness and truth of our cause" by hosting Ungerleider. Hildesheimer simply dismissed Hirsch's complaint. He stressed that he had no intention of sanctioning such a union, but that refusing to see Ungerleider would have demonstrated a real lack of common decency (*derekh erets*).[44] Indeed, Hildesheimer had friendships with several nonobservant Jews. His correspondence demonstrates that even when he was vitriolic in denouncing his opponents' religious views, he was careful to distinguish between the person and the person's views.[45]

Hildesheimer's openness in dealing with nonobservant Jews on matters of communal concern is demonstrated clearly by his support of a proposal for the establishment of a Jewish orphanage in Jerusalem. In 1872, Heinrich Graetz and two companions toured Israel. One was Gottschalk Lewy, a friend of Hildesheimer's. Upon their return, the three men issued a report describing the depressed economic and social condition of the Jewish settlement.[46] Particularly disturbing to Hildesheimer was their description of the number of orphans who were neglected, both spiritually and physically, by the existing Jewish communities in Israel.

Hildesheimer had long toiled on behalf of the Jewish settlement in Israel and throughout his career had raised significant funds to support it. As early as 1858, he and his brother-in-law, Joseph Hirsch, had established the Society for the Support of *Erets Yisrael*, which supplied housing for Jews living in the old city of Jerusalem. His strong attachment to the "Land of His Fathers" was reflected even more visibly in 1882 when, at a Berlin meeting of Jewish representatives gathered from all over the world to deal with the problem of Russian Jewish refugees fleeing from the 1881 pogroms, Hildesheimer was the only delegate to recommend that the stream of refugees be directed toward Israel, not America. In 1885 he wrote: "America or Palestine—on religious grounds I plead for Palestine."[47] And again, in 1894, Hildesheimer wrote: "Israel is our homeland and—especially during a time of anti-Semitism—our only hope.[48]

Hildesheimer was deeply disturbed by Graetz's report, and he wholeheartedly supported Graetz's suggestion that an orphanage be established to ensure proper care for these youngsters. In a memorandum circulated in December 1872, Hildesheimer called for the immediate establishment of these orphanages in Israel. Because he distrusted the means of distribution used by the rabbis in Israel, Hildesheimer advocated placing the administration of the orphanages in the hands of a committee located in Europe, which, in turn, would appoint a local committee in Israel to administer the orphanage. Finally, in accordance with Graetz's suggestion, Hildesheimer stated that while the education of these youths would be based upon the "Holy Torah," secular subjects would be added to the curriculum to ensure that these youngsters would be able to lead independent lives.[49]

There was opposition to Hildesheimer's proposal. Rabbis in Israel were adamant in their critique of Hildesheimer's proposed orphanage, both because it threatened their autonomy and because of the proposed religious and secular curriculum of the school. Hildesheimer replied that the world was changing and that "the need for this knowledge [i.e., secular] grows every day."[50] More important for purposes of this study, however, is that opposition to this plan arose in Europe not because of the proposal's merits or demerits but because the "heretic Heinrich Graetz" had first proposed it.[51] Hirsch wrote to Hildesheimer:

> I feel myself obligated to inform you . . . that the idea to establish an orphanage in Israel both to rescue the orphans from the hands of the missionaries and to raise the level of culture is the idea of Graetz. . . . A man like this is not fit to be trusted by us.[52]

Hildesheimer responded both to Hirsch and other critics who opposed supporting any plan Graetz advocated by reconfirming his opinion that Graetz was a "religious heretic." No one, Hildesheimer stated, had fought Graetz and his heresy as adamantly as he.[53] Yet he wrote:

> A grave situation has arisen in opposition to my program among circles who do not wish to distinguish between the heresies of Graetz and his reports regarding established facts in our times; and there are great dangers bound up with this approach.[54]

Hildesheimer stressed the importance of distinguishing between a man's religious views and other aspects of his person. Though a man such as Graetz might hold, in his opinion, despicable religious beliefs injurious to the continuity of Judaism, Hildesheimer did not hold that one should therefore totally isolate oneself from such a Jew. He put it bluntly: "The truth is the truth even if it be on the side of our opponents."[55]

Hildesheimer's proposed orphanage never achieved fruition, and ultimately he abandoned his efforts on its behalf. Nevertheless this episode, his reservations concerning secession, and his participation in the Alliance indicate that his position regarding the non-Orthodox Jewish world differed from Hirsch's. His was a very real and strong sense of both the Jewish people and their religion.

III.

Esriel Hildesheimer was a man of unbending religious principle who refused to cooperate with or acknowledge the legitimacy of non-Orthodox religious bodies on matters of religious import. While a proponent of modern culture, he was not in sympathy with that spirit of the time which advanced a benign attitude toward religious pluralism. On the other hand, he was not a narrow, rigid sectarian. His love of the people Israel caused him to participate, whenever possible, with his fellow Jews, both Orthodox and non-Orthodox, on matters of common concern. By refusing to adopt a totally sectarian stance, Hildesheimer telescoped a vision of modern Orthodoxy that permitted it to participate in the total Jewish world while allowing it to remain true to its own principles.

1. See Jacob Katz, *Out of the Ghetto* (Cambridge: Harvard University Press, 1973).
2. Charles Liebman, "Orthodoxy in American Jewish Life," in *The Jewish Community in America*, ed. Marshall Sklare (New York: Behrman, 1974), 134.
3. Katz, *Out of the Ghetto*, chapter 9. For example, see Leo Levi, "The Relationship of the Orthodox to Heterodox Organizations," TRADITION 9 (Fall 1967): 95–102. Several other articles relating to this question have appeared in TRADITION throughout the last decade.
4. Mordechai Eliav, *Jewish Education in Germany during the Era of Haskalah and Emancipation* (Hebrew) (Jerusalem: Sivan Press, 1969), 227–39.
5. Both Ettlinger and Bernays, who were also the teachers of Samson Raphael Hirsch, were unique among the Orthodox rabbis of their day, for they preached and taught in German, not Yiddish.
6. Meir Hildesheimer, "The Rabbi and His Student" (Hebrew), *HaMaayan* (1972): 41.
7. Meir Hildesheimer, "Contributions towards a Portrait of Esriel Hildesheimer" (Hebrew), *Sinai* (1961): 69.
8. Cited by Zvi Benjamin Urbach, "A Biography of Rabbi Esriel Hildesheimer in His Hometown of Halberstadt," in *Festschrift for Yehiel Jacob Weinberg* (Hebrew) (Jerusalem, 1969), 232.
9. Azriel Hildesheimer, ed., "Rabbi Esriel Hildesheimer on Zacharias Frankel and the Jewish Theological Seminary in Breslau" (Hebrew), *HaMaayan* (1953): 65, hereafter referred to as "Hildesheimer on Frankel."
10. Urbach, "A Biography of Rabbi Esriel Hildesheimer in His Hometown of Halberstadt," 234–35.
11. Mordechai Eliav, ed., *Rabbiner Esriel Hildesheimer Briefe* (Jerusalem, 1965), 17 (Hebrew section). Hereafter referred to as *Hildesheimer Briefe*.
12. Esriel Hildesheimer, *Responsa* (Tel Aviv, 1969), 1:11–14.
13. "Hildesheimer on Frankel," 69.
14. Meir Hildesheimer, "Writings Regarding the Founding of the Berlin Rabbinical Seminary" (Hebrew), *HaMaayan* (1974): 29.
15. "Hildesheimer on Frankel," 71–72. Hildesheimer wrote, "So long as Graetz remains in the institution we will never give our approval to the students educated there."
16. Meir Hildesheimer, "Contributions towards a Portrait of Esriel Hildesheimer," 78.
17. "Hildesheimer on Frankel," 68–69.
18. Meir Hildesheimer, ed., "Writings Regarding the Rabbinical Seminary," 13.
19. "Hildesheimer on Frankel," 66.
20. Hermann Schwab, *The History of Orthodox Jewry in Germany*, trans. Irene R. Birnbaum (London, 1950), 95.

21. *Hildesheimer Briefe*, 195–97.

22. Schwab, *The History of Orthodox Jewry in Germany*, 60.

23. Salo Baron, "Freedom and Constraint in the Jewish Community," in *Essays and Studies in Memory of Linda R. Miller*, ed. Israel Davidson (New York, 1938), 12.

24. Schwab, *The History of Orthodox Jewry in Germany*, 66.

25. Baron, "Freedom and Constraint in the Jewish Community," 12–13.

26. Ibid., 14. For a fuller discussion of this whole matter against the background of the times, see Uriel Tal, *Christians and Jews in Germany: Religion, Politics, and Ideology in the Second Reich, 1870–1914*, trans. Noah Jacobs (Ithaca: Cornell University Press, 1975), chapter 2.

27. Schwab, *The History of Orthodox Jewry in Germany*, 68–69.

28. Ismar Schorsch, *Jewish Reactions to German Anti-Semitism, 1870–71* (New York: Columbia University Press, 1972), 10.

29. Quoted in Baron, "Freedom and Constraint in the Jewish Community," 15.

30. *Hildesheimer Briefe*, 109.

31. Isaac Unna, "Ezriel [*sic*] Hildesheimer," in *Jewish Leaders* , ed. Leo Jung (New York, 1953), 227.

32. Quoted in Meir Hildesheimer, "Contributions towards a Portrait of Esriel Hildesheimer," 72.

33. Esriel Hildesheimer, *Rabbiner Dr. I. Hildesheimer: Gesammelte Aufsätze*, ed. Meir Hildesheimer (Frankfurt, 1923), "Das biblisch-talmudische Recht."

34. Isaac Unna, "Ezriel Hildesheimer," 226.

35. Azriel Hildesheimer, ed., "A Selection of Letters between Rabbi Esriel Hildesheimer and Samson Raphael Hirsch and His Supporters" (Hebrew), *Yad Shaul* (Tel Aviv, 1953), 236.

36. Ibid., 236–38. Also see Schwab, *The History of Orthodox Jewry in Germany*, chapter 9.

37. Ibid., 238.

38. Ibid., 233.

39. Ibid., 240.

40. Quoted by Isaac Heinemann, "Rabbi Marcus Horovitz," in *Jewish Leaders*, ed. Jung, 263.

41. Azriel Hildesheimer, ed., "An Exchange of Letters between Esriel Hildesheimer and Samson Raphael Hirsch on Matters Relating to the Land of Israel" (Hebrew), *HaMaayan* (1954): 50. Hereafter cited as "Hildesheimer and Hirsch on Israel."

42. Ibid., 48–49.

43. Ibid., 48–50.

44. *Hildesheimer Briefe*, 199.

45. See Schorsch, *Jewish Reactions to German Anti-Semitism*, 35, where he describes Hildesheimer's friendship with Samuel Kristeller, a nonobservant Jew. Also note his attitude toward Graetz as described below.

46. This report is found in J. Meisl, *Heinrich Graetz* (Berlin, 1917), 101–5, 142–51.

47. *Hildesheimer Briefe*, 205.

48. Ibid., 244.

49. "Hildesheimer and Hirsch on Israel," 41.

50. *Hildesheimer Briefe*, 54 (Hebrew section).

51. "Hildesheimer and Hirsch on Israel," 44.

52. Ibid., 45.

53. *Hildesheimer Briefe*, 90–91.

54. "Hildesheimer and Hirsch on Israel," 44.

55. *Hildesheimer Briefe*, 48 (Hebrew section).

2

German Orthodox Rabbinical Writings on the Jewish Textual Education of Women

The Views of Rabbi Samson Raphael Hirsch and Rabbi Esriel Hildesheimer

Kol kevudah bat melekh penimah (Psalm 45:14) have been understood by the rabbis in Shevuot 30a as meaning "The king's daughter is all glorious within," and the phrase has regularly been employed in rabbinic literature to justify the position that the legitimate venue for the activity of women is a domestic one. Consequently, it is small wonder that the sphere of classical Jewish textual study has been the near-exclusive province of men throughout Jewish history, for the mastery of this literature has profound implications for the exercise of public positions of power and authority within the traditional Jewish world.

As Paula Hyman has pointed out, "Jewish women . . . chafed under these gender divisions and the consequent educational restrictions of traditional Jewish society." After all, "According to *halakha* (Jewish law) women were exempt from the study of Torah, that is, the texts of the Hebrew Bible and of rabbinic learning, whose mastery conferred status upon Jewish men."[1] In a traditional Jewish world, where the will of God was seen as being expressed in these classical writings, the refusal to allow women access to these textual sources meant that women were unable to attain the public status and authority such study conferred upon men. Indeed, this stance made it well-nigh impossible for women to exercise public political power in traditional Jewish religious society throughout history.

The primary traditional warrants that exclude women from access to classical Jewish textual study are found in several places in the Talmud. For example, in Berakhot 20b and Kiddushin 34a the Talmud teaches that women are under no obligation to study Torah. Furthermore, in Babylonian Talmud Tractate Kiddushin 29b, the rabbis, basing themselves on the biblical verse "And you shall teach them to your children [*l'va'nekha*]," note that the last word in that verse should actually be rendered as "your sons, and not your daughters [*v'lo liv'no'te-kha*]." Consequently, a father was responsible for teaching Torah only to his sons, not to his daughters.

As a result of these sentiments, the statement of the talmudic sage Rabbi Ben Azzai in Sotah 20a, "A man is obligated to teach his daughter Torah," has generally not been cited in traditional Jewish circles as providing a justification for establishing schools for the textual education of girls. Rather, the position adopted by Rabbi Eliezer on the following page of the Talmud (Sotah 2lb)—"Anyone who teaches his daughter Torah, it is as if he taught her sexual licentiousness"—has more often been cited as justifying the denial of access to the study of Torah for women.[2]

In light of these views, the primary position assigned women in the formal Jewish educational process was unsurprisingly that of domestic facilitator for husbands and sons. Women were not traditionally designated as active participants in Jewish study. Berakhot 17a justifies and reflects this stance toward female gender roles: "Whereby do women gain merit? By making their sons go to synagogue to learn Scripture and their sons to the House of Study to learn Mishnah and waiting for their husbands until they return home from the House of Study."

Despite these traditional warrants and stances, the last two hundred years have witnessed a near revolutionary change in the status of the textual education that Jewish women have received, even in many traditional Jewish precincts. This essay describes the attitudes that two great leaders of Modern Orthodox Judaism adopted toward the Jewish education of women. I will look specifically at the writings of Rabbi Samson Raphael Hirsch (1808–88) of Frankfurt, the great champion of Neo-orthodox Judaism in the modern world, and Rabbi Esriel Hildesheimer (1820–99) of Berlin, founder of the first Orthodox rabbinical seminary on German soil. While their positions will hardly seem sufficient by present-day standards of gender equality, their stances nevertheless established a pathway that later generations would expand. As a result, classical textual education would become a reality for ever-increasing numbers of Jewish women, thereby making it possible for the voices of women and their concerns to be heard in the public square of Jewish communal religious life.

With the advent of the Enlightenment political structures in the West and their attendant emphasis upon increasing equality even in the realm of gender, trends in the larger world supported a shift in educational policy toward girls and women even as gender role divisions were maintained. As Hyman has observed, "Middle-class Jewish women in Western societies happily claimed the new definitions of female responsibility for religious socialization of the young." Jewish women eagerly embraced "the modern expectation that women would serve as the primary inculcators of Jewish consciousness in their children, just as Western bourgeois culture saw mothers as the first teachers of moral values to the younger generation."[3] While these attitudes assigned women a role that was primarily domestic, they also helped facilitate a situation in which women would no longer be totally excluded from the realm of Jewish textual study. Indeed, it was in Germany that these modernist sensibilities were paramount and where modern Judaism was born. There, a number of Orthodox rabbis such as Hirsch and Hildesheimer began to issue legal rulings and establish educational institutions that relaxed the prohibitions that prevented women from engaging in the formal study of Torah.

In order to place the words and deeds of these Orthodox leaders in the German historical context, it is instructive to cite the observations of Mordecai Breuer, who, in characterizing the state of attitudes and practice concerning the formal Jewish education of women and girls that marked the German Orthodox community of that period, wrote:

> The most significant and far-reaching success of Orthodox education proved to be the complete reorganization of education for girls. Before the age of emancipation the education and training of female youth had been a matter exclusively for the parental home. There had been no formal education for girls and women. According to tradition the study of the Oral Law and intensive occupation with the Bible were mandatory only for men. At the end of the nineteenth century, the Orthodox press could still write, "A few years ago, as is well known, it was still customary among all Jews to exclude females from the study of Torah."[4]

The person perhaps most responsible for this change, as Breuer states, was Samson Raphael Hirsch. About Hirsch, he writes, "It was unthinkable for Hirsch to undertake the founding of a school for boys without at the same time being concerned about instruction for girls."[5]

Of course, Hirsch was not the first Jew—not even the first Orthodox one—to make such changes in the course of education for women. As Mordecai Eliav has reported, as early as 1769 German *maskilim* (Enlighteners) demanded that Jewish girls receive formal instruction in Hebrew, and the call for women to receive formal education grew exponentially in Germany in the closing years of the eighteenth century and in the first years of the nineteenth century.[6] The influence of this larger trend in the Jewish world was also felt in Orthodox precincts of the community, and in 1827 the first Orthodox elementary school in Germany to combine secular with religious subjects in its curriculum—Hasharat Zevi in Halberstadt— opened its doors to girls thirty-one years after it first began.[7]

Both Rabbi Hirsch, who was raised in an atmosphere that he described as *"erleuchtet religioes* [enlightened religious]," an approach that combined strict adherence to Jewish law and belief in its divine origins with an embrace of modern culture, and Rabbi Hildesheimer, who was educated in Halberstadt at Hasharat Zevi, may have been predisposed by upbringing and schooling to adopt a positive attitude toward modern culture and the formal education of women. This distinguished them from their medieval forebears as well as from rabbinic peers in Eastern Europe.

Hirsch, a prolific author and charismatic personality, served as the rabbi of the *lsraelitische Religionsgesellschaft* (IRG) in Frankfurt, a separatist Orthodox community, where he built communal organizations based upon Orthodox principles and beliefs and waged constant attacks upon the Reform movement. In his 1842 *Horeb: A Philosophy of Jewish Laws and Observances*, an exposition of the precepts and obligations incumbent upon all Jews, Hirsch outlined his views concerning the issue of women and Torah study. In the pages of *Horeb*, a biblical term for Mt. Sinai, the site of revelation, Hirsch maintained that women in the modern setting required formal Jewish education despite the negative statements contained in the tradition that inveighed against offering such schooling to women.

Hirsch began by placing his stance on behalf of the formal Jewish education of women within a larger overarching educational context. At the outset of his argument, he stated that the Jew "must study for practical life—that is the fundamental principle of the law. With attentive mind and with receptive heart," he told his reader, "you must study in order to practice." The purpose of Jewish learning was not *Wissenschaft*— academic study unconnected to life. Rather, the goal of Jewish study was

Religionsunterricht—religious instruction designed to motivate the student to act. For this reason, Hirsch wrote:

> No less should Israel's daughters learn the content of the Written Law and the duties which they have to perform in their lifetime as daughter and young woman, as mother and housewife. Many times have Israel's daughters saved the purity of the Jewish life and spirit. The deliverance from Egypt itself was won by the women; and it is by the pious and virtuous women of Israel that the Jewish spirit and Jewish life can and will again be revived.[8]

Just as the pious acts of its women rescued Israel in the past, so Hirsch posited that the present and future revival of the Jewish people is and would be dependent upon the pure deeds of its women. However, Hirsch went on to contend that Torah knowledge alone would enable women to accomplish such deeds. The redemption of Israel was contingent upon the ability of women to acquire knowledge of Torah. Such education for women—formal study of the Written Law—was surely necessary in a modern context that fostered the assimilation of Jewish youth and where the continued allegiance of boys and girls alike to the Jewish religion was inextricably tied to the efforts of the mother to instruct her offspring and create a Jewish home.

Hirsch made clear precisely what this education for girls meant in the discussion he put forth, again in the pages of *Horeb*, regarding "general subjects of instruction for Jewish youth." It was the duty of parents to see to it that their sons were well versed in "1) Hebrew language, 2) Vernacular, 3) *Torah* (Pentateuch), *Nevi'im* (Prophets), and *Kethuvim* (Writings), 4) Nature and man (Sciences), 5) History, 6) Right living (teaching of duties) from the Written and Oral Law, and 7) Writing and Arithmetic." He stated that while "we have tried to trace the general course for boys, the same holds good for girls." This meant that "1–5 and 7 remain somewhat simplified, but for 6 only systematic instruction in the duties of her future life is required."[9]

In his commentary on the traditional Jewish prayer book, Hirsch explains more fully what "somewhat simplified" instruction for women means, and he defines his position regarding "Right living (teaching of duties) from the Written and Oral Law" more precisely by delimiting the areas of Torah study open to women. The expansiveness implied in his previous writings on the topic in *Horeb* is here circumscribed and confined to "non-specialized" areas of "Torah study." Women are not permitted to engage in "theoretical knowledge of the Law," that is, Talmud and the Oral Law. Commenting upon the second paragraph of the *Sh'ma*, the major creedal statement of Jewish faith recited daily by the traditional Jew in morning and evening prayers, he writes:

> "*V'limad'tem otam et b'neichem*—and you should teach them to your sons" (Deut. 11:19)—The term *limud* is more comprehensive than *shinun*. We believe that the Halacha bases its statement *b'neichem v'lo banoteichem*—your sons and not your daughters (Kiddushin 29b), limiting the commandment to teach the Torah to the instruction of our sons exclusive of our daughters, on the sentence *V'limad'tem otam et b'neichem* and not on the sentence *v'shinantam l'vanekha*—(Deut. 6:6). The fact is that while women are not to be exposed to specialized Torah study or theoretical knowledge of the Law, which are reserved for the Jewish man, such understanding of our sacred literature as can teach the fear of the Lord and the conscientious fulfillment of our duty, and all such knowledge as is essential to the adequate expression of our tasks should indeed form part of the mental and spiritual training not only of our sons, but of our daughters as well. This is indicated also by the commandment pertaining to *Hakhel* (Deut. 31:12—Gather together the people).[10]

While Hirsch has here restricted the study of Torah for women to "non-specialized" areas, it is equally important to note that he does not forbid Torah study for women altogether. Not only "our sons, but our daughters" must learn "fear of the Lord," and they must attain "all such knowledge as is essential" in order to fulfill their tasks as wives and mothers. While this viewpoint hardly embraces a contemporary notion of gender equality, it did allow for the formal instruction of women in certain classical Jewish texts. Indeed, Hirsch elucidates his position in several places in his biblical commentary.

Writing on the commandment of *Hakhel* in Deuteronomy 31:12, which reads, "Gather together [*Hakhel*] all the people, the men and the women and the children and the stranger that is within your gates that they may hear [*l'ma'an yish'm'u*] and that they may learn [*u'l'ma'an yil'm'du*] and fear [*v'yar'u*] the Lord your God and conscientiously fulfill all the words of this Torah," he states, "*Hakhel* is one of the 'positive time-bound commandments' which apply also to women."[11] While women are often exempt from such commandments, their inclusion in the commandment of *Hakhel* indicates that women, no less than men, are required to "hear" the commandments and understand their obligations to fulfill the law. Commenting specifically on the words "that they may hear and that they may learn," Hirsch states that in both "the most general [public] assembly of the nation" and "the home" the Jewish man and Jewish woman must engage in "the ever progressive study of the Torah." Such study will "increase and fortify their fear of God" and thereby cause man and woman to realize "the culminating aim of all the institutions of Torah," the fulfillment of "the whole Torah faithfully and conscientiously." Furthermore, he then refers his reader to his previous commentary on Deuteronomy 11:19, where he fully explicates the "relation of women to the study of Torah."[12]

In his extended note on the verse "*V'limad'tem otam et b'neichem*" (Deuteronomy 11:19), Hirsch begins by echoing what he wrote in his remarks on these words in the second paragraph of the *Sh'ma* in his prayer book commentary and states, in accord with his understanding of the passage in Kiddushin 29b, "that women are only not to be directed to the scientific study of the Law." Such study is admittedly the exclusive province of men. However, the commandment of *Hakhel* in Deuteronomy 31:12—with its demand that all Jews "fear God" and fulfill "the words of this Torah"—requires an "understanding of Jewish Scripture" and "knowledge of the Torah" that can be realized only through "the education of the intellect and the feelings of our daughters as much as of our sons."

Having made this assertion, Hirsch is aware that such instruction for women runs counter to the stance that many traditionalists continued to adopt on this subject, and he clearly feels constrained to provide ample textual justifications for his position. He therefore cites a number of arguments and counterarguments to support the formal textual education of women. Hirsch notes that the Talmud in Hagiga 3a, commenting upon Deuteronomy 31:12, states, "Men come to learn, women come to listen." On the basis of this rabbinic text, one might suppose that women cannot or ought not to receive any formal Jewish textual instruction. However, Hirsch completely rejects this understanding of

Hagiga 3a and contends that a complete reading of the Hagiga text in light of the rabbinic commentaries upon it yields a different conclusion. Indeed, he points out that Rashi (Rabbi Solomon ben Isaac of Troyes, 1040–1105, the leading classical commentator on the Bible and Talmud) and the *Tosafot* (medieval commentators on the Talmud), writing on the phrase *"l'ma'an yish'm'u* [that they may hear]," in Hagiga 3a, state that these words do "not mean just hearing, but a proper competent understanding, to be taken as 'learning.'" Women, like men, can thus engage in textual "learning." Hirsch further cites the Mishnah in Nedarim 35b, where it states, "Yet he may teach Scripture [*Mikra*] to his daughters," as an explicit warrant for the practice of providing courses in *Tanakh* (Hebrew Bible) for girls, as well as the Gemara in Nedarim 37b, where the Sages assume that "accentuation of Scripture [*pisuk ta'a'mim*]" can be taught to daughters as well as to sons, to legitimate once again his position that women can be instructed in the Bible. In addition, Hirsch contends that the statement of Joseph Karo (1488–1575, author of the premiere code of Jewish Law, the *Shulchan Aruch*), in his commentary on the late medieval Jewish law code, the *Tur, Orah Hayyim* 47, "Women are required [to study] the Written Torah and the laws which apply to them," provides a further warrant for this practice. Finally, Hirsch concludes this note by observing, "It has been the practice from time immemorial—in proof of which there is a whole literature in Yiddish written predominantly for women—to give women a knowledge of biblical and liturgical writings and a general knowledge and understanding of the Torah and the rabbinic teachings."[13]

As we assess the stance that Hirsch put forth on the subject of classical Jewish textual education for women, it is clear that he confined such "learning" to the Written Law, that is, the texts of the Bible and other nonlegal texts in the Jewish literary tradition. Furthermore, he did not surrender or modify the traditional domestic role that Jewish society assigned women. Nevertheless, Hirsch did allow Jewish women contact with the classical literary legacy of the Jewish people, and his views and the institutions he created for the formal education of girls as well as boys at the schools of his congregation in Frankfurt contained seeds for greater inclusion and change that would grow and develop in the subsequent century. We turn now to his colleague Esriel Hildesheimer to assess the viewpoint and stance of his contemporary on this topic.

Hildesheimer adopted a position on the matter of women and Torah study that was akin to, if not identical with, the position advanced by Hirsch. As stated above, Hildesheimer attended the first coeducational Orthodox elementary school in Germany, and he received his rabbinical ordination, as did Hirsch, from Rabbi Jacob Ettlinger (1798–1871) of Altona, who countenanced the Jewish education of girls.[14] His experience as a child, his study with Rabbi Ettlinger, and his affirmative approach to secular knowledge—and surely his commitment to Orthodox Judaism—all clearly informed his particular position regarding the issue of Torah education for girls.

In a pamphlet Hildesheimer wrote in 1871, *Etwas über den Religionsunterricht der Mädchen* (A few words regarding the religious instruction of girls), he began by citing the talmudic commentary found in Shevuot 30a on Psalm 45:14 and asserted, "The king's daughter is all glorious within." The strength and glory of the Jewish woman is an inward one, and her domain is the domestic. In a highly romantic and traditionally gendered patriarchal vision of the roles assigned the woman, Hildesheimer described in four pages the central role that "the Jewish mother" played in rearing her "beloved children," instructing them in the words of the *Sh'ma* and teaching them the fundamentals of Jewish faith. The Jewish woman is the linchpin in establishing the peace and harmony of the home, the foundation upon which the true teachings of Israel are constructed and in which the most enduring memory and knowledge of Judaism are implanted for children. Echoing Hirsch—whose school in Frankfurt he cited as a model for the type of education that ought to be provided to both boys and girls—Hildesheimer claimed that it was as necessary to educate these girls in Bible and Hebrew as it was to educate boys, for "if it is true that knowledge is power, then the Jewish knowledge of our wives and young ladies will contribute to an invincible Jewish power—to a power in the home, in Jewish family life, and to a priceless influence in the area of the education of our sons."[15]

The argument Hildesheimer constructed in advocating for the necessity of providing formal education for Jewish women can surely be characterized as reflecting the traditional patriarchal notion that the appropriate gender role for women is a domestic one. Undoubtedly, Hildesheimer himself had internalized this view of gender as natural and correct. Indeed, he concluded his remarks with a paean in praise of the Jewish woman by citing Genesis 12:16, where it is written, "And because of her [Sarah], it went well with Abram," and Baba Mezia 59a, "Let a man be ever careful to honor his wife, because God's blessing is found in a man's house only for the sake of his wife." Such sentiments only reinforce the assertion that Hildesheimer shared in the traditional as well as dominant contemporary cultural worldview, as Marion Kaplan has phrased it, that the "family remained a central focus for the expression of Jewish feeling and commitment" and that the role of the woman in facilitating and achieving this for her husband and for her children was "primary."[16]

At the same time, Hildesheimer was well aware that a number of traditionalists still opposed any change in Jewish educational life that would countenance the textual education of women. This may well be a factor in why he was so careful, as was Hirsch, to couch his argument in what can be labeled "instrumental-pragmatic" terms, that is, that educating young women in this way was not an end in itself but a means to provide for the Jewish education and identity of the young in a world where the lure of assimilation for the Jewish middle and upper middle classes was all too strong. Hildesheimer therefore cited many of the traditional warrants from rabbinic literature to support this innovation, as Hirsch had.[17]

Having provided this backdrop for advocating the formal education of Jewish girls, Hildesheimer then laid out the curriculum in the Berlin *Gemeinde Adass Yisroel* congregational school that he headed. In the course of study, young women were taught the Pentateuch, Prophets, Hebrew language and grammar, Jewish history, the grace after meals, *Pirkei Avot* (Ethics of the Fathers), and basic prayers and blessings for Sabbath and daily devotions. However, they were not taught, as the boys were, Talmud or Codes of Jewish Law.[18]

Seventeen years later, in an 1888 letter he wrote in response to questions his pupil Josef Rosenfeld had posed to him, Hildesheimer again maintained that instruction of girls in Bible was permitted by the Talmud and Codes. Moreover, such education was not only sanctioned by classical rabbinic warrants. Rather, Hildesheimer insisted that "the education of a child, and naturally of a girl as well, rests in the first place upon an ethical consciousness and on the promotion of a sense of morality that can only be attained through knowledge of the original [biblical] text." He further observed, "I am acquainted with many cases where such instruction was so eminently successful that the girls were able to instruct their sons in biblical knowledge."[19]

In these writings, Hildesheimer, like Hirsch, never countenanced the study of Talmud and Codes for Jewish women. Nor was the study of Torah deemed important for women as individuals in their own right. Rather, their study of Torah was proclaimed crucial for instrumental reasons. It would allow women to fulfill their roles as helpmeets for their husbands as well as the part they would play as educators of "our sons." As wives and mothers, these girls would grow up to play the pivotal role in ensuring a true Torah consciousness in home and family life. Hildesheimer recognized that the religious education of girls was desirable on ethical grounds as well. After all, "the promotion of a sense of morality . . . can only be attained through knowledge of the original [biblical] text." Hildesheimer, like Hirsch, thus allowed for women to study the Written Law and nonlegalistic texts on moral-religious as well instrumental-prudential grounds.

As has been observed above, this stance toward the textual education of women that Hirsch and Hildesheimer advanced is hardly as inclusive or radical as a present-day advocate of gender equality might desire. Furthermore, both evidenced a highly traditional attitude regarding the domestic gender role they assigned women. For both men, the role appropriate for women was one limited to the domestic realm alone.

Nevertheless, in adopting the positions they did concerning the permissibility and need that women receive formal education in the text of the Bible as well as exposure to ethical resources within Jewish tradition, Hirsch and Hildesheimer reflected attitudes regarding the position and role of women derived from the larger German society. Moreover, their stances represented a departure from traditional Jewish communal norms that denied women formal educational access to all classical textual learning. In this sense, their posture and practice in this area had far more revolutionary implications for the public roles women would one day assume as a result of expanded educational prospects than either of these men probably ever imagined. Furthermore, their position on this topic foreshadowed what would become popularized in other precincts of the Orthodox world only fifty years later, even in Eastern Europe.

In *Gender and Assimilation in Modern Jewish History*, Paula Hyman points out that in 1933, Israel ben Meir HaCohen (1880–1933), better known as the Hafetz Hayyim, arguably the most outstanding moralist and Jewish legal authority of his day in Poland, himself "advocated formal Jewish education for women in response to the conditions of the time." Indeed, she quotes from his commentary on Sotah 20a, where the Hafetz Hayyim writes on the talmudic passage, "One who teaches his daughter Torah, it is as if he teaches her sexual licentiousness." He states, "It is surely a great *mitzvah* (commandment) to teach girls the Pentateuch and also the other books of Scripture (the Prophets and Writings) and the ethics of the rabbis . . . so that our holy faith will be verified for them. Because if not, the girls are likely to stray completely from the path of the Lord and transgress the foundations of our religion, God forbid."[20]

The attitudes adopted by Hildesheimer and Hirsch had by then become the common views of a much wider Orthodox Jewish audience, for many of the same reasons that had motivated the German rabbis discussed in this essay. These men would not extend their permission on this matter to include study of the Oral Law for women. Yet their decision to allow for women's formal study of the Written Law as well as their exposure to the ethical teachings of the tradition represented an expansion in this area of Jewish law and thus constitutes an important chapter in the evolving role of women in Jewish religious and communal life.

NOTES

1. Paula E. Hyman, *Gender and Assimilation in Modern Jewish History: The Roles and Representation of Women* (Seattle: University of Washington Press, 1995), 54.
2. For a fuller understanding of these passages from Sotah, see Judith Hauptman, *Rereading the Rabbis: A Woman's Voice* (Boulder: Westview Press, 1998), 22–23, and Judith Romney Wegner, *Chattel or Person? The Status of Women in the Mishnah* (New York: Oxford University Press, 1988), 161.
3. Hyman, *Gender and Assimilation in Modern Jewish History*, 30, 33.
4. Mordecai Breuer, *Modernity within Tradition: The Social History of Orthodox Jewry in Imperial Germany* (New York: Columbia University Press, 1992), 120–21.
5. Ibid., 123.
6. Mordecai Eliav, *Jewish Education in Germany in the Period of Emancipation and Enlightenment* (Hebrew) (Jerusalem: Sivan Press, 1960), 19.
7. Ibid., 156–57.
8. Samson Raphael Hirsch, *Horeb: A Philosophy of Jewish Laws and Observances* (London: Soncino Press, 1962), 2:370–71.
9. Ibid., 411–12.

10. Samson Raphael Hirsch, *The Hirsch Siddur: The Order of Prayers for the Whole Year* (Jerusalem: Feldheim, 5729/1969), 122.

11. Samson Raphael Hirsch, *The Pentateuch—Deuteronomy* (London: Isaac Levy, 1962), 612.

12. Ibid., 612–13.

13. Ibid., 189–90.

14. For Ettlinger's position on the education of women, see Judith Bleuch, "Jacob Ettlinger, His Life and Works: The Emergence of Modern Orthodoxy in Germany" (PhD diss., New York University, 1974), 265–66.

15. Israel Hildesheimer, *Etwas über den Religionsunterricht der Mädchen* (Berlin: M. Driesner, 1871), 8.

16. Marion A. Kaplan, *The Making of the Jewish Middle Class: Women, Family, and Identity in Imperial Germany* (New York: Oxford University Press, 1991), 70.

17. Hildesheimer, *Etwas über den Religionsunterricht der Mädchen*, 7. In a lengthy footnote, Hildesheimer cites the *Turei Zahav* on *Yoreh De'ah* 246 and the Sotah texts found in the Talmud to support his stance.

18. Ibid., 13–14.

19. Mordecai Eliav, ed., *Rabbiner Esriel Hildesheimer Briefe* (Jerusalem: Verlag Rubin Mass, 1965), 233–34.

20. Hyman, *Gender and Assimilation in Modern Jewish History*, 60.

3

Rabbi Samson Raphael Hirsch to Liepman Phillip Prins of Amsterdam

An 1873 Responsum on Education

Sociologists of religion have routinely noted that the term "secularization" has provided a powerful ideal type for analyzing and illuminating the course and direction of personal and communal religious life in the modern Occident. In employing this term, sociologists do not contend that religion disappears from modern life. Rather, they utilize this notion to indicate that, in the modern setting, religion comes to be confined to ever more discrete precincts. Areas of life that were formerly under the sway of religious imperatives and sensibilities no longer are, and most individuals, and the communities to which they belong, are no longer guided in these areas by traditional religious norms and values. In such a setting, religion increasingly comes to be compartmentalized and restricted. People belong to multiple cultural worlds, and there are often great differences between the values and norms that mark those worlds. In such a situation, the dissonance between the values advanced in the formal educational institutions of a traditional religious community and the values that obtain in other sectors of society to which the religious individual is exposed is often quite pronounced. For these reasons, the modern situation often makes it difficult for traditional religions to maintain themselves and transmit a holistic heritage to future generations.

Such considerations provide a significant framework of analysis for the responsum by Rabbi Samson Raphael Hirsch (1808–88) that is presented in this article. Rabbi Hirsch was acutely aware of these matters, and the viewpoints he advanced in this responsum show that he was fully appreciative of the heavy and unusual burden the modern setting imposed upon the Jewish school as a transmitter of Jewish values and identity. Rabbi Hirsch is of course famed as the foremost proponent of the "*Torah* '*im derekh erets*" philosophy that spawned Modern Orthodox Judaism. A brilliant ideologue as well as a charismatic figure who served as the rabbi of the *Israelitische Religionsgesellschaft* in Frankfurt from 1851 until his death, Rabbi Hirsch was convinced that traditional Jewish observance and belief were compatible with modern Western culture. A prolific author who wrote on a broad array of topics in a number of literary genres, Rabbi Hirsch enjoyed unparalleled fame and prestige as the foremost leader of traditional Judaism in his time and place. His correspondence was vast, and Jews worldwide wrote to Rabbi Hirsch for his legal rulings and opinions on a wide array of topics.[1]

Among these persons was the famed Amsterdam Orthodox philanthropist Liepman Phillip Prins (1835–1915). Prins turned to Rabbi Hirsch more than once as he sought support and advice on Jewish public affairs in general and on behalf of the Jewish educational institutions he helped establish in particular. On one occasion, for example, Prins asked Rabbi Hirsch to provide the Orthodox Amsterdam community with a curricular model for the day school they were about to create.[2]

In the specific responsum presented in translation below, Prins posed a different educational question to Rabbi Hirsch. In this instance, he solicited Rabbi Hirsch's opinion as to the obligation Jewish tradition imposed upon wealthy and influential members of the community to provide their own children with a Torah education. Prins took it for granted that such people were required by tradition to maintain communal educational institutions for the offspring of less affluent as well as indigent Jews, and in this responsum Rabbi Hirsch explicitly agreed with this position and labeled such support for the children of the less affluent as "an act of loving kindness." But Prins clearly wanted to impress upon members of his own socioeconomic class their personal responsibility to educate their own children in traditional Jewish texts and teachings, and he hoped that the viewpoint Rabbi Hirsch would express on this matter would aid him in this effort.[3]

The response Rabbi Hirsch provided Prins surely did not disappoint him. Indeed, the Hirsch responsum buoyed Prins's position and strengthened Prins's resolve to provide a meaningful Jewish education for the children of all Jews as well as his conviction that authentic Jewish instruction for the children of the well-to-do and powerful was particularly critical in the present-day era of modern Europe. After all, there was an overarching social-religious-intellectual cohesion that marked the Jewish world of medieval Europe. That world was not marked by the secularization of the modern situation. The values present in the Jewish home were consistent with those that obtained in the marketplace and the synagogue as well as in the formal educational institutions of the community. With the advent of the modern West, such cohesion—for the reasons put forth in the opening paragraph of this essay—no longer existed, and the children of the wealthy were even more exposed than other Jewish children to the lures of a non-Jewish world. Without a vibrant and vital Jewish education, these children and the aid they might one day provide for the Jewish people and Jewish life would disappear. In his responsum, Rabbi Hirsch therefore insisted that these wealthy and powerful individuals were required to provide for the Jewish education of their own children, and he assigned absolute priority to this obligation for the Torah education of the offspring of the affluent.

In adopting this stance, Rabbi Hirsch showed significant religious insight and sociological sagacity. The policy statement he put forth in this particular writing is of ongoing religious and sociological significance for committed modern Jews because the thoughts Rabbi Hirsch here put forth in his social context are reflective of our own world as well. He correctly pointed out the crucial role that education plays in fostering and transmitting Jewish values to each new generation of Jews. Rabbi Hirsch also underscored the role that Jewish schools were called upon to play in the differentiated setting of the modern world if Jewish continuity and teachings were to be maintained and passed on to a Jewish community that no longer enjoyed the political hegemony and cultural and religious cohesion that characterized European Jewish life in the Middle Ages. In the contemporary setting of the modern Occident, the Hirsch responsum remains of enduring worth as Jews continue to grapple with the challenges and burdens confronting formal Jewish education today. It is fitting that the thoughts Rabbi Hirsch expressed on this occasion be disseminated to a wider audience through the translation that now follows.

A Letter from Rabbi Samson Raphael Hirsch of Frankfurt to the Honorable Liepman Phillip Prins of Amsterdam, May 29, 1873

Your Excellency turned to me with the following question and requested an expression of my opinion on it—"Is it the obligation of the leaders of a community among the people Israel, after they have provided for the Torah education of the children of the poor and the middle-income [members of the community], to do the same for the children of the well-to-do? Is this matter not important, if not to a greater extent, at least to the same extent as the concern for matters of the synagogue and other interests of the community?"

In connection with this, I am honored to respond: The concern for the Torah education of all the youth of the community, with no distinction between rich and poor, is not only a portion of the obligations thrust upon the leaders of a community; rather, it stands, without doubt, in first place among their obligations, and other matters retreat before it. Leaders of a community who do not do everything in their power to see to it that all the children of the community, rich and poor, can study Torah as required, have failed to fulfill the obligation that they took upon themselves before God on a matter that is of supreme import and the greatest holiness. The law of Torah obligates us, as well as those responsible for the administration of the affairs of a community, concerning the absolute importance of this matter on the basis of the following sources:

1) "Teachers for children are appointed in every city, and if any city does not have a teacher for children within it, a ban is pronounced upon the inhabitants of the city until they appoint a teacher for the young. And if they do not make such an appointment, they are destroying the city, that is, they are undermining rather than sustaining the future existence of the city. For the world is sustained only by the breath of schoolchildren." (*Yoreh De'ah* 245:7.)

2) "Every father is obligated to hire a teacher for his son. Comment [by Rema–Rabbi Moses Isserles]—and we compel him to hire a teacher for his son, and if he is not in the city and he has means, if it is possible to inform him, they inform him, and if not, his funds are expropriated and a teacher for his son is hired." (Ibid. 245:4.)

3) "The residents of a city compel one another jointly to hire a teacher for their children" (Ibid. 245:15).

From these laws it is absolutely clear that the Torah education of the children of the affluent is not a private concern of their parents alone. The Torah education of children is a public concern attached to the entire community. The wealthy members of a community have a mutual claim upon one another to arrange for a comprehensive Torah education for their children, making use of their fiscal resources. At the same time, they are obligated to be concerned about the Torah education of the children of the poor. According to the commentary of Rashi on Nedarim 81a, the phrase "take heed of the children of the poor" does not at all mean that we fulfill the obligation of concern for a Torah education through a specific program of study for the children of the poor. Rather, its sole intent is to protect the children of the poor from abandonment, "that it will not be trivial in our sight to teach them Torah." This caution receives double force in that it emphasizes that it is precisely from the children of the poor that great Torah scholars frequently emerge.

Yet, without a doubt, the first obligation of the affluent and a commandment directed towards Heaven is the concern that the Torah education of their own children takes precedence over the education of the poor. The commandment to teach Torah to their own children assails them at the start, as it is the first commandment of the father with respect to his son and his obligation to bequeath Torah to his sons after him. Indeed, the commandment to teach Torah to the children of the poor may be thrust upon them indirectly only through the commandment of *tsedaqah*. Thus a Jewish law states unambiguously, "One is obligated to hire a teacher for his son to teach him. However, he is not obligated to hire for the son of his friend" (*Yoreh De'ah* 245:4). Hence, the wealth of the affluent, from which tax money is taken for the needs of the community, is subject first and foremost to the Torah education of their own children, and only afterwards to the children of the poor. The leaders of the community who are called upon to administer the community and who are obligated according to Jewish law as explicated above to demand from the affluent father that he maintain Torah education from his wealth—it is incumbent upon them to use the funds of the wealthy first and foremost for the necessity of Torah education for the sons of the wealthy themselves and only afterwards for the children of the poor.

This and more. It is clear and obvious according to the law that the holiness of the house of study is greater than the sanctity of the synagogue, for in a time of need it is permissible to transform our synagogues into houses of study (*Orah Hayyim* 153:1), and in a time of emergency it is even permissible to sell our Torah scrolls if it is necessary for the maintenance of Torah education (*Yoreh De'ah* 270:1). From this, it is also evident that a concern for the Torah education of the children of the rich and poor alike is not only a matter comparable in importance to other affairs of the community; rather, the extent of its importance, its essentiality and its urgency, exceeds all else. For the synagogues as well as all the other religious institutions of the community will lose all their value and prestige, and the glory of our synagogues and our scrolls of Torah—their significance and content—will be reduced to objects of scorn and derision if we are not concerned with establishing schools which will raise our children to be faithful heart and soul to Judaism and to be sanctified in those synagogues for the sake of this Torah, in accord with all its statutes and judgments, from a state of understanding and enthusiasm, and for the sake of being servants of God in truth in the life of Israel, a life of Torah and commandments.

And that which has been true at all times has been elevated into a matter of unparalleled importance at the present moment. The holy concerns of Judaism will, God forbid, be abandoned completely if we do not succeed in arousing enthusiasm among the children of the affluent for Torah and worship and if we do not raise them to become proper Jews. For they are those most exposed to the great temptations of the time, and they are likely to be the first who will be lost to the community of Israel if they do not acquire a broad knowledge through the spirit of an illuminating and exciting Torah. In this way, they will display an honor and an enthusiastic love that elevates the prestige of Torah, and they will not, from a lack of knowledge, distort and abandon her in life. The study of Torah alone will permit their rescue, and this will be only if the affluent members of our community and their children return and understand the honor that stems from being among those who are learned and who revere the Torah and those who study it. Then, members of our middle class as well will preserve their faith in God and His Torah, and the decisive influence upon our communities will be in the hands of those who are devoted in nobility and enthusiasm for the cause of Torah and its holiness. In our day, concern for the Torah education of the poor is an act of loving kindness. However, the concern for the Torah education of the wealthy is an act of rescue for the sake of God and His Torah.

I hope that the leaders of your community succeed in this great act of rescue for your community. May God extend His help and bestow blessing upon all the works of your hands.

NOTES

1. For a volume of his halakhic writings, see Samson Raphael Hirsch, *Shemesh Marpeh*.
2. On Prins and his life and writings, see *Liepman Phillip Prins: His Scholarly Correspondence*, ed. Mayer Herskovics and Els Bendheim (Hoboken: Ktav, 1992) (Hebrew). For Prins's correspondence with Rabbi Hirsch on the matter of curriculum, see Letter 4 in Herskovics and Bendheim.
3. Letter 5 in Herskovics and Bendheim. This responsum can also be found in *Shemesh Marpeh*, no. 53.

4

An Ideology for the Liberal Jewish Day School

A Philosophical-Sociological Investigation

Liberal day schools (those affiliated with the PARDES—the Progressive
Association of Reform Day Schools, RAVSAK—the Network of community day schools, and the Solomon Schechter Day School Association)
have since their earliest days championed the ideology of integration
and have made integration of subjects with one another a cornerstone of
their curriculum. Indeed, virtually every day school includes integration
as part of its mission, and most see integration as an important part of
teaching and learning (even if they struggle with how to accomplish this
goal). In recent years, the ideology that integration represents has been
called into question, and educators and educational scholars have begun
exploring an alternative ideology and curriculum model that stresses the
dynamic "interaction"[1] among aspects of the day school curriculum (see
Zeldin, 1998).

　This article intends to describe the historical context that initially led
to the integrative model that characterized the modern Jewish situation
and informed Jewish education in the West throughout the nineteenth
century and during most of the twentieth. I will then explore the contemporary sociological and intellectual currents that have caused a philosophical notion of "interaction" between minority and majority cultures
to emerge in what has been labeled a "postmodern" world. Having analyzed the conditions that have advanced the "interactive model," and having described the philosophical basis that has informed it, I will then cite
and reproduce a philosophical reflection and a textual example provided
and discussed by Alan Mittleman that will show how this model might
be applied so as to inform the classroom situation that liberal Jewish day
schools confront as they attempt to meet the challenge of educating and
preparing students to navigate the shoals of an increasingly complex and
diverse North American world.

The Universalism of Enlightenment and the Direction of Modern Jewish Thought and Education

As Friedrich Nietzsche (1966) observed in 1885, "The Jews . . . are beyond doubt the strongest, toughest, and purest race now living in Europe. . . . Meanwhile, they [the Jews] want and wish . . . to be absorbed and assimilated" (187). Nietzsche's comment is certainly an exaggerated one. Most occidental Jews during the last two centuries have neither actively desired nor been prepared to surrender their identity as Jews. In fact, one of the great fictions of modern Jewish self-understanding has been the tendency to believe that the rate of actual Jewish conversion to Christianity, particularly in Germany during the nineteenth century, has been strikingly high. (For a sober assessment of the phenomenon and actual rates of Jewish apostasy, see Endelman 1987.) Yet it is undeniably true that from the onset of Enlightenment and Emancipation in the West at the beginning of the 1800s until our own day, the single most dominant cultural characteristic of Western Jews has been the desire to participate fully in the life of the larger host society and culture. Jewish eagerness to receive the cultural, political, economic, and social rewards of the modern world has known virtually no bounds. The need to define the relationship between the poles of "Judaism, Jewish traditions, and Jewish identity" on the one hand and "modernity" on the other has informed Jewish leaders and thinkers across denominational lines. It has led virtually all Jewish ideologues, liberal and Orthodox alike, to ignore the "divided passions" such twin commitments might engender and has caused them to proclaim instead a strong affinity for the teachings of Judaism and the ethos of the West. (An explication of this impulse to see Jewish tradition and Western values as absolutely compatible even within the precincts of Jewish Orthodoxy can be found in Kurzweil 1986.)

There are undoubtedly several reasons for this proclamation of identity and compatibility between Western and Jewish values. However, foremost among them has been the Jewish desire to reap the rewards such a proclamation would grant Jews as members of a minority community seeking to participate in the life of a majority population. After all, modern Judaism—and Reform in particular—was born in a German crucible of "messianic expectations." When Israel Jacobson, the father of Reform Judaism, dedicated the first Reform synagogue, the Temple of Jacob, in

Seesen, Germany, on July 17, 1810, a contemporary account reported that "hundreds of persons of distinguished rank, scholars, Jewish, Protestant, and Catholic clergymen, officials, businessmen of all kinds," were in attendance. The event displayed the universalistic aspirations of the dawning era, and a commentator upon it was visibly moved by the spirit of concord and "uniform tolerance" that marked the day and its participants. In a burst of unconcealed enthusiasm, he rapturously asked, "Where could one have seen a similar day on which Jews and Christians celebrated together in a common service in the presence of more than forty clergymen of both religions, and then sat down to eat and rejoice together in intimate company?" (see Plaut 1963, 27–30).

This episode bespeaks the universalistic hopes and commitments of the day and affirms that the utopianism inherent in an enlightened vision of the world was capable of being transformed into reality. Jews would no longer view themselves or be regarded as "Others," as part of a distinct ethnic-national-religious community. Rather, they would define themselves and be seen as individual citizens of a modern nation-state whose religion happened to be Jewish. The universalism inherent in this approach as well as the practical benefits to be derived from it are unmistakable. It is a Judaism informed by an Enlightenment faith in the power of autonomy and reason as well as reliance on the innate goodness of humanity. It reflects a world in which the social and religious insights of each generation are regarded as representing an improvement over the preceding one. The confidence these Jews possessed in the icons of occidental culture and their determination to demonstrate the confluence between Judaism and the West cannot be exaggerated. They have certainly informed the "integrative model" that has guided liberal Judaism for so much of its history.

Pedagogy played a central role in nineteenth-century Jewish attempts to realize this vision of a world where Jews and Christians could live as equals. In keeping with Enlightenment philosophy's emphasis upon the perfectibility of humanity through reason and education, the Jewish community attempted to realize its hopes for integration and advancement into the larger society through the reform of its educational system. The approach to education these Jewish leaders of the 1800s took was strongly informed by the concept of Bildung, a notion that dominated the world of nineteenth-century German culture. As George L. Mosse (1985) has observed, "The word *Bildung* combines the meaning carried by the English

word *education* with notions of character formation and moral education."
It suggested a philosophical view of lofty human potential. Bildung was a
natural outgrowth of the Enlightenment, with its stress on the individual
and reason, as well as romanticism. Its function was "to lead the individual from superstition to enlightenment." It was, in addition, an approach
to education that would allow the "inequality between men" to be overcome. As such, it "might also work to transcend the differences between
the Jewish and the German middle classes. The centrality of the ideal of
Bildung in German-Jewish consciousness must be understood from the
very beginning . . . [as] fundamental to the search for a new Jewish identity after emancipation" (3).

The first practical applications by the Jewish community of this
Enlightenment-derived philosophy of education can be seen in the creation of schools by German *maskilim* (Jewish Enlighteners) and reformers
at the end of the eighteenth century and the beginning of the nineteenth.
Hasharat Zvi, an elementary school established in Halberstadt in 1796,
exemplifies the trends toward change that marked Jewish educational
institutions during this period as well as the "integrative model" that
was to characterize and inform Jewish schools for so much of the modern period. Zvi Hirsch Katzlin, the founder of this school, was a wealthy
and religiously observant Jewish businessman. He bequeathed funds in
his will for the creation of a school that would combine Jewish learning
with a secular curriculum and would prepare students for occupations in
general German society. Like other Jews of his economic and social class
who were eager to receive the benefits proffered by the French Revolution, Katzlin was an enthusiastic proponent of the Emancipation. He was
convinced that the acquisition of one's "equal rights" depended on a mastery of the German language, as well as a knowledge of general subjects
and professions. However, he was equally concerned that Jewish children
should retain their identity as Jews. As a result, Hasharat Zvi was opened
and the curriculum was one where the students received instruction in
both Jewish and general subjects. The integrative vision that propelled
the school's benefactor can be seen in the school's motto—"A blending of
eternal religious verities with popular enlightenment in accord with the
spirit of the time." Hasharat Zvi was certainly more traditional than comparable educational institutions established by liberal Jews in the 1800s.
However, like its more liberal sister institutions of the next century, it

shared in an Enlightenment vision that the values of Judaism, taught in a progressive spirit, and the teachings of the secular world were complementary, not dissonant. The "integrative model" informed its curriculum and was typical of the tone that marked all German-Jewish schools, not just liberal ones, during the nineteenth century. The vision of integration, while certainly strongly advanced by Reformers, was sufficiently vital to inform virtually all modernist sectors of Judaism during the 1800s (see Eliav 1960, 156ff., for a description of Hasharat Zvi and the philosophy of "integration" characteristic of German-Jewish educational institutions of the period; see also Feiner 2004 for historical treatment of the Haskalah).

This ideological vision was not confined to Germany, but manifested itself on American's shores as well throughout the nineteenth and twentieth centuries. The German Jews who came to the United States in the nineteenth century brought views of a nonparticularistic universal-rational religion with them. These Jews, both by background and the promise of future reward within the American societal context, were predisposed to eschew Jewish particularistic values that, because they emphasized group distinctiveness, would have retarded their progress in the United States. The ethos of American Jews and the Reform Judaism that was dominant in that era—expressed in documents like the Pittsburgh Platform of 1885— was one that rejected particularistic values and Jewish uniqueness. These Jews purged "oriental" patterns of worship from the synagogue, devised a liturgy almost wholly universalistic in orientation, abandoned dietary laws, and rapidly conformed to the cultural patterns and mores of the United States.

With the onset of Jewish immigration from Eastern Europe in the late nineteenth and early twentieth centuries, a different type of Jew came to North America. These Jews deliberately avoided and were purposefully excluded from the Reform community and its Germanic culture. It would be a mistake to claim, on the basis of these differences, that these Eastern European Jews were not as enamored as their German American brothers and sisters of the model of integration. For their aim, like their German Jewish predecessors, was to acculturate. Drawn to America by its promise of a brighter future, these immigrants and their progeny did not possess a commitment to Jewish religious values and practices that would have hindered their acculturation. They quickly abandoned observance of the Sabbath and dietary laws outside of the home, and their failure to construct ritual baths or Jewish day schools indicates not only their economic status but also their lack of attachment to either traditional Jewish learning or laws of family purity (see Hertzberg 1989; Liebman 1973, 42ff.; for more recent works see Diner 2003; Sarna 2004).

These Jews possessed a universalistic orientation that allowed them to forge a Judaism that was seen as totally compatible with American life and values. They established systems of religious thought and practice—Reform and Conservative Judaism—that applauded the virtues of democracy and the American way of life. Indeed, an offshoot of Conservative Judaism, Reconstructionism, accorded the status of *sancta* to such American festivals as Thanksgiving, Labor Day, and the Fourth of July. Even when a highly particularistic vision of Judaism such as Zionism was affirmed, it was articulated so that Justice Brandeis as well as many American rabbis could both equate the *halutzim* of Palestine with America's Pilgrim fathers and proclaim that the values of Zionism and those of American democracy were one and the same. (See Brandeis's famous statement on this point in Hertzberg 1959, 519–20, where he states, "Let no American imagine that Zionism is inconsistent with Patriotism. Multiple loyalties are objectionable only if they are inconsistent. . . . There is no inconsistency between loyalty to America and loyalty to Jewry. The Jewish spirit . . . is essentially modern and essentially American.") Indeed, Jewish particularity was largely justified by these committed Jews through the creation of apologetic works that either demonstrated the affinities between American and Jewish teachings or "proved" Judaism's decisive impact upon this or that element of American history or civilization. Such claims to Jewish influence on the values of the United States, as well as the notion of compatibility between American and Jewish values, undoubtedly contain more than a kernel of truth. It reflects how highly the American Jew prized the United States and its values. It bespeaks the heritage bequeathed American Jews by their German predecessors as well as the common response offered by both these acculturated Jewish communities to the lure of the West. Most significantly for our purposes, it demonstrates the strength and vitality that the ideology of integration held for these immigrant Jews and their progeny as they sought security and advancement on the North American continent. How this model surrendered its monopoly over the hearts and minds of significant numbers of American Jews, and the ideological basis for this shift to an interactive model that would permit a greater sense of Jewish ethnicity with distinctive values to emerge, will be the focus of the next section of this essay.

A Shift in Paradigms

In recent years, American society has witnessed a shift in attitudes and values concerning ethnicity and race. Michael Novak (1972) coined the phrase "the new ethnicity" to characterize what he saw as a sense of discomfort that ethnic Americans were beginning to feel with the prevailing model of behavior, attitudes, and values that they, as their ancestors before them, were expected to emulate. The dominant cultural image of the ideal American—established by the British American upper-class elements who founded this nation—no longer seemed compelling. As Eugene Borowitz (1972) explained,

> Today [humanity] needs people who are creatively alienated. To be satisfied with our situation is either to have bad values or to understand grossly what [persons] can do. . . . Creative alienation implies sufficient withdrawal from our society to judge it critically, but also the way and flexibility to keep finding and trying ways to correct it. I think Jewishness offers a unique means of gaining and maintaining such creative alienation. This was not its primary role in the lives of our parents and grandparents. (209)

Jews, like other ethnics in the United States, were no longer infatuated with the model of the "melting pot." Many began to feel the "creative alienation" of which Borowitz spoke, and their dissatisfaction led many of them to appreciate the wisdom of Judaism and affirm their Jewish heritage. These Jews began to wonder why the writings of Emerson or Thoreau should be deemed superior to the rabbis of the Talmud or Maimonides in constructing the human spirit. Such changed attitudes toward ethnicity in the larger culture have surely served as a source for the curricular debates over multiculturalism that have embroiled American college campuses for decades. (Here I emphasize the "positive" contributions multiculturalism can and does make to our society; for examples critical of the disintegrative trends of "multiculturalism," see Berry 2002; D'Souza 1991; Huntington 1996; Schlesinger 1998.) They have also promoted a transformation in attitudes that many Jews possess regarding Judaism and its teachings and have caused Jews to explore their own culture and religion as a source of identity and meaning in an increasingly perplexing world. Jewish day schools, at their best, have emerged out of this impulse.[2] Thus the very impulse that has given rise to our day schools has been an interactive, not an integrative, one. Indeed, the ideology that allowed liberal Jewish day schools to open presupposes a different relationship and attitude toward American culture than the "melting pot" metaphor that informed our community in the first half of this century.

Alan Dershowitz's book *Chutzpah* is a prime illustration of how the position and values of the Jewish community in the United States have been transformed. In a telling reminiscence, Dershowitz recalls that in his first day

> as a law student at Yale, I read a Supreme Court decision [*West Virginia State Board of Education v. Barnette* (1944)] involving a compulsory flag salute during World War II, to which some Jehovah's Witnesses objected on religious grounds. The majority agreed with the religious objectors, but Justice Felix Frankfurter dissented . . . on the ground that patriotism during wartime is more important than religious liberty. (48)

Frankfurter, in the case, wrote a dissent that James O. Freedman (1990), the first Jewish president of Dartmouth College, has described as "one of the most confessional and emotional of Supreme Court opinions." Frankfurter wrote,

> One who belongs to the most vilified and persecuted minority in history is not likely to be insensible to the freedoms guaranteed by our Constitution. Were my purely personal attitude relevant I should wholeheartedly associate myself with the general libertarian views in the Court's opinion. . . . But as judges we are neither Jew nor Gentile, neither Catholic nor agnostic. We owe equal attachment to the constitution and are equally bound by our judicial obligation whether we derive our citizenship from the earliest or latest immigrants to these shores.

Frankfurter's dissent in *Barnette* was consistent with the position he had adopted in a similar case three years earlier. In that instance, Chief Justice Hughes had assigned Frankfurter the majority opinion in *Minersville*

School District v. Gobitis (1940), a case "upholding the constitutionality of a statue requiring all students, including the children of Jehovah's Witnesses," to salute the flag, an act the Witnesses viewed as blasphemous. The chief justice had chosen Frankfurter for the task, Hughes recalled, "because of Frankfurter's emotional description, in conference, of the 'role of the public school in instilling love of country' based upon his own experiences as a [Jewish] immigrant child" (see Freedman 1990).

Dershowitz (1991), the child of Orthodox Jewish parents raised and educated in a highly Jewish Brooklyn enclave, comments that he read the 1943 opinion "in astonishment. As a twenty-one-year-old student, I simply couldn't identify with it. I didn't feel 'vilified' or 'persecuted,' or even as part of a 'minority.'" Indeed, the only "insensitivity" Dershowitz observed in these cases was that Frankfurter was "quite 'insensible' to the religious freedoms of the Jehovah's Witnesses" (48).

The gap between the opinions of Frankfurter and Dershowitz is emblematic of the transition that marks many American Jews' attitudes toward this country's values. Frankfurter, the product of an immigrant Jewish community that took to heart the image of a melting pot, could permit no emphasis on particularism. Frankfurter felt he had to insist upon the adoption of "neutral, universal" values as the only ones that could legitimately guide American society. His vision of Judaism, like countless others of his generation, was one that affirmed complete compatibility between American and Jewish values. Such a vision allowed no room for the expression of independent Jewish values and interests.

In contrast, Dershowitz, raised in a post-Holocaust generation that was no longer dominated numerically by an immigrant population, displays a different sensibility. Dershowitz does not fear affirming his or others' particularities. In a pluralistic contemporary America, such a position on the part of a member of an ethnic group is not only defensible, it is demanded by a free and open society where values of tolerance and diversity would flourish and ensure a healthy democracy. Dershowitz represents a shift in how American Jews approach the issue of American values in a present-day setting. His reading of American society today affirms that legitimacy of distinctive Jewish values and interests within an American context.

This changed perspective has been promoted by trends the sociologist Peter Berger identifies as present in the larger culture. In *The Heretical Imperative*, Berger (1975) points out that the quintessential feature of modern Western culture is that *haeresis*, option or choice, has become inescapable. The condition that characterizes modernity is that options and choices that were once unthinkable have now become acceptable in ways that would have been unimaginable a generation earlier. Choices increase at a dizzying pace. People leave their native towns, women become clergy, gays and lesbians "step out of the closet" and are wooed by presidential candidates as they seek elective office. Such examples can be multiplied a thousandfold. It is, as Berger sees it, the mark of the modern world. Modernity is marked, in his felicitous phrase, by the move "from fate to choice" (see especially 29–30).

The pluralism of the modern world no longer permits "reason" to speak in the monotone that Kant envisioned. Enlightenment confidence that "reason" can yield a set of prescriptions that all "rational persons" will acknowledge as universally true is hardly shared in the contemporary situation. "Reason" cannot prescribe "truth" for all persons nor can it necessarily move persons to act. The central belief that marked modern thought was a faith in the hegemony of reason and the capacity of reason to form a "universal person" bereft of particularistic attachments or commitments. The recognition that ours is a world marked by choice, by a "heretical imperative" that elicits diverse commitments and values on the part of disparate communities, challenges the ideological foundation of the modern world, a foundation that saw truth as emanating from a single rational source. Our sociological situation and our historical experiences undermine the faith of the Enlightenment. The heretical imperative, and the sociological-historical recognition that ideas and values cannot be totally separated from the diverse communities and cultures that promote them has yielded a different perspective on the world for contemporary persons.

This movement, as Berger describes it, is liberating. It frees people from the shackles of a stultified culture and tradition that define roles and expectations in a narrow and confining way. It also leaves people feeling bewildered or, as Berger states in another of his works, "homeless." In *The Homeless Mind*, Berger, Berger, and Kellner (1973) argue that the modern condition of choice, the displacement that marks the upwardly mobile as they move from place to place in search of career and opportunity, has also left many persons without a secure sense of roots and stability. Ethical and spiritual purpose does not appear to have emerged out of the rationalist ethos of an Enlightenment world. While many have been liberated from "tribal brotherhood," still more have experienced the anomie and alienation of "universal otherhood" (see Nelson, 1969). Restriction and uncertainty have been introduced into the minds and hearts of many.

The paradox of the modern world is that it both destroys and engenders community and tradition. It releases the bonds and frameworks that tied persons to the practices and perceptions of the past while simultaneously allowing them to experiment with and return to a tradition they may never have known in order to discover the security and warmth such tradition promises to offer. Berger's (1979) analysis, in the case of Jews, helps explain why we have entered a postmodern situation in which antipodean currents—where record rates of nonaffiliation and abandonment of Jewish religion and identity compete with intense pockets of Jewish commitment and knowledge—mark the contemporary American Jewish situation. The pluralism of the modern situation and the bewildering variety of choices that modernity provides leads many to abandon Judaism. Simultaneously, it causes others, living within a pluralistic framework, to seek out Judaism for the sense of wisdom, security, and identity that Jewish tradition and religion can offer to its committed adherents. This was not its function even forty years ago. Berger's analysis hopefully illuminates and explains the move from a model of integration to one of interaction between the teachings of tradition and the values of the modern world on the part of significant numbers of ethnics and minorities in American society.

Among Jews, another significant cause for this change in attitude has undoubtedly been the Holocaust. Simply put, the Holocaust has rocked the confidence Jews formerly had in the goodness of humanity and the moral progress of civilization. Such beliefs must now be tempered by recognition that the human capacity for evil, as for goodness, is virtually infinite. As Irving Greenberg has written, "There is the shock of recognition that the humanistic revolt . . . is now revealed to sustain a capacity for death and demonic evil" (Greenberg 1977, 15).

Borowitz (1987) echoes Greenberg's sentiments and contends that the modern Jew, living in a post-Holocaust situation, must recognize the limits of Enlightenment thought. In the twentieth century, reason and reliance on the innate goodness of humanity have shown themselves to be "unreliable, if not destructive" (265). As he writes elsewhere, "I think it is only an understatement to say that, in our day, self-confidence in humanism is ludicrous. . . . Secularity no longer is self-assured and triumphant. If anything, its moral collapse has been so thorough-going that it threatens to destroy whatever little faith in humankind we can still manage to muster" (Borowitz 1974, 300).

The need to oppose evil resolutely means that ethical warrants for guiding human values and actions must be produced. Religion addresses this need and is entitled to an independent voice in the contemporary setting precisely because of the confidence in the tradition from which it speaks. In a bewildering world of choices and indecision, religion offers the surest compass for navigating through the shoals of contemporary moral claims. In sum, contemporary history has effectively undermined the confidence in human judgment that formerly undergirded modern thought. This, in turn, has brought about a renewed appreciation of the independent power and truth of religion in a postmodern situation. The power of the integrative ideal no longer seems as compelling as it did to earlier generations of liberal Jews (Borowitz, 1991).

Nevertheless, for liberal Jews this turn in modern thought does not signal a total retreat from the insights and affirmations derived from an Enlightenment vision of the world. Modern-day liberal Jews reject the religious fundamentalism that appears to dominate so many sectors of the Jewish world today, even as we turn with new respect to examine the wisdom and power of Jewish religious tradition. For liberal Judaism, the concept of "the self" as well as the rights of conscience and the practice of democracy and pluralism this concept entails must continue to be incorporated into our ideology. An abandonment of this legacy can neither be countenanced nor imagined. This belief in the importance of the individual and the concomitant commitments to democracy and pluralism that this concept engenders constitute irreversible elements in the philosophy of contemporary liberal Judaism. They establish an ongoing interactive dialectic between the values of tradition and the teachings of modernity in the life of contemporary liberal Judaism. However, the dialectic itself mutes and shapes the notion of "self" that emerges. In the postmodern setting, it is essential to rethink the meaning of even this concept in Jewish terms, and it is in teachings of Jewish tradition as interpreted by Martin Buber (1958) that the contours and shape of a Jewish concept of "self" appear.

Buber (1958), drawing heavily on the teachings of the rabbis, taught throughout his work that the meaning and purpose of human existence is found in the fundamentally social nature of reality. The individual is "human" primarily because he or she is capable of entering into dialogic relationship with another person and with God. In a word, the individual is able to communicate. Authentic being consists in being known and knowing that one is being known. One is permitted to say "I" only because there are "Thous." As Buber wrote, "I become through my relation to the Thou; as I become I, I say Thou. *All real living is meeting*" (11; emphasis added). Persons live in a state of mutually independent interdependence.

> A Person makes his appearance by entering into relation with other persons. . . . He who takes his stand in relation shares in a reality, that is, in a being, that neither merely belongs to him nor merely lies outside of him. All reality is an activity in which I share without being able to appropriate it for myself. Where there is not sharing there is no reality. Where there is self-appropriation there is no reality. The more direct the contact with the Thou, the fuller is the sharing. (63)

One is made fully human through others. Our unique characters, which make each of us individual, make us essentially other. Yet our uniqueness, our being for ourselves, constitutively leads us to be for others. Neither the solitary individual nor the social aggregate is the irreducible datum of human existence. We are persons because we can claim and respond, address and be addressed. We are persons because we are responsible to and for others. We are persons because we live in community.

Judaism provides a powerfully communitarian notion of "self" and sense of morality that is at odds with the disintegrative tendencies of an excessive Kantian individualism that has proven insufficient to provide for a social cohesion that the contemporary world, and particularly the Jewish community, so desperately needs. In the present situation—both sociologically and philosophically—the task confronting individual persons is not primarily one of affirming autonomy and individual personhood. It is the challenge of creating institutions in which Jews and all persons can have a sense of confidence and hope. This is the task confronting our educational institutions, and it lends a sense of urgency to our efforts. The integrity and wisdom of Jewish tradition and our attempts to reconstitute Jewish community in our modern situation of choice and fragmentation can contribute much to individual Jews and the Jewish community in a world that all too often flounders in its quest for values and identity. By creating schools, and providing a model of Judaism that is not identical to but interacts with the larger world of values and culture of which we are a part, Judaism may make its greatest contribution to individual Jews and our larger society.

Having now indicated the sociological, historical, and philosophical reasons for this shift from an integrative to an interactive model for understanding the relationships of Jews and Jewish tradition to the modern world, I now turn to several rabbinic texts that can provide a model for how this interactive approach might be applied to the classroom of the liberal Jewish day school.

The Interactive Model in Action—A Textual Application

The question of how persons ought to live in community and what their responsibilities are to society is one of the most pressing of our age. How do we balance a legitimate concern with autonomy and the rights of an individual with the responsibilities which devolve upon us as members of a community? It is a dilemma that is addressed in both Western and Jewish thought. A consideration of how modern Western political thought as opposed to Jewish tradition deals with this problem will reveal a great deal about how an interactionist, as opposed to an integrative, model might approach this question in the day school setting.

In the integrationist mode, the teacher would assume or seek to demonstrate that the values and teachings of Jewish tradition and those of Western culture are either identical or complementary on this or virtually any other topic. The teacher might even attempt to show how the values of the former are derived from the sentiments of the latter. The interactionist model, on the other hand, would compel the teacher to investigate each tradition separately and seek initially to discover the independent integrity of each tradition. The dialectical nature of the relationship between these two great traditions would be emphasized. Complementarity or identity might result from such investigation. Conversely, the tensions between these different systems of thought might also be presented to the students so that they could ultimately make informed decisions about which system of thought each would consider more apposite to a particular problem or situation. Professor Alan Mittleman (1993) of the Jewish Theological Seminary offers an instructive example as to how this might be done. In his brilliant article, "From Private Rights to Public Good," he contrasts what modern Western thought has to say about the relationship of the individual to society and the concomitant rights and obligations this might entail with the position of Jewish tradition on this issue. Mittleman's piece and a presentation of a Talmudic textual analysis he provides in his article will guide us in this deliberation.

Modern Western political thought has traditionally centered around the importance of the individual. From Locke through Nozick, one strand of classical liberal political theory has envisioned the polity as a voluntary contract entered into by free, independent individuals who are endowed prior to their political relationship with natural rights. This means, as Locke articulated it, that persons enter into political relationships because this permits them to secure a more effective defense of their natural rights than they would possess in a state of nature. The political order has as its sole purpose the protection of the natural rights of the individual. Communal interference in the life of the individual is justified only when it prevents wrongdoers from infringing upon the liberty of others. The purpose of the community is exclusively prophylactic. Hence the powers of the community over the individual are severely limited.

In the twentieth century, the foremost exponent of this line of thought has been the Harvard philosopher Robert Nozick. In *Anarchy, State and Utopia*, Nozick (1974) has offered a philosophical defense of the "minimal state." He argues that the state bears no "corporate responsibility" to its citizens. Instead, a "state should do no more than is necessary to enable citizens to exercise their private rights." To coerce its citizenry in any way in order to act on behalf of the disadvantaged is to violate the state's only legitimate function—the protection of the rights of the individual and the preservation of individual human dignity. The "political individualism" that undergirds Nozick's notion of community would protect a physically debilitated and homeless beggar from those who would remove him from the sidewalk on a public street. However, while no one would take away his rights, his inability to exercise them would be of no concern to the state. The beggar and his kind may have the negative liberty of non-infringement, but not the positive liberty that is available only for the vigorous and determined. A communal obligation to provide a system of welfare and training for the exploited and oppressed in society would not exist in Nozick's state (26ff.).

To be fair, there are others within classical Western thought who provide an alternative to the philosophical tradition of Locke and the excessive and atomistic individualism he offered.[3] Jean Jacques Rousseau was a contemporary critic of Locke and the political thinking associated with him. In contrast to Locke's thoroughgoing individualism, Rousseau taught that community is the product of a contract freely entered into by individuals who recognize an identity of interests among themselves and therefore voluntarily surrender their private desires to a universal desire to serve the whole. This creation of a "general will" forms the basis of the "social contract" that undergirds and legitimates government. Once established, the state is endowed with rights over the individual. Indeed, the individual is obligated to align his or her will with that of the general will so that freedom can be achieved. For those who cannot so believe, their fellow citizens "may compel [them] to be free." That is, the state has the right to compel the individual to conform to the general will. The coercive power of the state is virtually unlimited. In a century that has witnessed the excesses and cruelty of totalitarian regimes that have trampled on individual liberties, Rousseau's thought hardly provides a desirable alternative to the ideology of Locke and his intellectual followers. Neither negative nor positive liberty would necessarily be accorded the individual in Rousseau's community. There would be no institutional checks upon the coercive power of the State. The challenge that remains is one of fashioning a political philosophy that would provide a corrective to both the collectivism of Rousseau and the atomistic individualism of classical Western political theory. The goal would be to investigate Jewish tradition to see whether Jewish teachings could provide an alternative ground to the ones presented in Western thought.

The *mishnah*, in Baba Batra 1:5, as well as in the *gemara* upon it (Baba Batra 7b), offers such a text. It provides ample material for a discussion of how individual liberties might be balanced against the needs of the community. The *mishnah* states, "Everyone [that dwells within a courtyard] may be compelled to [contribute to the] building of a gatehouse and a door for the courtyard. Rabban Simeon b. Gamaliel says, 'Not all courtyards are such that they need a gatehouse.' Everyone [that dwells within town] may be compelled to [contribute to the] building of a wall for town. Rabban Simeon b. Gamaliel says, 'Not every town is such that it needs a wall.'" The *mishnah*, at the outset of each case, puts forth a principle of justified coercion. A recalcitrant resident of a courtyard as well as a recalcitrant resident of a town may be compelled (*kofin oto*) to participate in a capital improvement that is mandated by the general will of the community. However, the responsibility for and the costs of building the gatehouse in the first instance and the wall in the second must be fairly divided among all the residents to ensure that each benefits equally from the capital improvement that will be made. Individual desires can be subsumed by the collective will because it is assumed that each person should identify with the common interests of the community. The assumption is made that responsibilities and benefits will be arranged so that all gain and none loses. The *gemara*, in commenting on this *mishnah*, immediately addresses the public implications entailed by the construction of a gatehouse. After all, the structure will increase the privacy of the courtyard and may therefore prevent the poor from coming in to beg. Indeed, the *gemara* states that Elijah refused to visit a pious man after he constructed a gatehouse for this precise reason. It seems that the *gemara* finds the gatehouse morally problematic on this score. Yet, if this is so, how can the *mishnah* require the "recalcitrant neighbor or citizen" to participate in the construction of the gatehouse in the first place? There is an apparent contradiction between the pious man's morally objectionable action in building such a house and the *mishnah*'s stipulation that such a house represents a legitimate capital improvement. The *gemara* resolves this seeming contradiction by demanding that a gatehouse be built in such a way that it causes no problems for prospective beggars to enter the courtyard. The pious man had failed to provide his gatehouse with a latch or a handle so that the poor might enter! The *gemara* expands on the level of public obligation required of persons living in a courtyard. These residents are not only responsible to one another for capital improvements as the *mishnah* would have it. They are equally obligated not to impede the poor as they come to claim *tzedakah*!

Up to this point, the coercive powers of the community on the individual appear to be absolute. Jewish tradition and the "collective will" of Rousseau appear to be identical. However, in both cases the text moves to the concerns of Rabban Simeon b. Gamaliel. In both instances, he cautions that not all courtyards require a gatehouse nor do all towns require walls. The recalcitrant resident's obligation to participate in the construction of either is contingent not only upon the will of the community but also upon the ability of the community to indicate that there are other relevant concerns that mandate the building of the gatehouse in the first instance and the wall in the second. Hence the *gemara*, in its continued discussion of the *mishnah*, explains the reason for R. Simeon b. Gamaliel's objection in the first instance and produces a *baraita* that asserts that only courtyards that "abut on a public domain" require a gatehouse, for only there is the privacy of the residents compromised. The other rabbis disagree with Rabban Simeon b. Gamaliel and contend that the "privacy rights" of individuals who reside in a courtyard are so great that even when a courtyard does not abut on a public domain, there always exists the possibility that a crowd of people could force their way in and disrupt the tranquility of the residents. Consequently, all residents of the courtyard may be compelled to share in the construction of the gatehouse. The courtyard community, as envisioned in the *mishnah* and *gemara*, reflects a delicate balance of private and public concerns.

This sensibility is evinced as well in the *gemara*'s discussion of the obligation imposed upon all residents to contribute to the construction of a city wall. As in the first case, R. Simeon b. Gamaliel asserts that in some instances a person need not be obligated to share in the construction of a wall. This is when a city does not lie on the frontier. In such cases the town will not be subject to attack. The rabbis dismiss R. Simeon b. Gamaliel's objection by asserting that all towns, not just those on the frontier, may legitimately require such walls, as all cities are potentially liable to attack from roving bands. However, the *gemara* shows great concern for how the tax designed for the construction of the wall should be levied. Should it be a tax imposed equally upon all residents of the city, rich and poor alike, since all will lose from an attack? Or should those closer to the wall and hence more vulnerable to attack pay more than those who dwell closer to the center of the city? The *gemara* resolves this by asserting that while all are obligated to pay a tax for the construction of the wall, "a poor man," in the words of the *tosafot* on this *gemara*, "at the edge of the town pays more than a rich man near downtown, but a rich man regardless of location will always pay more than a poor man." All are obligated to provide for the public good. This provides for the dignity of each individual. At the same time, the individual is not seen as an autonomous being. The individual is self-located in community. As Buber (1958) would have it, "We are persons because we dwell in community."

The analysis Mittleman provides of the Talmudic source demonstrates that Jewish tradition possesses a rich concept of persons and community. The common good is a regulative principle of political obligation. The community is more than a conglomeration of individual selves. It is an association of mutually obligated, interdependent selves who participate in a common good. It calls for a notion of self-in-society, an interrelated and derivative self that provides a palliative to what many see as the corrosive individualism of classical liberalism. At the same time, it provides for the dignity of the individual and an affirmation of the individual's position in society in a way that is distinct from the collectivism of a Rousseau.

Such an investigation reflects the shift to the interactionist model described in the first two sections of this article and indicates how the interactionist model might be applied in a day school setting. Jewish tradition is no longer assumed to be identical with Western values and perspectives. Indeed, in the text under discussion in this article, it is seen as possessing certain values and principles that are at odds with the normative ethos of Western political philosophy. In this way, Jewish teachings stand apart from Western tradition and offer the educated Jew the privilege of a different perspective from which to think about notions of self and the relationship of that self to the demands of society. Jewish teachings, so viewed, embody the "creative alienation" of which Borowitz (1973) speaks, an alienation "that implies sufficient withdrawal from our society to judge it critically, but also the way and flexibility to keep finding and trying ways to correct it."

The interactionist model does not imply a retreat from the larger world in which we live. Nor does it demand we accept and apply Jewish values over against ones derived from the larger culture. In cases other than the one I have produced here, it might well be that the values of Western culture would be deemed superior to Jewish ones. In yet other instances, the values and teachings of these two systems of thought might be seen as complementary or even identical. What is critical is that the direction of Jewish experience and ideology in this century has allowed an approach to Jewish texts and values to emerge today in the American Jewish community that would not have been possible in earlier generations. As Jews concerned with the establishment and course of liberal Jewish day schools, we ought to be mindful of and applaud this shift. The "interactionist model" for Jewish education, as opposed to the "integrationist model," bespeaks the newly found confidence we Jews have in the power of our own tradition as well as the wisdom it has to offer our students as they ultimately go forth to confront and contribute to both the Jewish community and the larger world.

NOTES

1. The idea of curriculum interaction was first articulated by my colleague Michael Zeldin at a symposium on integration sponsored by Hebrew Union College–Jewish Institute of Religion in 1994.
2. I recognize that other factors—not the least of which is "flight" from the public schools—have also contributed greatly to the growth of day schools. However, one should not overstate such factors or underestimate the ones this article details in considering why day schools have emerged. Of course, a sociohistorical description of why day schools have arisen at this juncture in the American Jewish Experience is also a topic for a different article.
3. It should be noted that others within the tradition of Western liberal political thought such as Nozick's Harvard colleague John Rawls and New York University law professor Ronald Dworkin have been sensitive to the problems inherent in deriving a welfare-oriented social policy on the basis of the teachings of Locke. These men, in contrast to Nozick, have introduced a concept of "distributive justice" into their political thinking that attempts to mute what they deem the deleterious social consequences of classical liberal political teachings. However, they refuse to abandon the notion of an autonomous, atomistic "self" that also undergirds Rawls's thought. Consequently, they have been subjected to critique on the grounds that it is logically difficult to speak of a common good and communal obligation in a discourse that emphasizes private rights. My purpose here is not to engage in a discussion of all the nuances of contemporary liberal political thinking. Rather, it is simply to alert the interested reader to the complexities of this debate and to indicate that I am aware that contemporary liberal political theory has its own nuances and subtleties. However, for our purposes what remains vital is that the liberal political tradition in the West remains committed to an autonomous, unrelated notion of self regardless of the political stance that ultimately emerges. This, I argue, is distinct from the Jewish notion of self, presented above in the discussion of Buber (1958) and below in the discussion of the Talmudic text selected and analyzed by Mittleman (1993).

REFERENCES

Berger, P. 1979. *The Heretical Imperative: Contemporary Possibilities of Religious Affirmation*. Garden City NY: Anchor Books.

Berger, P., B. Berger, and H. Kellner. 1973. *The Homeless Mind: Modernization and Consciousness.* New York: Random House.

Berry, B. M. 2002. *Culture and Equality: An Egalitarian Critique of Multiculturalism.* Cambridge MA: Harvard University Press.

Borowitz, E. 1973. *The Masks Jews Wear.* New York: Simon and Schuster.

Borowitz, E. 1974. "God and Man in Judaism Today: A Reform Perspective." *Judaism* 23.

Borowitz, E. 1987. "Freedom." In *Contemporary Jewish Religious Thought,* ed. A. A. Cohen and P. Mendes-Flohr, 261–67. New York: Scribner's.

Borowitz, E. 1991. *Renewing the Covenant.* Philadelphia: Jewish Publication Society.

Buber, M. 1958. *I–thou.* Trans. R. G. Smith. New York: Scribner's.

Dershowitz, A. M. 1991. *Chutzpah.* Boston: Little, Brown.

Diner, H. 2003. *New Promised Land: A History of the Jews in America.* New York: Oxford University Press.

D'Souza, D. 1991. *Illiberal Education: The Politics of Race and Sex on Campus.* New York: Free Press.

Endelman, T., ed. 1987. *Jewish Apostasy in the Modern World.* New York: Holmes and Meier.

Eliav, M. 1960. *Jewish Education in Germany during the Period of Enlightenment and Emancipation.* Jerusalem: Sivan Press. In Hebrew.

Feiner, S. 2004. *The Jewish Enlightenment.* Philadelphia: University of Pennsylvania Press.

Freedman, J. O. 1990. "Insiders and Outsiders." Inaugural Lecture of the Center for American Jewish History at Temple University, November 12, 8–9.

Greenberg, I. 1977. "Cloud of Smoke, Pillar of Fire: Judaism, Christianity, and Modernity after the Holocaust." In *Auschwitz: Beginning of a New Era?* ed. E. Fleischner. New York: Ktav.

Hertzberg, A., ed. 1959. *The Zionist Idea.* New York: Harper Torchbooks.

Hertzberg, A. 1989. *The Jew in America.* New York: Simon and Schuster.

Huntington, S. P. 1996. *The Clash of Civilizations and the Remaking of World Order.* New York: Simon and Schuster.

Kurzweil, Z. 1986. *The Modernist Impulse in Traditional Judaism.* New York: Ktav.

Liebman, C. 1973. *The Ambivalent American Jew.* Philadelphia: Jewish Publication Society.

Minersville School District v. Gobitis (1940).

Mittleman, A. 1993. "From Private Rights to Public Good: The Communitarian Critique of Liberalism in Judaic Perspective." *Jewish Political Studies Review* 5, nos. 1–2: 79–93.

Mosse, G. L. 1985. *German Jews beyond Judaism.* Cincinnati: Hebrew Union College Press.

Nelson, B. 1969. *The Idea of Usury: From Tribal Brotherhood to Universal Otherhood*. Chicago: University of Chicago Press.

Nietzsche, F. 1966. *Beyond Good and Evil*. Trans. W. Kaufman. New York: Random House.

Novak, M. 1972. *The Rise of the Unmeltable Ethnics*. New York: Macmillan.

Nozick, R. 1974. *Anarchy, State, and Utopia*. New York: Basic Books.

Plaut, G. 1963. *The Rise of Reform Judaism*. New York: World Union for Progressive Judaism.

Sarna, J. 2004. *American Judaism: A History*. New Haven CT: Yale University Press.

Schlesinger, A., Jr. 1998. *The Disuniting of America: Reflections on a Multicultural Society*. New York: W. W. Norton.

West Virginia State Board of Education v. Barnette (1944).

Zeldin, M. 1998. "Integration and Interaction in the Jewish Day School." In *The Jewish Educational Leader's Handbook,* ed. R. Tornberg, 579–90. Denver: Alternatives in Religious Education.

5

Denominationalism

History and Hopes

Jewish religious denominationalism arose in Germany at the beginning of the nineteenth century as a way for the Jewish community to cope with the revolutionary political, cultural, religious, and social changes brought on by the onset of the modern world. While Moses Mendelssohn and his circle of *maskilim* (followers of the Jewish Enlightenment) represented the first individual responses to these dramatic changes through their affirmation of and participation in the culture of the larger German world in whose midst they dwelt, it was the Reform movement in the first decades of the 1800s that articulated the first communal denominational response to these transformations in Jewish life. Reform was, at first, a lay-led movement that aimed to recast traditional modes of Jewish worship in accord with nineteenth-century German standards of aesthetics.

The rise of *Wissenschaft des Judentums* (academic study of Judaism) introduced the idea that Judaism was not only *in* but *of* history, that is, that Judaism developed through time and had to be understood in its cultural context. This provided an ideological basis that would allow for the growth of non-Orthodox liberal movements in Germany. The Reform strand centered around Abraham Geiger and the Hochschule für die Wissenschaft des Judentums in Berlin. The positive-historical school, which would be a predecessor to Conservative Judaism, was more committed in principle to *halachah* (Jewish law) than its Reform counterpart was, and it was centered around the Breslau-based Positive-Historical Jewish Theological Seminary of Zacharias Frankel.

Cultural conditions in Germany were such that the ritual observance patterns among rabbis as well as lay adherents of these respective trends—ideological differences notwithstanding—were similar. Thus these two wings of German liberal Judaism functioned within a common institutional framework where graduates of both institutions joined the same rabbinical organization and served the same communal synagogues. At the same time, a distinct modern Orthodox movement arose in opposition to these liberal movements. Neo-Orthodoxy, as it came to be called, was devoted, in the words of its chief ideologue, Rabbi Samson Raphael Hirsch, to a philosophy of *Torah' im derech eretz*. What this meant was an affirmation of Western culture and mores combined with a commitment to the traditional ahistorical Jewish notion of divine revelation of Torah at Sinai and classical observance of Jewish halachic practice. Hirsch's colleague, Rabbi Esriel Hildesheimer, proceeded to establish a seminary in Berlin to serve this new movement. Denominational divisions in Germany were thus twofold—Orthodox and liberal. It would take America with its cultural-social divisions between the Jews of German descent and the Jews of Eastern European descent to foster the development of more than one non-Orthodox denomination.

American Developments

When Isaac Mayer Wise came to the United States and established the Union of American Hebrew Congregations in 1873 and the Hebrew Union College in 1875, he avoided the label "Reform" in the titles of his institutions because he did not believe that he was a creating a denominationally distinct form of American Judaism. Instead, his intention was to create an "American Judaism" for a German-speaking American Jewish community that was overwhelmingly Germanic and culturally homogeneous prior to 1881. Wise aspired to speak for all of American Judaism and even claimed that the Hebrew Union College would educate both Orthodox and Reform rabbis.

However, Wise's dream of a united American Jewish religious community vanished in the 1880s with the arrival of hundreds of thousands of Eastern European Jews to these shores. The cultural and religious cleavages between the Eastern European immigrants and their earlier-arriving German coreligionists were quite pronounced, and it soon became apparent that a union between these disparate groups was impossible. Liberal Judaism may have been possible in Germany, where cultural homogeneity promoted a similarity in observance that allowed two trends to coexist in the non-Orthodox camp without erupting into distinct denominations. But the differences between Eastern European and German Jews would not permit this coexistence in the United States, and soon two major non-

Orthodox denominations—Reform and Conservative—emerged at the end of the nineteenth century.

One infamous episode points to how the fissures caused by ethnic and religious divisions began to widen. In 1883, the Hebrew Union College ordained its first class of rabbis, and Jewish leaders throughout the United States were invited to the graduation ceremony. At a banquet held to celebrate the ordination, traditional Jewish dietary restrictions forbidding the mixing of milk and meat at the same meal were flouted, and all types of forbidden seafood were served. While most historians assert that what has come to be labeled as the infamous "*Trefa* Banquet" was the result of a caterer's error, there is no doubt that this banquet delivered a powerful message to Eastern European immigrants and other Jewish religious traditionalists. Judaism, at least as the Reform movement envisioned it, was no longer wedded to traditional Jewish law and practice. At this moment, American Jewish religious denominationalism was fully born.

The Reform movement gave explicit ideological expression to this denominational stance in the Pittsburgh Platform of 1885. Authored by the German-born Kaufmann Kohler, who would eventually succeed Wise as president of Hebrew Union College, this platform asserted that Judaism was a universal faith ever striving to be in accord with the postulates of reason. Kohler looked askance at Jewish ritual behaviors and was a fierce opponent of Jewish nationalism. The posture Kohler and the Reform movement now championed found practical liturgical expression within the walls of Reform temples. The removal of head coverings for men during worship now came to be a near-universal Reform custom, and in 1895, the *Union Prayer Book*—composed almost entirely in English and highly universalistic in its orientation—was adopted as the official liturgy of the Reform movement. Such steps on the part of the Reform movement were an anathema to Jews of Eastern European descent, who were then pouring onto American shores.

The Jewish Theological Seminary (JTS), which was first established in 1886 in opposition to Reform, flourished under the leadership of the Romanian-born scholar Solomon Schechter. Schechter articulated the twin ideological foundations upon which Conservative Judaism was to be established—a nonfundamentalist fidelity to Jewish law that recognized the historical character of Jewish tradition and law as well as an uncompromising devotion to "Catholic Israel," the community of the people Israel.

These ideological positions, combined with a warm embrace of cultural Zionism as well as an affirmation of modern American aesthetic standards and sensibilities, appealed to the Eastern European Jews and their children as they began their process of acculturation into American life.

The commitment of Conservative Judaism to Jewish law clearly differentiated it from the Reform movement. Yet the rise and growth of denominationally distinct forms of non-Orthodox Judaism in America almost a century ago resulted primarily from the sociological divide that marked the American Jewish community at that time. The religious attitudes and cultural patterns that divided first-generation American Jews of Eastern European and German descent were too large to bridge. Reform Judaism thus came to be the denominationally distinct expression of the "folk Judaism" of German Jews in this country, while the Conservative movement came to express the folk Judaism of Eastern European Jews and their descendants as they successfully integrated into American society.

Nevertheless, it is crucial to note that Jews of Eastern European background were as anxious to acculturate into America as the German Jews had been before them. As they did so, the cultural distance that separated them from their German Jewish coreligionists began to diminish, and Reform itself came to change as children of Eastern European Jews began to join Reform temples. As the Reform Columbus Platform of 1937 demonstrates, more positive attitudes toward religious ritual and Zionism began to make inroads in Reform Judaism through the leadership of figures such as Rabbis Samuel Cohon, Stephen Wise, and Abba Hillel Silver.

The 1934 publication of *Judaism as a Civilization* by Rabbi Mordecai Kaplan and the ideal of Jewish peoplehood that stood at the center of his Reconstructionist philosophy had a profound influence upon many in the Reform movement. Kaplan similarly exerted a powerful influence in the Conservative movement through his teaching at JTS, even as he initially opposed the creation of a distinct Reconstructionist movement during the first half of the twentieth century. The influence and numbers of Conservative Jews grew throughout most of the twentieth century, and Conservative Judaism became the dominant movement within American Judaism for most of this period. But at the same time, the divide among culturally homogeneous, non-Orthodox Jews on matters of observance and belief became narrower and narrower as the century progressed. This change would ultimately come to have a significant impact on minimizing distinctive denominational allegiances among American Jews.

This tale would not be complete without some attention being paid to Orthodox Judaism. During the 1920s and 1930s, Orthodox Judaism began to establish itself more securely in America. The Orthodox at this time represented the least successfully acculturated elements among the Jewish immigrants. However, under the leadership of Rabbi Bernard Revel, a nascent modern American Orthodoxy began to develop real roots. The establishment of Yeshiva College in New York in 1928 and the incorporation of the Rabbi Isaac Elchanan Theological Seminary into Yeshiva University provided an institutional framework that would later prove to be critical for the growth of Orthodox Judaism in the United States.

The birth of Yeshiva University in 1928 was complemented by the arrival of elite Orthodox scholars such as Rabbi Moses Soloveitchik and his son, Rabbi Joseph Baer Soloveitchik. These men were able to spread the influence of Orthodox Judaism among rabbis and laypersons alike. Perhaps the most significant of these Orthodox immigrant leaders was Rabbi Aaron Kotler, who established a traditional Orthodox yeshiva in Lakewood, New Jersey, in 1941 and who inspired his students to establish a network of Torah Umesorah Orthodox day schools throughout the United States long before parochial schools became part of the landscape of American education. The appearance of large numbers of Orthodox Hungarian Jews who entered America after World War II also contributed to the resurgence of Orthodox Judaism in this country during later decades. It laid the groundwork for the emergence of two types of Orthodox Judaism— modern and sectarian or ultra-Orthodox.

Contemporary Trends and Directions

By the 1960s, even as denominational allegiances remained strong, the sociological makeup of the community began to change. The American Jewish community was no longer an immigrant community seeking to adjust to the United States. Old ethnic patterns that formerly preserved and divided the Jewish religious community were no longer present, and the rivalry that had existed between American Jews of German and Eastern European descent was little more than a historical memory.

During this same period, America witnessed the emergence of "the new ethnicity." In the Jewish community this gave rise to new forms of

Jewish expression. The *havurah* movement offered Jews a way to be part of a religious practice outside the walls of a synagogue. Jewish feminism empowered women's voices in ways that were rarely heard in the hallowed halls of rabbinical seminaries. *The Jewish Catalog* became a mini best-seller and planted the seeds for a "do-it-yourself " Judaism that no longer made Jewish practice dependent on rabbis. The near-miraculous Israeli victory during the Six-Day War in 1967 also unleashed an enormous amount of pride among American Jews and led to a renewed sense, in the words of Rabbi Sidney Schwarz, of "tribal" Jewish commitment as well as newfound religious commitment among hundreds of thousands of American Jews.[1]

In short, the attitudes and beliefs that had so sharply divided Reform from Conservative Jews in the first half of the twentieth century now began to blur, and crossover between denominations was no longer unusual. The 1990 National Jewish Population Survey indicated that more than 700,000 of the million-plus persons who claimed to be Reform Jews stated that they had Conservative Jewish backgrounds.

Sidney Schwarz correctly notes in his discussion of "covenantal Jews" that this growing uniformity took place against an ever more intense universalistic backdrop in which Jews—particularly those who came to adulthood during the past twenty years—feel completely at home in America. For these Jews, tales of anti-Semitism and the memory of the Holocaust embody a distant past that has virtually no impact on promoting their allegiance as Jews. Indeed, as the election of Barack Obama as president indicates, older forms of prejudice and discrimination—while they have surely not disappeared—do not possess the power and influence they once did.

American Jews have now been fully accepted into American life, and Jews of all stripes and ethnic backgrounds as well as sexual orientations are now full participants in the cultural, social, political, and economic spheres of the United States. Ivy League colleges that formerly had strict quotas limiting Jewish admission now have Jewish presidents, and businesses like DuPont that once banned Jewish executives now frequently have Jewish CEOs.

As Jews have become fully accepted by Gentiles as social equals and as traditional Jewish attitudes that opposed exogamy have weakened, intermarriage rates have soared, and traditional Jewish communal attitudes opposing intermarriage have undergone revolutionary changes. Younger American Jews do not feel the sting of social anti-Semitism that their forebears did, and this makes their attitudes toward Israel and Jewish identity different than those of their parents and grandparents. Those Jews who seek out affiliation with the Jewish community do so with an indifference to denominations that was unknown earlier in the century. Indeed, the appeal of the individual rabbi and the ability of specific congregations to serve the personal religious and spiritual needs of congregants are far more important factors than denominational identification in attracting most non-Orthodox Jews to membership in particular synagogues.

In addition, there are new forms of Jewish identification being created by younger Jews that take place completely outside the realm of Jewish denominations. Reboot was founded in 2002 to appeal to "Jewishly un-connected cultural creatives" and it supports their development of new projects for both Jews and non-Jews. Storahtelling, founded in 1999, works with clergy, educators, and artists to make Torah more accessible to Jews through dramatic presentations. Even as print Jewish magazines have trouble staying financially solvent, *Tablet* has emerged as an online Jew-ish magazine with a wide and young Jewish following. Of the hundreds of new Jewish initiatives that have appeared in just the past decade, few of these phenomena are dependent on Jewish denominations, and almost all are transdenominational.

Nor is the cultural and religious excitement that marks present-day American Judaism limited to the few examples cited in the previous para-graph. There are larger trends that underscore the vibrancy of Jewish life in America, including the rapid and significant growth of Jewish day school education among a significant minority of non-Orthodox Jews in the United States, the explosion of Jewish studies programs at universi-ties, Birthright and the rise of trips to Israel, the dramatic growth of Jew-ish camping, the growth of Jewish renewal study centers, the appearance of the nondenominational Yeshivat Hadar in New York and the nonde-nominational rabbinical program at Boston Hebrew College, the rise of Jewish social action projects, and the appearance of Limmud conferences, where thousands of Jews come together each year to learn and socialize. Indeed, these developments can rightfully be described as contributing to a renaissance in Jewish religious and cultural life among a core minority of American Jews. Some look at these developments as signs of a golden age for Judaism in America, and the impact of such creativity and vitality has been felt both within and beyond denominational boundaries.

Judaism beyond Denominationalism

All these developments have promoted the growth of alternative modes of Jewish religious and cultural expression and have propelled many committed Jews to seek out Jewish community and religion apart from denominations in a manner that was unknown to earlier generations of American Jews. My own impression here comports with those of Schwarz, when he speaks optimistically and hopefully of the emergence of significant pockets of "covenantal Jews" whose activity in the community is quite independent of the structures of Jewish denominations.[2]

For all the reasons cited above, more American Jews are indifferent to denominational labels in their highly eclectic and idiosyncratic search for meaning and community. To employ Leo Baeck's felicitous phrase, more and more Jews are likely to move away from "an adjectival Judaism," in other words, a Judaism where the adjective—whether it be Reform, Conservative, Reconstructionist, Renewal, or Orthodox—is more important than the noun, Judaism. They will not hesitate to shop among movements and individual rabbis and religious teachers as they engage in their own personal religious and communal quests. The distinctions in theology and ideology that are so crucial to the elite leaders of the different movements are increasingly irrelevant to these Jews. Many of the debates that occupy the leaders of these movements are regarded by most Jews as needlessly divisive and extraneous to the larger task of creating a Judaism that is vital and vibrant in the face of the challenges that modern-day America presents to Jewish life and commitment.

Of course, denominations are in no immediate danger of extinction. Any elementary course on sociology can tell us that well-established and powerful institutions do not simply disappear. Furthermore, the movements themselves and their institutions are not blind to these trends, and they strive mightily to reinvent and adapt themselves to these forces of change. The current preference of Jewish foundations for cross-denominational collaboration has led to unprecedented institutional cooperation between JTS (Conservative) and Hebrew Union College–Jewish Institute of Religion (HUC-JIR; Reform) in innovative programs sponsored by the United Jewish Appeal (UJA) of New York, the Charles and Lynn Schusterman Family Foundation, and the Jim Joseph Foundation. As a result, some of the most significant transdenominational programs for the renewal and reconfiguration of synagogue life are taking place within denomination-ally sponsored structures. Synagogue 3000, which has done cutting-edge work with synagogue transformation, was cofounded by professors from the American Jewish University (Conservative) and HUC-JIR (Reform). The Institute of Jewish Spirituality is doing important training of clergy in meditation and mindfulness, and they work in close cooperation with American rabbinic seminaries. JTS, the Reconstructionist Rabbinical College, and HUC-JIR are also collaborating in the area of health and healing. In the Reform movement, Rabbi Rick Jacobs, president of the Union for Reform Judaism, has insisted that the movement heed these trends. He has initiated a number of programs to address Jews within and beyond Reform synagogues and has not hesitated to enlist the support of scholars and teachers from places like the Shalom Hartman Institute in support of these initiatives. The bottom line: the denominational centers of American Judaism are striving to adapt to the new post-denominational reality.

However, all of this begs the question of whether such adaptation is as rapid and flexible as it ought to be to meet the needs of the hour. After all, the larger and more pervasive reality at play in American Judaism today as reported in all surveys of the American Jewish community indicates that "unaffiliated" is the largest growing category among contemporary American Jews, even as many of these Jews seek spiritual meaning and renewal. The 2012 New York UJA demographic study indicates that denominational affiliation in the New York metropolitan area among Reform and Conservative Jews has decreased over the past decade, and record numbers of Jews now define themselves as "just Jewish" or nondenominational. Crossover among denominations is more common than ever for thousands of Jews, as it is for millions of non-Jewish Christian Americans as well. Indeed, a recently conducted U.S. religious landscape survey indicates that no more than 25 percent of American Christians remain in the Protestant or Catholic denomination into which they were born.[3] Jewish indifference to denominations and crossover among denominations therefore reflects larger trends in American society.

Many commentators suggest that not only is the heyday of Jewish religious denominationalism in the United States over, but they also predict that the non-Orthodox movements in Judaism (Conservative, Reconstructionist, and Reform) will one day merge and that sectarian Orthodox Judaism will triumph over more modern manifestations of Orthodox Judaism found in institutions like Yeshivat Chovevei Torah. From this perspective, the prospects of maintaining traditional Jewish denominational patterns do not appear particularly bright, and there is surely a great deal of evidence to suggest that this assessment may well be right. Yet even as the trials facing Jewish religious denominations today are admittedly great, the challenges in forging meaningful expressions of Judaism for millions of Jews without the support of national denominations may well be even greater. After all, denominations still possess great resources, and the programs that emerge from their institutions would be hard to duplicate by the innumerable Jewish start-ups that currently dot the communal landscape.

Still, given the current access to the tools of mass communication and social media, a power shift has taken place in society. Institutions and movements no longer own their own messages, nor do they have a complete monopoly over knowledge. Jews—and, for that matter, even synagogues—need no longer rely solely on their rabbis or their denominational movements for knowledge. The web and a wide variety of teachers available in every community provide viable options for Jewish learning. Additionally, through the wonders of technology, groups can easily form without organizations. Online Jewish communities like My Jewish Portal and Our Jewish Community are more common than ever and promise to grow over the next decade. Ours is a world of niche markets and customer customization. People coalesce around interests and values, not institutions. People seek personalization rather than institutional affiliation. No wonder numbers in denominations have declined. Synagogues and movements need to respond to these changed realities. They need to reach out to people beyond the synagogue in informal settings where people gather, like coffee shops and shopping malls. They also need to find ways of fostering participation and engagement in the community without insisting on the payment of membership dues.

Sidney Schwarz, in his "Jewish Megatrends," gives a compelling rationale for why we must make such adaptations.[4] While I am highly sympathetic to Schwarz's call, I would still ask, does the emerging symmetry between universal and Jewish values bode well for the ongoing vitality of Jewish life in this country? American Jews have overwhelmingly internalized the dominant values of their host society. We in the liberal Jewish community and movements are decidedly universalistic in our orientations. Even our particularistic affirmations are made in the service of a universal cause. Whether such affirmations will prove strong enough to sustain a cultural and religious identity in the future is open to debate. Jews have been blessed with freedom in this country. Whether such blessing will strengthen Jewish commitments, values, and identity or whether America will be the solvent in which Jewish continuity dissolves remains to be seen. The resiliency of Judaism as it confronts the future will surely be tested.

As we move into the twenty-first century, the tasks that confront traditional religious movements in the modern American context—whatever the ideological distinctions and organizational commitments that mark and sometimes divide them—are essentially identical. The challenge that confronts all of them is how to make Judaism relevant, compelling, joyous, meaningful, welcoming, comforting, and challenging to American Jews who, as "sovereign selves," have infinite options open before them. Both within and beyond denominations we must ask boldly whether Judaism can succeed in doing this for large numbers of Jews.

American Judaism today stands at a crossroads where trends of weakened Jewish commitment and attachment compete with pockets of intense Jewish revival and knowledge—and all this takes place across denominational boundaries and institutional lines. The task of all Jews will be to strengthen these pockets of revival and knowledge. This task will compel us to recognize that such revival and knowledge must take place both within and beyond the denominational universe. The future of Judaism in the United States depends on the ability of all Jews, regardless of denominational identification, to maintain and revitalize Jewish religious tradition in light of the conditions that confront our community today.

NOTES

1. For the use and meaning of the term *tribal* in relationship to Jews and Judaism, see the essay by Sidney Schwarz, "Jewish Megatrends," in his book *Jewish Megatrends: Charting the Course of the American Jewish Future* (Woodstock, VT: Jewish Lights, 2013), 10ff.

2. Ibid. Again, see the Schwarz discussion of and employment of the term *covenantal Jews* in his insightful essay to which I react and upon which I draw in this article.

3. Pew Forum on Religion and Public Life, "U.S. Religious Landscape Survey" (2008), 22.

4. For the complete presentation of Schwarz's argument and thoughts, see "Jewish Megatrends," 3–39.

6

The Integrity of Reform within *Kelal Yisra-el*

"When is God exalted?" a famous midrash asks. The answer, it states, is "when all Israel is bound up in a single fellowship—*ba-aguda achat*."[1] Few ideas in Judaism are as compelling as the belief in a united Jewish people. Certainly none has received or has continued to evoke as much hyperbolic obeisance. All generations of Jews, the Talmud teaches, stood together at Sinai. When Moses addresses the people toward the end of the book of Deuteronomy in *parashat Nitsavim*, which begins with the sentence, "All of you are standing here this day before the Lord your God," the rabbis have suggested that the phrase that concludes that thought, "from your hewer of wood to your drawer of water," reemphasizes the notion that every Jew—past, present, and future—stands united with all others in covenant before God. For the "hewer of wood," it is said, refers to Abraham, the progenitor of our people who chopped wood in preparation for the sacrifice of his son Isaac at Mount Moriah, and the "drawer of water" is none other than Elijah, who will draw from the wellsprings of salvation and announce the coming of the Messiah at the end of history.[2] All Israel shares a mystical bond that transcends time and space. This metaphysical hope is expressed theologically in the literature of *Agada* and *Kabbala* through the concept of *Knesset Yisra-el*, "the Communion of Israel," which is employed to personify both Israel and its faithfulness in its relationship with God.

The notion of a united Jewish collectivity is not confined by the rabbis to the spiritual and mystical realm alone. There is a social dimension to this idea as well, a dimension that is captured in the well-known talmudic statement "All Israel is responsible for one another."[3] The reality of kinship among all Jews and the sense of concern for each other's welfare that this reality entails are reflected in Hebrew through the term *Kelal Yisra-el*, "the community of Israel." It refers to the totality of the Jewish people, not just a segment of it. *Kelal Yisra-el*, as it is generally understood, is a broad-based term, an inclusionary one that emphasizes the shared sense of consciousness and relatedness that infuses all of Jewish life.

This stress upon the inclusive nature of the term *Kelal Yisra-el* tends to obscure a second way in which this idea is utilized, particularly in our own day. For *Kelal Yisra-el*, inasmuch as it speaks to Jewish unity and responsibility, also imposes the obligation upon the community to rebuke sinful behavior when such behavior is perceived as threatening to the unity and stability of the Jewish people. Here the concept of *Kelal Yisra-el* is used in a limiting way as a tool of control. It is invoked in order to allow one group of Jews to brand another as deviants and to exclude them as sectarians. It is, in this sense, a term that attempts to establish and maintain boundaries of acceptable belief and practice within the community.

In speaking to you today on the integrity of Reform in relationship to *Kelal Yisra-el*, I draw specific attention to these two meanings of the term, for they are vital for an understanding of the context that has called forth this presentation. We are obligated, in addressing this topic, to acknowledge and confront fully the dispute that has brought the issue of Reform Judaism's relationship to *Kelal Yisra-el* to the forefront of the Conference at this time—that is, our passage of the resolution on patrilineality at our 1983 Los Angeles convention and the accolades of support and the howls of protest, all in the name of *Kelal Yisra-el*, that it has elicited. It would be disingenuous of us to claim that our adoption of the resolution on patrilineal status was not a major break with Jewish tradition in this area. During the two previous millennia, the principle that the mother, not the father, conferred Jewish status upon the offspring of a union was the norm among the people of Israel. On the other hand, proponents of the resolution, who constitute the overwhelming majority of the membership of this organization, contend that in an open American society where intermarriage between Jew and non-Jew is legion, such a resolution was amply justifiable. It is an important measure for the preservation of the Jewish people, for it helps, in the words of Alexander Schindler, to "make certain that the children issuing from such an intermarriage will be born Jewish."[4] The ambivalent and confusing wording of the text aside, it is clear that the Conference, in conferring Jewish status upon children born to Jewish fathers and Gentile mothers, intended to be inclusive and to identify as many persons as possible as Jews. Such a position was justified not only by an appeal to the Bible but, in view of the many children from such homes who entered our temples and religious schools, was seen as the most humane response we could offer in keeping with the highest values of our tradition. As such, the case has certainly been made that a decision on patrilineal status is consistent with the spirit of our movement. More significant, in light of our topic, is that these considerations have allowed the supporters of the resolution to argue on pragmatic, textual, and moral grounds that this decision was in the best interests of *Kelal Yisra-el*.[5]

Conversely, we are all aware that barely a week passes that some major journal of Jewish life and thought fails to include an article or an address excoriating us for the passage of this resolution. Some of these speeches and essays are the work of unthinking zealots. Others represent the labor of thoughtful people who, though sympathetic to our attempts and aims, remain convinced that our decision on this matter, however well-intentioned, is misguided. They contend that the Reform movement, through its affirmation of the principle of patrilineal status, has hopelessly splintered the Jewish people, and the destructive effects of our resolution will reverberate in a divided Jewish community for centuries to come. Even within our movement, support for the decision is by no means unanimous, and one need only recall the impassioned plea by Moshe Weiler against passage of this resolution at the Los Angeles meeting to be reminded of this. Our body, these critics assert, both within and without our movement, has condemned Reform to a position of sectarianism within the general Jewish community and, in the name of *Kelal Yisra-el*, they call upon us to rescind our resolution.[6]

It is with an awareness of this debate, which wracks much of the Jewish world, that I intend to deal with our subject. For we are not speaking today of *devarim be-alma*, theoretical matters that may be of little or no relationship to the world of praxis. Rather, in considering the integrity of Reform Judaism in relationship to *Kelal Yisra-el*, we are touching upon matters that are of the utmost importance and moment to the people we have chosen to serve, lead, and love: this people Israel. Mindful of the gravity of this topic, I employ the issue of patrilineality as a lens to focus my discussion of the relationship between our movement and *Kelal Yisra-el*. In so doing, I hope to share thoughts and considerations on this matter that, I trust, are not isolated ones. My desire is that you will recognize these reflections, in some measure, as your own and that you will therefore resonate to them.

I begin with a representative historical analysis, albeit selective, of the reactions Reform has elicited from Orthodox rabbinical leaders during the last two centuries concerning religious matters. The topic that we have under discussion today does not arise *de nova* in a historical vacuum. There are parallels to it in the recent past and there are lessons that these parallels suggest about our relationship as Reform Jews with *Kelal Yisra-el*.

With the rise of the Reform movement in Germany at the beginning of the nineteenth century, the ire of the traditional rabbinate was aroused. Infuriated by innovations in prayer and ritual that the Reformers introduced in Hamburg during the second decade of the 1800s, the rabbinate excoriated the Reformers despite the Reformers' care to legitimate their changes in Jewish ritual and custom on the basis of warrants drawn from halachic precedent. The attacks of many of these rabbis were collected in a very famous pamphlet, *Eleh Divrei ha-Berit* (These are the words of the Covenant), which enjoyed a wide circulation among the European Orthodox rabbinate for decades after its appearance. Rabbi Moses Schreiber, the undisputed leader and architect of traditionalist Orthodoxy in Hungary during this time, was foremost among the rabbis whose opinions were gathered in this book. Schreiber, also referred to as the Hatam Sofer, condemned the "pernicious" deeds of the leaders of the Hamburg Temple. The rabbinate, he claimed, would be duty-bound, if it possessed the power (which it did not), to excommunicate the Reformers from the community. In his view, by denying the divinity and transgressing the authority of the Oral Law, the Reformers were persons of no religion. Consequently, to excommunicate them from *Kelal Yisra-el* would simply be putting distance between them and the community, a policy the Reformers themselves had already established by their refusal to accept what he regarded as the *'ikar*, the principled foundation, of Jewish faith, i.e., *Torah mipi haGevura*, Torah from the mouth of the Almighty. It was the Reformers' rejection of theological doctrine, and not just their deviations from what Schreiber considered to be authentic Jewish practice, that formed an essential basis for his rejection and condemnation of Reform.[7] It is this emphasis upon belief that must be highlighted here. For, as we shall see, this serves as the ultimate foundation for the Orthodox refusal to grant a principled recognition to any Jewish religious act performed under non-Orthodox rabbinic auspices. The Hatam Sofer's writings already lay out the major parameters of the Orthodox case against Reform. They allow the Orthodox to assert that proper membership in *Kelal Yisra-el* involves assent to the dogmatic assumption that all of the Torah, both Written and Oral, was delivered to Moses at Sinai. To deny this, as Rabbi Samson Raphael Hirsch was to observe of the Reformers over fifty years later, was to separate oneself from the community.[8]

In the 1840s, Rabbi Zvi Hirsch Chajes of Zolkiew, one of the foremost rabbinic scholars of his generation, issued a blistering polemic against the Reformers. The polemic, *Minchat Kena-ot*, appeared originally in 1845, and Rabbi Chajes added an excursus to it in 1849. Focusing on the Reform rabbinical conferences that met in Germany between 1844 and 1846, Chajes attacked the Reformers as *madichim* and *mumarim*, terms traditionally reserved for apostates in medieval rabbinic literature. Chajes was particularly agitated by the debate concerning the issue of mixed marriage that took place at the Brunswick Conference. The rabbis assembled there agreed to a motion that read, "Members of monotheistic religions in general are not forbidden to marry if the parents are permitted by the laws of the state to bring up children from such wedlock in the Jewish religion." Such permission, it should be noted, was not given in Germany at this time. The intent of the resolution, in large measure, was thus clearly rhetorical. Nevertheless, Chajes viewed this resolution as a serious and unforgivable breach of Jewish tradition. He contended that it was a holy duty for the Orthodox to separate themselves from these people on account of such deviations from and perversions of tradition. He not only proscribed marriages between Orthodox and non-Orthodox Jews, but even forbade Orthodox Jews to visit the Reformers in their homes. Testimony offered by Reform Jews was not to be considered valid in a Jewish court of law. Chajes even declared the children of Reform Jews to be *mamzerim* (illegitimate) because of their parents' refusal to obey traditional laws of family purity.[9] Chajes's polemic against the Reformers was not an isolated one. Further examples from the Orthodox literature of this period could certainly be adduced to affirm this point. Suffice it to say that the posture adopted by Rabbi Solomon Eger of Posen, who wrote that the Orthodox were obligated to "separate them [Reform Jews] from Israel, for in no wise are they to be considered as belonging to the people Israel,"[10] is representative of the sentiments expressed by a significant number of Orthodox leaders throughout the nineteenth century.

Nevertheless, it must be noted that the overwhelming majority of Orthodox rabbis rejected the position that marriage with Reform Jews was forbidden. The halachic axiom that anyone born of a Jewish mother was a

Jew prevented them from actually defining Reform Jews out of the community on this most basic level. While their absolute commitment to belief in the divinity of the entire Written and Oral Laws as the sine qua non for an authentic religious Judaism prompted them to view Reform Judaism as illegitimate, it also compelled them to recognize that Reform Jews were Jews, albeit sinning ones. This gives the lie to the often-repeated canard that the Orthodox do not consider Reform Jews to be Jewish. It should not obscure the fact that the leaders of Orthodoxy, in response to what they deemed to be the needs of the hour, elevated dogma to a position of supreme importance in their hierarchy of values.

The implications of Orthodoxy's insistence upon dogmatic commitment as a prerequisite for inclusion in the ranks of legitimate Jewish religious leadership, particularly in an era where intermarriage is common, become apparent when we move to the twentieth century and consider several responsa issued by representative Orthodox rabbinic leaders on the issue of conversion to Judaism performed under non-Orthodox auspices. The *Seridei Esh*, Rabbi Yehiel Yaakov Weinberg, the last head of the Orthodox *Rabbinerseminar* in Berlin prior to its destruction by the Nazis, admitted that there were occasions when liberal rabbis conducted conversions in a halachically prescribed manner. He recognized that European liberal rabbis often required ritual circumcision (*mila*), ritual immersion (*tevila*), and some form of "the acceptance of the yoke of the commandments" (*kabalat 'ol mitzvot*) in performing the conversion ceremony. Nevertheless, all conversions performed by these rabbis before a liberal *beit bin* remained, in his opinion, "meaningless exercises." Such conversions, he claimed, "appear ridiculous to the best of Christians as well. A Jew who marries a convert of this type knows that he is throwing dirt in the face of his fellow creatures."[11] Therefore, we see that even when a non-Orthodox rabbi fulfills all the ritual requirements in the performance of a conversion he, and certainly she, cannot be accorded legitimacy by his Orthodox counterparts.

The writings of two major modern Orthodox rabbis, Moshe Feinstein, who died recently, and J. David Bleich, a Rosh Yeshiva at Yeshiva University's Rabbi Isaac Elchanan Theological Seminary, indicate explicitly why this is so. In one responsum, Rabbi Feinstein ruled that it was not permissible to bury a woman in a Jewish cemetery who had been converted to Judaism by a Conservative rabbi. The ultimate reason for this was "that the rabbinic court of the Conservative is unfit [*pesulin*] to be a *beit din* as they [Conservative rabbis] deny [*koferin*] many of the principles of Judaism." The testimony of Conservative rabbis is thus invalid, "for anyone who accepts the shameful title 'Conservative' upon himself is assumed to be *mufkar* [lawless] in regard to many of the prohibitions in the Torah and to be in apostasy [*kefira*] against many of the principles of Judaism. Consequently, it is evident that no conversion performed by a Conservative rabbi has any legal standing."[12] Such disqualification applies all the more so to Reform rabbis. In another responsum, Rabbi Feinstein asserted, "Even if no one witnesses their transgressions of Torah, the name 'Reform' testifies to the fact that they are heretics," and, therefore, unfit to conduct conversions.[13] As Rabbi Bleich succinctly puts it, "The halacha recognizes the validity of a conversion only if it is performed in the presence of a qualified *beit din*." This means, according to Rabbi Bleich, that an individual member of a *beit din* "need not necessarily be an ordained rabbi." He (and note that I use only the male gender here, for a woman, by his definition, could not possibly serve as a member of a *beit din* that was to supervise a conversion) must, however, "be committed to the acceptance of Torah—both Written and Oral—in its entirety. One who refuses to accept the divinity and binding authority of even the most minor detail of halacha is, *ipso facto*, disqualified. Ideological adherents of Reform and Conservatism fall into this category."[14]

The line from the Hatam Sofer in the nineteenth century to Rabbis Bleich and Feinstein in the twentieth is complete. Orthodoxy holds a principled objection to Reform. They hold a view of revelation that does not allow them to accept the validity of the principle of religious pluralism. This causes them to define us and any innovations or practices we might introduce institutionally into Jewish religious life as invalid. This is precisely why compromise in areas such as *ishut*, personal status, is not just difficult, but virtually impossible to attain on anything other than a personal, case-by-case, ad hoc level.

And what of the term *Kelal Yisra-el*? Our discussion thus far indicates that there is no clear referent for it. Inclusion for us as a movement would be dependent upon not only amending our practices but also a fideistic affirmation of *Torah miSinai*. In light of this, no action we could ever take, short of a decision to dissolve ourselves as a movement, would legitimate Reform religiously as part of *Kelal Yisra-el* as the Orthodox define it. The role that Reform plays institutionally in enhancing our people's position in the political and social realms can and has been acknowledged. On rare occasions some Orthodox leaders even concede that we have prevented some Jews from assimilating into non-Jewish society.[15] None of this should obscure the truth that no religious integrity is ever accorded Reform, from an Orthodox perspective, within *Kelal Yisra-el.*

We come now to the dilemma of how we as Reform Jews, leaving the Orthodox aside, approach the notion of *Kelal Yisra-el* with a genuine sense of integrity and responsibility. The concept reminds us that we do not live in isolation. We are not the first generation of Jews, nor will we be the last. We are heirs to a tradition, and we pledge ourselves to transmit it to our descendants after us. Judaism, like any other religion, must be seen in this sense as a "system of symbols which acts to establish powerful, pervasive, and long-lasting moods and motivation."[16] *Kelal Yisra-el* recalls to us that Judaism partakes of an ethos, that we as Reform Jews are part of a cultural system that has its boundaries. The concept intimates to us that there are limits to what we can define as authentic Judaism. It warns us that some changes are so radical that they rupture our linkage to the past and thus our identity in the present. In short, *Kelal Yisra-el* does not allow us to surrender to what the Catholic theologian David Tracy has labeled a "relaxed pluralism" where everything we might propose or do as a body is responsible and/or acceptable.[17]

Yet we as Reform Jews also refuse to accept a monolithic Judaism. Judaism does not speak, nor has it ever spoken, in a single, stagnant voice. Adaptation and change are characteristic of our religion. *Our* sense of the demands of the time, as well as our feelings of compassion and justice— themselves informed by the tradition—grant us, as they have past generations of Jews, the courage and confidence to be. "It is time to serve the Lord," the rabbis have observed, "make void thy law."[18] There is a dialectic in Reform, as in all Judaism, between the past contents of our traditions and our insights into the needs of the present. Wrestling with both ends of this dialectic as our ancestors did permits us to produce innovation and, in so doing, to serve God and the people Israel in full conscience and with religious devotion. Jacob Toury, the Tel Aviv University historian, has pointed out that intermarriage and abandonment of Jewish identity almost always went hand in hand during the previous century in Germany.[19] How best to serve our God and the people Israel in an age when intermarriage no longer necessarily signifies a desire to leave the community must be and, appropriately, has been the subject of creative and often painful debate and decision in our ranks. Our resolution on patrilineality has certainly been one of the fruits of this struggle.

Let us, for the moment, turn our thoughts away from the issue of patrilineality to another that was, at one stage of our history, probably more controversial than patrilineality is today, to see how this dialectic of tradition and conscience played itself out within Reform deliberations in the past. I refer to the issue of the ordination of women as rabbis. Again, my intent is not to give a comprehensive historical treatment of the topic. Rather, I would point out to you that when Martha Neumark enrolled at the College in Cincinnati, Jacob Lauterbach, in a letter to the president and his colleagues on the faculty dated December 12, 1921, objected to the ordination of Neumark, or any other woman, as a rabbi in Israel. He observed, "It is contrary to all Jewish tradition and Jewish religious teaching to have women perform the functions of rabbis in Israel." Two months later, on January 30, 1922, the minutes of a faculty meeting indicate that the issue of women's ordination was a main item on the faculty's agenda and the following statement is recorded: "Dr. Lauterbach does not think it wise to make such a radical departure from Jewish tradition *because it creates a schism.*" In other words, *Kelal Yisra-el,* in Dr. Lauterbach's opinion, would be shattered by such an unprecedented step as the ordination of female rabbis.[20]

Lest anyone think that Professor Lauterbach was mistaken in his view that the ordination of women as rabbis would further fragment the religious unity of the Jewish people, I would refer you to an article that appeared on June 18, 1986, in the *New York Times.* This article, which begins with the headline "Issue of Women as Rabbis Breaks Up Jewish Unit," reports that "the Jewish commission that has approved rabbis as chaplains for the United States Armed Forces since World War I broke up yesterday over whether a rabbi who is a woman can serve as a military chaplain." Rabbi Louis Bernstein, the president of the Orthodox Rabbinical Council of America, protested the fact that our body, the Central Conference of American Rabbis, endorsed the application of our colleague, Rabbi Julie Schwartz, who had applied and is currently serving as a chaplain in the United States Navy. Our Conference had taken this step, apart from the Commission on Chaplaincy of the Jewish Welfare Board, on account of the Commission's refusal to act, "because of Orthodox opposition," upon Rabbi Schwartz's application. Commenting upon this, Rabbi Bernstein is reported as saying, "When they endorsed a woman, we said: 'That's it. The Commission on Jewish Chaplaincy of the JWB is finished.'" This decision to withdraw from the Commission, according to the newspaper account, won the unanimous support of his two hundred Orthodox colleagues gathered in Baltimore for the fiftieth convention of the RCA. Rabbi Bernstein is further quoted as saying, "We do not want to splinter the Jewish community any further than it is. But it is quite clear that this was imposed on us and left us with little choice. Orthodox Judaism cannot accept women rabbis."[21]

In light of this reaction by Rabbi Bernstein and the Rabbinical Council of America to a woman serving as a Jewish chaplain in the United States Armed Forces, can anyone doubt that Professor Lauterbach was correct in observing over sixty years ago that a decision to extend ordination to women would be viewed as a serious and irreparable break with tradition? Given the overwhelming Orthodox halachic consensus that women cannot be counted in a *minyan* (prayer quorum), cannot serve as *shelichei tsibur* (prayer leaders), may not officiate at weddings, may not serve as witnesses at weddings and conversions, and may not either issue a *get* or serve as witnesses in a Jewish divorce proceeding, how could we not have anticipated that such a negative response to the issue of women as rabbis would ultimately be forthcoming from even the most moderate of Orthodox rabbinical bodies? In electing to affirm the right of women to be ordained as rabbis, our movement did depart from tradition in a serious and significant way. Our decision in this area, along with that of the Reconstructionist and now the Conservative movements, did constitute a radical departure from the past practices of *Kelal Yisra-el*. In view of the dialectic interplay between tradition and conscience that I have said characterizes our movement at its best, how and why did we do this?

The question is largely rhetorical, and the reason for our departure from what was admittedly the previous tradition of our people in this area is, at least to me, obvious. The failure of past generations of males to accord women the right to rabbinical ordination and the refusal to permit women to function in public roles of prestige and power were certainly the products of rules produced by a patriarchal culture over 1,500 years ago. In the light of historical context, these disabilities that were attached to women in the public arena are perfectly comprehensible. However, it is impossible for us to contend, and I would hope there would be no dissent from this in our body, that such discriminations against women represented the will of God. To have denied women their legitimate right of access to any public role in Judaism would have been, in light of our own principles of conscience and religious belief, a moral blunder of incalculable proportions. Our movement was the first religious body in Judaism to ordain women as rabbis because we knew it was right. It might have taken Reform over a century to take this first step in redressing the wrongs our men had perpetrated against our women in this area. However, make no mistake about it. Our decision to ordain women as rabbis and to accord women the same public status that had previously been reserved exclusively for men was not, as some critics charge, simply a concession to a modern ideal of "gender equality,"[22] although changes in our culture undoubtedly created the context in which such a decision could be made. Instead, our actions in this area represent a deeply felt religious conviction on our part. Our own sense of compassion and justice required us to affirm the religious vision of humanity implied in Genesis 1:27, *zachar unekeiva bera-am*, that God created men and women in the divine image. The *telos* of Judaism, with its stress upon the dignity of both men and women, compelled us to do what we knew was right. The right of women to be ordained as rabbis was, and remains, a moral imperative for us. It was the morally unambivalent nature of this issue and the genuine spirit of humaneness informing our religion that legitimated our departure from the past ways of our people and allowed us to insist that it was an ethical mandate for all Israel to move in our direction.

The decision to accord Jewish status to the daughters and sons of Jewish fathers and non-Jewish mothers, another admittedly radical departure from our people's tradition, has not commanded the same unanimity of assent among the members of our Conference. This past month there was an article in a Los Angeles Jewish newspaper by a prominent Reform rabbi calling upon us to rethink our stance upon patrilineality.[23] The reason for this ambivalence about our decision, even within our own movement, is that the moral dimensions of this issue are not as evident to all the members of this body. Even among many who support the resolution, there seems to be a sense of unease with it. The concept of *Kelal Yisra-el*, in the absence of an unmistakable moral imperative, seems to cause some of us to doubt the wisdom and necessity for the resolution. The concept of *Kelal Yisra-el*, combined with our allegiance to the principles of conscience and freedom, ensures that tension will always mark our decision-making processes within Reform. No facile philosophical or theological reasoning will ever afford most of us an easy resolution to the challenges and problems that confront our movement except in the rarest of cases.

The tension inherent in this method of arriving at a decision need not be construed as a weakness. This dialectic between tradition, the past practices and beliefs of our people, and the dictates of conscience in a contemporary setting grant us an elasticity and freedom in our decision-making which is the real strength of our movement. It allows a multiplicity of views to emerge on a single issue. In the case of our decision on patrilineality, it permits the majority of the Conference to claim that a broad definition of *Kelal Yisra-el* was simultaneously affirmed and created with the passage of this resolution. *Kelal Yisra-el* is an inclusive entity that seeks to embrace all children of Jewish parents as Jews.

My purpose here is not to contend that a single definition of *Kelal Yisra-el* is authoritative. It should be clear, and in a post-Holocaust world I say this with considerable pain, that the concept of *Kelal Yisra-el* and the image of Jewish unity it evokes is much more a fervent desire and pious wish than it is a description of contemporary, or past, Jewish reality. By indicating some of the ways in which *Kelal Yisra-el* is understood by members of the Conference, I hope I have demonstrated that Reform Judaism, to be true to itself, must affirm the right and reality of pluralism. I do not mean that we as Reform Jews must retreat into a world of privacies where all meanings are assigned by the individual. I do mean that we must live in mutual respect with one another and that the integrity of Reform Judaism is dependent upon an acknowledgment that Judaism can flourish only when it creates a culture in which many modes of discourse are developed and legitimated.

The implications that such an affirmation holds for us within the Conference are clear. We know that the ability to stand in relation to others is essential if true dialogue is to occur. Accordingly, we must cultivate the ability to listen and to empathize with the position of the other. If and when such affirmation of ourselves and others as fully equal partners will occur, we will not need to fear conflict or confrontation. Arguments need not be shunned; they are necessary for serious conversation.

The true spirit of *Kelal Yisra-el* must be grounded in and propelled by *Ahavat Yisra-el*, the sense of love, concern, and mutual caring every Jew ought to have for one another. If these conditions are present, then conflict and dispute can prove to be liberating possibilities. They can grant free rein to the imagination and allow the potential for transformation. At the least they can command tolerance. Such openness is what we demand of ourselves. It is what we seek, to no avail, I am afraid, from most of the Orthodox.

I say much of this in a spirit of sadness. My own family background, my own ties of friendship to many in the Orthodox community, my own sense of respect for the men whose writings I study, my own sense of personal Jewish religious practice and authenticity—all these factors combine to make me lament many of the directions I have mapped out today. Too much of my own psyche, my own heart, resides in another region to grant me satisfaction with many of the conclusions I have arrived at in preparing for this moment.

Our tradition is not monolithic, and no one faction within world Jewry possesses a monopoly over the texts of our tradition. They are our inheritance, and our right to interpret them in accordance with the dictates of our conscience cannot be denied us. This right certainly will not prevent us from working with more traditionalist segments of the Jewish people on a variety of social and communal issues. It also will allow us to construct with Orthodox colleagues personal relationships that can build bridges toward mutual respect and understanding. And if this goal cannot be attained, then we can attempt to achieve civility in our relationship with the Orthodox. To do less would be to obviate our responsibility to the Jewish people. What we cannot achieve is the total respect and legitimacy that we would require from the Orthodox for a true religious dialogue to take place. To deceive ourselves in this way is to demean the integrity of Reform as a religious movement.

As David Tracy has observed, "The corruptions of pluralistic tolerance are real enough. Yet . . . these corruptions pale beside the outright oppression inflicted by the self-righteous upon all . . . who do not share their univocal ideologies. . . . Monists in every movement of thought need not trouble with a messy pluralism. They already know the truth."[24] It is a truth that sets them free from the world and allows them to ignore the pain that they may inflict upon the individual in their zeal. In a world where many suffer the lash of discrimination and the hurt that comes from exclusion, such insensitivity cannot be forgiven.

I close with one final comment. When I was a boy, no Jewish ceremony had a greater impact upon me than the ritual of *duchanen*, which took place in my family's synagogue, as in all traditional synagogues in the Diaspora, during the *Musaf* service on the three pilgrimage festivals of Passover, Shavuot, and Sukkot. As the priests would bless the people, a sense of *kedusha*, of holiness and mystery, would pervade the room. I recall that ceremony at this moment because the priests, immediately prior to their recitation of the priestly benediction, would recite the words, "Blessed are You, O Lord our God, Ruler of the Universe, who has sanctified us with the holiness of Aaron and commanded us *levarech et amo Yisra-el be-ahava*—to bless God's people Israel with love." It is the only *beracha*, blessing, that I am aware of that demands love, *ahava*, as an essential component in its fulfillment. Action and intention must be one. The priest must bless this people Israel "with love." Otherwise, the mitzvah is not complete. In an unredeemed world we cannot strive for less. In serving this people Israel out of love and with compassion, we do honor to ourselves and make our most enduring contribution to *Kelal Yisra-el*. Let the worst accusation hurled against us as a movement be this—that we are attempting to serve this people Israel with too much love, too much compassion. "*Eimatai hu yitaleh?*—When is God exalted?" It is then that God is exalted.

ACKNOWLEDGMENTS

I would like to acknowledge the help and support that my colleagues at HUC-JIR, Los Angeles, have given me in the writing of this essay. Their nurturance makes intellectual and religious discourse a delight, and I am most appreciative that "my portion" has been found among them. I would particularly thank Rabbis Stanley Chyet and Michael Signer, who spent considerable time with me discussing issues of style and substance surrounding this address. I also appreciate the comments and criticisms of my friends Rabbis Kerry Baker of Seattle and Robert Levine of Danbury, Connecticut, who aided me in formulating several of the ideas expressed in this talk. A special debt of gratitude for her forbearance is owed to my wife, Rabbi Jacqueline Koch Ellenson, who dialogued with me "endlessly" on the content and tone of this piece. Finally, I would suggest that the reader of this paper consult the editorial written by Rabbi Jacob Staub in the March 1986 issue of the *Reconstructionist* for views similar to the ones I express in this paper. I thank him for stimulating my thinking on this subject.

1. *Leviticus Rabba* 30.
2. This commentary is drawn from Simeon Maslin, "Hewers of Wood, Drawers of Water, and We," *CCAR Journal* (Fall 1975): 1–6.
3. Shevuot 39a.
4. "Issue of Women as Rabbis Breaks Up Jewish Unit," *New York Times,* May 23, 1982.
5. Two thoughtful essays written in support of the resolution have been authored by Sheldon Zimmerman, "Raising the Standard" (*Moment* [September 1983]: 32–34), and Jacob Staub, "A Reconstructionist View on Patrilineal Descent" (*Judaism* [Winter 1985]: 97–106). A very penetrating article from a theological perspective has been written by Conservative rabbi M. H. Vogel, "The Resolution on Patrilineal Descent" (*Modern Judaism* [May 1986]: 127–56).
6. This point is made clearly and forcefully by Jakob J. Petuchowski in his article "Toward Sectarianism," *Moment* (September 1983): 34–36. Robert Gordis has recently called upon Reform to rescind the resolution on Patrilineality in his piece, "To Move Forward, Take One Step Back: A Plea to the Reform Movement," *Moment* (May 1986): 56–61.
7. These views of the Hatam Sofer are taken from the researches of Jacob Katz in his article "Kavim lebiyografiya shel he-Chatam Sofer" (Towards a biography of the Hatam Sofer), in *Studies in Mysticism and Religion Presented to Gershom G. Scholem,* ed. E. E. Urbach, R. J. Zwi Werblowsky, and Ch. Wirszubski (Jerusalem: Magnes Press, 1967), 115–61.
8. For a description of Hirsch's position, see David Ellenson, "A Response by Modern Orthodoxy to Jewish Religious Pluralism," *Tradition* (Spring 1979): 83–84.
9. Zvi Hirsch Chajes, *Minchat Kena-ot in Kol Sifrei Maharitz Chajes* (All the writings of Zvi Hirsch Chajes), 2 vols. (Jerusalem: 1958), 2:1003, 1007–9.
10. *Iggerot Soferim,* 4 parts (Letters of the Sofers), ed. S. Sofer (Tel Aviv: Sinai, 1970), 1–84.
11. Yechiel Ya-akov Weinberg, *Seridei Esh* iii, no. 100.
12. Moshe Feinstein, *Iggerot Mosheh, Yoreh De-a,* no. 160.
13. Ibid., *Even ha-Ezer* iii, no. 2.
14. J. David Bleich, "Parameters and Limits of Communal Unity from the Perspectives of Jewish Law," *Journal of Halakha and the Contemporary Society* (Fall 1983): 13–14.
15. See the speech delivered by Rabbi Walter Wurzburger to the Central Conference of American Rabbis at Snowmass, Colorado, on June 26, 1986. It is also instructive to read "Symposium—The State of Orthodoxy," *Tradition* 20 (1982): 3–83, where many of the leaders of modern Orthodox Judaism make these same points.
16. Clifford Geertz, *The Interpretation of Cultures* (New York: Basic Books, 1973), 90.

17. Tracy has a prolonged discussion of the idea of pluralism in his book *The Ana-logical Imagination: Christian Theology and the Culture of Pluralism* (New York: Crossroad, 1981), 446–55. The term *relaxed pluralism* is found on p. 451.

18. Berakhot 9:5.

19. Jacob Toury, *Bein mahapecha, re-aktsya, ve-eman tsipatsya* (Between revolution, reaction, and emancipation) (Tel Aviv: Tel Aviv University Press, 1983), 40.

20. I am grateful to my student Shoshanah Perry, who brought these documents to my attention in a term paper she wrote on "Hebrew Union College and the Ordination of Women as Rabbis," in a seminar Stanley Chyet and I taught on "Reform Judaism" in the spring 1986 term at the Los Angeles school of HUC-JIR.

21. *New York Times*, June 18, 1986, 16.

22. This point has been made by Rabbi David Novak in his essay "Women in the Rabbinate?" *Judaism* 33, no.1 (1984): 39-49.

23. Daniel Polish, *Jewish Journal of Greater Los Angeles,* March 28–April 3, 1986, 14.

24. Tracy, *The Analogical Imagination*, 451.

TWO

Searching for a Balanced Theology

7

A Theology of Fear

The Search for a Liberal Jewish Paradigm

The dilemma confronting humanity on the issue of weapons of mass destruction is monstrous. We face possible extinction of the planet if disarmament does not occur. Simultaneously, there is an understandable reluctance—given the lessons of aggression and destruction in human history—on the part of present-day super and regional powers to surrender their arsenals for fear that the "other side" will not do so. Solutions are not simple or easily discovered. Guidelines must be forthcoming, for the "fate of the earth," in Jonathan Schell's felicitous phrase, hangs in the balance.

This essay will explore representative writings of liberal Jewish thought during the past century. The goal is to extrapolate positions that are illustrative of the spectrum of opinions on the issue of omnicide. The effort, however, will be more than descriptive. Through critical evaluation of the various postures, the goal will be to cull insights that might provide hope and guidance for humanity in the midst of our plight.

Franz Rosenzweig

At one end of the continuum of liberal Jewish opinion stand those thinkers whose views on war and peace can be said to lead to a position approximating the pacifistic. Foremost among these is Franz Rosenzweig (1886–1929), the famed German theologian whose thought has had a profound impact upon the American rabbinate. Rosenzweig saw the calendrical cycle of Sabbaths and holidays with their attendant liturgies as embodying the "essence" of Judaism, and the Jewish people as celebrating the existence of eternity within historical time. On the Sabbath, for example, the Jew, through the recitation of a liturgy that centers on the themes of Creation, Revelation, and Redemption, lives *sub-specie aeternitatis*, in the realm of eternity, and not *sub-specie temporis*, in the mundane sphere of the temporal. Similarly, the Jew steps beyond the constraints of time imposed upon him as a human being and encounters the eternal God through the yearly observance and repetition of the holidays. In short, Judaism requires the Jew to participate in an "eternal present" and, as such, allows the Jew to be part of an eternal people that transcend history. The Jewish people, forever basking in the rays of God's eternal presence, are removed, in Rosenzweig's opinion, from the passages of flux and succession that constitute the life of other nations. Situated beyond time, the Jewish people "must forget the world's growth, must cease to think thereon."[1]

The implications that this theological posture held for Rosenzweig's views on war and peace were immense. For while such a stance need not necessarily evolve into political quiescence, in Rosenzweig's case it did mean that the Jewish people needed to retreat from the political concerns of this world and focus instead upon preserving itself spiritually. "Because the Jewish people," Rosenzweig wrote, "is beyond the contradiction that constitutes the vital drive in the life of nations, . . . it knows nothing of war." The Jew, he continued, "in the whole Christian world . . . is practically the only human being who cannot take war seriously, and this makes him the only genuine pacifist. For this reason, and because he experiences perfect community in his spiritual year, he remains remote from the chronology of the rest of the world." Judaism and the Jew are "outside of time agitated by wars."[2] Rosenzweig's view of war and peace and that of Jewish noninvolvement in—one could almost say indifference to—this struggle is understandable, stemming as it does from a pre-Holocaust and pre-State of Israel Jewish thinker. However, his view is widely separated from the intense political concerns of contemporary proponents of a unilateral and total elimination of nuclear, chemical, and biological weapons and is obviously open to modern Jewish charges of irrelevancy and danger in an era when Jews, out of moral necessity, have entered into the realm of power politics. Indeed, Emil Fackenheim, commenting upon this aspect of Rosenzweig's thought, has critically noted that "an absolute transcendence of time, that is, a Judaism of liturgical and holiday cycles which refuses to participate in the political and moral questions of this world, is not attainable in our time."[3] At a moment in history when nuclear apocalypse threatens, a Rosenzweigian type of pacifism that both ignores and retreats from the demands of the day is a luxury whose price Judaism cannot afford to pay.

Rosenzweig's vision of Judaism as a religion unconcerned with the burdens of this world and history was opposed by Abraham Joshua Heschel (1905–1972), professor of Jewish mysticism and ethics at the Jewish Theological Seminary of America for over two decades. To be sure, Heschel, like Rosenzweig, focused upon Judaism as a religion of "timelessness." Jewish tradition, he taught, instructs humanity on "how to experience the taste of eternity or eternal life in time."[4] For "to men with God time is eternity in disguise."[5] Even when he dealt with the concrete phenomenon of the rebirth of the State of Israel and attempted to find a place for it in his theology, Heschel viewed it through the lens of eternity, just as Rosenzweig viewed the calendar and liturgy of Judaism. Thus when he authored his work on the state and its significance to religious Judaism, he entitled it *Israel*, with the subtitle, *An Echo of Eternity*. Nevertheless, drawing upon his own roots as a scion of a Hasidic rabbinic dynasty, Heschel emphasized that the traditional Jewish belief in *tikkun olam* (the restoration of the world) obligated each Jew to participate in this world's affairs through what he labeled, in an inspired phrase paraphrasing Kierkegaard, a "leap of action."[6] In opposition to Rosenzweig, Heschel regarded Judaism as being very much involved in politics and saw that arena as one wherein the Jew could fulfill his duties as a member of the Jewish people. This undoubtedly accounts for a great deal of Heschel's own political activism.

Heschel lived in an era unlike that of Rosenzweig's. He knew the Holocaust firsthand, and in his own lifetime he experienced the exhilaration and rebirth of the State of Israel. As an American, he participated in the struggle for civil rights for blacks and other minority groups during the 1960s, and he witnessed and protested entry into the Vietnam War. Most significantly for this chapter, Heschel also lived at the time of Hiroshima and Nagasaki, as well as the proliferation of nuclear weaponry. Writing with a Heideggerian sense of facticity, Heschel knew that the challenge of the nuclear age could not be avoided.

> When Israel approached Sinai, God lifted up the mountain and held it over their heads, saying: "Either you accept the Torah or be crushed beneath the mountain." The mountain of history is over our heads again. . . . Men all over the world have a dreadful sense in common, the

fear of total annihilation. An apocalyptic monster has descended upon the world, and there is nowhere to go, nowhere to hide.[7]

Humanity, in its freedom, was compelled to meet this test successfully. Yet, aware of the finite nature of the human species, Heschel warned that humanity might not be up to the task. In an autobiographical fragment, Heschel recalled the experience he had as a child of seven when reading the biblical story relating the sacrifice of Isaac by his father, Abraham:

> Isaac was on his way to Mount Moriah with his father; then he lay on the altar, bound, waiting to be sacrificed. My heart began to beat even faster; it actually sobbed with pity for Isaac. Behold, Abraham now lifted the knife. And now my heart froze within me with fright. Suddenly the voice of the angel was heard: "Abraham, lay not thy hand upon the lad, for now I know that thou fearest God." And here I, crying, broke out in tears. "Why are you crying?" asked the rabbi. "You know that Isaac was not killed."
>
> And I said to him, still weeping, "But, Rabbi, supposing the angel had come a second too late?" The rabbi comforted me and calmed me, saying that an angel cannot come late.[8]

Heschel then concluded with the following observation: "An angel cannot be late, but man, made of flesh and blood, may be." Despite such caution, Heschel would not surrender to despair, and he refused to acknowledge that humanity was incapable of forging peace. Deeply religious, Heschel was convinced that God was benevolent and that persons created in God's image were partners with God in the work of creation. This meant that humanity not only had the freedom but possessed the ability to establish peace and break with millennia-old habits of enmity and bloodshed. Thus Heschel was not despondent about prospects for making peace. "Fundamentally," he said, "I am an optimist about all of us, against my better judgment. This is because we have a Father who cares. Our task is to be deserving of His care."[9] So blessed by God, humanity's ability to attain peace—despite centuries of proof to the contrary—was not, in Heschel's view, illusory. In these sentiments, he echoed Hermann Cohen (1842–1919), the great German philosopher of neo-Kantianism whose thought was prominent in the Berlin intellectual and religious circles of Heschel's student years.[10]

Cohen, like Heschel later, recognized that humanity was far removed from the ideal of peace and wrote of the reality of conflict between persons and nations throughout history. However, he postulated that one "should not despair" on account of this, for "the style of the prophets avoids such pessimism." To be sure, "War . . . marks the historical cycle of any nation's existence." Nevertheless, Cohen believed that humanity was capable of "sloughing off" this form of existence and "arising," instead, to a "new life . . . of morality," one in which war would "disappear" and life would be "lived in harmony and justice."[11] As the idea of God gave Cohen "the confidence that morality will become reality on earth,"[12] Cohen optimistically posited that humanity could transform the world of "is," a world of war, tensions, and conflicts, into a realm of "ought," a reality of tranquility and peace.

The seminal influence Cohen had on Heschel in this matter is clear. Heschel, too, claimed that the prophets taught that a world wherein all persons lived in "a relationship of reverence for each other" was possible.[13] They foresaw the day when all would acknowledge that "might is not supreme, . . . the sword is an abomination, . . . violence is obscene."[14] War, from the perspective of the prophets, was not simply immoral. It was also futile and absurd, destined to be repeated until nations came to recognize the basic truth that the "other," as a being created in God's likeness, was endowed with infinite worth and dignity. The task of Judaism was to spread this teaching and, in so doing, help to establish conditions that would cause others to believe in the possibility of peace. Without such faith, Heschel believed that conflict between nations could not be avoided. "Worse than war is the belief in the inevitability of war," Heschel wrote,[15] for such despair would only be self-fulfilling and lead to a tragic denouement. Instead, humanity had to be convinced of the truth of prophetic teaching and accept the fact that release from the quagmire of seemingly never-ending wars was not a utopian hope. Only if humanity willed it could peace reign among nations.

Heschel's faith that peace, albeit difficult, was attainable is embodied in a story he told of Rabbi Ben Zion Uziel, a leading Sephardic rabbi in Tel Aviv. In 1929, in the midst of an Arab-Jewish riot in the Tel Aviv–Jaffa area, Rabbi Uziel positioned himself between Arabs and Jews and asked each side to cease fire. He then addressed himself to the Arabs in a sympathetic manner and said, "Our common father, Abraham, the father of

Isaac and Ishmael, when he saw his nephew Lot was causing him trouble, claiming that there was not enough room for both his flocks and Abraham's flocks to live together, said to him: 'Let there be no quarrel between you and me, and between your shepherds and my shepherds, for we are people like brothers.' We also say to you, the land can sustain all of us and provide for us in plenty. Let us, then, stop fighting each other, for we, too, are people like brothers." The Arabs, after hearing Rabbi Uziel's words, dispersed quietly. Heschel then ended the tale with the following statement: "Men of goodwill will never cease to pray that the logic of peace may prevail over the epidemic of suspicion."[16]

As this story suggests, the real enemy that humanity confronts in its efforts to eradicate war is not another people. It is the distrust and hatred, the evil, that seem to adhere in the nature of existence and foster conditions of tension that transcend national boundaries and particularistic groupings. Heschel nonetheless asserted that as partners with God in the work of creation, humanity possesses the ability to overcome all this strife and establish, in its stead, tranquility and understanding. His rendition of a wise and gentle rabbi resolving disputes between two bitter enemies simply reflects his belief in the eventual positive evolution of human interaction. In extrapolating a position on nuclear weapons from Heschel's writings, it seems obvious that he would have condemned their employment in any capacity as being not only idiotic and immoral but sinful. For even the threatened use of nuclear arms would inexorably move humanity on to renewed conflict and would hasten the destruction of creation itself. It would retard humanity's obligation to participate in a healing process that our situation so desperately requires.

Heschel's commitment to the Jewish religious tradition, it would seem, leads to a type of "pacifism" on the nuclear question similar to that of Rosenzweig's. However, this should not obscure the fact that the sense of activism that animates it is radically distinct from that of the older German thinker. Consequently, Heschel's position is essentially impervious to the kind of criticism Fackenheim hurled at Rosenzweig. Instead, it is the absolute fideism of Heschel's posture—the belief that humanity can refrain from traditional forms of aggressive behavior and establish prophetic visions of peace—that leaves his thought, however inspirational, vulnerable to criticism. The story of Rabbi Uziel and the Arabs can hardly be regarded as anything other than exceptional. Heschel's account of war and peace thus does not fail because of its perception of what ought to be. Rather, his approach is to be faulted for not fully confronting what is, for ignoring the realities of history and psychology. To base nuclear policy on the assumption that discord can be resolved and harmony established through goodness and reason is to act recklessly in a premessianic world that empirically accords more respect to power than to kindness. Indeed, it is precisely on these grounds that a Richard Rubenstein would adopt a policy position on the nuclear arms race diametrically opposed to that of a Heschel, and his voice, something of a lone one in the liberal Jewish camp, deserves a hearing.

Richard Rubenstein

Richard Rubenstein (b. 1924), a professor at Florida State University in Tallahassee, received his rabbinical ordination at the Jewish Theological Seminary and completed his doctorate at Harvard in religious thought and psychology. He first gained widespread public attention as a "Death-of-God" theologian in the 1960s, and his *After Auschwitz* has continued to command a following in religious studies circles. Rubenstein has published extensively, and a revised version of his Harvard dissertation, "The Religious Imagination," offers a Freudian interpretation of rabbinic literature. Indeed, it is obvious, when reading Rubenstein's analysis of the nuclear issue, that Sigmund Freud's view of humanity has had a considerable impact upon Rubenstein's thought and that Rubenstein's position on this matter cannot be understood without recourse to him. Consequently, it is vital to take note of a correspondence Freud had in 1932 with Albert Einstein. In that correspondence Freud revealed his own attitude, one which Rubenstein obviously shares, about the prospects for the attainment of peace in this world. On July 30 of that year, Einstein asked Freud, "Is it possible to control man's mental evolution so as to make him proof against the psychosis of hate and destructiveness?" Freud, in response, stated that "there is no likelihood of our being able to suppress humanity's aggressive tendencies. . . . The ideal conditions would obviously be found in a community where every man subordinated his instinctive life to the dictates of reason. Nothing less than this could bring about so thorough and durable a union between men. . . . But surely such a hope is utopian."[17]

Rubenstein, grounding his argument upon these Freudian views, dismisses as futile any attempt to forge peace on the basis of notions such as mutual respect and goodwill among nations. These efforts, however well-intentioned, ignore the psychological realities of human existence. For people, by nature, are aggressive, and the strongest instinct they possess is that of survival. "Rights do not belong to men by nature," Rubenstein writes. "All that men possess by nature is the necessity to participate in the incessant life and death struggle for existence of any animal." To gloss over this and to establish a nuclear policy in the hope that humans will somehow suppress their aggressive impulses is, from Rubenstein's perspective, just so much wishful thinking. Instead, Rubenstein advises policy makers to recognize aggression as an ineradicable part of human behavior and to acknowledge that only the instinct for survival can possibly keep it in check. To do otherwise is to desire what never was and never will be. To formulate policy on any other basis is, in the contemporary situation, to act irresponsibly and suicidally. Rather, in full cognizance of humanity's capacity for violence, one should create policy in accordance with the insight that "the power to injure remains the most important credible deterrent to a would-be aggressor's violence."[18] Only if there is sufficient fear on one party's part that its own existence will be threatened should it use violence against a second party—assuming there is a fear that the second party possesses enough power to retaliate in kind—would the first party refrain from doing so. The instinct for survival is the only force more powerful than the drive for dominance.

Applying these arguments to the nuclear arms situation, Rubenstein initially notes the novelty of the present setting in human history.

In warfare and weapon making, practical reason may have reached its limits. Mass destruction only makes sense to a warring power if it can survive as a viable society. Nuclear warfare renders such an outcome uncertain. . . . For any large-scale war now entails the possibility that nuclear weapons could terminate all life on earth, if not as a direct result of the initial assaults on population centers, then as a result of the predictable aftereffects.[19]

The specter of total destruction does not lead Rubenstein to conclude that nuclear weapons should therefore be destroyed. While humanity's capacity for total destruction of the planet might supply a new ingredient in the modern situation, the realities of human aggression nevertheless remain constant. The only prophylactic against them is a policy of deterrence.

Disarmament is useless, for no nation would ever trust another nation to fulfill its commitment truthfully. In the Hobbesian universe of Richard Rubenstein, where each side of a nuclear power struggle could assume that only an instinct for survival would outweigh visions of aggrandizement, the threat of total nuclear retaliation would be the one course sufficient to dissuade a would-be attacker from attempting to launch a nuclear attack on its opponent. Given the nature of the world, the existence of nuclear weapons—in that they make victory in war virtually impossible to attain— ironically heightens the prospects for peace. The nature of Rubenstein's position in this regard is seen in the concluding pages of his autobiography, *Power Struggle*. Standing at the top of Masada with his son Jeremy, Rubenstein muses:

> As J stood there, I wondered about the future. Was Israel's return after two thousand years of wandering and misery but the prelude to a final nuclear holocaust? After Auschwitz, it is inconceivable that the Israelis would consent to their own annihilation. . . .
>
> For years there have been persistent rumors of Israeli nuclear weapons. I have no hard facts, but it is inconceivable that the Israelis could have listened to threats of annihilation for twenty-five years without producing their own doomsday weapon.[20] Faced with the destruction of the only political entity they can trust to defend their existence and dignity, the State of Israel, they would unleash their bombs on Cairo, Alexandria, Amman, and Damascus in certain knowledge that the extinction of Haifa, Tel Aviv, and Jerusalem would swiftly follow. *There is a limit to the pressure the Arabs can exert.* . . .
>
> Yet, as I thought of Israel's deadly peril, I was mildly optimistic. *Nuclear terror may offer the only credible guarantee of peace.* For twenty centuries it has been possible to slaughter Jews at will. *More often than not there was gain in the bloody venture for the slaughterers.* In the century par excellence of broken promises and broken trust, the dearer it becomes to eliminate Jews, the greater the likelihood that peace will someday come to the Holy Land and all of its peoples.[21]

Rubenstein's position thus turns out to be a simple one. Remove the incentive for war, that is, "gain"—through the prospect of total destruction— and a "credible guarantee of peace" will be achieved.

Rubenstein's solution to the nuclear predicament is open to question on two major grounds. The first is that Rubenstein's stratagem for peace, predicated as it is on the assumption that the only thing unique about the modern era is the increased ability of humanity to unleash destruction, assumes that human instincts and behaviors have not changed. If this is true, why should it then be assumed that opposing sides in a nuclear age will surrender the belief that nuclear wars, like other wars in the past, can be won? After all, with proper technological advancements, it is conceivable that one nation's scientific knowledge and capabilities could so far outstrip a rival's that victory, even in the case of a nuclear war, could be envisioned as attainable by a nation's leaders. Indeed, given pronouncements made by leaders, such a scenario hardly appears fantastical. Thus there is no reason to assume, along with Rubenstein, that humanity's instinct for survival will suddenly allow it to develop the imagination that nuclear attacks cannot be withstood. The possibility of war, therefore, is not lessened by the ever-escalating manufacture and development of nuclear weapons, which a policy of deterrence would inevitably dictate. Instead, the risks such wars would entail are only heightened.[22]

An even more telling negative response to Rubenstein's posture is a development of relatively recent vintage on the world scene. Rubenstein's reliance on deterrence as an adequate means for ensuring peace is based upon the contention that the human desire for survival is so great that no one would knowingly prefer a total nuclear conflagration to the continued existence of this planet. However, in a time when thousands of young Shiite Muslims willingly sacrificed their lives at the behest of an Ayatollah Khomeini in order to earn a martyr's death in the landmines of a Middle Eastern desert, no such confident pronouncement can be easily made. Deterrence, in short, is effective so long as one's opponents fear death for themselves, their families, their nations, or the world. In the case of religious fanatics who possess no such fear—in fact, who are convinced that such destruction would lead to a place in Paradise—the prospect of global annihilation hardly provides an obstacle to nuclear war. Moreover, given the reality of nuclear proliferation, the prospects of regional powers fed by bullyboy dictators for obtaining a nuclear arsenal are great. Rubenstein's contention that deterrence offers the "only credible guarantee of peace" is suspect. It presupposes that the world is and will be ruled exclusively by rational people who will maintain total control over nuclear weapons forever. In a world of madmen, this posture cannot be maintained with absolute certainty. In light of the nature of our world, an unwillingness to work toward disarmament is insane.

It seems that we have returned to our original dilemma and that the positions of Heschel at one end and Rubenstein at the other both contain serious flaws. It is imperative to move beyond the Scylla of an unwarranted faith in humanity's capacity to subdue its instincts and pursue peace and the Charybdis of an exclusive policy of deterrence which, without any real basis, insists that humanity, in its quest for survival, will not commit a suicidal act. The issue is certainly not easily resolved. However, by taking elements from each of these approaches as reflected in the writings of other modern Jewish thinkers, some directions for navigating humanity's way out of this complex and hellish maze may yet emerge.

Hans Jonas

Hans Jonas (1903–89) for many years enjoyed a worldwide reputation as one of the foremost scholars of Gnosticism and early Christianity. A former student of both Rudolf Bultmann and Martin Heidegger, Jonas also attended the Hochschule für die Wissenschaft des Judentums (the Liberal Rabbinic Seminary) in Berlin. Forced to flee from his German homeland as a result of Nazi persecution, Jonas served in the Jewish Brigade of the British army during World War II and ultimately came to the United States, where he renewed his academic career and gained prominence not only as a student of the early centuries of the Common Era but as a philosopher as well.

In a seminal essay, "The Concept of Responsibility: An Inquiry into the Foundations of an Ethics for Our Age," Jonas argues that the rise of modern technology, with its unprecedented capacity for power and destruction, has changed "the nature and scope of human action . . . decisively."[23] While past systems of morality centered on concepts such as love and reverence, Jonas contends that it is insufficient to ground systems of morality in such sentiments any longer. Instead, "responsibility" must now lie at the heart of a mature and just ethics for the nuclear age. And this "responsibility," he asserts, is nothing less than the preservation of human existence now and in the future. This is the transcendent moral obligation imposed upon humanity at a time when the whole human enterprise is jeopardized by nuclear weaponry. Unlike Rubenstein, Jonas sees the obligation to live as a moral one, and rejects the notion that it is simply a psychological instinct. However, like Rubenstein, Jonas claims that humanity can no longer depend upon the Good, the *bonum*, to motivate it to behave in a proper and responsible moral manner. Moreover, he stated this despite the fact that he recognized that rare individuals will be led to do the morally proper thing by such a motive. Indeed, in an autobiographical reminiscence akin to the story Heschel told of Rabbi Uziel, Jonas stated:

> When in 1945 I reentered a vanquished Germany as a member of the Jewish Brigade in the British Army, I had to decide whom of my former teachers in philosophy I could in good conscience visit, and whom not. It turned out that the "no" fell on my main teacher . . . who by the criteria which then had to govern my choice had failed the human test of time; whereas the "yes" included the much lesser figure of a rather narrow traditionalist Kantian persuasion, who meant little to me philosophically but of whose record in those dark years I heard admirable things. When I did visit him and congratulated him on the courage of his principled stand, he said a memorable thing. "Jonas," he said, "I tell you this; without Kant's teaching I couldn't have done it."[24]

Jonas conceded that some human beings are capable of heroic deeds. He acknowledged that there are individuals who, recognizing the *bonum*, act in accordance with the categorical imperative that a situation reveals. Thus Jonas did not display the cynicism of Rubenstein. Nevertheless, such deeds are all too rare. Previous systems of morality are outmoded, Jonas argued, not only for this reason but because they did not have to accept the full weight of responsibility that a system of ethics has to bear today. As he phrased it, "Responsibility with a never-known burden has moved into the center of political morality," for the complete annihilation of the planet is now possible.[25] An ethic for a nuclear age must confront the possibility that there will be no future. Since the *bonum* as a motivating force has been shown historically to be insufficient to ensure that future, then perhaps, Jonas reasoned, fear of the *malum* (the bad) will do so.

In an essay entitled "Responsibility Today: The Ethics of an Endangered Future,"[26] Jonas argued that at present "we need the discovery of our duties." It is the threat to the continued existence of humanity that marks the modern setting and provides the starting point for contemporary ethical reflection. Unfortunately, "the perception of the *malum* is infinitely easier to us than the perception of the *bonum*; it is more direct, more compelling, less given to differences of opinion. . . . It is forced upon us by the . . . presence of evil." Jonas concluded, "Therefore moral philosophy must consult our fears prior to our wishes. . . . And although the heuristics of fear is not the last word in the search for goodness, it is at least an extremely useful first word."

Nuclear weapons have introduced a *novum* into history. Every political leader must now consider the possibility that a wrong decision could signal the end of the planet. This, however, gave Jonas cause for hope.

> Let us return once again to the heuristics of fear I am suggesting. For many the apocalyptic potential of our technology is concentrated in the atom bomb. . . . But it has one consolation: It lies in the realm of choice. Certain acts of certain actors can bring about catastrophe—but they can also remain undone. Nuclear weapons can even be abolished. . . . (The prospect is admittedly small.) Anyway, decisions still play a role—and in those fear. Not that this can be trusted; but we *can*, in principle, be *lucky* because the use is not *necessary* in principle, that is, not impelled by the production of the thing as such (which rather aims at obviating the necessity of its use).[27]

Jonas, like Rubenstein, did not trust, as Heschel did, in the power of goodness to move humanity. His own experience of Nazi Germany—above all, the performance of his teacher Martin Heidegger—undoubtedly prevented him from sharing Heschel's moral optimism. It is his moral pessimism—one could almost say his Gnostic-like vision that morality can emerge from the dark places of the soul—that gave him cause for hope.

Humanity has one primary moral obligation—the preservation of the planet and the life that dwells in it. The destruction of the earth is not "an inevitable *fatum*."[28] This is a moral statement, because it recognizes that humanity possesses the ability to choose between life and death. Jonas, like Rubenstein, was able to advocate deterrence, though he did not do so on the basis of assuming that humanity's psychological desire for survival was stronger than its impulse toward aggression. Rather, he did so because he believed that humanity was sufficiently fearful—had the requisite moral imagination—to conjure up the image of a world destroyed by nuclear attacks and to know that such destruction would be a moral abomination. Mutually ensured destruction allows humanity to refuse to empty its weapons. Simultaneously, Jonas's writings permit humanity to consider attempts at disarmament as more than pious wishes. While he conceded that it is unlikely that nuclear powers will pursue this option, it is possible, for humans do possess both moral choice and vision. It is this posture which distinguishes Jonas from Rubenstein and identifies him with the cardinal thrust of the Jewish religious tradition.

Martin Buber

Lest this middle path mapped out by Jonas appear inconsistent, it will be instructive to turn to themes on war and peace in the work of Martin Buber (1878–1965), for Buber, more than any other modern Jewish thinker, uses the metaphor of the "narrow ridge" to symbolize the precarious nature of human decision making. Buber, who earned worldwide prominence for his most famous book, *I and Thou*, as well as countless other publications, was an active Zionist. Consequently, after the Nazis rose to power in Germany, Buber immigrated in 1938 to Palestine, where he served as professor of social philosophy at the Hebrew University. In addition, he was active in numerous social and political causes both in Israel and abroad, and his stances on issues such as Arab-Jewish relations and the Eichmann trial (which he opposed) generated tremendous controversies. His work serves to clarify and amplify the nature of the positions as staked out by Jonas, and his thought provides a fitting conclusion to the positions surveyed in this essay.

For Buber, the meaning and purpose of human existence is found in the fundamentally social nature of reality. The individual is "human" primarily because he is capable of entering into dialogic relationship both with other persons and with God. In a word, the individual is able to communicate. Authentic being consists in being known and knowing that one is being known. One is permitted to say "I" only because there are "Thous." As Buber wrote:

I become through my relation to the *Thou*; as I become *I*, I say *Thou*. All real living is meeting.[29]

A person makes his appearance by entering into relation with other persons. . . . He who takes his stand in relation shares in reality, that is, in a being, that neither merely belongs to him nor merely lies outside him. All reality is an activity in which I share without being able to appropriate it for myself. *Where there is not sharing there is no reality. Where there is self-appropriation there is no reality.* The more direct the contact with the Thou, the fuller is the sharing.[30]

One is made fully human through others—in a reciprocal dependent independence. Our unique characters, which make each of us individuals, make us essentially other. Yet our uniqueness, our being for ourselves, constitutively leads us to be for others. Neither the solitary individual nor the social aggregate is the irreducible datum of human existence. Instead, the fundamental reality is the individual person acting in relation to other persons or God. We are persons because we can claim and respond, address and be addressed. We are persons because we are responsible to others. We are persons because we live in community.

True community, where persons both retain their individuality and realize their responsibility for others, forms the backdrop for Buber's views on war and peace, for such a community leads the way to peace and freedom. The decisive test for community was not, however, life within the community alone. Rather, it was at the edge of the community, at the boundaries that separated one group from another. As "righteousness itself can only become wholly visible in the structures of the life of the people," it is incumbent upon a people to make peace wherever "we are destined to do so: in the active life of our own community and in that aspect of it which can actively help to determine its relationship to another community."[31] The practical application of this for Buber was the nature of the relationship he attempted to forge with his Arab neighbors in the Middle East. He felt it imperative that Jew and Arab live not only next to but with each other. In describing his role and membership in Ihud (Unity), a group which strove for rapprochement between Arab and Jew, Buber said to Mahatma Gandhi, "I belong to a group of people who . . . have not ceased to strive for the conclusion of a genuine peace between Jew and Arab. By a genuine peace we . . . infer that both peoples should develop the land without one imposing its will on the other. . . . This appeared to us to be very difficult, but not impossible."[32] Like both Heschel and Jonas, Buber posited that humanity had the ability to transform visions of peace into a reality. However, as his writings indicate, he recognized that the contingencies of the human situation provided parameters for this goal that sometimes made the attainment of peace an impossibility.

Humanity, Buber observed, had a violent side to its nature. Thus when Gandhi, in a 1938 letter to Buber, claimed, "India is by nature nonviolent," Buber refused to grant credibility to Gandhi's assertion.[33] Contemporary events only support the wisdom of Buber's refusal. Instead, Buber countered by pointing out to Gandhi that the world humanity inhabits is an imperfect one. Violence, evil, destruction exist; and they are not endemic to a single individual or nation. Consequently, Buber felt compelled to reject Gandhi's suggestion that the Jews employ *satayagraha* (soul-force) as a form of nonviolent resistance to Nazi persecutions of the Jews. Instead, he maintained that the Jews, of course, "do not want force. . . . From time immemorial we have proclaimed the teaching of justice and peace. . . . Thus we cannot desire to use force. No one who counts himself in the ranks of Israel can desire to use force." Despite this, the Jews "have not proclaimed, as did Jesus, the son of our people, and as you do, the teaching of nonviolence, because *we believe that sometimes a man must use force to save himself or even more his children.*"[34] Judaism does not abjure force, the use of violence, to combat wrong. While hardly desirable or even the first recourse in a confrontation with evil, it must still remain available as a final option in our dealings in a world where aggression against the innocent exists. Of course, one employs such force with a great deal of hesitancy. Nevertheless, its use, real or perceived, may be the only just course a community can adopt when confronting a particular situation. Buber's position can be summarized by the following statement:

> For I cannot help withstanding evil when I see that it is about to destroy the good. I am forced to withstand the evil in the world just as the evil within myself. I can only strive not to have to do so by force. . . . But if there is no other way of preventing the evil destroying the good, I trust I shall use force and give myself into God's hands.[35]

The purpose of ethics and the guidance that ethical reflection provides are herein revealed. Ethics must guide the relationships between persons and nations amidst the demands of life. They can neither retreat behind the garb of a pious optimism nor cloak themselves in the vestments of an ostensibly realistic psychological reductionism. Instead, they must provide direction for the world as it is—with all of its complexities and inconsistencies. This is why ethical decisions, in the final analysis, have to be made by persons addressing and caring for others in real situations. They cannot be left to computers, nor can they be preprogrammed and packaged. Thus, in extrapolating a position on the nuclear issue from Buber's writings, it is clear that one cannot simply glorify humanity, optimistically ignore the persistence of human evil, and thereby advocate a policy of disarmament as the answer to the nuclear dilemma. Nor can one posit that humanity is guided by instincts of survival and aggression alone, thereby arriving at the conclusion that only a policy of deterrence will be sufficient to resolve the nuclear issue. Ethical decisions, in facing hard matters such as this, do not have the luxury of dealing in black and white. Violence, or its implied threat, cannot responsibly be forsworn. As Buber observed:

> In order to preserve the community of men, we are often compelled to accept wrongs. . . . But what matters is that in every hour of decision we are aware of our responsibility and summon our conscience to weigh exactly how much is necessary to preserve the community, and accept just so much and no more; . . . that we . . . struggle with destiny in fear and trembling.[36]

Buber's thought, when applied to the question of omnicide, can be interpreted as having the same themes contained in Jonas's writings. The writings of Jonas and Buber have the virtue of sensitizing humanity to the multilayered nature of this problem. The paradigm they provide indicates that liberal Jewish thought in the current setting has moved beyond the unbridled faith in humanity that marked liberal Jewish thinkers in the pre-Holocaust Jewish world.[37] Theirs is a paradigm that acknowledges the reality of evil in the world while, at the same time, refusing to surrender a cautious optimism about the possibility of human goodness. Monovalent decisions regarding weapons of mass destruction cannot be made. Peace must be pursued on the levels of both disarmament and deterrence. Policy has to be subtle, polyvocal, and flexible, sensitive to all the nuances involved and outlined in this chapter. This is certainly frightening: The chance that this planet could be destroyed and the inability, in the face of that fact, to derive a single response to this crisis of unparalleled proportions has to strike fear into the hearts and minds of every human being. A theology of fear is unavoidable in our day.

NOTES

1. Franz Rosenzweig, *The Star of Redemption*, trans. W. W. Hallo (New York: Holt, Rinehart and Winston, 1971), 328.

2. Ibid., 332.

3. Emil L. Fackenheim, *To Mend the World: Foundation of Post-Holocaust Thought* (New York: Schocken, 1982), 324.

4. Abraham Joshua Heschel, *The Sabbath: Its Meaning for Modern Man* (New York: Farrar, Straus and Young, 1951), 74.

5. Ibid., 100.

6. Abraham Joshua Heschel, *God in Search of Man* (Northvale NJ: Jason Aronson, 1955/1987), 282.

7. Abraham Joshua Heschel, *The Insecurity of Freedom: Essays on Human Existence* (New York: Farrar, Straus and Giroux, 1966), 179.

8. Abraham Joshua Heschel, "The Moral Outrage of Vietnam," in Robert McAfee Brown et al., *Vietnam: Crisis of Conscience* (New York: Associated Press, 1967), 51–52. Much of this discussion on Heschel is based on Morton C. Fierman, "Ideas on Peace in the Theology of Abraham Joshua Heschel," California State University Seminar Papers Series (Fullerton CA, November 1974), no. 8.

9. Interview in the *Los Angeles Times* (October 4, 1970).

10. During the same period when Heschel was a student at the University of Berlin, Rabbi Joseph Soloveitchek was writing his doctoral dissertation there on the writings of Cohen. This is indicative of the influence of Cohen's thought on those who were within the ambit of German Judaism during those years. Heschel was certainly included among those numbers.

11. Hermann Cohen, *Reason and Hope: Selections from the Jewish Writings of Hermann Cohen*, trans. and ed. Eva Jospe (New York: Norton, 1971), 110–21.

12. Ibid., 5.

13. Abraham Joshua Heschel, *The Prophets* (New York: Harper and Row, 1962/1967), 160.

14. Heschel, "The Moral Outrage of Vietnam," 60.

15. Abraham Joshua Heschel, *Israel: An Echo of Eternity* (New York: Farrar, Straus and Giroux, 1969), 175–78.

16. Ibid.

17. Quoted in Otto Nathan and Heinz Norden, *Einstein on Peace* (New York: Simon and Schuster, 1968). Einstein's quote is found on p. 190 and Freud's statement on pp. 199–200.

18. Richard L. Rubenstein, *The Cunning of History: Holocaust and the American Future* (New York: Harper and Row, 1975), 89.

19. Richard L. Rubenstein, *The Age of Triage: Fear and Hope in Our Overcrowded World* (Boston: Beacon Press, 1968), 33.

20. *Time*, in a June 1985 issue, stated that Israel does possess such a nuclear weapon. In addition, Shai Feldman, *Israeli Nuclear Deterrence: A Strategy for the 1980s* (New York: Columbia University Press, 1982), argues that Israeli possession of nuclear arms and a concomitant policy of deterrence that accompanies it is the surest safeguard for peace in the Middle East. Abba Eban, *The New Diplomacy: International Affairs in the Modern Age* (New York: Random House, 1983), makes the same argument concerning the efficacy of the policy of deterrence in ensuring peace between the superpowers.

21. Richard Rubenstein, *Power Struggle* (New York: Scribner's, 1974), 192–93.

22. I would like to thank my colleague Norman Mirsky at Hebrew Union College–Jewish Institute of Religion at Los Angeles for this insight.

23. Hans Jonas, *On Faith, Reason, and Responsibility* (Claremont CA.: Institute for Antiquity and Christianity, 1981), 81.

24. As quoted by Fackenheim in *To Mend the World,* 269.

25. Jonas, *On Faith, Reason, and Responsibility,* 99.

26. Ibid., 73.

27. Ibid., 78.

28. Ibid., 79.

29. Martin Buber, *I-Thou,* trans. by Ronald G. Smith (New York: Scribner's, 1958), 11.

30. Ibid., 63.

31. As cited by Maurice Friedman, in *Martin Buber: The Life of Dialogue* (New York: Harper, 1960), 144.

32. Ibid., 144–45.

33. Martin Buber and Judah Leon Magnes, *Two Letters to Gandhi* (Jerusalem: Reuben Mass, April 1939), 20.

34. Ibid., 19–20.

35. Ibid., 21.

36. As cited by Friedman in *Martin Buber,* 145.

37. The most cogent statement of this reversal is found in Eugene Borowitz, "Rethinking the Reform Jewish Theory of Social Action," *Journal of Reform Judaism* (Fall 1980): 1–19.

8

Eugene B. Borowitz

A Tribute on the Occasion of His 70th Birthday

In the summer of 1969, while waiting for a friend at a Greyhound Bus Station in Lynchburg in my native Virginia, I perused a rack of paperback books in the station's gift shop. I had just completed an undergraduate seminar on "Modern Christian Religious Existentialism," and my eyes raced to a work entitled *A Layman's Guide to Religious Existentialism*. To this day, I have no idea why this book was placed among the rows of pulp novels that otherwise dominated the stand. However, it was there, in that most unlikely setting, that I was first introduced to the name and writings of Eugene Borowitz. As I read the pages, I was struck by the clarity, precision, passion, and accessibility of the author's words. Furthermore, as a young Jew, I was gratified that amidst all the Christian theologians explicated in the work, there were Jewish ones as well.

Particularly striking was a chapter on a German Jewish theologian named Franz Rosenzweig. It was with a mixed sense of gratitude, relief, and excitement that I devoured this chapter. I was elated to find a Jew who was such a significant participant in this emotionally and intellectually compelling contemporary religious dialogue. Borowitz's exposition of Rosenzweig's thought meant a great deal to me on an intellectual level. More significantly, I was grateful for the guidance to be gained in a modern idiom from a Jewish thinker on eternal questions of religious faith and doubt. Several years later, when as a second-year rabbinical student at the Hebrew Union College–Jewish Institute of Religion in New York I attended Eugene Borowitz's lectures on "Modern Jewish Religious Thought," I was given a vocabulary to name and define the religious struggle I was then experiencing. In his initial lecture in the course, Rabbi Borowitz said clearly and simply, "The problem of modern Jewish thought is one of how we affirm the best of what the modern world has taught us while simultaneously maintaining our commitment to the covenantal tradition that is at the base of genuine Jewish belief and practice. In a sentence, how can we simultaneously be 'modern' and 'authentically Jewish'?"

It is the challenge of defining and understanding this dialectical interplay between the poles of "tradition" and "modernity" that lies at the heart of modern Jewish thought, and Eugene Borowitz has been foremost among Jewish thinkers of his generation in explicating the nature and directions of the multiple responses that have been offered to meet this challenge. His books, articles, and lectures have been instrumental in encouraging the American Jewish community to take theology and issues of religious faith seriously. He has described the parameters of modern Jewish thought and chronicled its developments in the twentieth century. Most significantly, he has also sought to provide some answers to the dilemmas posed by this modern chapter in the history of Jewish religious thought. My own experience that day in Lynchburg was neither isolated nor unique but one that many other modern Jews have experienced through dialogue and discussion with the words and writings of Borowitz. This article, a companion piece to one I have recently written with my colleague Lori Krafte-Jacobs on Borowitz and his thought, is intended to provide further insight into the development of that thought and to measure the dimensions of Borowitz's contributions to Jewish religious thinking in our day.

Early Thought

Born in Columbus, Ohio, in 1924, Borowitz was educated as an undergraduate at the Ohio State University. In 1948, he was ordained a rabbi by the Hebrew Union College in Cincinnati and in 1950 received the degree of Doctor of Hebrew Letters from Hebrew Union College for a dissertation in the field of rabbinic thought. In the 1950s he served as founding rabbi of the Community Synagogue in Port Washington, Long Island, New York, and was enrolled in the Columbia-Union joint PhD program in religion, where he completed all work except for the dissertation. When Borowitz assumed the position as director of religious education for the Union of American Hebrew Congregations, he agreed to switch to Columbia's doctoral program in education and ultimately received an EdD. In 1962 Borowitz joined the faculty of the Hebrew Union College–Jewish Institute of Religion in New York, where he continues to serve as Sigmund L. Falk Distinguished Professor of Jewish Education and Religious Thought. His editorship of *Sh'ma: A Journal of Jewish Responsibility* and his many writings, lectures, and teaching positions have made him a preeminent contemporary Jewish religious thinker and leader.

Throughout the 1950s and 1960s Borowitz published numerous articles in journals such as *Commentary, Judaism*, and the *Journal of the Central Conference of American Rabbis*. His impact on the religious thought of the American Jewish community was intensified by his publication of three books in 1968 and 1969. In *A New Jewish Theology in the Making*, Borowitz built upon the foundations he had initially established in *A Layman's Guide to Religious Existentialism*. Whereas the latter book had primarily focused upon non-Jewish theologians, *A New Jewish Theology in the Making* systematically presented and evaluated the particularistic reality of a twentieth-century tradition of Jewish religious thought. Borowitz took great care to describe this tradition in all its richness and variety. By lucidly explicating the thought systems constructed by the major Jewish theologians of our era, Borowitz was able to illuminate the directions of that tradition, reflect upon his own indebtedness to it, and lay the groundwork for his own dissent from it. In *A New Jewish Theology in the Making*, as well as in the other two works he published in those years— *How Can a Jew Speak of Faith Today* and *Choosing a Sex Ethic*—Borowitz argued that the religious rationalism that dominated an earlier generation of Jewish thinkers had come to an end. As Borowitz himself later testified in *Renewing the Covenant* (1991), he had, at this stage in his development, already come to reject his liberal predecessors' assertion that there was a conceptual core to Jewish religiosity that had to serve as the foundation for Jewish theological reflection. Instead, in his own gropings to articulate a new non-Orthodox theology, Borowitz incorporated what he termed "a recognized truth in the general culture . . . a root belief that personal dignity means having substantial self-determination."

Borowitz thus turned to religious existentialism—particularly as expressed in Martin Buber's philosophy of dialogue and relation—as the most compelling and attractive methodological approach Jewish thinkers could employ in addressing issues of contemporary religious and communal concern. Furthermore, as he was to demonstrate in his books of those years, traditional thinkers in the community, such as Heschel and Soloveitchik, had similarly moved beyond the Kantianism of their own youth and had come to embrace elements of religious existentialism in their own attempts to describe Jewish religious faith and practice. In explicating the thought of these two exemplars of traditional Judaism, Borowitz was displaying another proclivity of his own thought. The Jewish theology he was struggling to express was not intended to be a sectarian one, reserved only for members of the Reform community. Instead, he was attempting to address a broad swath of American Jewry who, regardless of denominational label, made their Jewish decisions in large measure on the basis of personal freedom. His presentation of the positions of Heschel and Soloveitchik, representative as they were of the traditionalist camps in American Judaism, reflected Borowitz's own desire to speak to the reality that marked the spiritual and communal lives of vast numbers of American Jews across denominational lines.

Existentialist Outlook

Borowitz expressed these thoughts with striking and characteristic clarity in 1974 when he received the National Book Award in the field of Jewish thought for *The Masks Jews Wear*. Borowitz, in accepting the award, stated in a speech printed in that year's *Jewish Book Annual*, "I should like to see in this honor a sign that, after 25 years of labor, the existentialist interpretation of Judaism has become accepted among American Jews." He noted that in his own "groping for a post-rationalist, post-naturalistic way of thinking about Judaism," he had come to be attracted to "the broad-scale literary, philosophic and theological currents loosely united under the term 'existentialist.'" These currents, he continued, had been treated with contempt—or what was even worse, totally ignored—by his own teachers during his six years of study for the rabbinate. These men were still attuned to the philosophies of Kant and Hegel, and the twentieth-century Jewish thinkers they applauded—Cohen and Baeck—were men informed by the thought of these "Teutonic geniuses" and "the schools derived from them." Indeed, Borowitz observed that many of these men who had been his own teachers "still seem to think that Judaism must essentially have to do with ideas or concepts, much as Hermann Cohen interpreted it half a century or so ago. They are puzzled if not disdainful when one tries to speak of Jewishness, as I have done in *The Masks Jews Wear* in terms of the ground of the self."

Emphasis upon "self" and the key role that modern culture played in informing this dimension of Borowitz's theological project should not obscure the very real limits he placed around the existentialist approach he had come to adopt as the most promising method for the creation of a modern Jewish theology. In that same 1974 speech, he wrote, "When being Jewish is primarily a matter of where one grounds one's self, then Jewishness is involved in all one's life and surely requires explicit, particular expression in much of it." Borowitz's appreciation of pluralism applauded "the many options available in traditional and modern ways of expressing one's Jewishness" and asserted that an existentialist Jewish faith must "motivate us to Jewish living." Highly critical of a "mindless existentialism" that would abandon traditional Jewish "learning and analysis to whatever feels good Jewishly," Borowitz demanded that Jews take responsibility for the study and practice of tradition.

In concluding his remarks that night in 1974, Borowitz asserted, "The thinker's . . . job is to give this [modern Jewish] way of living the comprehensibility of sensitive, thoughtful language—at least, so I now understand my task. To complete such a statement of modern Jewishness—I do not know whether I am capable of carrying out so ambitious a project. But I am emboldened by the honor here bestowed upon me and encouraged by the many blessings God has given me day by day, and especially, this one. So I propose to see what I can manage to do about this in the years ahead."

The task of modern Jewish thought, as Borowitz so aptly phrased it twenty years ago, is not simply one of framing and facing "intellectual options." Instead, "We need to guide Jews in the difficult art of maintaining an intense loyalty to Jewish tradition, that is, of living by a deeply Jewish faith, while freely assessing the virtues of the various modern ways of interpreting it—and within this continuous dialectic process to find the personal and conceptual integrity of what it means to be a modern Jew." For Borowitz, the challenges of measuring this dialectic and explicating its applications in the lives of Jews were to become the central foci of his activities and writings over the next two decades.

Later Works

Borowitz's insistence that Jewish thought be linked to Jewish action can be seen in the flurry of activities in which he engaged and in the spate of books he produced shortly after the publication of *The Masks Jews Wear*. In that book, Borowitz had argued that American Jewish life was fundamentally more religious and spiritual than most American Jews would openly acknowledge. Beneath the veneer of an ostensibly secular life, the Jewish community remained attuned to the hum of divine imperatives. His sociological-religious frame of analysis in that book blossomed five years later in 1978 into *Reform Judaism Today*, his three-volume commentary on the 1976 Reform Movement's San Francisco Centenary Perspective.

Borowitz had served as chair of the Central Conference of American Rabbis' Committee that wrote this successor statement to the 1885 Pittsburgh Platform and the 1937 Columbus Platform, and it was fitting that he offer the exegesis upon it. The most striking feature of his commentary, from one perspective, is the degree to which Borowitz located the Reform movement at the center of American Jewish life. Borowitz not only demonstrated how the contemporary Reform movement's position on the doctrines of God, Torah, and Israel had abandoned the sectarian postures of a classical American Reform Judaism. He also argued that Reform Judaism and its liberal attitudes toward an observance of the tradition had come to inform almost all precincts of American Jewish life, inasmuch as most American Jews were now self-consciously self-determining. The problem of Jewish thought that still had to be addressed more fully was one of linking this commitment to self-assertion to a ground for Jewish action.

In order to provide some answers for these problems, Borowitz turned, as he had in the 1960s, with characteristic openness to the writings of Jewish and Christian theologians for guidance. In 1980 he wrote *Contemporary Christologies: A Jewish Response*. This book was the outgrowth of an address he was invited to deliver at the predominantly Christian American Theological Association, and in it he asserted that Jews could recognize and learn from these modern Christian writings directed to the service of God, even though a Jew might detect in them tonal elements distinct from the commanding-forgiving rhythms of a Jewish view of the Divine. In addition, 1983 witnessed Borowitz's publication of *Choices in Modern Jewish Thought*, a revision and reformulation of his earlier *A New Jewish Theology in the Making*. Finally, in 1984 and 1985 Borowitz published *Liberal Judaism* and *Explaining Reform Judaism*, a children's textbook written with Naomi Patz. Published by the Union of American Hebrew Congregations, both reflected Borowitz's continuing quest not only to articulate an authentic liberal Jewish faith for American Jews but also, in so doing, to provide these Jews with guidance in the practical realms of life's demands and complexities.

Borowitz's theological projects, and his concern for their practical applications, reached their crescendo in two works published in 1990 and 1991. The first year saw his publication of forty-one papers collected under the title *Exploring Jewish Ethics: Papers on Covenant Responsibility*, while the latter was the occasion for his most comprehensive, mature, and systematic theological statement, *Renewing the Covenant: A Theology for the Postmodern Jew*. In his preface to *Renewing the Covenant*, Borowitz observed, "For all its reach, this book deals with but one aspect of my theology. To my surprise and consternation, the theological task I early set for myself refused to remain unified, but ramified into three independent, if correlated, foci of interest: (1) the response to our culture, (2) the dialogue with Jewish tradition, and (3) the testing of these ideas in Jewish action."

Exploring Jewish Ethics, in Borowitz's own view, is the fulfillment of the third item on his agenda, while *Renewing the Covenant* represents his attempt to mediate the relationship between Judaism and contemporary culture. The two books, as Borowitz himself has maintained, must be seen as companion volumes. These works reflect his intensity, and the reader cannot fail to admire the personal witness he offers in both of them. Here, as in all his books, one appreciates Borowitz's clarity and candor, the directness with which he allows the reader to share not only in his struggles and his doubts, but also in his certainties and his faith. Borowitz's ability to allow the intelligent lay reader to follow his arguments and the humility his efforts reflect cannot help but command sympathy and respect from even the most ardent critic. These are works that express liberal religious thought and ethics, with all their "hesitancy," at their authentic best. *Exploring Jewish Ethics* and *Renewing the Covenant* permit one to see how Borowitz strives to allow God's presence to enter and direct his life, no matter how painstaking and uncertain the process.

Failure of Secularism

In *Renewing the Covenant* Borowitz argues that the major motivation for the invigoration of Jewish religious life in our time is the spiritual crisis that has beset all of Western religion as a result of a growing recognition that a secular ground for values is no longer possible. Borowitz argues that the confidence our forebears exhibited in the power of the Enlightenment and the certitude they displayed about the adequacy of reason as a ground for human values can no longer be sustained. The utter evil of the Holocaust has forced Jews and others to a radical reassessment of the humanistic heritage of the Enlightenment and compelled many of them to face the limits of tolerance and relativism. The horror of the Holocaust and the failure of some later commentators upon it to draw a categorical distinction between Nazis and their victims, between genocidal death camp operators and their Jewish prey, has compelled many contemporary Jews to assert that modernity is not messianic. The moral nihilism of the modern world and the inability, in light of the Holocaust, to sustain a faith in humanity as an adequate source of values have led, Borowitz avers, to the creation of a postmodern religious situation for many Jews. It is one where an unbridled modernist confidence in reason must be tempered.

The contemporary world, as Borowitz sees it, has been plunged into a spiritual crisis that stems from the recognition that it is now impossible to maintain that there is a commanding secular ground for values. Yet ethical foundations for distinguishing between good and evil—between the Nazi ss officer and his Jewish victim—must be constructed and moral absolutes must be maintained. The need to oppose evil resolutely means that ethical warrants for guiding human values and actions must be produced. Religion addresses this need and is entitled to an independent voice in the contemporary setting precisely because of the confidence in the tradition from which it speaks. In a bewildering world of choices and indecision, religion offers the surest compass for navigating the shoals of competing moral claims. In offering this analysis of the postmodern religious situation, Borowitz is arguing that the desire on the part of Jews to affirm a normative ethics has led them back to God. However, unlike earlier Kantian approaches that marked the writings of men such as Hermann Cohen, Borowitz points out that the move from ethics to God no longer engenders an idealistic construction of God. Instead, this movement from the moral to the Divine in postmodern Jewish faith has been marked by a belief in a personal deity Who is at once transcendent and immanent. In sum, *Renewing the Covenant* contends that contemporary history has effectively undermined the confidence in human judgment that previously undergirded modern thought. This, in turn, has led to a renewed appreciation of the truth and power of religion in a postmodern situation.

Role of Autonomy

Nevertheless, Borowitz is not prepared to retreat totally from the insights and affirmations of an Enlightenment world. The one survivor of modernist religiosity, in his view, is the concept of "the self." Autonomy is so firmly rooted in the contemporary Jewish condition, so unalienable a right, that its surrender would be unthinkable. Borowitz asserts that the ongoing affirmation of this concept remains crucial for present-day liberal Jews. They reject the religious fundamentalism that appears to dominate so many sectors of the Jewish world today, even as they turn with a new respect to examine the wisdom and power of Jewish religious tradition. For liberal Judaism, Jewish spirituality must incorporate the rights of conscience and the practice of democracy and pluralism. An abandonment of this legacy bequeathed by modernity and the Enlightenment to the contemporary postmodern Jew can be neither countenanced nor imagined. It is an irreversible element in the nature and character of present-day liberal Judaism.

Borowitz's commitment to the concept of "self" must therefore be acknowledged if one is to grasp the nature of his Jewish theological position. Even so, such recognition should not obscure the distinct way in which he employs the concept. In contrast to his modernist predecessors who "considered it axiomatic that contemporary Jewish thought must be constructed on the basis of universal selfhood," Borowitz claims that in the postmodern setting it is essential to "rethink" the meaning of this concept in Jewish terms. Simply put, "Jewish selfhood arises within the people of Israel and its Covenant with God." It is a "self that is autonomous yet so fundamentally shaped by the Covenant that whatever issues from its depths will have authentic Jewish character. The secular concept of self must be transformed in terms of its Covenantal context." For Borowitz, only a selfhood radically grounded in God and community can mandate postmodern Jewish duty. *Renewing the Covenant* is the statement of a mature theologian. In it one can identify the dialectical themes of Covenant and self, God and community, that Borowitz has emphasized throughout his theological writings. Here those themes find their ultimate definition. How they find normative expression remains the task of *Exploring Jewish Ethics*.

Borowitz affirms over and over again throughout the pages of *Exploring Jewish Ethics* that Judaism provides a powerful communitarian ethos and sense of morality that can inform the life of the postmodern Jew. The integrity and wisdom of the Jewish ethical tradition can also contribute much to a modern society that all too frequently flounders in its quest for values and direction. In business, government, and intergroup relations the distinctive Jewish emphasis upon everyday life and the command to infuse that life with the sanctity of God's holiness promote a moral attitude that society sorely needs. This does not mean that ethical conflicts can be avoided. Indeed, Borowitz frequently notes that it is precisely the distance which often exists between the ethical prescriptions of Judaism and the practices of a surrounding society—whether in Israel or the Diaspora—that permits Judaism to fulfill its highest role by pricking the conscience of a contemporary world.

Ethical Guidelines

Exploring Jewish Ethics also does not shrink from displaying the ongoing dialectical tensions that exist among the poles of autonomy, community, and Jewish tradition to which Borowitz feels bound. There is a palpable sense of struggle among the various competing pulls that each of them, at times, exerts. Most striking is the valence Borowitz assigns in so many places to the moral sensibilities and consensus of the contemporary Jewish community. In response to his own theology, Borowitz permits the Covenantal community within which he stands as a Jew to inform his moral judgments. His variegated responses on matters of sexual morality reflect this. For example, the community's overwhelming affirmation of the principle of gender equality makes any defense of traditional attitudes and laws that would discriminate in any way against women intolerable. Conversely, Borowitz's judgment concerning the Covenantal community's commitment to the ideal of the procreative, heterosexual family causes him to argue that avowed homosexuals should not be ordained as rabbis. These contrasting positions bespeak the dialectical nature of his own approach to Jewish ethics. It is one in which "autonomy is not subservient to [Jewish law] . . . but at the same time, the law, in all its details, does not hesitate to make its claims on the autonomous Jewish self." The seeming paradoxes in the normative positions Borowitz enunciates in such matters reflects his own understanding of the theological task as unending. This is precisely why it is best validated by a community seeking to live it through time. What is clear at one moment may be murky at another. However, with all the ambiguities that mark Judaism and the Jewish moral enterprise as Borowitz portrays them, what is undeniable is that the Jewish self cannot vitiate the ultimacy and urgency of human responsibility and the moral passion that emanates from a Jewish religious posture.

In his *Contemporary Christologies*, Borowitz concluded with a "personal reflection" and a "blessing" of thanks for the Divine wisdom the Christian theologians he had studied imparted to him. I would now do no less. As a student at the College–Institute, I remember how Eugene Borowitz stood out as a rabbi. His academic role as professor was always properly subordinated to his vocation as a *moreh derekh* (spiritual guide). One could never escape the passion, commitment, and love he displayed for God and the Jewish people, for persons and the imperatives of the Covenantal tradition. As Rabbi Borowitz celebrates his seventieth birthday, and as I and others would express gratitude for all he has taught and will continue to teach, I invoke the words our Tradition prescribes upon seeing a person distinguished in the study of Torah. "Praised are You, Lord our God, Ruler of the universe, Who has given a share of Divine wisdom to those who revere You." May the passion and the intellect with which Rabbi Borowitz has challenged and directed the Jewish community continue unabated for years to come. May his "dialogue with tradition," the attempt to derive from Jewish law "the ground of [his] theology," achieve completion and publication along with his numerous other projects. May Eugene Borowitz, and the work of his mind and heart, grace our community and our world in the years ahead. *'Ad me'ah v'esrim*—until one hundred and twenty!

9

Laws and Judgments as a "Bridge to a Better World"

Parashat Mishpatim (Exodus 21:1–24:18)

In Judaism, as in every religion, teachings collide with one another. Yet it would seem that the Jewish attitude toward homosexuality, on the basis of two passages found in Leviticus as well as later Jewish exegesis on these passages, is unequivocally negative. The first passage, Leviticus 18:22, states, "Do not lie with a male as one lies with a woman—it is an abomination," and the second, contained in Leviticus 20:13, asserts: "If a man lies with a male as one lies with a woman, the two of them have done an abhorrent thing. They shall be put to death."

The simple meaning of these texts appears quite clear. Rabbi Tzvi Weinreb, executive vice president of the Orthodox Union, built on these Levitical statements in an op-ed, "Orthodox Response to Same-Sex Marriage," in the *New York Jewish Week* (March 26, 2004), and has summarized the position of traditional Judaism on homosexual behavior as "clear and unambiguous, terse and absolute. Homosexual behavior between males or between females is absolutely forbidden by Jewish law, beginning with the biblical imperative, alluded to numerous times in the Talmud and codified in the Shulchan Aruch." Indeed, such behavior, "an act characterized as an 'abomination,' is prima facie disgusting," maintains Rabbi Norman Lamm, former president of Yeshiva University, in his article "Judaism and the Modern Attitude to Homosexuality" in the 1974 *Encyclopaedia Judaica Yearbook*.

As the famed legal philosopher Ronald Dworkin explains in his *Philosophy of Law*, in a chapter entitled "Is Law a System of Rules?" "Rules are applicable in an 'all or nothing' fashion. If the facts a rule stipulates are given, then the rule is valid, in which case the answer it supplies must be accepted." The biblical "rules" expressed in these Levitical passages that prohibit male-male sexual relations seem clear-cut and negative and the consequences attached to the rules so seemingly absolutely condemnatory of homosexual relations that the positions advanced by Rabbi Weinraub and Rabbi Lamm appear incontrovertible.

Nevertheless, "the plain meaning" of such biblical statutes and the attitudes that flow from them have not gone unchallenged on either religious or moral grounds. One way in which such challenges have taken place is through engagement in reinterpretation of these passages. For example, scholars such as Rabbi Steve Greenberg and Rabbi Bradley Artson have provided alternative readings of these texts. Rabbi Greenberg, an Orthodox rabbi, in his *Wrestling with God and Men: Homosexuality in the Jewish Tradition* contends that Leviticus 18:22, "Do not lie with a male as one lies with a woman—it is an abomination," should be understood as "And [either a female or] a male you shall not sexually penetrate to humiliate—it is abhorrent." As Rabbi Greenberg reads Leviticus, the verses in question are not about anatomy. Rather, they prohibit exploitative sexual relations and demand that sexual partners treat one another with respect.

In another effort to reinterpret these texts, Rabbi Artson, director of the Conservative movement's Ziegler School of Rabbinic Studies, in a responsum he authored, contextualizes the Levitical prohibitions. He argues that they must be viewed against an ancient Near Eastern background in which same-sex male relations were part of idolatrous practices of pagan religious cults. The proscriptions in Leviticus are primarily part of a fundamental biblical polemic against idolatry, not homosexuality per se. Both these readings—and others not cited—possess the virtue of approaching the Levitical texts in such a way that they can no longer be viewed as blanket condemnations of all homosexual relations. These efforts at reinterpretation can be applauded because they seek new meanings in these ancient texts, meanings that empty these passages of a contemporary justification for discrimination and violence directed against homosexuals

Yet as laudatory as these attempts are, such examples of reinterpretation may not be sufficiently satisfactory. Although Rabbi Greenberg and Rabbi Artson object to the consequences that flow from Leviticus 18:22 and Leviticus 20:13 and therefore offer alternative readings so that new outcomes can flow from the texts, the harsh precision and the overt homophobia of the Levitical text seems so palpable that it is difficult to feel sanguine about reinterpretation as a method to obviate the traditional understandings and implications of these texts.

Catholic scholar Elizabeth Schussler-Fiorenza has suggested a more methodologically radical theological solution in her powerful book *In Memory of Her*. She argues that reinterpretation does not always constitute an adequate means for dealing with ethically troublesome texts. Instead, she boldly states that an axiom that guides her own work is that the divinity and authority of any passage in Scripture that diminishes the humanity of another ought to be questioned altogether. In short, her book suggests that the process of reinterpretation is sometimes unduly limiting and that another scheme must be discovered for rectifying morally problematic passages in Holy Scripture, a scheme that requires looking elsewhere in Scripture at alternative texts that can provide for a principled correction of morally repugnant passages.

Two passages in *Parashat Mishpatim* embody overarching principles of judgment that provide correctives to the Levitical texts cited earlier, and they offer a way of providing for the emergence of a more just and different Jewish teaching regarding homosexuality. Exodus 22:20 states, "You shall not wrong a stranger or oppress him, for you were strangers in the land of Egypt," and in Exodus 23:9, the Torah proclaims, "You shall not oppress a stranger, for you know the feelings of a stranger, having yourselves been strangers in the land of Egypt."

The attitudes contained in these passages indicate that the experience of oppression demands sensitivity and response on the part of Jews to the needs of others. They reveal a wide-ranging philosophy that lies at the heart of Judaism and embody a crucial teaching that is instructive and determinative for the formulation of Jewish actions and deeds. They indicate that the Torah itself provides overarching attitudes and principles that can and should surmount these specifically vile rules that diminish the humanity of LGBT people. As the medieval Spanish rabbi Ibn Ezra states *"I'kar kol ha-mitzvot l'yasher ha-lev*—the essential purpose of all the commandments is to make the heart upright" (Ibn Ezra, Commentary on Deuteronomy 5:18). In short, the overarching principles contained in these passages can trump the rules contained in Leviticus and provide for repair and improvement of the text and the world.

Modern writings in the philosophy of law clarify this point, dictating how legal systems achieve this constructive task by distinguishing between the weight attached to conflicting rules on the one hand and principles on the other that are both found within the same legal system—as the aforementioned passages in Leviticus and Deuteronomy are. As Dworkin himself has argued, "principles," in contrast to "rules," are general notions—often moral ones—embedded in a legal system that possess a *gravitas* that a rule alone simply does not. Although the weight assigned a principle cannot always be determined exactly, principles are generally decisive in rendering judgment.

This understanding that Dworkin provides regarding the role that "principles" in contrast to "rules" occupy in the legal system is expanded on and clarified in the work of the late professor Robert Cover of Yale. In his insightful article "Nomos and Narrative," Cover argued that law itself functions in two modes, one "imperialistic" and the other "jurisgenerative." The imperialistic approach is marked by an emphasis on authority and the application and enforcement of rules. This is undoubtedly the manner in which virtually all devotees of Jewish law—even liberal ones—have understood halakhah. Indeed, this is what has led exegetes such as Rabbi Greenberg and Rabbi Artson to wrestle with the "rules" in Leviticus as they have.

However, the latter mode of jurisgenesis that Cover has adumbrated seems more promising for our enterprise. In this mode, law is viewed as embodying a *paidea*—the highest educational ideal of the community—that is embedded in a master narrative of the community, and the ongoing rendering of judgments attempts to give this *paidea* ever more exact and just application over time. So perceived, law constitutes a "bridge to a better world."

In this way, Cover provides for a theoretical approach to the issues of Jewish law—including judgments regarding homosexuality—that reinterpretation does not. For law "is not merely a system of rules" nor is Torah—the Teaching, as Franz Rosenzweig once labeled it, that guides the life of the Jewish people. Instead, Torah and the normative guidance the Teaching contained in Torah provides must be situated in a larger context of narrative discourse and meaning. This approach "privileges" principles over rules, and in this instance, it means that Torah must be viewed in an expansive manner. From this perspective, there is no doubt that the broad ethical principles contained in Exodus should by necessity take legitimate religious legal precedence over the narrow proscriptions provided in Leviticus.

For Jews, the primary orienting narrative of "discourse and meaning" that the Bible provides tells of how an enslaved Jewish people went beyond the "narrow straits" in which the Egyptians had confined them as they celebrated a journey "from degradation to freedom." The Exodus passages cited from *Parashat Mishpatim* indicate that rejoicing in that freedom for themselves alone was not enough. Instead, the principles that animate that narrative—as *Parashat Mishpatim* suggests—provide a different religious imperative. Jews, precisely because their narrative reminds them over and over again that they "were strangers in the land of Egypt" and therefore know "the feelings of a stranger," must have empathy for others and alleviate the venomous impacts that accompany acts and attitudes of discrimination and oppression against others. A messianic goal—the creation of a more just world—lies at the heart of the Jewish story, and the responsibility imposed on each generation of Jews is to allow that goal to be more fully approximated even if that means that we must change traditional beliefs and understandings of Jewish law.

Parashat Mishpatim teaches that a "more inclusive and tolerant Judaism" must be forged, a Judaism in which the *paidea* of justice and redemption for the oppressed will be achieved. The principles expressed in Exodus 22:20 and 23:10 demand that Jews and others not discriminate against LGBT persons or tolerate readings of the Torah that would legitimate such discrimination. Instead, these principles demand a reading of Jewish tradition that requires that the LGBT community receive the same privileges and entitlements that heterosexuals enjoy. This position is surely the most religiously compelling one for Jews to adopt in regard to the LGBT community in our day, as Jews seek to realize the moral obligations that the narrative and principles in our Torah impose on our community.

10

Heschel and the Roots of *Kavanah*

Responsibility and *Kavanah* in Postwar America

The second half of the life of Abraham Joshua Heschel was spent in the United States. During the thirty-two years that elapsed from his arrival as part of the Refugee Scholars Project of Hebrew Union College until his premature death at sixty-five in 1972, Heschel rose to great prominence among North American Jewry. His legacy has been enduring and his impact profound.[1]

Heschel's view of Jewish life in the America of the 1950s and 1960s combined enthusiasm and dismay. His enthusiasm was sparked by the renaissance of interest in Judaism he identified in the younger generation. In 1962, in fact, he proclaimed, "We are living through one of the great hours of history. The false gods are crumbling, and the hearts are hungry for the voice of God."[2] In 1965 he expressed amazement that "together with a decline of affection for being a Jew on the part of our older people we witness a rise of appreciation on the part of many of our younger people ... [who are] disturbed at parents who are spiritually insolvent. They seek direction, affirmation; they reject complacency and empty generosity."[3] Comments to this effect can be found in Heschel's writings from the mid-1950s on.[4]

Although he was buoyed by evidence of a search for spiritual meaning among the younger generation, Heschel was greatly dismayed both by the state of the established Jewish community as well as by the state of contemporary religion and of American society in general. Already in 1948 he had bemoaned what he called "the banalization of Judaism ... the tumult of arrogant not-knowing and not wanting to know."[5] In unpublished remarks made in 1955, Heschel is recorded as having excoriated much of what he saw in Jewish life in postwar America and as having added that had he grown up in the modern American synagogue, he probably would not have remained.[6] One such child of the 1950s, Arnold Eisen, wrote of the exhilaration, inspiration, and surprise he experienced upon reading these first words of *God in Search of Man*:

> It is customary to blame secular science and anti-religious philosophy for the eclipse of religion in modern society. It would be more honest to blame religion for its own defeats. Religion declined not because it was refuted, but because it became irrelevant, dull, oppressive, insipid.[7]

Heschel's enthusiasm and his dismay shared a common source: his sense that the enormous potential offered by North America was being squandered. In his view, laxity was being promoted rather than liberty, entertainment rather than celebration,[8] vulgarity instead of seriousness of purpose, and platitudes in place of genuine gratitude. Heschel was not afraid to frame his critique in prophetic terms:

> To paraphrase the words of the prophet Isaiah: What to me is the multitude of your organizations? says the Lord. I have had enough of your vicarious loyalty. Bring no more vain offerings: generosity without wisdom is an evasion, an alibi for conscience.[9]

In this article we will emphasize two of the concepts that played a central role in the mature Heschel's spiritual and social agenda: responsibility and *kavanah*. Although these are by no means the only themes to be found in Heschel's work, they are of particular interest. An analysis of the early material presented here will raise the question of the origins of these particular Heschelian concerns.

The very last days of Abraham Joshua Heschel say much about how the concept of personal responsibility had become a central tenet of his life. The last known photograph of Heschel shows him and Daniel Berrigan on their way to Philip Berrigan's release from the Danbury Correctional Institute on 20 December 1972. Heschel had decided that his teaching, research, and even his health were less urgently significant than his involvement in the great social struggles of the day—in this case, his commitment to Clergy Concerned About Vietnam.[10]

Throughout his final years Heschel was to be found calling for an end to apathy and intransigence. He was at the forefront of the civil rights move-

ment and, in addition to many other involvements, was also a voice of conscience for Soviet Jewry and a vociferous opponent of the war in Vietnam.

The classic Heschelian statement on responsibility is to be found in the
English version of his work on the prophets:

> Above all, the prophets remind us of the moral state of a people: Few
> are guilty, but all are responsible. If we admit that the individual is in
> some measure conditioned or affected by the spirit of society, an indi-
> vidual's crime discloses society's corruption.[11]

This statement was later to reappear with relation to race[12] and Vietnam.[13] Time and again, Heschel prevailed upon his fellow Jews and his
fellow Americans to hear the call to action and not to shirk responsibility.
In a rare autobiographical passage, he recalled his fear as a seven-year-old
upon studying the tale of the Binding of Isaac that the angel might inter-
vene too late. With a mixture of sadness and outrage, Heschel added: "An
angel cannot be late, but man, made of flesh and blood, may be."[14] For
Heschel, responsibility is not some abstract commitment. It is an urgent
and relentless call, and if it remains unheeded, the implications are omi-
nous indeed.

In order to find a useful translation of the second of the concepts under
discussion, one may consult the dictionary of philosophical terms compiled
by Heschel himself in 1941, not long after his arrival at the Hebrew Union
College in Cincinnati. In that work *kavanah* is translated as "intention;
methodicalness; attention; aim, purpose, meaning, significance; turning
toward a certain place."[15] Heschel used that term often and for a variety
of purposes. It is not surprising to find considerable attention paid to the
concept in Heschel's leading work on prayer, *Man's Quest for God*. In fact,
two mini-chapters in different sections of that work bear the same title:
"The Nature of *Kavanah*."[16] The entire book is suffused with discussions
of this term, which Heschel renders in English as "inner devotion."[17]

At one juncture in *Quest* Heschel makes a thinly veiled pejorative reference to Mordecai Kaplan and Reconstructionism, indicating that "there
are some people who believe that the only way to revitalize the synagogue
is to minimize the importance of prayer and to convert the synagogue
into a social center." His refutation of this position demonstrates the significance Heschel attached to *kavanah*: "A synagogue in which men no

longer aspire to prayer is not a compromise, but a defeat; a perversion, not a concession. To pray with *kavanah* (inner devotion) may be difficult; to pray without it is ludicrous."[18] Heschel was keen to suggest that *kavanah* was in essence the same whether it was being applied to prayer or in a wider sense: "Our great problem . . . is how not to let the principle of regularity impair the power of spontaneity (*kavanah*). It is a problem that concerns not only prayer but the whole sphere of Jewish observance."[19] Later in the work we find *kavanah* described as "more than a touch of emotion," but rather as "insight, appreciation." It is the "unique task" of the rabbi "to be a source of inspiration, to endow others with a sense of *kavanah*."[20] The term comes to refer to all that is opposed to a dry instrumentalist reading of the function and purpose of Judaism. A stultified and stagnant Judaism must give way to a Judaism of *kavanah*, which is taken to include a number of desiderata: inner devotion, insight, appreciation, spontaneity, and more.

Kavanah was pressed into service in the cause of Heschelian polemics. The motivation for his fervent opposition to symbolic thinking remains a matter of debate.[21] In any case, it is clear that this constituted one of Heschel's most persistent peeves. He was keen to emphasize the "difference between symbolic understanding and what tradition means by *kavanah*":

> *Kavanah* is awareness of the will of God rather than awareness of the reason of a mitzvah. Awareness of symbolic meaning is awareness of a specific idea; *kavanah* is awareness of an ineffable situation. . . . It is *kavanah* rather than symbolic understanding that evokes in us ultimate joy at the moment of doing a mitzvah.[22]

Heschel is sensitive to the possibility that a notion of inwardness might be used to brand traditional Judaism as a religion of mechanical performance and conformity as opposed to one of intentional and meaningful deed, or alternatively that a misreading of *kavanah* could be used to encourage antinomian trends. In the course of one year—1953—we find Heschel exhorting the Conservative rabbinate to serve as exemplars of *kavanah*, while warning the Reform rabbinate of its dangers. In this latter address, he launched a blistering attack against the notion that Judaism can be understood exclusively in terms of intention, with action relegated to obsolescence or to the category of custom and ceremony. He asks whether the statement that God wants the heart can be taken to mean that He asks for the heart only. Unlike certain Oriental traditions, and also unlike Paul and Kant, Judaism rejects the notion that the right intention by itself can suffice. Indeed, "the crisis of ethics has its root in formalism, in the view that the essence of the good is in the good intention. Seeing how difficult it is to attain it, modern man despaired. In the name of good intentions, evil was fostered."[23]

This assault on a notion of unrealized intention was not sufficient. Heschel also rejected the trend to replace disembodied ethical probity with "customs and ceremonies." By relating to Jewish observance as a subject of anthropological interest, a heavy price was to be paid: "A religious act is something in which the soul must be able to participate; out of which inner devotion, *kavanah*, must evolve. But what *kavanah* could I entertain if entering the sukkah is a mere ceremony?"[24] In Heschel's very last work we find mention of the relation between performance of the deed and the intention behind the deed. While legalists have pondered what a person should do, and philosophers and kabbalists alike have debated what a person should think, "Hasidim have chiefly been absorbed by the problem of how a man should think while acting."[25] In the parallel Yiddish volume, the allusion to *kavanah* is quite explicit, and the question of whether mitzvot require *kavanah* is explicitly mentioned.[26] Until the last period of his life, this question remained in his thoughts.

If one book from Heschel's mature oeuvre were to be chosen as his major theological work, it would be that same work which had evoked such a strong response in the young Arnold Eisen: *God in Search of Man*.[27] We find *kavanah* playing a prominent role in that work: the tension between *kavanah* and deed is listed as one of the key exemplars of "a polarity which lies at the very heart of Judaism."[28]

Two chapters of *God in Search of Man* are devoted to *kavanah*, and each of them presents a central problem associated with the concept. Chapter 38, "The Problem of Integrity," grapples with a major religious challenge, highlighted most particularly in the Hasidic tradition: "If *kavanah* is as intrinsic to the service of God as impartiality of judgment is to scientific investigation; if, in other words, it is not only essential what one does but also what one is motivated by, the possibility of true service, of genuine piety may be questioned."[29] Heschel marshals a range of sources, predominantly from Hasidic literature but also from Rabbinic and medieval texts, in order to grapple with the eternal quest for religious integrity.

Chapter 31 is entitled "*Kavanah*." After briefly reviewing the term's etymology and commonly accepted meanings, Heschel goes on to emphasize *kavanah*'s dimensions of attentiveness, appreciation, and integration, before he ends the chapter with a section entitled "Beyond *Kavanah*." Here he is keen to assert that the mitzvah is not coterminous with its intention: "A mitzvah is neither a substitute for thought nor an expression of *kavanah*. A mitzvah is an act in which we go beyond the scope of our thought and intention."[30] It appears that the same concerns he had expressed in his 1953 speeches to Reform and Conservative rabbis were still exercising Heschel. On the one hand, he is aware that an emphasis on intention might be interpreted as an excuse for not performing *mitzvot*. On the other, he is critical of an approach to religious life that douses the fire of intensity and purpose.

Poised between the Scylla and Charybdis of a spiritualized abstract Judaism on one side and religious behaviorism on the other, Heschel ends the chapter by championing a third way: "When superimposed as a yoke, as a dogma, as a fear, religion tends to violate rather than to nurture the spirit of man. Religion must be an altar upon which the fire of the soul may be kindled in holiness."[31] Appended to this closing sentence we find the longest footnote in the entire book, running from page 317 through page 319. Just as remarkably, the genre discussed in the footnote is neither ethical literature nor Hasidic teachings. Instead, the footnote relates to *halakhic* discourse, citing "an ancient controversy among scholars of Jewish law" as to whether the presence of "*kavanah*—of the right intention in carrying out one's duty—is absolutely required for the performance of all religious acts." The classic example of this question which Heschel chooses to mention is that of the person who inadvertently hears the Shofar blown on Rosh Hashanah—does physical performance of the act without intention constitute its fulfillment?

Reviewing examples taken from the Temple cult and from the Laws of Divorce, Heschel presents a relatively detailed survey of the different views relating to the necessity of intention for the validity of the performance of commandments. He provides the following summary: "the presence of proper intention is required for the act; the presence of improper intention (in some cases) invalidates the act; lack or absence of intention, proper or improper, while not desirable, does not invalidate the act." The last section of the footnote leans heavily on Joseph Engel's *Athvan Deoraitha*. Engel, who has been described as "one of the most brilliant and underestimated figures of the pre–World War II generation,"[32] was without a doubt beyond the reach of the great majority of Heschel's readership. Neither he nor the close *halakhic* argumentation in which he specialized would have been familiar or accessible to most modern Jews (let alone non-Jews) in America in the 1950s. Nevertheless, he closes the mammoth footnote with a conclusion taken directly from that work:

> . . . the deed without the *kavanah* is considered as if it had been done with *kavanah*, for where no intention is consciously entertained, it may be assumed the deed was done for its proper purpose. Consequently, in the case of improper intention, wherein that assumption cannot be maintained, the deed is not valid because of the absence of *kavanah*.[33]

The message at the heart of this footnote is of keen relevance to American Jewish life in Heschel's day (and in ours). He is suggesting that performance without explicit intention is to be preferred over performance when accompanied by a perverse or contrary motivation. Whether this last possibility represents a sideswipe at such approaches as Reconstructionism, which offered a model of religious performance devoid of a basis in Faith, remains an open question.[34]

Yet, however the content of the note is understood, its form and length are remarkable. This is a long *halakhic* excursus at the heart of a work which, while replete with sources, contains very few which exemplify the argumentation of Jewish law.

From Heschel's perspective, both *kavanah* and responsibility served as rallying calls for an alternative to the mediocrity and apathy of much of American Jewry in the postwar period. What can be learned about the provenance of these terms in Heschel's lexicon? What are the earliest traces of this concern? Perhaps they belong to the American phase in his career, or perhaps the seeds were planted during his decade in Weimar Germany during the Nazi rise to power. However, it is our assertion that the roots of Heschel's concern with these notions go back still further—back to Warsaw, the city of his birth. The remainder of this article will demonstrate this claim by presenting and analyzing two remarkable Hebrew notes his older contemporary Shalom Joseph Halevi Feigenbaum wrote in response to two questions Heschel posed on the issues of *kavanah* and responsibility when he was yet a teenager in Poland.

Heschel the Teenage Halakhist, Kavanah, *and Responsibility*

At the age of fifteen, Abraham Joshua Heschel (1907–1972) was first published. The piece, two short paragraphs in length, was followed in subsequent months by two others, all of them in the *Bet Midrash* section of the journal known as *Shaarei Torah*.[35] Although the existence of these pieces has been noted by Heschel's biographers, little interest has been shown in them.[36] It is our view that a renewed interest in this earliest layer of Heschel's life and work may yield useful insights.

We turn now to a remarkable piece of literary evidence from this early stage of Heschel's intellectual and religious development that bears on our topic in this essay. The article in question is a piece comprising two responsa by Rabbi Shalom Joseph Halevi Feigenbaum, which was published in the same journal, *Shaarei Torah*, in the Tevet-Adar edition for the year 5684 (1924).[37] These two responsa are dedicated to "the learned and acute descendant of illustrious lineage, Mr. Abraham Heschel, may his light shine, from Warsaw," and they relate to questions posed by Heschel, who was then seventeen.

Of particular interest here are Heschel's questions. To be sure, they are not framed in the young Heschel's own style: we have to rely on the accuracy of Feigenbaum's account. Nonetheless, an echo of Heschel's teenage voice—a voice in transition to maturity—may be heard here.

In the first of these two responsa, Feigenbaum states that Heschel asked him the following question. Inasmuch as the question appears to reflect the words of Heschel himself, it is worthwhile to translate this part of the query in full. Heschel is reported as asking:

There is an individual whom [the congregation] honored during Sukkot by having him serve as *shaliach tzibur* (prayer leader) for the recitation of *Hallel* (Psalms of Praise) and the waving of the lulav and etrog [as mandated by Jewish law during that part of the prayer service]. However, he has not yet recited the blessing, "*al n'tilat lulav*—on the taking of the lulav," and he wants to wait and not recite the blessing that accompanies the act [of taking (*l'kikhah*) the lulav] until a beautiful etrog

(*etrog m'hudar*) arrives after the prayers are recited. Is it permissible for the [*shaliach tzibur*] who leads in the recitation of Hallel and the ritual of waving the lulav [*na'anu'im* that takes place during the recitation of this prayer] to state explicitly that he will intentionally not fulfill the halakhic obligation to [recite the blessing associated with *l'kikhah*—the taking of the lulav—even as he fulfills the ritual of waving the lulav] until the "beautiful etrog" arrives?[38]

There are a number of Jewish legal concerns that are involved in this question, and they reflect the world of halakhic discourse in which Heschel was raised. Heschel knew that Leviticus 23:40, which states, "On the first day (of Sukkot), you shall take (*l'kakhtem*) [1] the product of *hadar* (goodly) trees, [2] branches of palm trees, [3] boughs of leafy trees, and [4] willows of the brook, and you shall rejoice before the Lord your God seven days," demanded that each Jew recite a blessing over the Four Species (Kinds) mentioned in this verse. However, as the response Feigenbaum issued to the question posed by his young student indicates, Heschel was keenly aware that rabbinic literature described the fulfillment of this commandment in a multilayered and nuanced way.

Within Jewish legal tradition, one major ritual issue surrounding the fulfillment of the Levitical commandment is whether the *na'anu'im* are an integral part of the commandment; another revolves around the "quality of beauty" (*hadar*) that the Four Species—unquestionably the etrog— must or ought to possess. While a description of all the laws surrounding this ritual are surely beyond this paper, some understanding of these particular strands of Jewish law is most helpful for illuminating the concerns that occupied the teenage Heschel.

As the Bible makes clear, "taking" of the lulav is surely a required part of the commandment. Therefore, in Peshahim 7b, the Talmud holds that the act of taking (*l'kikhah*) the lulav in hand requires that the blessing of "*al n'tilat lulav*—on the taking of the lulav," be recited immediately prior to lifting the lulav. This follows from the explicit words found in Leviticus 23:40, "You shall take." It is a biblical commandment. In contrast, most authorities regard the "waving—*na'anu'im*" as a rabbinic commandment. The *halakhic* issue that remains is whether the waving (*na'anu'im*) is nevertheless regarded as part of the mitzvah of "taking," or whether it is an act separate and apart. No less an authority than the Rosh (Rabbi Asher ben Yehiel, fourteenth century) considers the *na'anu'im* to be a separate requirement and he therefore—in keeping with the logic of Pesachim 7b—states that the blessing must be recited immediately prior to grasping the lulav. He allows for recitation of the blessing prior to the "waving" only if an individual has for some reason failed to recite the blessing prior to the "taking." On the other hand, authoritative legal figures such as Maimonides (Hilchot Lulav 7:9) and the Ran (Rabbi Nissim Gerondi, fourteenth century) regard the act of "waving"—albeit a rabbinic enactment—as an essential part of the "taking," and allow for the blessing to take place subsequent to the "taking." Nevertheless, both camps would assert—whatever the differences that divide them concerning the constituent parts of the commandment—that the recitation of the blessing over the lulav and etrog take place prior to the "*na'anu'im*" of the Hallel. Thus it would seem that there is no way to delay offering the blessing prior to the "waving" of the Four Species during the Hallel service if one serves publicly as *shaliach tzibur*. As Rabbi Feigenbaum observed in the first part of his responsum, inasmuch as the Four Species are in the hands of the *shaliach tzibur* during the recitation of the Hallel, "in my humble opinion, it is impossible" for the *shaliach tzibur* to avoid the commandment of "taking the Four Species—*n'tilat arba minim*,"—and presumably reciting the blessing over them beforehand.

However, this discussion does not settle the matter. Rosh (Sukkah 3:33) states that an individual fulfills a mitzvah in an optimal way, "*min hamuvhar*," in Hebrew, by observing the highest standard of the commandment. From this perspective, there is some possibility for delaying the recitation of the blessing even after lifting the lulav if the highest standard has yet to be observed. In the case of the Four Species, the Talmud does assert that such a "highest standard" exists. Based on Leviticus 23:40, which describes the etrog as "*p'ri eitz hadar*—the product of a goodly (*hadar*) tree," the rabbis, in Sukkah 31a, all concur that the etrog must be *m'hudar* (beautiful) if it is to be ritually qualified for use during Sukkot. Furthermore, in Sukkah 29b, the rabbis state that a lulav that is "dry—*yavesh*" is rendered invalid for ritual use, as they assert that lulav as well as the etrog must possess the trait of "*hadar*—beauty," and, in Sukkah 31a, they extend this standard of *hadar* to all of the Four Species. Otherwise, the species are ritually disqualified for usage in the performance of the commandment. Consequently, as Rabbi Feigenbaum notes at the conclusion of his responsum, it is "possible to say that one can delay [recitation of the blessing] so that one can fulfill the essence of the commandment of 'taking' by employing 'beautiful species—*m'hudarim*.'" There are warrants in Jewish law that would allow for postponement of offering the blessing in light of the conditions that Heschel outlined in his question to his rabbi—especially since every single Jewish legal source agrees that the etrog must be *m'hudar*.

Before commenting on the significance of these halakhic considerations for our essay, it should also be noted that Heschel's question itself may well reflect a literary trope that he adapted from his Hasidic background and that it does not reflect an actual situation in which either Heschel or someone else was involved. In his *Circle of the Baal Shem Tov: Studies in Hasidism*, Heschel, years later, related a story regarding Rabbi David Ostrer, a Hasid who would visit the Baal Shem Tov each year during Sukkot.[39] When the Baal Shem fell ill, Ostrer asked whom he should now turn to as "his master." The Baal Shem told him he should seek out the Maggid of Mezritch and R. Pinchas of Koretz. As Ostrer was accustomed to sending a beautiful etrog each year to the Baal Shem Tov, he now had one sent to both the Maggid and R. Pinchas. However, Ostrer went to the court of the Maggid, for R. Pinchas did not yet "preside" over a court of disciples "in the first years after the death of the Baal Shem." Heschel then continues his narrative with the following tale:

> It once happened that the Gentile messenger bearing the etrog was delayed, so that he still had not arrived in Koretz the day before Sukkot. Heavy rains and flooded roads, which had contributed to a general shortage of etrogs, now left the community of Koretz without a single one!
>
> The congregation was already in the midst of their prayers on the morning of the first day of Sukkot, when R. David's messenger at last arrived. R. Pinchas made the blessing over the etrog [after he had put it together with the palm branch, myrtles, and willows, comprising the four kinds of plants used on Sukkot]. Subsequently, the rest of the congregation also fulfilled the commandment of the "four kinds." R. Pinchas then went to the prayer-reader's stand, recited the *Hallel* psalms, and made the required *na'anu'im* [while reciting the Hallel psalms, the "four kinds" are "shaken" in sequence toward all directions of the compass, as well as upward and downward, reflecting the omnipresence of the Divine].

R. Pinchas remarked that until then he had not wished to take upon himself the onus of being a leader, but during the holidays he had recognized that a pact had been made in Heaven for him to accept the yoke. From that point on, he began to "preside."[40]

To be sure, there are significant differences between the question posed in the responsum and the story told in the Hasidic tale. In the Koretz story, there was not a single etrog available prior to the holiday. In the responsum, etrogim were available. The issue was whether the prayer-leader could both lead the service and intentionally delay his recitation of the blessing over the "Four Species," aware that a more "beautiful" etrog that would allow him as an individual to fulfill the commandments of the holiday more fully would soon arrive. In the Hasidic story, the matter of delaying recitation of the blessing was also not at issue. Finally, in the tale, the appearance of the messenger just at the moment that was required for the recitation of the blessing was taken as a divine sign that Heaven desired that R. Pinchas "accept the yoke" of public leadership over a circle of disciples in his native city of Koretz. While it may be that the literary trope suggested by this story did not prompt Heschel to ask his rabbi the *halakhic* query he posed, the parallel between the story—which surely was known to Heschel from his youth—and the question he asked are clearly striking and do not allow us to rule out the possibility that the question was inspired by the story.

Whatever the case, it is evident that the notion of intentionality and responsibility in matters of prayer and leadership and the problems associated with them had begun to occupy Heschel even during his youth and that he drew upon and expressed these tropes in a *halakhic* genre. However one would adjudicate the *halakhic* arguments and counterarguments that mark the question of whether lack of appropriate intentionality (*kavanah*) can allow a *shaliach tzibur* to delay the recitation of a blessing over the Four Species, the fact that he posed this question as a seventeen-year-old indicates that his concern with the issue of *kavanah* and religious devotion had its roots in his youth. What would ultimately lead Heschel to label this requirement as "attentiveness to God" beyond the demands of "paying attention to the text of the liturgy or to the performance of the mitzvah"[41] had already begun to occupy him during his formative years.

The second question the teenage Heschel posed to Rabbi Feigenbaum indicates that his adult concern for the issue of responsibility also found expression in his adolescence. In this responsum, Feigenbaum reports that Heschel asked him for an explication of the Talmudic principle, "Sin, in order that your friend may gain merit—*hato k'dei she'yizkeh haverkha*" (Shabbat 4a). As Feigenbaum wrote, "And he (Heschel) asked in addition, whether (*ha*) the principle, 'We do not say to man, Sin, in order that your friend may gain merit,' [is actionable] even [in an instance] where the many will derive merit [from the sinful act performed by the individual]."[42]

In the Talmudic passage (Shabbat 4a) where this principle is found, the issue revolves around the case of an individual who, in ignorance of Jewish law, placed a loaf of bread in an oven and thereby violated the prohibition that forbids baking on the Sabbath. During the course of the discussion, Rabbi Shila raises the possibility that an individual other than the one who placed the loaf in the oven ought to commit the "minor sin" of removing the loaf from the oven in order to "rescue" his unaware friend from the "more severe sin" of baking on the Sabbath. Rabbi Shesheth, however, immediately objects, stating, "Is a person then told, 'Sin, in order that your friend gain merit'?"

The concern voiced in this responsum may or may not have been directly related to the issue raised in the first question Heschel posed to Feigenbaum. To be sure, it is admittedly unlikely that the concerns voiced in this responsum were linked to the first question Heschel posed about *kavanah*. After all, neither Heschel nor Feigenbaum made any such direct linkage, and it is surely possible to treat both matters separately. However, it is possible that Heschel posed this additional question to his rabbi because he wanted to clarify the responsibility that the *shaliach tzibur* had to the entire congregation. After all, if the *shaliach tzibur* led the congregation in prayer and recited the *brachah* over the *arba minim* prior to the *Hallel* for the sake of leading the community in prayer while at the same time wishing he could have delayed recitation of the blessing until the "choice etrog (*m'hudar*)" arrived, he would surely have committed the "sin" of reciting a blessing that lacked appropriate *kavanah*. The responsibility to lead the congregation in prayer and thereby grant merit to the community may have well have been employed as a sufficient justification to permit the commission of what could then have been labeled "a minor transgression."

The issue involved here is one of responsibility—of whether individual piety and observance can be sacrificed in specific and discrete instances for the sake of a greater good. The principle invoked by Rabbi Shesheth seems to affirm that this is categorically forbidden. However, there are a number of passages in the Talmud and in later Jewish legal literature (e.g., Berachot 47b and the *Tosafot* on Shabbat 4a among others) cited by Feigenbaum in his response to Heschel that indicate that a "sinful act" by an individual can be countenanced in instances where the larger community will derive benefit from a relatively "minor transgression." Moreover, one sees this principle invoked quite often in the responsa literature to countenance a "sinful act" on the part of an individual or a rabbinic court of three for the sake of the merit that such an act will bestow upon other individuals or the larger Jewish community. For instance, Rabbi David Tzvi Hoffmann (1843–1921) of Berlin, in his *Melammed L'ho'il, Yoreh De'ah* #83, deals with the question of whether a rabbinic court ought to commit "the minor sin" of accepting an individual who is likely to be nonobservant subsequent to his conversion for the sake of his Jewish wife and the children who will issue from the union. R. Hoffmann cites the dictum of R. Shesheth in Shabbat 4a as offering a possible warrant for not accepting the man. However, he cites the *Tosafot* (medieval commentators on the Talmud) on this dictum in Shabbat 4a as providing grounds for the rabbinic court to commit what R. Hoffman labels the "minor sin" (*issura zuta*) of accepting this man into Judaism for the sake of the greater benefits that will flow to the woman, the children, and the larger Jewish community from his acceptance as a convert.

Clearly, this principle places responsibility upon the individual Jew to engage in a "moral calculus" that can require the Jew to commit a "minor infraction" of the law for the sake of the advantages that such an act will confer upon either the larger community or specific individuals. This principle evokes an unavoidable burden of responsibility, and the query Heschel posed to his rabbis indicates that he was sensitive to this concern from his earliest years in Poland.

Any claim that the issue of *halakhic* responsibility is identical to the later Heschel's emphasis on social responsibility is unsupportable, and unnecessary, as there is little doubt that the historical experience of prewar Berlin and postwar America had a profound impact on Heschel. Indeed, it is possible to demonstrate that much of Heschel's distinctive emphasis on the need for daring action in pursuit of justice was a relatively late development.

One important source mandating an approach that may be termed "moral interventionism" is Psalm 119:126. As Heschel pointed out in a small chapter devoted to this verse in his work on Rabbinic theology, the meaning of this verse is susceptible to a variety of interpretations. We may render it here as: It is time to act for the Lord / for the Lord to work; make void Your Torah / they have made void Your Torah.

This verse was introduced explicitly into Heschel's repertoire only in the 1960s, and it may be seen as a biblical foil to his growing political activism. He devoted a mini-chapter of his work on Rabbinic theology to the verse,[43] in which he noted that it "served as a firm foundation for a modest measure of flexibility in the legal construction of mitzvoth."[44] Yet, as the chapter proceeds, the interpretations seem less and less modest. In the fifth of five interpretations of the verse, Heschel enumerates a number of bold legal decisions predicated on the notion, to quote Rashi on Berakhot 54a, that "There are times when one cancels the words of Torah in order to act for the Lord." Having mentioned some of the classical applications of the legal principle, such as greeting on the Sabbath and committing the Oral Law to writing, Heschel then brings a tradition from Mishnah Keritot, according to which Rabban Simeon ben Gamaliel changed the price and scope of a bird sacrifice in the Temple in a year when prices were prohibitively high, explaining his social intervention with reference to our verse.[45]

Heschel's next comment is of great significance: "This fifth interpretation is audacious, and it should not be entrusted to any but the wisest of Sages, who truly understand contemporary times."[46] The risk inherent in the provision of a mandate for overruling the strictures of *halakhah* is self-evident: who is to decide when a particular situation justifies the abrogation of norms? A special capacity to fathom the times in which we live, specifically bestowed upon the elite of each generation, is necessary to ensure that this *halakhic* flexibility does not lead to licentiousness. At the end of this chapter, Heschel brings in *halakhic* applications of the verse from Maimonides and readings of a quite different nature in the name of the Baal Shem Tov and the Kotzker Rebbe.

Heschel's growing involvement in his later years with life outside his study room forced him to confront many issues relating to his commitments as a traditional Jew. One example may prove instructive. Heschel was pictured next to Rabbi Maurice Eisendrath of the Union of American Hebrew Congregations (Reform) carrying a Torah scroll in an antiwar mobilization at Arlington Cemetery. Many Orthodox Jews protested that this represented a clear infraction of Jewish law. Heschel was at pains to offer a defense for his actions using both *halakhic* and other criteria.[47] In his last works, too, we find Heschel struggling with the question of how to deal with a conflict between the word of God and the demands of Torah.

Rather than suggesting a direct continuity between Warsaw and New York, it is our intention to point out that the roots of Heschel's call for social involvement and responsibility run deep. We do not suggest that Heschel's concern with responsibility in Warsaw in the 1920s is identical with the mature Heschel's call for action in postwar America. However, the questions of the teenage Heschel may be read as foreshadowing his later passions.

In fact, these early writings do unquestionably indicate that Heschel had already begun to consider the themes of intention and responsibility during his Warsaw youth. The concerns voiced in these legal writings anticipate what would be a lifetime of reflection on these notions, and the adult Heschel would articulate these matters in a voice that possessed unparalleled depth, and in a life that would provide unsurpassed inspiration for countless American decades later.

Writing in postwar America, Abraham Joshua Heschel stated, "Teaching a child is in a sense preparing him for adolescence. We have to teach him ideas which he can carry over to maturity."[48] It appears that some of the ideas and insights to which the young Heschel was exposed did indeed carry over into his later life and provided the basis for what was to follow. Arthur Green has shown how a reading of his early poetry can yield many insights into Heschel's life project,[49] and we hope that in this article an even earlier stratum can be considered worthy of interest. Heschel's methodology and terminology were to change during his long journey from Muranowska Street via Vilna, Berlin, and London, all the way to Selma, Alabama, and the Vatican. We are grateful for the opportunity to present some of the legal and ethical questions that occupied the mind of the youth described simply as "Abraham Heschel of Warsaw." We have tried to demonstrate that despite the differences of context and genre separating Warsaw and New York City, core insights such as the centrality of *kavanah* and the importance of responsibility were established during Heschel's earliest years.

ACKNOWLEDGMENT

Michael Marmur co-authored this article, and I am grateful for his permission to include it in this volume.

NOTES

1. See Michael A. Meyer, "The Refugee Scholars Project of the Hebrew Union College," in *A Bicentennial Festschrift for Jacob Rader Marcus,* ed. Bertram W. Korn (New York: Ktav, 1976), 359–75. See also S. Daniel Breslauer, "The Impact of Abraham Joshua Heschel as Jewish Leader in the American Jewish Community from the 1960s to His Death: A Social, Psychological, and Intellectual Study" (PhD diss., Brandeis University, 1974); Hillel Goldberg, "Abraham Joshua Heschel and His Times," *Midstream* 28, no. 4 (1982): 36–42; Hillel Goldberg, *Between Berlin and Slobodka: Jewish Transition Figures from Eastern Europe* (Hoboken NJ: Ktav, 1989), especially 115–36; Robert G. Goldy, *The Emergence of Jewish Theology in America* (Bloomington: Indiana University Press, 1990); Edward K. Kaplan, *Holiness in Words: Abraham Joshua Heschel's Poetics of Piety* (Albany: State University of New York Press, 1996), 7–18; and most comprehensively, Edward K. Kaplan, *Spiritual Radical: Abraham Joshua Heschel in America* (New Haven: Yale University Press, 2007). For compelling evidence of the impact of Heschel on rabbinical students in the 1960s, see Charles S. Liebman, "The Training of American Rabbis," *American Jewish Year Book* 69 (1968): 84–85.

2. "Idols in the Temples," in *The Insecurity of Freedom* (Philadelphia: Jewish Publication Society, 1966), 66.

3. "Existence and Celebration," in *Moral Grandeur and Spiritual Audacity,* ed. Susannah Heschel (New York: Farrar, Straus and Giroux, 1996), 27.

4. See "Teaching Religion to American Jews" [1956] as reprinted in *Moral Grandeur,* 148.

5. Quoted in Morris M. Faierstein, "Abraham Joshua Heschel and the Holocaust," *Modern Judaism* 19 (1999): 269.

6. Samuel H. Dresner, *Heschel, Hasidism, and Halakha* (New York: Fordham University Press, 2002), 92.

7. *God in Search of Man* (New York: Farrar, Straus and Cudahy, 1956), 3. Arnold M. Eisen, *Taking Hold of Torah: Jewish Commitment and Community in America* (Bloomington: Indiana University Press, 1997), 17–18. The comment is worth recording here: "'My God!' I exclaimed. . . . 'He's been to my shul!' Heschel knew! I noted excitedly that he had not excluded Judaism from the category of religion gone stale. My anger was legitimate. I was not supposed to be tolerant of what I saw all around me!"

8. See "Carl Stern's Interview with Dr. Heschel" (1972) as reprinted in *Moral Grandeur*, 412.

9. "Existence and Celebration," 27.

10. Heschel chose to close *The Insecurity of Freedom* with a translation of the last chapter of his 1934 biography of Maimonides, which he wrote in Germany. The account of the late Maimonides spending more and more time engaged in the ills of his patients and away from his books mirrored his own journey from the book-filled study to the barricades. See *The Insecurity of Freedom*, 285–98.

11. Heschel, *The Prophets* (Philadelphia: Jewish Publication Society, 1962), 16.

12. "Religion and Race" (1963) as reprinted in *The Insecurity of Freedom*, 93.

13. "The Reasons for My Involvement in the Peace Movement" (1973) as reprinted in *Moral Grandeur*, 225.

14. "A Prayer for Peace" (1971) as reprinted in *Moral Grandeur*, 232.

15. *A Concise Dictionary of Hebrew Philosophical Terms* (mimeographed, Cincinnati, 1941), 34.

16. *Man's Quest for God: Studies in Prayer and Symbolism* (New York: Charles Scribner's Sons, 1954), 11–14, 84–85.

17. Ibid., 34, 53, 64.

18. Ibid., 53. See Mordecai M. Kaplan, *Judaism as a Civilization* [1934] (Philadelphia: Jewish Publication Society, 1984), 425–30; Mel Scult, *Judaism Faces the Twentieth Century: A Biography of Mordecai M. Kaplan* (Detroit: Wayne State University Press, 1993), 154–78; David Kaufman, *Shul with A Pool* (Hanover NH: Brandeis University Press/University Press of New England, 1999), especially 242–74.

19. *Man's Quest for God*, 65. See also Heschel's *Heavenly Torah: As Refracted through the Generations* (New York: Continuum, 2005), 200–207. The Hebrew original of this section was published in 1962. See Gordon Tucker's comment, 204n37.

20. *Man's Quest for God*, 85. Significantly, this comment was originally made in a 1953 address to the Rabbinical Assembly of America. See "The Spirit of Jewish Prayer" (1953) as reprinted in *Moral Grandeur*, 121. See also Kaplan, *Spiritual Radical*, 146–56.

21. See Aaron L. Mackler, "Symbols, Reality, and God: Heschel's Rejection of a Tillichian Understanding of Religious Symbols," *Judaism* 40, no. 3 (1991): 290–300; Edward K. Kaplan, *Holiness in Words*, 75–89; Michael Marmur, "In Search of Heschel," *Shofar* 26, no. 1 (2007): 38–40.

22. *Man's Quest for God*, 136–137. The complex question of what Heschel has in mind in his disparaging remarks about "symbolic thinking" lie outside the range of this article.

23. "Toward an Understanding of Halacha" (1953) as reprinted in *Moral Grandeur*, 140.

24. Ibid., 143.

25. *A Passion for Truth* (New York: Farrar, Straus and Giroux, 1973), 42.

26. *Kotzk: The Struggle for Integrity* (Tel Aviv: Ha-Menorah, 1973), 35–37.

27. Interestingly, Eisen himself has warned against "undue concentration" on this work and calls for a shift "away from an exclusive reliance on *Search*." See Arnold Eisen, "Re-reading Heschel on the Commandments," *Modern Judaism* 9, no. 1 (1989): 1–3. For an early example of the view regarding *Search* as Heschel's *Summa*, see Franklin Sherman, "Abraham Joshua Heschel: Spokesman for Jewish Faith," *Lutheran World* 10 (1963): 400–408.

28. *Search*, 341.

29. Ibid., 387.

30. Ibid., 316.

31. Ibid., 317.

32. Norman Lamm, *Seventy Faces: Articles of Faith* (Hoboken NJ: Ktav, 2001), 1:61. The passage in question is from *Athvan Deoraitha* (Lemberg, 1891), chapter 23, from 35b. Heschel provides a highly selective reading of Engel's argument.

33. *God in Search of Man*, 319.

34. Particularly interesting in this light is a phrase employed by Heschel in a private letter to Kaplan in February 1943 [located in the Heschel Papers, box 2, at the Jewish Theological Seminary Archives in New York]. He asserts that despite their differences, "the community of *kavanah* is more decisive than the difference of *nusach*."

35. The conditions in which these pieces were written have been evoked by Heschel's biographers and are the subject of a forthcoming article by Michael Marmur, "Heschel the Teenage Halakhist in Warsaw." Having been tutored first by Bezalel Levy and then by the noted rabbi Menaheim Zemba, Heschel was also linked with the Metivta Yeshiva in Warsaw. The journal *Sha'arei Torah* had its offices on 4 Muranowska Street near—and actually on the same street as—the Heschel family home. Originally, Rabbi Shlomo Altman had established *Bet Midrash* as a separate publication in 1922, designed to challenge young men studying at the Metivta and elsewhere to sharpen their pilpulistic skills and demonstrate their capacity for *halakhic* creativity. Soon the decision was made to publish *Bet Midrash as* a supplement to *Sha'arei Torah,* a publication established in 1913 by Yitzhak Hacohen Feigenbaum and continued by his son, Yisrael Isser Feigenbaum. During the year 5683 (1922–23) five editions of *Sha'arei Torah* with the *Bet Midrash* supplement were published. Heschel, who turned sixteen in the course of that year, published in three successive editions of the journal. It may be the case that this consistency says something about the regard in which he was held, at least by the editor of *Bet Midrash*, Rabbi Shlomo Altman. It is clear from comments made in the journal that competition among young scholars to have their novellae published was fierce. In the Av 5682 (1922) edition, Altman issued a stern warning that any attempts to apply undue pressure so that a particular piece be included would come to nought. To give a sense of how remarkable the appearance of three consecutive pieces by one young man was, it is worth noting that in those three editions, thirty-eight young scholars published in

Bet Midrash; only Heschel and one other young man, Isaac Katz of Rippin, had three pieces published. Another young man, Mendel Sirkes of Warsaw, however, had five pieces published in the space of two years. Most of the students just had one piece included by the editor. In 1922 we find the journal offering a prize of two thousand marks to the provider of the most convincing and harmonious explanation of a *halakhic* conundrum. For a brief mention of this journal and the circle of R. Isaac Feigenbaum and for much useful information, see Abraham Zemba, "Metivta of Warsaw," in *Jewish Institutions of Higher Learning in Europe: Their Development and Destruction* [Hebrew], ed. Samuel K. Mirsky (New York: Ogen, 1956), 363–80.

36. Edward K. Kaplan and Samuel H. Dresner, *Abraham Joshua Heschel: Prophetic Witness* (New Haven: Yale University Press, 1998), 38–50.

37. Feigenbaum, an inhabitant of Lokacz, was associated with *Sha'arei Torah* from 1910, the year in which the publication first appeared. He was one of its most prolific contributors. In 1931 he published a selection of responsa, all of which are dedicated to rabbis and emerging scholars. See *Meshiv Shalom* (Bilgoray: Kronenberg, 1931). It is interesting to note that Feigenbaum did not include the present responsa in his collection.

38. This is our translation of the text, which is taken from the journal *Sha'arei Torah,* aleph.

39. See Abraham Joshua Heschel, *The Circle of the Baal Shem Tov: Studies in Hasidism,* ed. Samuel H. Dresner (Chicago: University of Chicago Press, 1985), 9–10. The article on R. Pinchas of Koritz was originally published in Hebrew, "Letoldot R. Pinchas MiKoritz," in *Alei Ayin: Essays in Honor of Zalman Shicken* (Jerusalem: Schocken Press, 1948–52), 213–44.

40. Ibid.

41. *God in Search of Man,* 315.

42. This is our translation/explication of the text, which is taken from the journal *Sha'arei Torah,* bet.

43. *Torah min Hashamayim be-Aspeklaria Shel Ha-Dorot* (New York and Jerusalem: Jewish Theological Seminary, 1995), 3:120–22. Quotations from this work are taken from Gordon Tucker, ed., *Heavenly Torah,* 736–739. See also ibid., 594. The full extent of Heschel's deployment of this verse falls beyond the scope of our current article.

44. Tucker, ed., *Heavenly Torah,* 736.

45. Ibid., 738. In a footnote Heschel points out that according to one commentary this was not a onetime ruling.

46. Ibid.

47. See *Spiritual Radical,* 323–24.

48. A. J. Heschel, "Jewish Education" [1953] as reprinted in *The Insecurity of Freedom,* 235. In a 1956 article ("Confusion of Good and Evil," as reprinted in *Insecurity of Freedom,* 139), Heschel paraphrases a tradition from *Midrash Tehillim*

and adds his own interpretation: *"There is not a single mitzvah which we fulfill perfectly . . . except circumcision and the Torah that we study in our childhood,* for these two acts are not infringed upon by 'alien thoughts' or impure motivations." This statement implied a special status to the material considered in this article. It refers to a period before puberty and complexity changed the nature of his study.

49. Arthur Green, "Three Warsaw Mystics," *Jerusalem Studies in Jewish Thought* 13 (1996): 1–58. For the translated poems, see *The Ineffable Name of God: Man,* trans. Morton M. Leifman (London: Continuum, 2004).

11

Rabbi Hayim David Halevi on Christians and Christianity

An Analysis of Selected Legal Writings of an Israeli Authority

The genre of Jewish legal literature labeled "responsa"—all the issues raised by postmodernism regarding "essentialist postures" notwithstanding—constitute a powerfully idiomatic Jewish language. For the uninitiated in this literature, responsa can best be understood as technical legal documents—case discussions and their "holdings," in modern Western jurisprudential nomenclature—that rabbis throughout the centuries have used to apply the insights, meanings, norms, and precedents provided by the literary and legal texts of the Jewish past (namely, Bible, Talmud, codes of law, and other responsa) to the issues of the age. Simply put, for over a thousand years leading rabbinic jurist-legislators have employed responsa to issue authoritative renderings of Jewish law to rabbinic colleagues for application in particular cases. A single responsum must be seen as part of a vast body of Jewish case law that stretches over the centuries. It is the crossroads where text and context meet in the ongoing tradition of Jewish legal hermeneutics.

In this essay, I will provide an analysis of a legal writing authored by Rabbi Hayim David Halevi (1924–98) on the relationship between Judaism and Christianity. Rabbi Halevi was the outstanding pupil of the famed Chief Sephardic Rabbi of Israel Ben Zion Meir Hai Ouziel and studied with his mentor for many years at the prestigious Yeshivat Porat Yosef in Jerusalem. He later served as Chief Sephardic Rabbi of Tel Aviv-Jaffa, and he was one of the most prolific and famous rabbinic authorities in Israel.

The legal writing under consideration in this essay reveals the complex attitudes this traditional Israeli Sephardic rabbi, who received no formal secular education, possessed regarding the Church and Christians. The changes in positions Rabbi Halevi adopted toward Christians and the Church are contained in various parts of his nine-volume collection of

responsa entitled *'Aseh l'kha rav*. While I will focus on a responsum entitled "Concerning the Relationships between Jews and Non-Jews," I will
also contextualize this particular writing by placing it against the backdrop
of several other responsa that both Rabbi Halevi and a major rival, Rabbi
Ovadiah Yosef, former Chief Sephardic Rabbi of Israel and founder and
head of the Israeli Shas political party, wrote relating to this broad topic.[1]

To provide a framework for comprehending the nature and for illu-
minating the significance of the positions Rabbi Halevi advanced in his
responsum, I turn to a distinction Michael Signer has drawn in a lecture,
"Body and Soul: Interreligious Dialogue in the Theology of Abraham
Joshua Heschel," delivered in Warsaw on 7 June 2008.[2] In this lecture,
Signer offers an analysis of a letter that Rabbi Heschel sent to Augustine
Cardinal Bea on 22 May 1962, as well as the 1966 address "No Religion
Is an Island," which Heschel delivered as his inaugural lecture as Henry
Emerson Fosdick Visiting Professor at Union Theological Seminary.

At the conclusion of his remarks, Signer noted that Heschel called for
"a revolution in language" in interreligious discourse. He pointed out that
Heschel called for Jews and Christians in interreligious dialogue "to be of
'help to one another.'" In explicating the meaning of this phrase, Signer
called for "a shift in the discursive style that Jews and Christians have
utilized in their communication to one another." Signer concluded: "The
political power of either flattery or refutation moves humans to split their
communicative patterns into an inner and outer discourse. The inner discourse is one of triumph while the outer discourse is purely utilitarian and
aims at manipulating the other."

This distinction between "inner" and "outer" modes of Jewish discourse
is both provocative and suggestive, though not absolute. As such, it provides an illuminating starting point for comprehending the writings under
consideration in this essay. In his legal work, Rabbi Halevi clearly engages
in an "inner discourse" in an idiomatic Jewish legal genre. However, we
will see that his work ultimately reflects neither "manipulation" nor "triumph." On the contrary, it bespeaks an evolving understanding of and
even the development of an attitude of appreciation for Christians and the
Church. The complexity of the positions he advances demonstrates that
even in an internal mode of discourse, a sensitive religious leader can come
to understand that both Jews and Christians are commanded to recognize that God addresses Jew and gentile alike in a manner that asks mem-

bers of both faith traditions "to demand justice, to promote compassion, and to develop an empathy for those who struggle to remain faithful to the living God." As Signer observes, quoting Heschel, "Religion is not an end, but a process." The legal writings presented in this essay capture this ethos of development and progression as they sometimes appear even in the most traditional precincts of the modern Jewish world.

Background to Rabbi Halevi's Mature Views

In the first volume of 'Aseh l'kha rav, Responsum 59, Rabbi Halevi was asked by a Jewish tourist who "came to visit in a church" whether Jewish "entry into a church was permitted for purposes of a visit only."[3] In order to comprehend the answer that Rabbi Halevi offered in this instance, it is necessary to understand that the Christian belief in the Trinity is theologically problematic from a Jewish perspective. Judaism requires that Jews affirm a belief in the "Absolute Oneness" (Achdut) of God. The Trinitarian conception of the deity—as the Father, the Son, and the Holy Spirit— was therefore understood by no less an authority than Maimonides as a form of idolatry,[4] for Maimonides held that the doctrine of the Trinity compromised the standard of Achdut that Judaism established as necessary for a faith to be defined as monotheistic.[5]

Rabbi Halevi was aware of this Maimonidean stance concerning Christianity. At the same time, he knew that other rabbinic authorities took a less severe stance on this question. These authorities would not consign Christianity to the category of idolatry, nor would they accept a definition of Christians as idol worshippers. In a comment on Sanhedrin 63b, Rabbi Isaac of late twelfth-century France, the nephew of Rabbenu Tam, spoke of Christians and Christianity in the following terms: "Although they [i.e., Christians] mention the name of Heaven, meaning thereby Jesus of Nazareth, they do not at all events mention a strange deity, and moreover, they mean thereby the Maker of Heaven and Earth too; and despite the fact that they associate the name of Heaven with an alien deity, we do not find that it is forbidden to cause gentiles to make such an association . . . since such an association (Shituf) is not forbidden to the sons of Noah [i.e., gentiles]."[6]

In adopting this position, Rabbi Isaac adopted a perspective that removed Christians from the category of "idol worshippers." While Trinitarianism remained a forbidden theological posture for Jews, adherence to this notion by Christians was deemed an acceptable form of monotheism as this doctrine fell under the rabbinic category of *Shituf* (Associationism). Indeed, Rabbi Menachem Ha-Me'iri of early fourteenth-century Provence expanded upon this doctrine and stated explicitly that contemporary Christians "recognize the Godhead" and "believe in God's existence, His unity and power, although they misconceive some points according to our belief."[7] He further declared that his Christian peers did not fall under the category of "idol worshippers" and stated, "Now idolatry has disappeared from most places."[8] This trajectory found later expression in Jewish legal writings and Rabbi Yehuda Ashkenazi, writing on Christians and Christianity in his commentary on the *Shulhan Aruch, Yoreh De'ah* 151:2, asserted, "In our era . . . when the gentiles in whose midst we dwell . . . [speak of God], their intention is directed towards the One Who made Heaven and Earth, albeit that they associate another personality with God. However, this does not constitute a violation of Leviticus 19:14, 'You shall not place a stumbling block before the blind,' for non-Jews are not warned against such Associationism (*Shituf*)."[9]

Returning to the responsum itself, Rabbi Halevi—despite the various postures displayed in Jewish law toward Christianity—held that Jewish law on the question of whether a Jew could enter a church for purposes of a tourist visit was nonetheless clear: entry into a church was absolutely forbidden. He maintained that this was because a Jew is forbidden to enter "a house of idol worship even after the idolatry is removed."[10] In advancing this ruling, Rabbi Halevi indicated that he relied upon Maimonides. He observed that the Mishneh Torah held that a Jew was prohibited from entering a city where there was a house of idol worship. Halevi reasoned that if it was forbidden to even enter a city where such a building exists, then it was surely forbidden to enter the church itself. Indeed, Rabbi Halevi asserted that the only exception to such entry into a church for a Jew was when life itself was at stake—that is, one could enter a church in order to save a life.[11]

Rabbi Halevi further stated that he did not believe, as his questioner did, that the rabbinic principle, "on account of the ways of peace" (*mipnei darkhei shalom*), should constitute grounds for easing this prohibition. While the Talmud and early rabbinic literature had ruled that this principle could be evoked to demand, among other things, that a Jew care for gentile poor, eulogize and bury gentile dead, and offer comfort to gentiles who were engaged in mourning,[12] Rabbi Halevi did not believe that this principle could be extended to justify Jewish entry into a church.[13]

Rabbi Halevi explained his stance by advancing the following argument. He acknowledged that contemporary Christians were not idolaters, as Christians—unlike Jews—are not commanded concerning the absolute Unity and Oneness of God (*Achdut*). Rather, they are required to affirm the existence (*Metziut*) of God alone. Consequently, *Shituf* (Associationism) was permitted them as a form of monotheism. However, *Shituf* is not permitted Jews. For Jews, *Shituf* constitutes idolatry as it violates the standard of affirming the "Absolute Oneness" (*Achdut*) of God that Jewish tradition requires of Jews.[14]

Rabbi Halevi then asserted that the specific issue of whether a Jewish tourist could enter a church for purposes of "enjoyment" rather than "ritual worship" depended entirely upon the uses that contemporary Christians make of the church. Citing Avodah Zarah 3 as precedent, he noted that the Talmud permitted a Jew to enter a bath where there was a statue of Aphrodite that was intended only for beautification, not worship. Therefore, Rabbi Halevi reasoned by analogy that a Jew could enter a museum or private home where crosses and other Christian artifacts stand, for these ritual items are intended for aesthetic purposes alone. However, if the church was employed for contemporary Christian worship, then it was forbidden for a Jew to cross its threshold, for a Christian house of worship was—for a Jew—idolatrous.[15]

In making these statements, Rabbi Halevi indicated that he did not agree that the refusal of a Jew to enter a church used for Christian worship should be regarded as an insult to Christians or Christianity. Rabbi Halevi therefore asked why this failure to enter a church used for Christian worship should be construed as injuring or insulting anyone. He asked, "If a Jew refuses to eat non-kosher food, does this injure anyone?" Having presented this example, Rabbi Halevi therefore contended that he saw no reason why a Jew should be required, "on account of the ways of peace," to surrender "his faith and his principles" and enter the church. He insisted that the prohibition against Jewish entry into a church used for Christian worship entailed no act of "religious or national discrimination" against Christianity or Christians and only allowed the Jew to affirm the integrity of the Jewish theological position regarding monotheism for Jews.[16] With this observation, his first responsum came to an end.

Years later, Rabbi Halevi was asked once again whether a Jew was allowed to enter a church that was not used for ritual purposes. Here the questioner asked whether it was permissible to enter into a church as a tourist, "as one who goes into a museum." He ruled once again that it was certainly not forbidden for a Jew to enter a church for purposes of tourism. However, this time he added another consideration. He cited another authority who stated, "There is no prohibition against praying in a structure where idol worship took place, even if such worship was fixed."[17] Consequently, inasmuch as "temporary prayer" was allowed in a building that had formerly been used for "forbidden worship," he contended that it was certainly permitted to enter a church for purposes of appreciating its architectural structure. In moving from Rabbi Halevi's first to second responsum on this subject, one observes a slight softening of his view of a church as "a house of idolatry" for Jews, an evolution that would be— as will be shown below—more fully developed in later years. Had the beginnings of this change not been evidenced here, Rabbi Halevi could not have even countenanced the possibility that a Jew could recite "temporary prayer" in a church.

Before turning to the responsum, "Concerning the Relationships between Jews and Non-Jews," which represents the attitudes that the fully mature Rabbi Halevi adopted on the question of the relationship between Judaism and Christianity, it will be instructive to examine the ruling that his chief rival, Rabbi Ovadiah Yosef, put forth on the same question of whether a Jew could visit a church. The posture Rabbi Yosef assumed on this matter and the contrasts between his reasoning and citations and those of Rabbi Halevi—despite overlaps between them—will provide an important framework not only for appreciating the slightly changed tone that marked Rabbi Halevi's later ruling on this question, but also for illuminating the precise nature of the positions that Rabbi Halevi put forth in his final responsum on the subject.

In his responsa collection, *Y'haveh Daat* 4:45, Rabbi Yosef was asked the exact question, "Is it permissible for a Jew to visit a Christian church," that had been put to Rabbi Halevi. In his response, Rabbi Yosef began by observing that the Talmud (Avodah Zarah 17a) states that it is forbidden to even approach the entrance of a house of idol worship. Furthermore, Maimonides, commenting on the Mishnah found on Avodah Zarah 11b, says as we saw above—that all non-Jewish houses of prayer in gentile cities are by definition "houses of idolatry." Ideally, Jews should not even live in such cities. However, "on account of our sins, we are compelled against our will to dwell in the lands of idol worshipers."[18] If the law is such that we should not even live in such cities, then it is certainly forbidden—where Jews are not compelled to do so—for Jews to enter a church,[19] for Christians, he ruled, basing himself upon Maimonides in *Hilchot Ma'acha'lot Asurot* 11, are idolaters. Their churches are houses of idolatry, and it is therefore forbidden for a Jew to enter a church under any conditions.

To underscore this point, Rabbi Yosef turned to the writings of Judah the Pious (twelfth–thirteenth centuries), who, in his *Sefer Hasidim* 435, told the following story. Judah wrote, "A gentile owed a Jew a financial debt, and when the Jew attempted to collect the debt, the gentile fled to his house of worship [in order to escape the Jew, as the Jew would not follow him there as his house of prayer was a place of idolatry that it was forbidden the Jew to enter]." However, once the Jew, Rabbi Judah reported, did follow after him and entered the church in order to collect the debt, the Jew then repented this deed and approached a Sage to ask what he should do as an act of repentance for this violation. The Sage told him that he should fast each year on the anniversary of his having entered the church as an act of remorse, and this he did all his days.[20]

Rabbi Yosef then cited other authorities to further bolster his stance. Among them were Rabbi Hayim Palagi of Izmir, Turkey (d. 1873), who ruled in his responsa collection (*Hayyim Ba-yad* 26) that "there was a severe prohibition against entering their houses of worship," and Rabbi David Zilberstein who (in his *Sh'vilei David* 145) ruled that entry into a Christian church was an "*issur torah*," a prohibition decreed by the Torah itself. Indeed, Rabbi Yosef stated that Rabbi Zilberstein held that a Jew could not enter a church even when there was a fear that this would arouse enmity (*eivah*) on the part of gentiles against Jews. And when Rabbi Eliezer Deutsch of Hungary (1850–1916) was asked, in his *P'ri Hasadeh* 2:4, whether it was appropriate that Jews of public prominence had entered a church to attend a memorial ceremony for a non-Jewish national leader, he asserted that even this act of respect for a deceased gentile violated a "grave prohibition" (*issur hamur*). Rabbi Yosef also ruled, as Rabbi Deutsch had, that the prohibition was so great that it could not be waived even in a place where "enmity" would result. Indeed, as Rabbi Yosef approvingly reported, Rabbi Deutsch contended that Jews who had entered a church for any reason needed to engage in an act of repentance. Rabbi Yosef therefore concluded that it was absolutely forbidden for a Jew to enter a church under any conditions and that Jewish tourists should not be swayed by any lenient ruling on this question and enter either past or present Christian houses of worship.[21] The uncompromising positions Rabbi Yosef put forth in this responsum only underscore the contrast between his posture and that of the fully mature Rabbi Halevi on the issue of Judaism's attitudes toward Christianity and Christians.

Rabbi Halevi's Mature Views on Christians and the Church

In Kislev 5748 (December 1987), Rabbi Halevi delivered what would be his definitive statement on Christians and Christianity, "Concerning the Relationships between Jews and Non-Jews." At the outset, he asserted that he deliberately chose not to focus in the traditional way on the halakhic category, "on account of the ways of peace," as a warrant for an inclusive approach to this topic.[22] Rabbi Halevi did this because he contended that most of the laws that fall under this category are irrelevant for deducing a proper Jewish attitude toward Christianity and Islam and Christians and Muslims for contemporary Jews who live in the sovereign Jewish State of Israel. This was because the bulk of laws that fall under the category, "on account of the ways of peace," addressed Jewish life under the conditions of the Diaspora, conditions under which the Jewish community was reduced to a distinct and sometimes powerless minority. As a result, the directives that fell under this category and instructed Jews to behave in charitable ways toward their gentile neighbors were often primarily motivated by pragmatic considerations that would allow the Jew to live in harmony with more powerful gentile neighbors. Rabbi Halevi did not dismiss such pragmatic motivations as frivolous or unimportant. However, it is clear that he wanted to discover a moral as opposed to a pragmatic posture to undergird a present-day Jewish attitude toward the other Abrahamic faiths and their adherents. Rabbi Halevi desired to affirm a stance that was consonant with both the politically sovereign status Jews now enjoyed as a majority population in the State of Israel and the ethos contained in the Israeli Declaration of Independence that stated, "Complete social and political equality will be established among all her citizens regardless of religion, race, or sex." Rabbi Halevi embraced this affirmation and asserted that Israel must be committed to all its citizenry, including gentiles, and must extend all the same rights to them that were granted to Jews.[23]

This does not mean that Rabbi Halevi totally ignored the category, "on account of the ways of peace." Indeed, he turned to Maimonides, *Hilchot Avodah Zarah* 9:5, where it states that gentile poor are to be supported along with Jewish poor "on account of the ways of peace." Rabbi Halevi also took note of the fact that the law immediately following, contained in *Hilchot Avodah Zarah* 9:6, seemed to circumscribe the application of this principle because Maimonides stated there that these directives based on the principle, "on account of the ways of peace," applied only when Jews dwelt as a minority in the midst of a majority culture or when gentiles had sovereignty in the Land of Israel. As Maimonides wrote, "These rules only apply when the people Israel are exiled among the nations, or when the gentiles have power over the people of Israel. However, when Israel has power over them, it is forbidden to allow gentiles to dwell among us."[24]

However, Rabbi Halevi asserted that these last strictures contained in 9:6 of the Rambam were not applicable in the contemporary setting while the instructions found in 9:5 that called upon the Jewish community to offer support to the poor "on account of the ways of peace" were actionable in the present-day State of Israel. Though one might suppose that these obligations would not be incumbent upon Jews in contemporary Israel inasmuch as Israel was now a sovereign nation, Rabbi Halevi contended that that was not so. He said that those who make this claim were mistaken since the Western world of democracy in which Israel participates has at its foundation the notion of equal rights among all persons. Rabbi Halevi stated that there is no place in a democratic state for religious discrimination and added that the world would simply not tolerate such behavior from the State of Israel. Consequently, Jews cannot be said to possess absolute sovereignty anywhere—even in the State of Israel. The ruling in *Hilchot Avodah Zarah* 9:6 was "non-actionable" in the present setting.[25]

Rabbi Halevi was not content to rest his argument upon what might be labeled a *realpolitik* approach. He further stated that all the decrees forbidding kindness and social interaction and support with gentiles found in ancient and medieval rabbinic tradition did not apply to contemporary gentiles for other reasons as well. Everything stated above in Maimonides and elsewhere in classical rabbinic sources applied only to those who were genuinely "idolaters," i.e., people who actually worshipped "statues and monuments." Yet, contemporary Muslims and Christians who live in the State of Israel obviously did not fall into this category. Islam was a form of pure monotheism, and Muslims no less than Jews worshipped the one God "Who created heaven and earth." Rabbi Halevi felt no need to engage in a lengthy discussion concerning the monotheistic status of Islam and did nothing more than advance the position that Muslims were not "idolaters."[26]

In regard to Christianity, Rabbi Halevi acknowledged that it might be possible to define Christianity as "idolatry." However, he asserted that that was not so in the contemporary era. To be sure, Rabbi Halevi introduced his discussion with a few general observations. He pointed out that Judaism has a "long and piercing account with Christianity as a religion." This is not only because much Jewish blood has been spilled in the name of Christianity. Rather, it is because Christianity "perverted the foundations of Judaism beyond recognition." The concept of the Trinity distorted the pure monotheism of Judaism with its belief that "God is One and God's Name is One." At a single blow, Christianity also uprooted those commandments and Jewish ways of life that served as the basis for the covenant that God established with the people Israel when Israel left Egypt.[27] His indictment of Christianity here at the outset of his discussion was certainly a strong one.

At the same time, Rabbi Halevi observed, Judaism is not a missionary religion. It pays no attention to any other faith. However, this is not the case with Christianity, which engages in vigorous proselytizing. Rabbi Halevi asserted that while Christianity may have denied any allegiance to the commandments, Jews should clearly appreciate Christianity. Through its missionary efforts, Christianity uprooted idolatry from the world and spread a permitted form of monotheism for gentiles throughout the world. Rabbi Halevi therefore drew a distinction between Christianity as a faith, on the one hand, and Christians, on the other. With Christianity as a religion, Jews have had a long and painful history. However, this is not so with the Christian man or woman. In fact, Judaism maintains, along with Ben Azzai, that its adherents ought to interact with Christians according to the great principle of the Torah ("You shall love your neighbor as you love yourself"), since all humanity is created in the image of God (Avot 3:14).[28]

Having opened his remarks in this way, Rabbi Halevi then continued with a lengthy discussion of whether Jewish law still regarded Christianity as a form of "idolatry." He acknowledged that there were surely elements of what could be labeled as *'avodah zarah* (idolatry) in Christianity—faith in the Trinity, for example, stands in opposition to belief in the unity of God. Furthermore, the multiplicity of icons and statues of saints and crucifixes could admittedly be regarded as "idolatrous." However, Rabbi Halevi insisted that the concept of "idolatry" had to be regarded in a nuanced and multilayered way. Indeed, he contended that what classical Jewish law condemned so uncompromisingly (*b'humrah rabah*) as "idolatry" was distinct from the Christian worship of God.[29]

Rabbi Halevi defended this position by constructing the following argument. He contended that the Talmud itself had already begun to develop the "first signs of greater moderation in later generations" that allowed for the creation of a novel legal category that would exempt many non-Jews from the category of "idol worshipper." Thus, in Hullin 13a, the Talmud, commenting upon the ruling that meat slaughtered by an "idol worshipper" is ritualistically impure and unfit for sale, distinguished between gentiles who are committed to idolatry in principle and gentiles who are not "genuine idolaters" but rather ones "who have inherited customs from their ancestors" (*she-minhag avoteihem b'ydeihem*).[30] Halevi claimed that the logic that even Maimonides put forth in his commentary on this Hullin passage should have compelled him to acknowledge that a logical distinction must be made between persons who hold a principled commitment to idol worship and attribute divinity and power to their idols, on the one hand, and those who simply follow the practices and customs that their sages instructed them to follow, on the other. Halevi stated that this latter group constitutes the majority of gentiles in the world.[31] Of these persons, as Rabbi Jochanan said, "Gentiles outside the Land of Israel are not actually idolaters. Rather, the custom of their ancestors is in their hands."[32]

Rabbi Halevi then followed this line of reasoning by noting that the *Tur, Yoreh De'ah* 148,[33] states that all the prohibitions that are prescribed for Jews toward idolaters are not applicable in "our age" (*ha-idana*).[34] He based this upon the Rashbam who cites Rashi, who states, "All is permitted, for they are not idolaters and they do not come and confess."[35] The *Bet Yosef*[36] also stated there that all the prohibitions listed in this chapter of the *Tur* are no longer in force, "as gentiles outside the land are not idolaters." Rather, they fall under the category of those in whom "the customs of their ancestors are in their hands."[37] Finally, in the *Shulchan Aruch*,

Yoreh Deʾah 148:12, Caro wrote, "At this time, they are not steeped in the nature of idolatry. Therefore, all is permitted."[38]

From all this, Rabbi Halevi concluded, "And if this is said regarding those who genuinely worship idols, i.e., those who worship icons and statues, it is all the more so in relationship to Christianity."[39] For Trinitarianism does not constitute idolatry for gentiles. It is a form of monotheism *(Shituf)* permitted to non-Jews. "No Christians in our day," Rabbi Halevi wrote, "are actually idol worshippers as were the gentiles whom the Talmud condemned during the Talmudic era." Moreover, he claimed that a literal belief in the Trinity had weakened among many Christians and that there were many Christians who understand this form of faith as nothing more than allegory.[40] Consequently, contemporary Christians clearly fall within the legal category of "the customs of their ancestors are in their hands." They were not and are not "idolaters." While Rabbi Halevi conceded that Maimonides refused to make this distinction, he also contended that Maimonides was virtually the only medieval legal authority not to apply the category of "the customs of their ancestors are in their hands" to contemporaneous Christians, and he looked to specific rulings issued by a variety of rabbis on a host of particular issues to demonstrate the correctness of this claim.[41]

In making this argument, Rabbi Halevi was grounding this part of his responsum on a particular traditional Jewish legal approach that Hebrew University professors Moshe Halbertal and Avishai Margalit have pointed out "involves changing the status of Christians without changing the status of Christianity." It is an approach that asserts that "the Christians were not devoted adherents of their religion but were simply following the customs of their ancestors. There is no change in the status of Christianity as an idolatrous religion; only the status of the Christians as loyal practitioners of this religion changed."[42] While this approach was clearly more tolerant than one that simply labeled Christians as "idolaters," Rabbi Halevi was not content with this position, and in the final pages of his responsum he advanced another posture that represents his views in their full development.

In *Idolatry,* Halbertal and Margalit point out that the great Provençal scholar Rabbi Menachem ben Solomon Meiri (1249–1316) (Ha-Meʾiri) advanced a Jewish position regarding Christianity that was distinct from the one discussed above. While that stance involved "changing the status of Christians without changing the status of Christianity," the posture Ha-Me'iri put forth reflected "a change in the status of Christianity itself." As Halbertal and Margalit view it, "The change in attitude toward Christianity stemmed not from the claim that Christians have monotheistic metaphysical beliefs but from a renewed understanding of idolatry as a lawless lifestyle." By creating a distinction "between monotheists and idolaters," Ha-Me'iri created "a new distinction between nations that are law-abiding and nations that are not." By putting forth this new mode of categorization, Ha-Me'iri was able to distinguish "Christians from the idolaters to whom the laws in tractate Avodah Zarah and in other parts of the Talmud apply." It is the matter of "degenerate lifestyle," not issues of "metaphysics," that defines "idolatry." Inasmuch as Christians "insist upon a moral lifestyle," Christianity is "a nonidolatrous religion."[43]

Halbertal and Margalit are undoubtedly correct in identifying the approach that Ha-Me'iri adopted toward Christianity as "a nonidolatrous religion" as a novel one in the Jewish legal tradition. Indeed, we will see that Rabbi Halevi justified his own approach to Christianity on the basis of Ha-Me'iri's teachings. At the same time, an examination of the final arguments he put forth in this responsum went beyond issues of "Christian lifestyle," and his presentation of Ha-Me'iri on this topic reflected a "metaphysical appreciation" of Christianity as well.

In a number of sections in his responsum dealing with various Talmudic interdictions against Jewish interactions with "idolaters," Rabbi Halevi asserted, based on his reading of Ha-Me'iri, that none of these prohibitions were in force in regard to Christians. Citing the opinions of Ha-Me'iri contained in his commentary on the first tractate of Avodah Zarah, Rabbi Halevi contended, "In our times, all [interactions with gentiles] are permitted, as [these prohibitions issued by the rabbis of the Talmud] applied only to their time . . . when they (i.e., non-Jews) worshipped the hosts of heaven—sun, moon, and stars."[44] While it is true that Ha-Me'iri claimed that Christians "erred" (*mishtabshin*) in regard to certain issues of faith, he also asserted that they nevertheless believed in the existence of God—His Unity and Power. Christian faith bore no resemblance to pagan religion, in which "idols of stone and wood" were worshipped. Contemporary Christians worshipped the God "Who created Heaven and Earth."[45] Rabbi Halevi could therefore assert that Christians believe in "the Exodus from Egypt, the renewal of the world, and in the fundamental principles of faith. Their every intention is toward the One who made Heaven and Earth."[46] His reading of Ha-Me'iri caused Rabbi Halevi to assume an attitude toward Christianity that did far more than simply acknowledge that Christians adopted a "moral lifestyle" incumbent upon all persons. His own theological sensibility allowed him to appreciate, as he felt Ha-Me'iri had, the "metaphysical truths" contained in the Christian faith as well.

Rabbi Halevi further contended that countless other Jewish legal authorities—among them Ovadiah Bartenora, Tosafot Yom Tov, and Moses Isserles—subsequent to Ha-Me'iri developed their teachings on Christianity in relationship to these theological understandings that Ha-Me'iri had advanced. These rabbis therefore asserted that the Christians in whose midst they dwelt were absolutely not 'ovdei' avodah zarah (idol worshippers). In the words of Isserles in his note on Orah Hayyim 126, "We are obligated to pray for their welfare."[47]

Rabbi Halevi went on to claim that instances of positive interaction with Christians in all facets of life constituted acts of Kiddush hashem (sanctification of the Name of God) that "adorn Israel." Rabbi Halevi cited numerous responsa by diverse rabbinical authorities who described specific deeds of charity and goodness toward Christians as ma'asei Kiddush hashem, actions that sanctified the Name of God in the world.[48]

Rabbi Halevi even asserted that Jews should accord Christians and Muslims the same treatment they would extend to Jews in areas of ethical obligation and concern. Based on the reasoning of Ha-Me'iri, Rabbi Halevi concluded his responsum by stating, "The legal category of 'idolater' does not apply to gentiles of our day. [Therefore], even if Israel was completely sovereign, we are in no way obligated to act towards contemporary gentiles as if the category of 'idolater' applied to them."[49] Furthermore, while "all relations between Jews and gentiles, whether in Israel or in the Diaspora, whether in societal relationship as a State to her gentile citizens, or whether in personal relationship between the Jew and his gentile neighbor or friend" must be conducted with fairness and integrity, this should not be based on the prudential halakhic category of "on account of the ways of peace" as some rabbis might maintain. Rather, "the maintenance and support of gentiles, visiting their sick, burying their dead, comforting their mourners, and all other duties" can and should be performed, Rabbi Halevi maintained, on the basis of an overarching teaching of "human ethical obligation" (hovah enosheet musarit) that animates and informs all of Jewish religious tradition.[50] In making this last point, Rabbi Halevi clearly extended his teachings beyond what Ha-Me'iri had advanced and held that Judaism possessed a universal moral posture that was consonant with the democratic ethos that marked the modern world. The expansiveness of his thought was clearly profound.

It is noteworthy that, in an addendum to his responsum, Rabbi Halevi reported that Professor Menachem Elon, the justice of the Israeli Supreme Court and the great student of Jewish law, objected to the position Rabbi Halevi had advanced in his presentation. While Justice Elon conceded that the approach of Ha-Me'iri did remove Christians "altogether from the category of idolaters," he nevertheless stated that Ha-Me'iri was alone in adopting this general stance. Indeed, Elon asserted that no other rabbinic authority did so, even though in specific instances they did rule leniently, as Rabbi Halevi correctly pointed out. Therefore, he asked, "How can we arrive at the overarching Jewish conclusion that Christians in our day can be removed from the category of 'idolaters'?"[51]

To this, Rabbi Halevi responded that it might be true that Ha-Me'iri was alone among all Jewish legal authorities in explicitly advancing an overarching position that removed Christians altogether from the category of "idolaters." However, Ha-Me'iri was hardly a minor authority. Furthermore, Rabbi Halevi would not concede that Rabbi Meiri was unique in his assertion that Christians do not fall within the category of "idolaters." He stated that countless rabbis, writing on particular issues, had asserted over and over again and in diverse sources drawn from different lands and times that Christians were not idolaters. Therefore, asked Rabbi Halevi, "What prevents us—on the basis of the same legal logic—from expanding these specific *hetarim* (permissions) and establishing the general principle that Ha-Me'iri had, one that affirms that Christians are not idolaters?" Therefore, Rabbi Halevi concluded, "I stand by my position" regarding Christians and Christianity.[52]

Conclusion

In summarizing and assessing the content and nature of the legal stances Rabbi Halevi put forth in his writings on Christians and Christianity, it is instructive to turn to a commentary that Avi Ravitsky of Hebrew University has written on the major responsum under consideration in this essay. A consideration of Ravitsky's commentary illuminates not only the broader dynamics at play in Rabbi Halevi's approach to Jewish law but also the significance of the latter's positions on this particular issue. In his article "'Ways of Peace' and the Status of Gentiles According to the Rambam: An Exchange of Letters with Rabbi Hayim David Halevi," Ravitsky observes that Rabbi Halevi prefers to interpret classical halakhic sources "according to their straightforward meaning." He does not attempt to impose upon them novel interpretations, "*midrash hadash.*" However, Ravitsky also notes that this "legal fundamentalism" does not prevent "R. Halevi from displaying flexibility and halakhic innovation. Indeed, exactly the opposite is the case. He 'neutralizes' the source and negates its contemporary relevance and authority."[53] The rabbinic interpreter must understand the meaning of the source precisely as it is and then determine carefully whether it is actually applicable in the contemporary situation.

Ravitsky defines this approach that characterizes Rabbi Halevi as one of "conservative audacity." Indeed, his "legal fundamentalism" and his refusal to provide "a new midrash" on the sources before him often allow him not only to "neutralize the earlier source," but "to display halakhic flexibility in response to a new [social-political-religious] reality."[54] Precedents contained in earlier writings are often deemed "irrelevant," as the circumstances that surrounded the source are completely different from those that obtain in the current situation. The vitality of Jewish law provides the rabbinic decisor with broad discretionary powers, as the rabbi has the right to assert that as "the contours and circumstances of life change," so the application of the law must change as well.[55]

In the examples presented in this essay, Rabbi Halevi therefore acknowledges that the sources do speak of "idolatry." There is no question that the Talmud and rabbinic tradition have stringent views on the topic. However, his analysis of these sources permits Rabbi Halevi to assign and limit the applications of these sources to a past when persons actually worshiped statues and masks. They do not refer to gentiles in our day, and they certainly cannot be applied to contemporary Muslims and Christians. In effect, his legal methodology facilitates innovation even as it affirms a fidelity to the tradition.

In Ravitsky's opinion, this is precisely what is most significant about his writings on Christians and Christianity. Indeed, his approach allowed Rabbi Halevi to contend that care for Christians and Muslims—indeed, all humans—stems from a worldview of "ethical human obligation" inherent in the tradition. This sense of moral obligation allows for a correction of the formal Jewish law beyond the pragmatic considerations inherent in the category, "on account of the ways of peace." Furthermore, this belief that Jewish tradition countenanced a spirit of "ethical human obligation" provided the basis for expanding the recognition of obligations toward gentiles in a broad and inclusive way not limited by specific matters defined in the Talmud. By asserting that "ethical human obligations" constitute an integral and overarching principle—a meta-principle—that informs and guides the Jewish legal tradition, Rabbi Halevi offered a "*hiddush hilchati*" (an halakhic innovation), and he had Judaism speak in a contemporary ethical voice that held, as Ravitsky puts it, "that universal obligations exceed the bounds of the halakhic formal command."[56]

The overarching developments that took place in the Sephardic sage's attitudes toward Christians and Christianity are noteworthy. While Rabbi Halevi "did not hesitate to rule that [Christian believers] were akin to idolaters in every way" in his earlier writings, he ultimately came to affirm that contemporary Christians "were not idolaters."[57] As Ravitsky states in his summation of Rabbi Halevi's work, "Over the passage of years there was a significant evolution in his opinions on these matters."[58] This essay certainly concurs in that assessment. Through an analysis of this Jewish mode of "internal discourse," we have seen that religious tradition, in the hands of a sensitive and bold interpreter, can be supple. The task of developing "empathy for those who struggle," in all religions, "to remain faithful to the living God" is an ongoing challenge for us all. In attempting to meet this challenge, I remain especially grateful that we have figures like Rabbi Halevi and my friend Rabbi Michael Signer, cited at the outset of this essay, to guide us.

NOTES

1. Two significant English language articles on R. Halevi are Marc Angel, "Rabbi Hayim David Halevy: A Leading Contemporary Rabbinic Thinker," *Jewish Book Annual* 52 (1994): 99–109; and Zvi Zohar, "Sephardic Religious Thought in Israel: Aspects of the Theology of Rabbi Hayim David Halevi," in *Critical Essays on Israeli Society, Religion, and Government*, ed. Kevin Avruch and Walter Zenner (Albany: SUNY Press, 1997), 115–36. In addition, I have written three essays in the past decade on elements of his thought. See David Ellenson, "Interpretive Fluidity and P'sak in a Case of *Pidyon Sh'vuyim*: An Analysis of a

Modern Israeli Responsum as Illuminated by the Thought of David Hartman," in *Judaism and Modernity: The Religious Philosophy of David Hartman*, ed. Jonathan Malino (Jerusalem: Shalom Hartman Institute, 2001), 341–67; "Jewish Legal Interpretation and Moral Values: Two Responsa by Rabbi Hayim David Halevi on the Obligations of the Israeli Government towards Its Minority Population," *Central Conference of American Rabbis' Journal* 48, no. 3 (Summer 2001): 5–20; and "A Portrait of the *Posek* as Modern Religious Leader: An Analysis of Selected Writings of Rabbi Hayim David Halevi," in *Jewish Religious Leadership: Image and Reality*, vol. 2, ed. Jack Wertheimer (New York: Jewish Theological Seminary, 2004), 673–93. Two books on Rabbi Halevi have also appeared. The first, an important and comprehensive book of essays, is *A Living Judaism: Essays on the Halakhic Thought of Rabbi Hayyim David Halevi* [Hebrew], ed. Zvi Zohar and Avi Sagi (Jerusalem: Shalom Hartman Institute and the Faculty of Law, Bar Ilan University, 2005). The second is written by Marc D. Angel with Hayyim Angel, *Rabbi Haim David Halevi: Gentle Scholar and Courageous Thinker* (Jerusalem: Urim Publications, 2006). Recent years have also seen two major scholarly works appear on Rabbi Yosef that merit attention: Benjamin Lau, *From "Maran" to "Maran": The Halakhic Philosophy of Rav Ovadiah Yosef* [Hebrew] (Tel Aviv: Miskal-Yedoth Ahronoth Books and Chemed Books, 2005), and Ariel Picard, *The Philosophy of Rabbi Ovadia Yosef in an Age of Transition* [Hebrew] (Ramat-Gan: Bar-Ilan University Press, 2007).

2. I would like to thank Michael Signer for sharing this as yet unpublished lecture with me in typescript. In that lecture, Signer reports that the letter between Rabbi Heschel and Cardinal Bea is being prepared for publication by Susannah Heschel. The Heschel essay, "No Religion Is an Island," appears in Abraham Joshua Heschel, *Moral Grandeur and Spiritual Audacity*, ed. Susannah Heschel (New York: Farrar, Straus and Giroux, 1996), 235–50.

3. *'Aseh l'kha rav* 1:59, p. 178.

4. See Maimonides, *Mishneh Torah, Hilchot Akum* 9:4 and *Peirush Hamishnah, Avodah Zarah* 1:3.

5. Moshe Halbertal and Avishai Margalit in *Idolatry* (Cambridge: Harvard University Press, 1993), 110–12, provide a philosophical explanation as to why Maimonides regarded the Christian concept of the Trinity as an unacceptable standard of monotheism for Jews. As they explain, Jewish belief "in the oneness of God [is] not merely denial of polytheism." Rather, the belief in *Achdut* as a requirement of monotheism for Jews demands the rejection of "Multiplicity," i.e., "not only the [rejection of the] belief in many gods," but the rejection of "an error that concerns God himself, which may be called 'internal polytheism.' The strict demand on unity implies a rejection of corporeality," for corporeality assumes that God is divisible, thus "vitiate[ing] God's perfection." After all, "the idea of matter is associated with decay, and it is also conceptually connected with finitude," and "decay and finitude" cannot be combined "with the idea of a

perfect God." Moreover, "corporeality entails divisibility, and hence the notion of a corporeal God undermines God's unity."

6. The text of Rabbi Isaac can be found in the *Tosafot* to Sanhedrin 63b and Bekhorot 2b. The translation is taken from Jacob Katz, *Exclusiveness and Tolerance: Jewish-Gentile Relations in Medieval and Modern Times* (New York: Schocken, 1969), 35.

7. This translation from Ha-Me'iri is found in Katz, *Exclusiveness and Tolerance*, 36.

8. Ibid., 121.

9. The translation of Rabbi Ashkenazi is mine.

10. *'Aseh l'kha rav* 1:59, p. 178.

11. Ibid., 178–79.

12. See Jerusalem Talmud, Gittin 5:9; Demaii 4:6; Avodah Zarah; and Babylonian Talmud, Gittin 63a; as well as Maimonides, *Mishneh Torah, Hilchot Melachim* 10:12.

13. *'Aseh l'kha rav* 1:59, p. 180.

14. Ibid., 181.

15. Ibid.

16. Ibid., 180.

17. *'Aseh l'kha rav* 4:53, p. 280.

18. *Y'haveh Da'at* 4:45, p. 235.

19. Rabbi Yosef goes on to cite numerous authorities—the Rashba, the Ritba, and the Rosh—who also all rule in this fashion on this matter.

20. *Y'haveh Da'at* 4:45, pp. 235–36. The phrasing here is mine.

21. Ibid., 237.

22. Another treatment of this responsum is found in Marc Angel, *Rabbi Haim David Halevi*, 190–93.

23. *'Aseh l'kha rav* 9:30, p. 61.

24. Ibid., 62.

25. Ibid., 63.

26. Ibid.

27. Ibid., 63, 64.

28. Ibid., 64–65.

29 Ibid., 65.

30. Ibid., 65–66.

31. Ibid., 66–67.

32. *Hullin* 13b.

33. The *Tur* is the great legal code of Rabbi Jacob ben Asher (1270–1340).

34. *'Aseh l'kha rav* 9:30, p. 66.

35. The Rashbam is Rabbi Samuel ben Meier, the grandson of Rashi and a medieval commentator on the Bible and the Talmud.

36. A commentary on the *Tur* written by Rabbi Joseph Caro between 1522–1544.

37. *'Aseh l'kha rav* 9:30, p. 66.

38. The *Shulchan Aruch* is the premiere code of Jewish law completed in 1564 by Joseph Caro.

39. *'Aseh l'kha rav* 9:30, p. 66.

40. Ibid., 67.

41. Halevi devotes a considerable number of pages to establishing this point and cites numerous authorities who issue *hetarim* (permissions) for Jews to interact with Christians on matters ranging from business dealings to selling them homes, from returning lost objects to them to praying for their health. However, R. Halevi concedes that the justification for these "leniencies" are based primarily either on the essentially pragmatic principle of "on account of the ways of peace," or as a result of the legal category, "the ways of their ancestors are in their hands." See his summations of these issues on pp. 67–72 of his responsum.

42. Halbertal and Margalit, *Idolatry*, 211–12.

43. Ibid., 212–13.

44. *'Aseh l'kha rav* 9:30, p. 68.

45. Ibid., 68 and 71.

46. Ibid., 71.

47. Ibid., 69 and 71.

48. Ibid., 70.

49. Ibid., 72.

50. Ibid., 73.

51. Ibid., 74.

52. Ibid., 75.

53. Avi Ravitsky, "'Ways of Peace' and the Status of Gentiles according to the Rambam: An Exchange of Letters with Rabbi Hayyim David Halevi," in Zohar and Sagi, *A Living Judaism*, 255–85, here 264.

54. Ibid., 260, 264.

55. Ibid., 265.

56. Ibid., 258.

57. Ibid., 257.

58. Ibid., 258.

12

Interreligious Learning and the Formation of Jewish Religious Identity

It is a social scientific truism that social, religious, and cultural identities are not simply established facts. They are produced and reproduced within a matrix of complex social, cultural, political, religious, and economic traditions and realities. Identity is embedded in life.

In commenting upon the Boys-Lee case study, "The Dynamics of Interreligious Learning,"[1] regarding the Catholic-Jewish Colloquium they conceived and supervised, I am mindful of this social scientific perspective. Furthermore, this perspective on identity formation teaches me that the confluence of attitudes and insights, positions, and feelings that I bring with me to this task of analysis and commentary are themselves informed by the multiplicity of forces that have shaped my own way of being in the world, my own multiple dimensions of identity. I am in large measure a person conscious of my minority cultural and religious status as a Jew raised to adulthood in the Southern Baptist environment of Newport News, Virginia. At the same time, I am a rabbi committed to the practice and transmission of Judaism to present and future generations and a professor trained and formed academically in the social sciences as well as religious thought and history through the joint Columbia-Union doctoral program in religion. My own identity, the myriad forces that shape it, and the diverse sensibilities that inform it are not so different from those of virtually all the Jewish participants in the Colloquium.

This reminds me, as I assess the Colloquium and ponder what it says about matters of religious identity formation in the modern world, that I myself as well as the participants in the Colloquium are products of a world in which a sense of "double consciousness" marks us. This phrase, which W. E. B. Dubois employed to describe the reality imposed by a modern American setting upon the consciousness of African Americans and other minority cultural and religious groups, refers to the sense modern persons possess of "always looking at one's self through the eyes of others" (Dubois 1965, 215, 218). As a result, the process of identity formation in the modern setting for both individuals and communities is transformed from what it had been in earlier epochs.

Today forces and realities that are more complex and plural than in the past shape the self as well as the community with which one identifies. This is so for two reasons. The first is that identity can no longer be constructed in isolation from a distant "other." Rather, both the self and the community are realized and established in confrontation with "others" who also inhabit our world. Propinquity and frequent communications among diverse persons and communities are among the marks of our times. The intimacy that such interactions foster falsifies, or at least calls into question, many of the certainties that formerly marked the process of identity formation in prior generations.

The second reason why the process of identity formation in the modern period is so distinct is that persons are fully aware that identity is in large measure socially constructed. Peter Berger has coined the felicitous phrase "the heretical imperative" to characterize this condition that informs virtually all persons and communities in the modern setting. *Hairesis* (option or choice) has become, in Berger's view, the quintessential feature of the modern Occident. It is inescapable. Persons are no longer born and socialized into a community as if by fate. Rather, identity—including religious identity—now becomes in large measure a matter of negotiation, an expression of choice among competing modes of identity, for individuals and communities alike. There is a self-consciousness, a self-recognition, and a self-awareness concerning the role played by society and culture in the establishment of both personal and communal identity that was absent from the world of our ancestors. For them, identity was seen as an "established fact," not the product of "social construction" and "choice" (Berger 1979). As Mary Douglas puts it, "We moderns [are quite self-conscious that we] operate in many different fields of symbolic action." In contrast, "for the Bushman, Dinka, and many primitive cultures, the field of symbolic action is one" (Douglas 1966, 68–69).

The very existence of the type of colloquium discussed in these pages, in which the identity of Christians and Jews is formed and reformed in the dialogical presence of the other, is itself a reflection of the consciousness and social reality that Dubois, Berger, and others contend is the hallmark of the modern situation. Indeed, Boys and Lee themselves testify to the accuracy of these accounts of the modern condition when they observe that the "pluralism" that dominates "our largely secular society . . . compounds the difficult task of forming people in the identity of a particular religious tradition" (p. 422). "Heresy" is now universal. The task of creating "sacred order" in the modern situation turns out to be complex and difficult. How interreligious learning not only reflects this fact but further complicates the task of identity formation in a modern setting of "tolerance and transformation" will constitute the focus of my remarks in this paper.

Formation of Communities

Communities, like individuals, have always, in part, defined themselves and established their identities by drawing boundaries that delineate between themselves and others. Social scientists from Durkheim through Erickson have routinely taken note of this phenomenon. In focusing on notions of social order and group cohesion, these scholars have observed that collectivities often posit or possess an opponent over against whom they have constructed their own sense of identity, their own way of being in the world. The group, by assigning the label of "other" to a rival group, helps to establish its own boundaries by defining specific norms and mores as acceptable forms of practice and belief. The range of beliefs and activities open to persons in the group is thereby limited, and the group is able to state precisely the limits of permissible behavior, belief, and activity for its members. The group, by defining its rival as other, helps to establish its own sense of cohesion and community.

A further word about this phenomenon of "drawing boundaries" will clarify the social mechanics that animate its function in the construction of identity. Designation of a rival group as "other" contributes, from the perspective of the social sciences, directly to the social task of boundary maintenance and subsequent identity formation. In order for one group to exist, there must be another. Social scientists dealing with identity formation routinely note that no group can even be conceived as a group except as set off by itself and made a group by other groups (Barth 1969). People who are members of one community routinely create boundaries between themselves as members of one group and others who are not members of the group. A "we-they dichotomy" is a crucial element among the social mechanisms that groups employ to construct their own identity (Cohen 1978, 379–403). In addition, precisely because groups need to draw boundaries in order to maintain a sense of identity and order for themselves, they are particularly zealous in establishing the limits of permissible behavior and belief in opposition to those beliefs and opinions that the group perceives as most threatening to its own sense of cohesion and identity. The applicability of these insights concerning the dynamics of identity formation and group cohesion are readily apparent when we begin to analyze elements and attitudes displayed by the participants as well as the organizers of the Colloquium.

Jews and Christians are formed, Amos Funkenstein claims, by religious traditions that are "tied to each other with . . . bonds of aversion and fascination, attraction and revulsion" (Boys and Lee, 428). The negative dimension of all this for forging a safe and confident venue for Jewish-Christian interreligious learning, as Boys and Lee note, is that Jews often only associate Christianity "with violence and persecution." Christians, along with their religion, become the preeminent "other" for all too many Jews, and Jewish identity—or at least elements of it—is constructed in opposition to the Christian and his/her Scripture and faith.

Boundary Maintenance and the Experience of the Jewish Participants

Many of the testimonies Jewish participants offered concerning the attitudes they brought with them to the Colloquium provide evidence of the impact of boundary maintenance and the necessity for maintaining the barriers erected by traditional Jewish attitudes concerning Christians and Christianity for the construction of a secure Jewish identity. For example, Lee's own "experiences of Catholics and the Catholic Church growing up in Boston had not predisposed her to Catholic-Jewish dialogue" (Boys and Lee, 421). Nor is this attitude atypical of that expressed by other Jews who engaged in the Colloquium. After all, the Christian Scripture, in the words of one Jewish participant, constituted a "forbidden book" (444).

In short, the challenge of creating a situation of Jewish-Christian interreligious learning and dialogue for contemporary Jews involved with and socialized into the Jewish community is that Jews are raised to think of Christians as persons who regard Jews as "deicides" and who think that the New Testament is above all an anti-Jewish tract. As one participant candidly observed, "We all carry scripts and to stop seeing ourselves and others in those ways is to start out on a journey that has no script and really is frightening, and that on some very basic level . . . [involves] a recrafting of self."

However, this recrafting of self, though frightening, is precisely what transpired in the setting of interreligious learning that Lee and Boys forged. The Colloquium, as the Jewish participants' statements indicate, fulfilled the goal Boys and Lee set of liberating Jews "from a view of Christianity as primarily predicated on rejection and persecution of Jews." Instead, as one Jewish member of the Colloquium so movingly and dramatically phrased it, he was finally able "to hear and understand Christian faith and spirituality in a very different and more open way" when a Christian colleague responded to his question, "Why do you need Jesus?" with the candid reply, "It isn't that we need Jesus. He just is." Or, as another Jewish participant phrased it in recounting her response to the meaning and import of Jesus for Catholics, "Listening to my new [Christian] colleagues that day brought an 'aha' of both understanding and appreciation which was both exhilarating and scary."

In making this assertion, this Jewish participant tacitly rejected the claim put forth over thirty years ago by the late Rabbi Joseph Soloveitchik in opposition to interreligious dialogue. Soloveitchik contended, "Each community is engaged in a singular . . . gesture reflecting the . . . nature of the act of faith itself and it is futile to try to find common denominators" (Soloveitchik 1964, 18–19). For the Jewish participant cited above, the Colloquium resulted in a transformed sense of being Jewish. Jewish identity was no longer dependent upon the rejection of the religiosity and the humanity of the Christian. Christians and their faith could now be seen in empathic hues and no longer confined simply to caricature and stereotype.

Interreligious learning in the presence of the "Christian other" demonstrated to the Jewish participants that Christianity meant and means more than the persecution of Jews. The Church, no matter how heinous its role in provoking anti-Jewish sentiment in the past, also has spoken to the religious and spiritual needs of those devoted to it. The educational environment of the Colloquium and the palpable reality of Christians who were "spiritual and faith oriented" allowed Jews "to discover new ways of seeking and connecting with spirituality and God within their own Jewish tradition." Most important, it permitted Jews, in constructing their own sense of identity, to begin to transcend "the perspective that we are victims and that Christians are potential perpetrators." This, in turn, held important implications for the construction of Jewish identity and self-understanding. As one participant said, "If I view myself as victim, then I actually practice Judaism differently."

Such testimonies indicate that Jewish participants began to recognize the *religious* character of Christianity, that is, the ability of the Church to move its people to profound assertions of faith and significant acts of piety. Such recognition allowed the Jewish participants to move beyond the total rejection of the "Christian other" in the construction of their own identity as Jews. It enabled them to see that neither Jewish pride nor Jewish identity needs to be constructed upon or bolstered by the rejection of the "Christian other." No longer need Jews assert that Christianity is morally and spiritually worthless as a result of its culpability in fostering anti-Jewish attitudes and actions as it has done all too often during the previous two millennia.

The "reconciliation" effected by the Colloquium "threw" its Jewish members "off balance." The vertigo the Colloquium engendered for its Jewish participants resulted from the reconceptualization and reassessment of Jewish self-understanding and identity the Colloquium demanded of its participants. The Christian now had to be seen not simply as another person who participated in the Colloquium. Indeed, there is no reason to suppose that the Jewish participant found this universalistic perspective especially challenging or troublesome even at the outset of the Colloquium. *Rather, the Colloquium compelled the Jews to see their Catholic colleagues and friends in all their particularity as "Christian men and women." The Jewish participant in the Colloquium was forced to recognize that individuals may be good, decent, and spiritual not in spite of but precisely because they are committed Christians.* Christianity, these Jewish participants came to understand, consists of more than a hatred for Jews. It comprises a force for good in the world. Constructing one's identity over against such persons is a much more complex and difficult task than establishing it over against a heinous caricature. It is no wonder, given the role that the Christian has traditionally played as the "preeminent other" for Jews in the construction of their own identity, that the effects of the Colloquium were "dizzying" upon the transformed sense of Jewish self-identity that emerged among its Jewish participants.

Boys and Lee, in planning the Colloquium, affirmed the insight of Diana Eck, whom they quote: "The theological task, and the task of a pluralist society, is to create the space and the means for the encounter of commitments, not to neutralize all commitments." It was thus their hope "that participants would leave the Colloquium with a deepened commitment to their own tradition—to have their own identity strengthened by sustained relationship with the other." Their aim was not to have the participants in the Colloquium surrender to what David Tracy has labeled a "relaxed pluralism" where everything is permitted and where boundaries are neither drawn nor commitments affirmed (Tracy 1985, 451). Rather, they demonstrated that standing in relationship to the other is essential if true dialogue and transformation among persons of "rival religious traditions" are to occur.

The participants—Jews and Catholics alike—transcended borders that precluded such conversation. The venue of a carefully and thoughtfully constructed setting for interreligious learning allowed them to cultivate the ability to listen to and empathize with positions advanced by those who had formerly been seen as preeminently other. The Colloquium demonstrated that when such affirmation and acknowledgment of the other as fully equal occur, identity can be transformed—not obliterated—and serious and respectful conversation can result. The modern situation—one of "heretical imperatives" and "double consciousness"—has made this possible.

The Catholic-Jewish Colloquium succeeded in transforming the identity of its participants because it established a setting in which caricatures of the "other" could no longer be maintained. These caricatures—so understandable in light of the historical circumstances which had forged and maintained the identity of Jews as a religious community distinct and apart from Christians—were initially softened and ultimately dissolved in the face of personal address and encounter.

The value of such dissolution is inestimable because, as Michael Wyschogrod has observed about Jewish intrareligious dialogue:

> There is a value in talking to one another in and by itself, apart from any "result" achieved. . . . To be with fellow [human beings] is to become aware of [their] mode of being in the world, of the reality of [their] being. . . . Let us realize that the alternative to speaking is violence. There is really no such thing as ignoring a fellow human being. Not to speak with my neighbors is a mode of relating to [them], and even if the mode does not immediately express itself in violence, it points onward because the alternative to speech is communication by deed, violent deed. (Wyschogrod 1983, 242)

When persons will not speak with the other, a dehumanization of the other easily arises and a demonization results. As a committed Jew, not only the past history of Jewish-Christian relations but recent events like the slaughter of Muslims engaged in prayer in Hebron in 1994 and the assassination of Prime Minister Yitzhak Rabin in 1995 all too painfully remind me of the tragedy that can ensue when the path of dialogue is not taken.

Colloquia and meetings like the one analyzed in this paper are more than exercises in which the identity of all those who participate is both strengthened and reformulated in the meeting with the other. They also embody additional moral and religious dimensions. By confronting the other in his or her full integrity as a person embedded in tradition, we—as persons informed by and conscious of the imperatives of the modern world—are each reminded of the ineffability of God and of the mystery and infinity that lie at the heart of religion and culture, history and memory. Our traditions and our symbols as well as our rituals—constructed and mediated as we are aware they are through human agency—are fragile and tentative gropings for the reality of the divine whose presence they purport to represent in the world. They are all penultimate. They point toward, but do not fully contain, the Divine, Whose plenitude is beyond all words and rituals. The Colloquium and the setting of interreligious learning it fostered teach us a great deal about how religious identity is constructed and transformed. More importantly, it testifies that members of each tradition can learn from one another even as the uniqueness of each community's own memory and identity are asserted and affirmed.

The enterprise of interreligious learning, so assessed, reflects more than the social dynamics involved in the process of forging a particular community's sense of religious identity. It also contributes to the creation of an atmosphere of mutual respect between former rivals who were all too often actual foes. Interreligious learning, carried out in the manner of the Catholic-Jewish Colloquium, permits its participants to forge a new sense of religious identity. It allows the Jew to assert, as Eugene Borowitz did in *Contemporary Christologies* over a decade ago, "To be sure, I see a substantial difference between my faith and that of the [Christian] theologians I have studied here, but I cannot say that their wisdom is only 'human wisdom.' They know a great deal about the God of my people and their knowledge has consequences for their lives [as well as my own] in ways . . . which are recognizably directed to God's service" (Borowitz 1980, 190).

NOTE

1. "The Dynamics of Interreligious Learning" in *Religious Education* 91 (Fall 1996): 420–66.

REFERENCES

Barth, F. 1969. *Ethnic Groups and Boundaries: The Social Organization of Culture*. London: Allen and Unwin.

Berger, Peter. 1979. *The Heretical Imperative*. Garden City NY: Anchor Books.

Borowitz, Eugene B. 1980. *Contemporary Christologies*. New York: Paulist Press.

Cohen, Ronald. 1978. "Ethnicity: Problem and Focus in Anthropology." *Annual Review of Anthropology* 7: 379–403.

Douglas, Mary. 1966. *Purity and Danger*. London: Routledge and Kegan Paul.

Dubois, W. E. B. 1965. *The Souls of Black Folks in Three Negro Classics*. New York: Avon Books.

Soloveitchik, Joseph. 1964. "Confrontation." *Tradition* 6: 5–30.

Tracy, David. 1985. *The Analogical Imagination*. New York: Crossroads.

Wyschogrod, Michael. 1983. *The Body of Faith*. New York: Seabury Press.

THREE

Visions for Israel

13

A Zionist Reading of Abraham Geiger and His Biblical Scholarship

Abraham Geiger (1810–74) of Breslau and Berlin was by any standards a scholar of prodigious proportions with an encyclopedic knowledge of Jewish sources. No area of Jewish learning was beyond his purview or expertise, and his publications span virtually every area of Jewish interest. At the same time, he was an activist who championed the cause of Jewish religious reform and who established, in 1872, the Hochschule für die Wissenschaft des Judentums, the major educational institution for the training of German and central European Reform rabbis. Geiger has modeled for many modern Jewish academics what it means to be an engaged scholar who attempts to be as dispassionate and objective in their scholarship as is humanly possible while having great concern for the practical life and vitality of contemporary Jewish life and Jewish spirit.

Tamara Cohn Eskenazi surely embodies the paradigm Geiger established in her own career and scholarship. Raised in Israel, hers is a life of engaged Jewish biblical scholarship and concern at its best. I am therefore delighted to dedicate this essay to Professor Eskenazi on the assessment that Zionist historians Menachem Soloveitchik and Zalman Rubashov offered of Geiger and his work on the Bible in their *Toldot bikoret hamikra—l'madaei ha-mikra (A History of Biblical Criticism—Part I of a Series in the Science of the Bible)*, published in Berlin by D'vir in 1925. This essay will not actually discuss Geiger's biblical studies per se. Rather, as a work of *Rezeptionsgeschichte*, this article will focus on how two Zionist students of modem biblical criticism in the generations after Geiger presented the legacy Geiger bequeathed the world in the area of biblical scholarship. As such, my hope is that this essay will provide a contribution to modern Zionist intellectual history and that it will express my esteem and regard for the manifold contributions Dr. Eskenazi has made to Jewish and academic life.

The Authors

In order to appreciate the nature of their summary and evaluation of Geiger on the Bible, it is necessary to provide background on both Soloveitchik and Rubashov. Menachem Soloveitchik, while perhaps distantly related to the famed family of Lithuanian rabbinic scholars, was not directly linked to them. Rather, Soloveitchik, who was born in Kovno in 1883 and died in Israel in 1957, was a prominent political figure and Zionist leader as well as biblical scholar. A scion of a distinguished and wealthy family, he was known to the larger world as Max Solieli, even as he published in Hebrew under the name Soloveitchik. As a young man, Solilei studied at the university in St. Petersburg and continued his education later at various institutions of higher learning in Germany. His particular interest was in the biblical period.

An active Zionist from his youth in Saint Petersburg, he was among the founders of the Russian-language Zionist journal *Jewish Life* in 1904. With the establishment of the state of Lithuania, Solieli was elected to its parliament (Seimas) and served as minister of Jewish affairs from 1919 to 1921. He proved adept as a leader of a community divided by ideological differences and as a defender of Jewish rights. Perhaps discouraged by efforts to curtail Jewish autonomy in Lithuania, in 1922 he left for London, where he served briefly as a member of the Zionist executive, resigning after about a year over differences with Chaim Weizmann. In 1923, Solieli moved to Berlin, where he was an editor of the *Encyclopedia Judaica* until 1933, overseeing articles devoted to the Bible and the ancient Near East. Solieli moved to Palestine in 1933 and settled in Haifa, where he held a number of leadership positions. With the establishment of the State of Israel in 1948, he was appointed director of Kol Yisra' el, the broadcast service of Israel. His publications include *Basic Problems of Biblical Science*, written in Russian in 1913, and, with Rubashov, *Toldot bikoret ha-Mikra*, the source for this essay.[1]

Zalman Rubashov (Shneur Zalman Rubashov), better known as Zalman Shazar, was president of Israel from 1963 to 1973. Shazar (an acronym for Shneur Zalman Rubashov) was born in Mir in the province of Minsk in 1889. In 1892, after a disastrous fire in Mir, his family moved to the nearby town of Stolbtsy, where Shazar received a *heder* education under the influence of Habad, in addition to being influenced by his parents' Zionism.

Shazar's writings span seventy years. His literary work took many forms, from poetry and autobiographical fiction, to scholarly treatises and journalistic articles. As early as his student days, Shazar had been drawn to the study of the Sabbatean movement and to biblical criticism. In the former he was attracted by the passion for national redemption, which he sensed as central within the mystic yearning of European Jewry in the dark days of the seventeenth century. He wrote his first article on the subject in *Ha-Shilo'ah* in 1913. His work on the subject of Jewish mysticism was published in the *Russian Jewish Encyclopedia* and was praised by Gershom Scholem.

In the field of biblical criticism, Shazar played a pioneering role in introducing this field to a Modern Hebrew language audience. He had himself studied biblical criticism at the University of Strasbourg, and in 1914 he translated the Russian essays of Solieli on the subject, *Basic Problems of Biblical Science*, into Hebrew.

Soloveitchik, Rubashov, and the Project of Biblical Criticism

In light of this brief biographical background, we can now assess how these two men—so devoted both to scholarship and to the cause of Zionism and the Jewish state—presented and analyzed the work of Abraham Geiger, whose scholarship they appreciated and admired even as they departed radically from the stance he adopted toward the matter of Jewish nationalism. To fully appreciate the presentation and analysis Soloveitchik and Rubashov offered of Geiger, it is instructive to view their writing on Geiger in the larger framework of their entire book. In the introduction to *Toldot bikoret ha-mikra*, they point out how difficult it had been to introduce biblical criticism into the Jewish world. Due to the centrality of the Bible in Western civilization, they contended that this field of study commanded great attention in the Western world. However, because the Bible, unlike, for example, Greek and Roman literature, was of religious significance and was therefore primarily within the province of the Church, such scholarship could not be separated from parochial religious concerns. Moreover, because such concerns were of practical significance to the lives of believers, it was difficult for such scholarship to be dispassionate, as the authors of these writings generally intended to promote particularistic religious viewpoints. Thus Soloveitchik and Rubashov maintained that Catholic and Protestant biblical scholars employed their researches in completely different ways, often to favor and defend the stances of one tradition as opposed to the other. In making this observation, the Jewish scholars surely seemed to imply that a Jewish approach to this topic might well be marked by the same confessional, if not tendentious, goals.[2]

Soloveitchik and Rubashov then turned to the matter of biblical criticism and its reception in Jewish circles. They noted that critical research by Jews in this field was virtually completely neglected (*nisharah be-emet bod'dah b'mo'adah*). They claimed that Jewish scholars had long feared that such a critical approach to the Bible would destroy the tradition. However, slowly, in the late eighteenth century and certainly in the nineteenth, the first representatives of the new spirit of criticism began to arise (*koh v'koh niru ha-natzigim harishonim, m'vasrei ha-shinui*). Judaism and its supporters could not remain isolated, hermetically sealed off from the surrounding influences of Western culture. The world of science and that of the Jewish world began to meet and encounter one another *panim el panim*, face to face. "Therefore the hour has approached where the barrier [between two worlds] must fall, [the barrier that separates the people] who are the creators [of the Bible] from their creation, and the scientific work that describes its context." Soloveitchik and Rubashov maintained that there was no need for committed Jews to fear this trend. Indeed, in a vein that reflects their own confidence in the all-encompassing strength of Jewish national revival in *Eretz Yisrael*, they maintained that new threads link modern critical biblical scholarship "with the remarkable period that is unfolding in the land of our ancestors (*'im tekufat mofeit b'eretz avot*)." Like the Protestant and Catholic scholars they referred to in their introduction, Soloveitchik and Rubashov, even as they were committed to the "objective" canons of modern scholarship, also believed that this scholarship could serve particular ends and values, i.e., the national project of the Jewish people as expressed in the Zionist movement. They asserted: "And from this consciousness the idea was born several years ago to attempt to present in a summary way the results of scientific biblical studies to a Hebrew audience (*U'mitokh hakarah zo nolad b'kirbeinu lifnei shanim ahadot ha-ra'ayon l'nasot la-geshet l'siduram shel ma-daei ha-mikra b'ivrit b'tzurat sikum*)."[3]

Soloveitchik and Rubashov stated that *Toldot bikoret ha-mikra* was to be organized and presented in the following manner. They claimed that their aim, first and foremost, was to present the complex findings related to the disciplines of critical biblical studies and criticism to a Hebrew-reading audience. This would allow the Jewish people to leave their isolation and allow Jews and Gentiles alike to recognize that the Bible occupied a proper place of honor among the classics of world literature and that the foundational narratives and teachings of the Jewish people were intimately connected to universalistic thought. They stated that their book was not directed principally at the scholar or researcher. Rather, they sought to address the "community of [Hebrew] readers, those who are lifting up the life and creation of the Hebrew nation in our generation (*kahal ha-korim, nosei hayyim v'ha-y'tzirah shel ha-uma ha-ivrit b'doreinu*)."[4] *Toldot bikoret ha-mikra* would allow these Jews to understand and appreciate the literary, religious, cultural, historical, and social dimensions of Jewish life during the period of the Bible.

Toldot bikoret ha-mikra: *Structure and Content*

Toldot bikoret ha-mikra is divided into three parts. The first part contains seven chapters that deal with the canonization of the Bible, critical observations on the process of canonization of the biblical text as presented in the Talmud, treatment of the Bible in medieval Babylon among the Geonim (Saadia figures here in a prominent way), Jewish biblical exegetes throughout history (ranging from figures in Spain such as lbn Ezra to men such as Rashi and Karo through Menasseh ben Israel), Christian exegetes, and Spinoza and his opinions on Scripture. In the second section of their book, Soloveitchik and Rubashov move directly to the field of "scientific criticism" (*ha-bikoret ha-mada'it*). This section deals with source-critical theory, the documentary hypothesis, and the work of Wellhausen and his school, the influence of archaeology on a scientific understanding of the Bible, and a concluding section on numerous other modern critics. It is only in the third section of their book that Soloveitchik and Rubashov return to the Jewish world and offer their analysis of Jewish biblical criticism in the nineteenth century.[5]

In this third section, entitled "Criticism in Israel during the Nineteenth Century," Soloveitchik and Rubashov preface their assessment of Geiger and provide the intellectual context for and understanding of his work on the Bible. They do so by explaining how a critical approach to the study of the Bible arose among Jews at the end of the eighteenth century and the first decades of the 1800s through a focus on the writings of

Moses Mendelssohn (1729–86) and Leopold Zunz (1795–1886).[6] Soloveit-chik and Rubashov were aware that rabbinical literature was traditionally the primary focus of religious study for Jews. After all, Judaism is not the religion of the Bible alone. *Sola scriptura* is alien to the Jewish religion. Rather, Judaism is the religion of the Bible as refracted through the lens of rabbinic interpretation and literature. The Bible *qua* Bible was therefore neglected as a primary object of study for Jews throughout the millennia. Instead, rabbinic literatures in all their varieties—law, narratives, codes, and commentaries—were traditionally the major foci of Jewish concerns.

As Soloveitchik and Rubashov argued, this Jewish concentration on rabbinic literature and relative neglect of the Bible began to change with the writings of Moses Mendelssohn and his circle. The 1781 Mendelssohn translation of the Bible into German was within two decades after its appearance universally present in virtually every German Jewish house-hold. Furthermore, the *Bi'ur*, the famed Hebrew commentary that Men-delssohn and his circle offered on the Bible, facilitated a greater interest among Jews in the Bible as a topic worthy of study in its own right. Johann Gottfried Eichhorn (1753–1827), a "father of Old Testament criticism," and other critical Christian scholars also had a great influence on the *Bi'ur*. Nevertheless, Mendelssohn, even as he was aware of Christian scholar-ship, still refrained from adopting a critical approach to the Bible. In his introduction to his *Bi'ur*, Soloveitchik and Rubashov quote Mendelssohn as saying that for secular non-Jewish critics, the Torah is nothing more than "a book of chronicles [required] for understanding the events of antiq-uity." However, "Even it is regarded in this way by the sages of the nations and their students, for us in the Household of Israel it is not so (*'im yita-khen zeh l'hachmei ha-amim v'talmideihem, lanu beit yisrael lo yitakhen*)."[7]

While the Mendelssohn translation and the *Bi'ur* did not fully embody a critical approach to Scripture, Soloveitchik and Rubashov pointed out that they were nevertheless vehicles that permitted the Jews to emerge from their previous cultural segregation and primary focus on rabbinic literature into the mainstream of German cultural life. The Mendelssohn Bible translation and biblical commentary facilitated the assimilation of German values and viewpoints on the part of German Jews and caused many of them to place an emphasis upon the Bible as opposed to rab-binic literature. While they were careful to point out that Mendelssohn could hardly be labeled a critical scholar of the Bible, his work nevertheless constituted a nascent turning point for an emerging Jewish interest in the Bible as a subject for serious consideration in its own right.[8]

However, it was to be several decades after Mendelssohn before this Jewish turning toward the Bible would be complete. Indeed, Soloveitchik and Rubashov observed that as the discipline of *Wissenschaft des Judentums* began to emerge, biblical criticism was not initially given a significant, if any, place in this burgeoning field of study. For example, they point out that when Eduard Gans, who stood at the head of the "Society for Culture and Scientific Study of the Jews" (*Verein fuer Kultur und Wissenschaft des Juden*), organized in Berlin in 1819, first advanced the notion of an academic study of Judaism, he did not mention biblical studies at all in his inaugural speech outlining the aims of the society.[9]

In featuring the work of the incomparable Leopold Zunz (1795–1886), the most magisterial and prolific scholar of Jewish studies during the nineteenth century, Soloveitchik and Rubashov reinforced the point they made regarding Gans when they stated that study of the Bible was not initially at the center of Jewish academic concerns in the early decades of the 1800s. They emphasized that Zunz did not devote his early scientific studies to the Bible but to medieval Jewish literature. Zunz, like other Jewish scholars, initially centered his work on the Talmud and other genres of rabbinic literature and placed them in primary focus even as he neglected the Bible as a topic for independent study. Soloveitchik and Rubashov claimed he did this not only because of the traditional Jewish concentration on rabbinic genres of literature but also because it was this literature, not the Bible, that distinguished Judaism from Christianity.[10]

Nevertheless, the impact of the modern world and the directions of nineteenth-century academic scholarship in the Western university upon Jewish scholars were unrelenting in transforming Jewish cultural and religious life. These forces opened the way for the field of biblical studies to gain more attention from Jewish researchers—including Zunz himself.[11]

Relying strongly upon the Mendelssohn translation, Zunz offered his own translation of the Bible in 1837–38. Shortly thereafter, he turned to the Tanakh itself. However, as Soloveitchik and Rubashov point out, Zunz did not choose to subject the first five books of the Bible to critical scrutiny. The classical Jewish religious commitment to the notion of Mosaic authorship of the *Humash* dissuaded him from moving in this direction. Instead, Zunz chose to investigate the later writings of the Bible, specifically Chronicles and parts of *Ketuvim*. Zunz claimed that parts of Psalms were surely written in Babylon during the Exile and that Ezra, Nehemiah, and Chronicles were divided at a later period in Jewish history. Originally, Zunz maintained that they constituted one book. Krochmal and Geiger both accepted these findings of Zunz, and it was upon these foundations that Zunz laid that Geiger constructed his own initial works in the field of Bible.[12]

Having constructed this context, Soloveitchik and Rubashov were now prepared to turn to Geiger. They pointed out that Geiger began his famed *Urschrift* by focusing on the period in Jewish history that marked the Jewish return from Exile in Babylonia through the period of the Hasmoneans.[13] In their summary of his researches on the Second Temple period, the authors of *Toldot bikoret ha-mikra* indicated that Geiger pointed out that the authors of Chronicles were *b'nei Tzadok*, Sadducees, from the priestly family, and their aim was to indicate to their contemporaries that the priesthood and temple worship were at the center of "Jewish national life" (*hayei ha-umah*).[14]

Foremost among the concerns of these priestly authors was the problem of intermarriage. In their view, these foreign women adversely affected the spirit of the people, and they reported that Geiger emphasized this element in his interpretations of these books. Thus Geiger pointed out changes that distinguished the approach and emphases found in Chronicles and Kings from the writings of the early prophets. For example, in 2 Kings 12.22, it is written of the servants who assassinated King Joash of Judah, "His courtiers formed a conspiracy against Joash and assassinated him at Beth-millo that leads down to Silla. The courtiers who assassinated him were Jozabad son of Shimeath and Jehozabad son of Shomer." In contrast, 2 Chron. 24.26 identifies the two assassins as Zabad son of Shimeath *the Ammonitess* and Jehozabad son of Shimrith *the Moabitess*. By explicitly pointing to the fact that the mothers of Zabad and Jehozabad were foreign women, Soloveitchik and Rubashov emphasized that Geiger argued that the author of Chronicles wanted to indicate that the evil that befell the land was the result of intermarrying with "the daughters of the land."[15]

Soloveitchik and Rubashov continued by pointing out that Geiger cited 1 Kings 11.1 to bolster this argument. There it is written, "King Solomon loved many foreign women in addition to Pharaoh's daughter—Moabite, Ammonite, Edomite, Phoenician, and Hittite women." In contrast, Geiger explained that 2 Chron. 8.11 omits mention of all foreign wives except Pharaoh's daughter when it states, "Solomon brought up Pharaoh's daughter from the City of David to the place he had built for her, for he said, 'No wife of mine shall dwell in a palace of King David of Israel, for [the area] is sacred since the Ark of the Lord has entered it.'" Geiger asserted that this was done so as to minimize the force of the precedent King Solomon represented for the men of this era regarding the legitimacy of intermarriage. Indeed, had the story of Pharaoh's daughter being married to Solomon not been so well known, Geiger was of the opinion that mention of this marriage would have been omitted altogether. However, that option was not possible given the widespread dissemination of this narrative among the people. Hence it was retained even as the author of Chronicles emphasized that her access to the sacred places of the Jewish people was circumscribed, i.e., she could not enter the palace of King David because it had housed the Ark of the Lord. From this and countless other examples that he brought, Soloveitchik and Rubashov stated that Geiger drew the following conclusion: "Every generation, every spiritual movement and every personality projected their own stances and views onto Scripture." In so doing, the "spiritual and national consciousness" of each generation served as a "crown" (*k'lil*) that supplemented the "holy legacy" it had received. In this way, Judaism and its adherents succeeded in making the traditions (*massoret*) they received from previous generations enduringly relevant. Geiger utilized the critical study of the Bible to maintain that the text was constantly created anew in the image and views provided by each succeeding generation (*b'tzilmah kidemutah*). Soloveitchik and Rubashov concluded from this: "And the entire book of Geiger is nothing more than a commentary upon this overarching rule (*v'kol hasefer shel Geiger eino ela peirush l'klal gadol zeh*)." Scholarship had surely been employed in the service of faith.[16]

Soloveitchik and Rubashov then emphasized that while Geiger devoted considerable attention to various translations of the Bible and argued that 1 Maccabees showed Sadduceean influence while 2 Maccabees displayed Pharisaic influence, they maintained that the bulk of his *Urschrift* was focused on changes that were present in the body of Scripture itself over the generations. The *Urschrift* demonstrated over and over again that each generation in Israel arrogated to itself the right of assessing "Holy Scripture" through its own spirit and from its own perspective. The Tanakh, as *sefer ha-sefarim*, the Book of Books, was "a living document intertwined with the soul of the people." They noted that Geiger especially emphasized that these changes were designed to "preserve the purity of the God concept (*lishmor 'al taharat ha-musag shel ha-elohut*)" and to protect "the honor of the people Israel (*she'mirat k'vod yisrael*)."[17]

In looking at this last claim, it is instructive to turn to the work of Nahum Sarna, who, in his essay "Abraham Geiger and Biblical Scholarship," asserted that Geiger, invoking Judah Halevi, believed that the Jews had an inherent capacity to grasp revelation and that this disposition was present not just in individuals but in the Jewish people as a whole. Sarna cites a famous passage in Geiger, who asks:

> How did it happen that such a people, a mere tribe surrounded by so many mightier nations, which had no opportunity of having an unobstructed view of the great events in the world, which had to fight many battles for its bare existence, which was confined within a limited territory and had to employ all its resources to defend itself against its powerful enemies—how did it happen that such a people rose to those sublime conceptions? It is an enigma in the world's history.[18]

Commenting upon this passage, Sarna observes, "Geiger here parts company with his contemporary Christian scholars, who saw in the biblical description of idolatry the true national religion [of the Jewish people]" and who viewed Israel's constant "infidelity" as "the fruit" of the increasingly retrograde beliefs that marked the Jewish people. Sarna contends that several Jewish scholars (including Jacob Agus and Joseph Klausner) "have noted the striking similarity between Geiger's idea of the original, intuitive, spontaneous, and national character of Israelite monotheism and the basic premise of the great *Toldot ha-emunah ha-yisraelit* (*The History of the Religion of Israel*) by Yehezkel Kaufmann." Sarna concludes by maintaining that in Geiger's scholarship "the history of the biblical text is interwoven with the history of the people."[19]

In offering this observation on Geiger's work, Sarna echoes elements of the assessment Soloveitchik and Rubashov had provided of Geiger more than half a century earlier. How ironic it is that Abraham Geiger, the great anti-nationalist, would be considered—in his biblical studies—a spiritual forerunner and ancestor of the great Hebrew University biblical scholar and Zionist Yehezkel Kaufmann. It is fascinating as well that Soloveitchik and Shazar regard Geiger as championing the Jewish national spirit by defending the honor of the Jewish people and by his claim that the Jews as a people possessed an original religious genius. In reflecting on Geiger and this aspect of his scholarly legacy, the treatment that the Zionists Soloveitchik and Rubashov accorded the anti-nationalist Geiger in the course of their writings on biblical criticism demonstrates that history, if not cunning, is at least paradoxical and that the muse of history surely possesses a sense of humor. The engagements of Geiger and his work in the enterprise of the Jewish people and the Jewish religion were profound, and they mirror the engagements of my friend Tamara Eskenazi, to whom this essay is dedicated.

NOTES

1. For these biographical data on Solieli, see *Encyclopaedia judaica* , *s.v.* 'Solieli (Soloveichik), Mordecai (Max); as well as Isaac Gruenbaum, "Dr. Menachem (Max) Soloveichik-Solieli," in *P'nei ha-dor* (Jerusalem, 5718/1956), 306–11 [Hebrew] and Alexander Manor, *Zalman Shazar: Yihudo v'ytzirato* (Tel Aviv, 5721/1961) [Hebrew].

2. See the introduction to M. Soloveitchik and Zalman Rubashov, *Toldot bikoret ha-mikra* (Berlin: D'vir, 5685–1925), 1.

3. Ibid., 1–2.

4. Ibid., 3.

5. Ibid., table of contents, v–vii.

6. Ibid., 125–27.

7. Ibid., 127.

8. Ibid., 125–26.

9. Ibid., 128.

10. Ibid.

11. Ibid., 125–29.

12. Ibid., 128–29.

13. Abraham Geiger, *Urschrift und Uebersetzungen der Bibel in iher Abhaengigkelt von der inneren Entwickelung des Judenthums* (Breslau: J. Hainauer, 1857).

14. Soloveitchik and Rubashov, *Toldot bikoret ha-mikra*, 129.

15. Ibid., 130.

16. Ibid.

17. Ibid., 131.

18. Cited in Nahum M. Sarna, "Abraham Geiger and Biblical Scholarship," in *New Perspectives on Abraham Geiger,* ed. Jakob J. Petuchowski (Cincinnati: Hebrew Union College Press, 1975), 24.

19. Ibid., 24–25.

14

National Sovereignty, Jewish Identity, and the "Sake of Heaven"

The Impact of Residence in Israel on Halakhic Rulings on Conversion

With the establishment of the State of Israel in 1948, Jews renewed their political sovereignty in their ancestral homeland. This transformation in the Jewish condition—in the State of Israel, the Jewish people were now in a position to craft public policy and they constituted a demographic majority—meant that conversion to Judaism in the State would take place within a social and political context that was substantively different from that which had obtained for the Jewish community throughout almost two thousand years of Diaspora life. With the advent of the Jewish State, conversion to Judaism would no longer take place in a setting where Jews were a minority—often a powerless one. This essay will demonstrate that in a significant number of instances this new reality led several chief Ashkenazic rabbis—and other Orthodox authorities as well—to expand traditional understandings of Jewish laws concerning conversion and to apply standards for conversion that prior to Jewish sovereignty would not have been seriously entertained by Orthodox figures.

In this essay, we will analyze selected legal writings authored by Ashkenazic Chief Rabbis Isaac Halevi Herzog, Isser Yehuda Unterman, and Shlomo Goren on the subject of conversion in the State of Israel, as well as the works of contemporary rabbinic figures who echo their views. We will show that the variable of Jewish "return to the Land" and subsequent residence there by persons desirous of converting to Judaism has served as a decisive factor in causing these Orthodox rabbis to issue judgments accepting these people into the Jewish fold. These rabbis have done this despite their (almost certainly correct) assumption that these converts would fail to observe classical Jewish law *in toto* subsequent to their conversion, a fact that outside of Israel would have made it very difficult for an Orthodox authority to sanction the conversion.

In offering our analysis of these writings and this phenomenon, we will show that the decisions these rabbis have made regarding conversion are informed above all by the facts that Israel is a Jewish state with a Jewish majority, and that these *poskim* in Israel are clearly making not only religious policy for a religious community, but public policy for a Jewish national entity blessed with political autonomy. While classic halakhic literature has long required that conversions be motivated exclusively "for the sake of heaven," the rabbis we will examine suggest that this criterion can be fulfilled by standards other than rigorous observance of the commandments. As we will see, life among the Jewish people in the Jewish State itself became a new and sufficient criterion to justify conversion. Thus once the State of Israel was created, the rabbis we will examine suggest, Jewish communities had a new criterion for fulfilling that most basic condition for conversion, and by implication, for redefining the very bedrock of what we might today call Jewish identity.

Chief Rabbi Isaac Halevi Herzog

After serving as rabbi of Belfast and Dublin, Rabbi Isaac Herzog (1888– 1959) was invited in 1936 to succeed Rabbi Abraham Isaac Kook as the second Ashkenazic chief rabbi of Israel. Rabbi Herzog wrote a number of responsa in which he insisted that genuine acceptance of all the commandments (*kabbalat 'ol mitzvot*) was a prerequisite for conversion. Indeed, in a number of instances, he contended that the various compromises entertained by some Orthodox rabbis for allowing nonobservant persons entry into the Jewish people were inappropriate. He frequently dismissed these "lenient rulings" on the grounds that those leniencies were created in a premodern setting where the Jewish community was traditionally observant. However, the changed sociological, cultural, and demographic realities of the modern era had diminished the power of Jewish communities to influence the practice of newly converted Jews. The now porous boundaries of Jewish communities in Europe had attenuated Jewish commitment and practice among countless Jews and the larger Jewish community itself was no longer predominantly observant. Therefore, the community could not realistically be expected to have the positive influence on converts that they might once have had, and no assumption could be made that the convert would likely adhere to the commandments. Consequently, a more stringent attitude regarding conversion to Judaism was required in his own day.[1]

In light of this tendency to restrictive rulings on his part, it is particularly fascinating to see how the existence of the State of Israel became a decisive factor for Rabbi Herzog in a number of his rulings in cases of conversion.[2] The language of a question submitted to him by an anonymous European rabbi living outside of Israel, dated December 23, 1948 (just months after Israel's Declaration of Independence, and while the War of Independence was still being fought), reveals the impact that the State in the aftermath of the Holocaust had upon his thinking in this area. His questioner wrote:

> Lately there has been an increase in the number of cases [in which] Jewish people in our country are married to non-Jewish women in their courts, and they now seek to convert them and marry them with *huppah* and *kiddushin* because they wish to immigrate to Israel.
>
> In general, [special consideration might be given] to these gentile women, since they saved their husbands from death during the Holocaust by their refusal to obey the Nazis' demands to divorce them. By doing so, they placed themselves in grave danger and were sent to concentration camps. . . .
>
> Until now, I have refused to bring these people under the wings of the Jewish people because their intention is not [to convert] for the sake of heaven, but rather, for the sake of *aliyah*, and in this, I followed the ruling of the *Shulhan Arukh* [*Yoreh Deah* 268:12] . . . I see the magnitude of the horrific tragedy for hundreds of families who wish to make *aliyah,* but, at the same time, my heart hesitates to take such responsibility upon myself [by converting these women to Judaism].

In considering the questioner's dilemma, Rabbi Herzog first addressed a few technical textual issues and then proceeded to the case at hand. While he asserted that those already married in civil courts were not converting "for the sake of marriage," Herzog also contended that he did not believe that these converts were converting "for the sake of heaven" as normative Jewish law would presumably demand. Rather, they were converting only because they wished to immigrate to the land of Israel. Yet he did not hesitate to "solve" this problem by offering a novel understanding and redefinition of how "conversion for the sake of heaven" could be understood. The responsum merits lengthy quotation:

> [Here] the concern is that their intention is [to convert] for the sake of making *aliyah* to Israel, [not for the sake of heaven]. However, this depends on the situation in your country. If the conditions are such that as foreigners they could not stay in your country, then it is obvious that their intention is not for the sake of heaven. Yet, if it were possible for them to remain in [their current] country, but they desire *Eretz Yisrael* [the Land of Israel], this can be seen as an intention "for the sake of heaven." For they are uprooting their dwelling places and abandoning their sources of income to migrate specifically . . . to the Land of Israel. Thus, it becomes clear that their desire is to cling to the Jewish people, in its Land. . . . And this is a good intention, and there is no need to prevent their conversion.

While Rabbi Herzog never explicitly states that the enormity of the human tragedy that would result from a failure to allow the conversion "trumps" the authority of the text of the *Shulhan Arukh*, he seems moved by the human dimension of the problem and responds by implicitly reconceptualizing the notion of "for the sake of heaven" in light of Israel's recent creation. Indeed, Rabbi Herzog seems to be implying that a commitment to the State of Israel constitutes a commitment to Judaism and the Jewish people sufficient to justify conversion. Indeed, joining the Zionist enterprise is "to serve heaven," whether or not the convert's intention is clearly to observe the commandments as Rabbi Herzog would surely prefer. Seemingly overwhelmed by the momentousness of Israel's creation just a few months earlier, Herzog concludes the responsum almost poetically by writing, "Signed with the blessing of Zion and Jerusalem, hoping to see you soon in our Holy City, May it Be Speedily Rebuilt."

Chief Rabbi Isser Yehuda Unterman

The daring and creative train of thought that Rabbi Herzog put forth in this particular responsum was echoed in the writings of his successor as chief Ashkenazic rabbi, Isser Yehuda Unterman (1886–1976). Born in Brest-Litovsk, Unterman had previously served as the head rabbi of Liverpool, and subsequently, as the chief rabbi of Tel Aviv (beginning in 1946). He served as chief rabbi of Israel from 1964 until 1972.

In an article on laws of conversion and their application written in the early 1970s, Rabbi Unterman dealt specifically with the question of potential candidates for conversion whom the rabbinic court suspects are most unlikely to observe the commandments subsequent to conversion. The occasion for his confronting this issue was the arrival on Israeli shores of a vast body of intermarried immigrants who were unfamiliar with Judaism and its practices. The question of converting these persons to Judaism, he noted, was not merely a theoretical one. It was "a practical one of pressing urgency" that demanded a policy position for the benefit of these people and the Israeli polity they had now entered.

As Rabbi Unterman wrote at the outset of his work regarding these persons, "The urgency informing this matter is that they are likely to be absorbed rapidly into the community and their [non-Jewish] origin will soon be forgotten." He stated that it was of great import for the Jewish community and State of Israel to find a positive solution that would resolve this dilemma despite two issues that explicitly disturbed him. First, he was unsettled by the fact that such conversions would be conducted in violation of the long-standing law that forbids conversion of a non-Jewish partner who does so in order to marry a Jewish man or woman.[3] Second, he knew full well that it was highly unlikely that there could be a genuine "acceptance of the yoke of the commandments" in the case of such a convert inasmuch as the would-be convert already lived with a Jewish partner who did not observe Jewish law. Therefore, these conversions would also violate the standard that insisted the prospective converts agree to the rigorous observance of Jewish law.[4]

Rabbi Unterman continued by acknowledging that most rabbis in the Diaspora were extremely stringent in not accepting persons such as these as converts. Indeed, he observed that when he had served as a rabbi in England prior to his *aliyah* he himself was very strict in not allowing such persons into the Jewish fold.[5] R. Unterman noted that there were two reasons to distinguish the situation and proper rabbinical response in the Diaspora from the situation and response in Israel. First, the sheer number of such cases in the Diaspora meant that if the rabbinate was lenient in accepting such persons, then intermarriage was likely to be seen as tolerated by the rabbis and would therefore increase. Second, he noted, the fact that converts to Judaism in the Diaspora remained in a Christian setting and were not disconnected from their former lives made them much less likely to make a full transition to committed Jewish life. All this applied to a Diaspora setting in which the "convert remained in the locale and atmosphere where he was raised and educated as a gentile." However, "when he is uprooted from his setting and comes to convert among us [in Israel] where he is far removed from his surroundings, it is well to examine [the situation differently]." Like Rabbi Herzog, he indicated that the profundity of the all-encompassing Jewish experience in the State of Israel and the theological significance of living attached to such experience created reason to be more lenient and welcoming than was the case outside the Land and State of Israel.[6]

Of course, R. Unterman was aware that most of these converts remained nonobservant even after their conversions. He noted that a number of authorities asserted, on the basis of Maimonides' statement that a conversion could not be affirmed as legally valid "until the righteousness of the convert was apparent—'ad she-yitba'rer tzidkato,"[7] that such "converts" should not be affirmed as Jewish as his or her nonobservance proved that "his righteousness" was most assuredly "not apparent." However, R. Unterman claimed that this Maimonidean passage could only be applied in an instance where converts reverted to "idolatry itself—la'a-vod 'avodah zarah." In Israel, "where there is no fear whatsoever of such idolatry," this passage is inapplicable, and there is no reason to be suspicious of these persons in that way whatsoever.

Furthermore, R. Unterman emphasized strongly that subsequent nonobservance of the commandments on the part of the convert in no way demonstrated that the intention of the "convert" was in fact insincere at the moment when he or she pledged to observe the Jewish faith. He stated that he found "astonishing" any ruling that would exclude these converts and their progeny from the Jewish fold on the basis of the claim that the convert was nonobservant after conversion. He stated forthrightly, "We have never heard of such a thing."

Rabbi Unterman contended that normative Jewish law asserted that a proper acceptance of the yoke of the commandments was effectuated when the convert, at the moment of conversion, "accepts upon himself with no mental reservations the observance of the commandments." Employing Maimonides, *Hilchot Issurei Bi'ah 13:17*, as a warrant, R. Unterman stated, "Even if a convert later transgresses the commandments, this does not legally impair his conversion." A convert, immediately after his immersion before proper witnesses, is a Jew, and if he subsequently violates Jewish law, then he is simply "a sinful Jew" (*Tosefta D'mai* 2:4). R. Unterman ruled that the betrothal of such a Jew is valid, "for after immersion, he is a Jew in every respect." Indeed, if one has already converted, "even [in an instance] where he does revert to idolatry, he is "a sinful and rebellious Jew—*yisrael mumar*" and his conversion cannot be undone.

In speaking specifically of the Russian immigrants who came to Israel as mixed couples, Rabbi Unterman stated that we should not be stringent with them as they "have come from there to here full of bitterness against the persecution of Jews and the calumnies issued against our holy religion" by their Gentile friends and relatives. When we accept them with kindness, "they connect to the Jewish people—*'am yehudi* with a full heart."[8] They are "partners in the suffering and degradations hurled at our people." Their attachment to the Jewish people in the Land of Israel demonstrates that "from a situation of degradation, the light of the people Israel has shone."[9]

The emphasis R. Unterman placed on the significance of peoplehood and land as decisive rationales for allowing these persons admittance into Judaism is evidenced in the following comment he added to support his position. He wrote, "In respect to the question before us, there is an additional reason that we are obligated to draw them near. For it is clear that those who have moved to the Land of Israel and distanced themselves from their original surroundings and who make themselves known as Jews in all their consciousness have no intention whatsoever of clinging to a foreign faith." There is no need to see whether these people display "their righteousness." Had they desired to cling to their faith of origin, they would never have agreed to come to Israel and live as a Jew among the Jewish people![10]

To be sure, Rabbi Unterman acknowledged that in this age it is as unlikely as the miracle of "the splitting of the Red Sea" that most converts will be observant. Nevertheless, "we are certainly obliged to take pity on the integrity of the family and look at its predicament from the viewpoint of our Holy Torah." The rabbinate should do nothing to distance Jews from participation in the community, particularly when the *halakhah* contains lenient precedents that allow the entry of such persons into the Jewish people.[11] While these people may well be nonobservant, this hardly demonstrated—in his opinion—that their intention was not "with a pure heart—*b'lev shalem*" at the moment they pledged to "cling to our holy religion and the Jewish nation and its future—*l'hidaveik b'dat kadsheinu u'va'uma ha'yisraelit u'va'atidah.*" Their presence in the State of Israel and the common fate and joined destiny they now share with the Jewish people provide a decisive warrant for their acceptance as converts into the Jewish religion.

Chief Rabbi Shlomo Goren

A product of a deeply Zionist family and a member of the Haganah, Rabbi Shlomo Goren (1917–94) served as the first chief rabbi of the Israel Defense Forces. Like Rabbi Unterman, he later served as chief rabbi of Tel Aviv, and following Rabbi Unterman, became Ashkenazic chief rabbi of the state in 1972. An acclaimed halakhic authority and the author of several significant volumes on Jewish law, Goren addressed the issue of conversion in celebrated cases throughout his career.

One of the most interesting for our purposes is the famed case involving Dr. Helen Seidman (1930–80). Dr. Seidman, a Unitarian, came to Israel from Bethesda, Maryland, as a tourist in 1964. Accompanied by her daughter, Seidman was drawn to Israel and to kibbutz life and settled in Kibbutz Nahal Oz. Eventually, she met a Jewish man and married him in a proxy marriage in Mexico.[12]

Dr. Seidman eventually decided that she wished to be converted to Judaism. However, as she was living in a nonreligious kibbutz where the laws of *kashrut* and Shabbat were not observed, it was patently obvious that virtually no Orthodox authority would convert her, as they would not regard such a proselyte as sincere in her intention to accept upon herself "the yoke of the commandments." Seidman therefore decided to convert under Reform auspices, and Reform rabbi Moshe Zemer of Tel Aviv instructed her and facilitated her conversion through the aegis of a Reform rabbinical court. Upon the completion of her conversion, Seidman applied for registration as a Jew in Israel. However, the Interior Ministry refused to grant her request. A court battle ensued, with the country's highest secular civil courts ruling that there was no legal basis for the Interior Ministry's actions. Ultimately, the Ministry was instructed to register Seidman as a Jew. However, the Orthodox Rabbinical establishment was absolutely unwilling to accede to this demand, and a political struggle between competing secular and Orthodox forces erupted, a struggle that threatened to topple a fragile governmental coalition among Orthodox and secular political parties within the Knesset.

It was against this backdrop of impending political crisis that Rabbi Goren, then the chief chaplain of the Israeli Defense Forces, met with Seidman. His meeting with her lasted approximately three hours, after which he assembled a *beit din* and hastily converted her. As Goren was an Orthodox rabbi of unquestionable stature, Seidman's conversion was now recognized by the Interior Ministry, and the political crisis was averted.

Goren's decision was very surprising, given his general position that Reform conversion was not to be considered conversion at all.[13] Unsurprisingly, the decision unleashed a storm of criticism from numerous Orthodox rabbinical colleagues. As might have been expected, they claimed that his decision to convert Helen Seidman was virtually incomprehensible, given that Jewish law required *kabbalat 'ol mitzvoth* (the acceptance of the yoke of the commandments) as a sine qua non for conversion. In attempting to understand what might have been the grounds for his decision to perform this conversion, some of his Orthodox critics suggested that behind the decision lay the belief that the standards for conversion could be different in Israel than they were in the Diaspora. Rabbi J. David Bleich offers the following summary of this understanding of Goren's motivations.[14]

A feature article appearing in the weekend supplement of *Ha-Tzofeh* 15 Sivan 5730 purports to give the rationale governing Rabbi Goren's actions in this case. It is reported that Rabbi Goren is of the belief that in Israel, prospective proselytes are to be viewed differently from the way in which they are regarded in the Diaspora.... It is suggested that proselytization was frowned upon by the Sages in the Diaspora but welcome in Israel. It is reported that Rabbi Goren, going a step further, asserts that in Israel sincerity of motivation may be dispensed with as a prior requirement for conversion.[15] In the Diaspora, converts motivated by reasons other than religious conviction cannot be accepted since doubts remain with regard to their future comportment; in Israel, where conversion entails not merely religious affiliation but national identification as well, such fears do not exist, contends Rabbi Goren. Hence, in his opinion, even converts prompted by self-serving motives may be accepted in Israel.

According to this interpretation of Goren, the decision that Rabbi Goren rendered in the Helen Seidman case indicates that he held that residence in the State of Israel was a decisive variable that allowed a prospective convert to be accepted into the Jewish fold even when it appeared unlikely that the convert would be observant of the commandments following her conversion. Like his predecessors Rabbis Herzog and Unterman, Rabbi Goren apparently felt that the decision on the part of the convert to live in the Jewish state meant that she would by definition be part of Jewish destiny. Her decision to live in Israel, a setting in which her identity as a Jew would be reinforced by her surroundings, was sufficient to justify her acceptance as a convert despite her level of observance.

The reasoning that supported Rabbi Goren's decision in the Seidman case as reported in *Ha-Tzofeh* was made completely explicit in an article, "Conversion in the Land [of Israel] and Outside the Land [of Israel]" that R. Goren wrote concerning the decision of an English rabbinic court not to sanction the conversion of Paula Cohen to Judaism. In that case, Rabbi Goren authorized the conversion of Mrs. Cohen despite the fact Mr. Cohen was a member of a non-religious kibbutz and despite the fact that she had married—in violation of Jewish law and as his last name suggests—a man of priestly descent. When the Cohen family subsequently moved to Manchester after a number of years in Israel and sought to register their children there in a school under Orthodox auspices, they were told that the conversion Mrs. Cohen had received from Rabbi Goren was valid only in Israel. The British *beit din* based this ruling on the conversion certificate itself, which contained the declaration, "This document has no legal validity in the Diaspora." Thus Mrs. Cohen was considered Jewish only in Israel, and this position was affirmed by an official document issued by the chief rabbinate.[16]

In his article on the topic, R. Goren explained the reasoning and sources that supported his decision and stated that during his tenure as chief rabbi all certificates of conversion that he certified contained a statement insisting that these conversions were valid in Israel alone. He further noted that he insisted all conversions that occurred under his authority as chief rabbi required the convert to take up permanent residence in the state, and asserted that this decision had a "significant halakhic foundation."[17] While he maintained that the Babylonian Talmud had a negative disposition to conversion in general, the Jerusalem Talmud had nothing negative to say either against "converts or those who converted them." R. Goren stated, "The Jerusalem Talmud adopts a positive and sympathetic approach to the institution of conversion," even when the conversion is seemingly motivated by love for a Jewish man or a Jewish woman.[18]

R. Goren claimed that the differences between the views of the Babylonian and Jerusalem Talmudic traditions were logical. The rabbis of the Jerusalem Talmud believed that when a conversion took place outside the Land of Israel the "convert would still remain within the bosom of his gentile family, and a serious fear existed that the male or female convert and their children would not sever themselves from the family, from their holidays, their festivals, and their ritual. They would continue to live as one family, and . . . their children would thus be raised in a gentile atmosphere. Therefore, no conversion there could be regarded as authentic."

In Israel, however, the situation was completely different. In contradistinction to the associational and kinship patterns that attached converts in the Diaspora to their family of origin, Rabbi Goren contended, converts to Judaism in Israel "were cut off completely from their gentile family and from their gentile existence. Their children did not even know that they came from a mixed family. Here the conversion is authentic and more certain from the standpoint of Judaism." From this perspective, it is "easy to understand why *Massechet Geirm* (The Tractate on Converts) 4 states, "Beloved is the land of Israel as it legitimates (*she'machsheret*) converts." In Israel, it is certain that converts "will live as Jews in every way."[19]

Contemporary Developments

The positions that Rabbis Herzog, Unterman, and Goren penned on conversion to Judaism in the Land of Israel have echoes in a number of more recent halakhic writings. This same view of Jewish nationalism as a determinative factor in causing rabbis to accept converts into Judaism can be seen in an article authored by Rabbi Yigal Ariel, the rabbi of the northern settlement of Nov in the Golan Heights, on the challenge posed by the large number of nonhalakhically Jewish Russian immigrants who have come to Israel in recent years.[20] Though Rabbi Ariel explicitly states that he sees himself as writing an exploratory study and not a formal responsum, the halakhic style he employs has significant legal resonance and overtones and indicates that he is setting forth a public policy pronouncement on what he regards as the optimal way in which to approach this problem.

R. Ariel notes that the Russian immigration to Israel has been massive and contends that "even those approaches and arguments which have not heretofore been the basis of law, might now, in this urgent time, be a basis for lenient rulings, using ex post facto justifications as ex ante solutions."[21] R. Ariel observes that these Russian *olim* are by and large not observant, and there is small prospect that they will become so. On the other hand, they are living as "Jews" in the Jewish state and their lot is intertwined with the Jewish people. The dilemma that confronts him is one of justifying the conversions of such people from the standpoint of Jewish law. As he points out at the conclusion of his article, "Conversion [of these immigrants is] not the problem of the immigrants, but the interest of the rabbinate, which is charged with saving Israeli society from a 'stumbling block' [wherein nonhalakhic 'Jews' would marry Jews of unquestioned status]."[22]

Rabbi Ariel is determined to construct an argument that will provide a solution to this dilemma. Like the authorities we cited above, he takes the approach that conversion is more than a religious act—it is a national one. Indeed, he suggested, there are two paradigms for conversion that exist in Jewish tradition. He describes the "conversion" of the biblical patriarch Abraham as "theological" in nature, and contrasts it to that of the biblical Moabite Ruth, which he regards, on the basis of her pledge, "Your people will be my people," as "national." R. Ariel thus argues that there is precedent for conversion based on "national" rather than "religious" commitments. While he observes that "the Russian immigrants do not know very much about Judaism," he also insists that "there is no doubt that they wish to become integrated into the nation and its land." Those who join the Jewish people as these immigrants have done by virtue of their becoming Israelis makes them eligible for conversion to Judaism.[23]

Of course, R. Ariel expresses the hope that these persons will one day come to embrace the Tradition and its practices. He does not see "conversion without acceptance of the *mitzvot*" as optimal. Nonetheless, the strength of the "nationalist dimension" that marks Judaism can allow for conversion of these people and "through this gateway to the Jewish people, the convert makes his way to Torah."[24]

R. Ariel further argues that the famous *baraita* from Yevamot 47a provides a warrant for this stance. In the passage, the prospective convert is asked, "What reason have you for desiring to become a proselyte; do you not know that Israel at the present time are persecuted and oppressed, despised, harassed and overcome by afflictions?" He states that this passage indicates that conversion to Judaism must be understood primarily from the perspective of nationhood, not theology.[25] While he apparently remains troubled that these people are unlikely to become observant Jews, he does not allow this concern to trump his determination to make them eligible for conversion. For theirs "is not an intentional [violation of the commandments]." They are to be considered as 'infants who were kidnapped,'"[26] and thus are not responsible for the sins they would commit as Jews after their ceremony of conversion inasmuch as "they [mistakenly] believe that a Judaism of the sort practiced by the majority of the people is sufficient."[27]

Ariel's views in his article on this question are reflected among other contemporary Israeli rabbis who view residence in the state as a decisive variable for admitting persons into the Jewish fold as converts. Rabbi Shlomo Rosenfeld, the head of the Hesder Yeshiva Shdemot-Nerya, also asserts that current realities in Israel require a fresh look at conversion policy. While his recommendations are not as far-reaching as those of R. Ariel, he does clearly state that the central challenge confronting the rabbinate is to honor halakhic precedent while at the same time recognizing that rabbis have a responsibility to all of Israeli society. He contends that life in a Jewish state makes a difference in how the laws of conversion ought to be applied. Rabbi Rosenfeld writes, "[The] complex situation is only growing more urgent. From a legal perspective, almost all these [non-converted people] can be citizens of the State. This state of affairs requires that we adopt an attitude of 'it is time to act.'"[28] Rabbi Ariel is clearly concerned here with the entire nation of Israel, not just the observant sectors of the community. Indeed, he remarks, "[We must] attend to them [i.e., the converts themselves] and thereby assist the entire Jewish nation. This is because mixed marriages and people's distancing themselves from the Jewish religion are liable to gnaw deeply into our collective."[29]

As for the problem of the converts' motivation and the centuries-old resistance to performing conversions for those already civilly married to nonobservant Jews, Rosenfeld states explicitly that immigration to Israel constitutes a factor that distinguishes these potential converts from others. "Their immigration to Israel and their desire to integrate into the life of the Jewish people here are reasons for greater consideration in the process of their conversion . . . as distinguished from other Israelis who met non-Jews in Israel or abroad [whose conversion was motivated by a desire to marry]."[30] His position is undoubtedly colored by his awareness that legal arbiters are engaged in public policy making and by a commitment on his part to the broader body politic of Israeli society. For him, the Zionist commitments of these immigrants constitute a justification for allowing their entry as converts into the Jewish people and religion.

Finally, we turn to Rabbi Yoel bin Nun, until recently the head of the Yeshiva at Kibbutz Ein Tzurim. Though recognized more as an exemplary teacher of the Bible than as a *posek*, Bin Nun is a charismatic leader with a huge following in Israel, particularly among many young people who see him as their primary religious authority. In an article published in *Eretz Acheret*,[31] Rabbi Bin Nun makes the familiar argument that the current legal structure in Israel was thoroughly unprepared to deal with the onslaught of hundreds of thousands of Russian immigrants who were halakhically non-Jewish. As long as conversions are handled on an individual basis with the classical standards traditionally employed in cases of conversion, he argues, the system will never keep up with the numbers of persons who desire to convert and the Jewish state will eventually absorb a significant number of non-Jews into its ranks. Like his colleagues cited above, R. Bin Nun believes that such a policy undermines the very purpose and nature of the Jewish state, and he thus takes the extraordinary step of proposing that a centralized and mass conversion process be instituted in order to bring these people formally into the Jewish fold.

While he does not specify precisely why, Rabbi Bin Nun sees the army— the most universal national socializing institution in the state—as the most suitable venue for this process. However, the issue of the venue for these conversions is not what is most significant. What is crucial to note is that by advocating such a mass ceremony of conversion, R. Bin Nun sidesteps the question of the observance level that will mark the prospective convert altogether. In his mind, the national needs of the Jewish people residing in their sovereign state require a radical approach to the issue of conversion. Mindful of this revolutionary posture, he nevertheless firmly advocates this stance and declares in his concluding sentence, "Courage, my colleagues, courage."

Conclusion

Though the creation of the State of Israel obviously changes much about the contemporary Jewish condition, one might have expected that the issue of conversion, one with which Jewish legal authorities have grappled for two millennia, was a relatively timeless matter that would not be dramatically affected by Jewish sovereignty. However, our analysis of the responsa of three Ashkenazi chief rabbis and several authorities who followed them indicates that even conversion has been palpably affected by the return of Jewish statehood.

The re-creation of the State of Israel has made the conversion crisis all the more pressing, due in large measure to the large numbers of not-technically-Jewish immigrants the state has had to absorb. The need to find a solution has surfaced profound questions about the process of Jewish law in a Jewish state. It appears from our survey that *poskim* in many instances are doing more than offering legal opinions in specific cases. Rather, they are shaping public policy as well for the first fully sovereign community that the Jews have had in two thousand years. These Orthodox authorities are clearly aware that they are not writing only for a narrow community of adherents who subscribe to their theologies and ways of life. Instead, they also view themselves as addressing a much larger Israeli Jewish community that consists of many nonobservant and religiously uninterested Jews. Furthermore, in the face of Jewish sovereignty, these Jewish leaders appear to regard conversion as more than a theological affirmation on the part of those whom they convert, and they recognize that there is now a national component to the decision to become Jewish that they cannot ignore. Consequently, even among the strictly Orthodox it appears that conversion policy is not monolithic. Indeed, the phenomenon of Jewish sovereignty appears to be so profound a variable that a number of these men have raised the possibility that factors involved in allowing for conversion in Israel might lead to a policy toward conversion that is distinct from that which should be adopted in the Diaspora.

Some of Israel's leading halakhic authorities have taken interesting and what seem to be surprising positions on each of these matters. As we have seen, some clearly understood their roles as public policy makers and not as halakhic decisors alone. They have acknowledged the possibility that halakhic policy in Israel might have to be different from that in the Diaspora, and they have boldly asserted that Jewish national independence makes manifest an entirely new way of legitimating conversion to Judaism.

Important and highly regarded though they are, we would not suggest that the authorities cited here represent the entirety of Israeli Orthodoxy. Indeed, there is reason to believe that the openness and creativity reflected in their work is not being embraced by some, perhaps most, of the religious leaders who have followed them. Will Israel's future religious leadership continue to see its national independence as a religiously significant datum? To that question, we do not yet have answers. What we do have is precedent from some of Israel's greatest authorities that demonstrates creativity, inclusiveness, and extraordinary courage on the issue of conversion to Judaism in the State of Israel.

ACKNOWLEDGMENT

Daniel Gordis co-authored this article, and I am grateful for his permission to include it in this volume.

NOTES

1. For examples of these attitudes on the part of Rabbi Herzog, see *Heikhal Yitzchak, Even HaEzer* 1, nos. 19–21. In addition, see the responsum he wrote in Yaakov Breisch, *Helkat Ya'akov*, no. 14, where Rabbi Herzog inveighs against conversion in the Diaspora.
2. *Heikhal Yitzchak, Even HaEzer* 1, no. 21.
3. *Shulchan Aruch, Yoreh De'ah* 268:12.
4. Isser Yehudah Unterman, "*Hilkhot Geirut Ve-Derekh Bitzu'an*—Laws of Conversion and Their Application," *Noam* 14 (5731): 1–9. This article is also cited at length in Menachem Finkelstein, *Ha-Giyyur—Halakhah ve-Ma'aseh*, 139n289.
5. Unterman, "*Hilkhot Geirut*," 1.
6. Ibid., 2.
7. *Hilchot Issurei Bi'ah* 13:17
8. Unterman, "*Hilkhot Geirut*," 5.
9. Ibid., 7.
10. Ibid., 2–3.
11. Ibid., 5ff.
12. As reported in the JTA, November 5, 1980, on the occasion of Dr. Seidman's death.
13. Cf., e.g., Shlomo Goren, *Torat Ha-Medinah* (Israel: Haidra Rabbah, 1986), 168: "Reform conversion has nothing in common with conversion to Judaism as it has been accepted in the Jewish people for 3,233 years." Indeed, most of Goren's chapter on conversion here (esp. 168–71) is devoted to the problem of Reform conversion and how to ensure that neither the Israeli courts nor Israel's Ministry of the Interior grant it any recognition.
14. J. David Bleich, "The Conversion Crisis: A Halakhic Analysis," in *The Conversion Crisis: Essays from the Pages of Tradition*, ed. Emanuel Feldman and Joel Wolowelsky (New York: Ktav, 1990), 36–37.

15. Goren here is reported to have cited the views of Rabbi Isser Yehudah Unterman from the *Noam* essay cited above in note 4.
16. Rabbi Shlomo Goren, "*Hagiyur ba'aretz u'va-hutz la'aretz*," in Goren, *Mishnat Ha-Medinah* (Jerusalem: 5749), 186.
17. Ibid.
18. Ibid., 188.
19. Ibid., 189.
20. Rabbi Yigal Ariel, "Conversion of Immigrants from the Former Soviet Union," [Hebrew] *Techumim* 12 (1992): 81–97.
21. Ibid., 82.
22. Ibid., 97.
23. Ibid., 89.
24. Ibid., 90.
25. Cf. Ibid., 91.
26. The phrase "*tinok she-nishbah bein ha-nochrim*," "an infant who was kidnapped [from among Jews and raised] among gentiles," appears twice in the Babylonian Talmud, both times in bt Shabbat 68b.
27. Ariel, "Conversion of Immigrants," 94. In taking this stance, R. Ariel is obviously stretching Jewish law beyond its "normal limits." After all, the category of "*tinok she-nishba*" classically refers to persons born of Jewish mothers who are raised outside the framework of traditional Jewish practice. In the case of these Russian converts, the rabbinic court would be bringing people born outside the Jewish faith into Judaism. Thus one might assume that the rabbinic court itself would be culpable for not informing the prospective convert of the punishments attached to nonobservance. In any event, the failure of R. Ariel to make this distinction explicit indicates how much his position is influenced by policy considerations and his desire to identify these people through conversion as "halakhic Jews."
28. Rabbi Shlomo Rosenfeld, "'A Time to Act' in the Conversion of Mixed [Marriage] Families," in *Techumin* 17 (1996): 223ff. The phrase employed here in the title, "It is time to act," is taken from the words found in Mishnah Berakhot 9:5 and bt Berakhot 54a, 63a, *inter alia*, where the ancient sages of the Talmud, writing on the phrase, "'It is time to act on behalf of the Lord,' they have violated your Torah," play with the word *violate* and read the word as an imperative, hence rendering the passage, "'It is time to act on behalf of the Lord,' Violate your Torah." This understanding has been employed by rabbis for centuries to allow for unprecedented flexibility in Jewish law when confronting an emergency situation of grave consequence.
29. Ibid., 224.
30. Ibid., 225.
31. Yoel Bin Nun, "We Should Perform Mass, Centralized Conversion," *Eretz Acheret*, no. 17 (Av-Elul 5763, July–August 2003): 68–69.

15

The Talmudic Principle "If One Comes Forth to Slay You, Forestall by Slaying Him" in Israeli Public Policy

A Responsum by Rabbi Hayim David Halevi

In an insightful article, "Physical Violence in Karo's *Shulhan Arukh*," Steven Passamaneck dealt at length with instances of "condonable violence" where "the self-defense or the protection of a person's—or a community's—interests" was involved. In that article, Passamaneck focused—among other texts—on Sanhedrin 72a, where the rabbinic principle, "If one comes forth to slay you, forestall by slaying him—*ha-ba l'hargekha, hashkeim l'hargo*," is found. In that paper, he dealt principally with the application of this principle to *private* life.[1]

In this essay, I am pleased to build upon this earlier study and discuss and analyze a responsum written by Rabbi Hayim David Halevi (1924–98) that will complement the Passamaneck study by dealing with the application of this principle found in Sanhedrin, "If one comes forth to slay you, forestall by slaying him," in matters of *public* policy. This essay will indicate how and when—and if—this norm could be applied to justify Jewish preemptory acts of self-defense in relationship to Arabs living within and beyond the borders of Israel.

As mentioned in an earlier chapter, Rabbi Halevi was the outstanding student of the famed Sephardic chief rabbi of Israel Ben Zion Meir Hai Ouziel and studied with his mentor for many years at the prestigious Yeshivat Porat Yosef. He later served as chief Sephardic rabbi of Tel Aviv-Jaffa and was one of the most prolific and famous rabbinic authorities in Israel during his lifetime. The responsum under consideration in this essay is the second responsum found in volume four of his collected responsa, *'Aseh l'kha rav*, a volume published in 5741 (1981).[2]

The Question

Rabbi Halevi reports at the outset of his responsum that he was asked to address an issue that was described as being of "great public policy importance" for the citizens of the Jewish state. The person who posed the query suggested that inasmuch as "each Arab is part of a larger public that despises us," then perhaps "it is permissible and perhaps even an obligation" to regard each Arab as falling under the category of "one who comes forth to slay you."

The questioner then posed a number of specific and highly detailed questions to Rabbi Halevi. They were designed to elicit a public policy statement as to the standpoint of Jewish law regarding the stance that the State of Israel and its Jewish majority should take toward its Arab minority population. The major questions were:

1. Does the Jewish legal norm of "If one comes forth to slay you . . ." apply to an individual who is likely to endanger your life? Or is it applicable only to specific circumstances where there is an immediate danger of violence? Or is the norm actionable only when there is a combination of both these factors—a dangerous individual and a dangerous situation?

2. Does the hostility of a given community (e.g., even when there is extreme hostility only on the part of a segment of that community) provide sufficient grounds for applying the principle of "one who comes forth to slay you" to every member of that community inasmuch as the specific individuals who constitute a threat cannot be precisely identified?

3. If the application of that principle is contingent upon specific circumstances—is there a definition of what constitutes such circumstances wherein it is permissible or even obligatory to make the rule of "If one comes forth to slay you" actionable?

4. In the Torah (*Exodus* 22:1ff.), it is written, "[If a thief be found breaking in, and be smitten so that he dies], *there shall be no blood shed for him* (i.e., the Torah does not hold culpable the individual who slays the thief). Rashi comments upon the phrase, "there shall be no blood shed for him," and states, "That is to say, the thief is to you as one who has no blood and no soul and it is permissi-

ble to slay him." Does not this comment of Rashi instruct us only concerning the right of self-defense? How can this understanding of the principle be extended to justify the slaying of all persons attached to a community that despises us, as some claim in applying this rule of "If one comes forth to slay you" to all Arabs living in Israel?

5. Is it proper to employ this rule as a decisive principle that should guide our political life, as some claim that "the recognition of our right to exist as a free nation in our land" is dependent upon our acknowledgment that acting upon this principle is demanded for the preservation of our nation?

6. Even if one acknowledges that there is an absolute right to self-defense, are there still no limits upon what constitutes legitimate self-defense, even according to this norm?

The remainder of this essay will indicate how Rabbi Halevi responded to these questions and present the policy position he advanced concerning what Israeli policy regarding the use of force toward its Arab population ought to be on the basis of his analysis of the talmudic rule found in Sanhedrin 72a and its subsequent discussion in Jewish literature.

The Initial Response of Rabbi Halevi and His Analysis of Sanhedrin 72a

As a preface to his responses to all these questions, Rabbi Halevi stated forthrightly and unequivocally, "I feel that I have an obligation to distance myself completely from those who contend [that the rule of 'If one comes forth to slay you' ought to be applied to all Arabs]. I am astonished by the suggestion that a legal sentence of death be applied to one and one-half million Arabs—the overwhelming majority of whom live in peace and tranquility despite their hostility for an Israel that they see as a conqueror—as a result of the terrorist activities of a minority."

Having explicitly stated his revulsion at the suggestion that the norm of "If one comes forth to slay you" could somehow be applied to justify a policy of legally sanctioned violence against all Arabs living in the State of Israel, Rabbi Halevi turned to an analysis and exegesis of the relevant rabbinic sources that led him to this conclusion. At the outset of his discussion, he cited two passages from *Sanhedrin* 72a, the *locus classicus*, for this warrant. The first passage he discussed states:

Raba said, "What is the reason for the law of breaking in (*ba ba-mahteret*)?" Because it is certain that no man is passive where his property is concerned. Therefore, the thief must have reasoned, "If I go there, the owner will oppose me and attempt to prevent me. However, if he does, I will kill him." Hence, the Torah decreed, "If one comes to slay you, forestall by slaying him"—*im ba l'horg'kha, hashkeim l'hor'go*.

Later in 72a, there is a second passage from the Gemara that reads:

Our Rabbis taught, "[If a thief be found breaking in and be smitten so that he dies], there shall be no blood shed for him, if the sun be risen upon him" (Exodus 22:1ff). . . . [This is the meaning]. If it is clear to you as the sun that his intentions are not peaceable, slay him. If not, do not slay him."

The Views of Rashi and the Meiri

Rabbi Halevi then offered his own analysis of the contrasting explanations that both Rashi and the Meiri offered for the norm, "If one comes forth to slay you," based on these passages in Sanhedrin. He immediately noted that Rashi attaches the principle of "If one comes forth to slay you" to the passage in Exodus 22:1ff. Hence, Rashi asks, "Why does the Torah state that 'no blood should be shed' [for one who is 'breaking in']? This is because, he states, "[the thief] is *like* one who has no blood and no soul and [the owner of the house is therefore] permitted to slay him." As there is a legal presumption (*hazakah*) that "no man stands by" passively when his property is in the process of bring stolen, it can be assumed that "the thief (the one who breaks in—*ba ba-mahteret*) [must be] prepared to kill the owner" in order to appropriate the property he intends to steal. The Torah therefore states, "There shall be no blood shed for him (the thief whom the householder slays in the process of his breaking in)."

In short, Rashi reasons that the intentions of the thief may be assumed to be homicidal, since the thief realizes that it may well be necessary to commit murder in order to secure his ill-gotten gains. The householder is permitted to slay the thief, for, from this perspective, his forceful response constitutes an act of self-defense and his act is justified, as the Talmud states, by the principle, "If one comes forth to slay you, forestall by slaying him."

However, Rabbi Halevi contended that the reading of the Talmud that Rashi provides on the basis of the Exodus passage is not as convincing as the explanation the Meiri offers. He pointed out that the Meiri disagrees with Rashi when the Meiri states that the source of the rule, "If one comes forth to slay you," does not emanate from the passages in Exodus 22. Rather, the Meiri claims it stems from a reading found in Midrash Tanhuma, where it states in *Parashat Pinhas* that God demands that the Israelites slay the Midianites, as "the Midianites are your enemies."[3] Here there is neither doubt about the murderous intention and attitude of the entire Midianite people regarding the Jews nor is there any question that God commands their destruction. There is an absolute certainty concerning the deeds they will attempt to carry out, and God therefore commands the people of Israel "to assail them." Rabbi Halevi asserts that "a preemptory strike" against a group is permissible (*r'sha'it*) only in instances such as this. Only then can the principle "If one comes to slay you" be considered actionable as regards a collective.

Following the Meiri, Rabbi Halevi therefore concluded that the rule "If one comes forth to slay you" can be applied only in an instance—regardless of whether it is an individual or a collective—where there is absolute certainty that there will be a murderous attack. Thus in Berakhot 58a, there is a tale told of Rabbi Shilo, who assassinated a Jewish informant who intended to slander him before the Roman authority and thereby endanger the entire community. The deed Rabbi Shilo performed was deemed justifiable homicide, that is, self-defense, on the basis of the rule "If one comes forth to slay you."

From all this, R. Halevi concluded that, in the contemporary setting, the application of the rule "If one comes forth to slay you," while sometimes actionable, is a matter of discretion (*r'shut*), not obligation (*hovah*). This is why Rashi states, "It is permitted to slay him," and why Maimonides, Laws of Theft 9:7 rules, "If a thief breaks in—*Ha-ba ba-mahteret*, . . . discretion is granted the householder to slay [the thief]." There is never an obligation to act upon this rule, even when its application is possible. "If one comes forth to slay you" provides for the option of preemptive force only in instances of imminent danger where it is certain that either an individual or a nation intends to attack and slay a blameless individual or collective. In such instances, the one who "comes forth to slay you"—either a single person or a group—is considered "*k'rodeph*—akin to a pursuer."

Consequently, Maimonides, in Laws of Theft 9:9, asserts, "He is akin to one who pursues his friend to murder him." Precisely because this person is "akin to a pursuer," it is "permissible," though never an "obligation," for the person or group that is attacked to rise up in self-defense on the basis of the rabbinic principle "If one comes forth to slay you."

The Application of the Rule of "If One Comes Forth to Slay You" to a "Hostile Public—Tsibur Oyein"

As a result of this discussion of the sources, R. Halevi stated that it was inconceivable that the rule "If one comes to slay you" should ever be construed as permitting, much less demanding, the murder of "any (*stam*) Arab." The status of "pursuer—*rodeph*" could never be applied to such an individual, nor could the status of "one who breaks in—*ba ba-mahteret*." Consequently, the rule "If one comes forth to slay you" can surely never be employed as a justification for the targeted assassination of an Arab where there is no good cause to believe that such a person intends to engage in and possesses the capacity to carry out an act of violence against individual Jews or the Jewish state.

Furthermore, while R. Halevi acknowledged that there is good reason to believe that the Arab community does possess an attitude of "general hostility" toward the Israeli Jewish population, one would still be mistaken in applying the rule derived from Numbers 25, "Assail the Midianites," as a license to slay an individual Arab for no just cause. Indeed, this warrant derived from Numbers applies to a group alone, and it cannot be actionable except in instances where "the leadership of the nation—*manhigut ha'am*" decides that "a particular people '*am m'suyam*" intends to wage war against Israel. In such a case, the Jewish people can engage in "a preemptive war," though here as well the warrant provided by Numbers 25 is limited to a war aimed at a collective, not an individual. Having discussed all these sources, R. Halevi was now ready to answer the specific questions posed to him at the outset of the responsum.

The Conclusions

In concluding his responsum, R. Halevi responded to the questions he was asked by stating immediately and unequivocally that the principle "If one comes forth to slay you" could be applied only in instances where it is absolutely certain that the individual intends to and is capable of committing murder, as was the case described in *Berakhot* 58a, where Rabbi Shilo slayed the would-be informant. Second, he ruled that it was never permitted to assassinate random individuals who are members of a community that "despises" your own community. There must be no doubt that the individuals who are the targets of "preemptory actions" both possess murderous sentiments and intend to act upon them. In such instances, preemptory actions of all types on the part of the government (e.g., restricting freedom of movement, not just "targeted assassinations" or acts involving the use of force) are permitted, since these actions constitute appropriate acts of self-defense.

R. Halevi also declared that it was futile to attempt to provide a precise definition of what the circumstances might be that would constitute the exact grounds for making the principle "If one comes forth to slay you" actionable. Nevertheless, R. Halevi was of the opinion that the grounds for the application of such a rule could be quite broad, for the very fact that the Talmud grants the householder the right to slay an intruder indicates that the Torah allows for a great degree of latitude in the application of this rule. Moreover, the principle "If one comes forth to slay you" should guide political policy no less than personal life. R. Halevi commented that this was so with all principles derived from the Torah, and he reiterated in the penultimate section of his responsum that the rule in Sanhedrin 72a provided a broad Jewish warrant for the position that an expansive variety of preemptory acts of force on the part of the government could be deemed morally acceptable under the conditions defined above as acts of self-defense. "Preemptory attacks" against terrorists and those who are known to provide active aid in support of terrorists and their cruel deeds—as opposed to all Arabs—were unquestionably justified by this rule. In the words of Steven Passamaneck, Rabbi Halevi affirmed that acts of "condonable violence," where "the self-defense or the protection of a community's interests" is involved, are justified by the rule in Sanhedrin 72a, "If one comes forth to slay you, forestall by slaying him."

Nevertheless, R. Halevi cautioned that Jewish law intended that this rule be applied only to actual cases of self-defense. Neither Rashi nor the Meiri nor any other halakhic authority could conceive this rule as supplying a justification for sanctioning the assassination of "innocent" individuals. In the final analysis, the application of this norm displays the flexibility and wisdom inherent in Jewish law. The employment of the rule "If one comes forth to slay you, forestall by slaying him" indicates that Jewish tradition allows for the judicious use of force in a world where predators exist.

NOTES

1. Steven Passamaneck, "Aspects of Physical Violence against Persons in Karo's *Shulkhan Arukh*," *Jewish Law Annual* 9 (1991), 5–106. His discussion of Sanhedrin 72a–b can be found on 56ff.

2. Two significant English language articles on R. Halevi are Marc Angel, "Rabbi Hayyim David Halevy: A Leading Contemporary Rabbinic Thinker," *Jewish Book Annual* 52 (1994): 99–109; Zvi Zohar, "Sephardic Religious Thought in Israel: Aspects of the Theology of Rabbi Haim David HaLevi," in *Critical Essays on Israeli Society, Religion, and Government*, ed. Kevin Avruch and Walter Zenner (Albany: SUNY Press, 1997), 115–36. In addition, I have written three essays on his thought. See David Ellenson, "Interpretive Fluidity and P'sak in a Case of *Pidyon Sh'vuyim*: An Analysis of a Modem Israeli Responsum as Illuminated by the Thought of David Hartman," in *Judaism and Modernity: The Religious Philosophy of David Hartman*, ed. Jonathan Malino (Jerusalem: Shalom Hartman Institute, 2001), 341–67; "Jewish Legal Interpretation and Moral Values: Two Responsa by Rabbi Hayyim David Halevi on the Obligations of the Israeli Government towards Its Minority Population," *CCAR Journal* (Summer 2001): 5–20; and "A Portrait of the Pasek as Modem Religious Leader: An Analysis of Selected Writings of Rabbi Hayyim David Halevi," in *Jewish Religious Leadership: Image and Reality*, ed. Jack Wertheimer (New York: Jewish Theological Seminary, 2004), 2:673–93.

3. Numbers 25:16–18 reads, "The Lord spoke to Moses, saying, 'Assail the Midianites and strike them, for they afflicted you by the conspiracies they practiced against you.'"

16

The Rock from Which They Were Cleft

A Review-Essay of Haim Amsalem's
Zera Yisrael and *Mekor Yisrael*

Over the last two decades more than a million people from the former Soviet Union have immigrated to Israel through the Law of Return, which grants citizenship to anyone (and their spouse) with at least one Jewish grandparent. This has facilitated the immigration of hundreds of thousands of people who are not recognized as Jews by Jewish law (*halakhah*). Although these immigrants and their children now identify with the Jewish people and live as Jews within the Jewish state, Israeli law—which defers to the rabbinic courts in these matters—does not allow them to marry full-fledged Jews in state-sanctioned weddings nor are they permitted burial in a Jewish cemetery.

Many of these Israeli citizens would like to convert to Judaism. However, the High Rabbinical Court of Israel has held that would-be converts not only have to affirm an obligation to observe every single commandment in the Torah, but that their conversions can be retroactively annulled if they subsequently fail to do so, thus placing the Jewish status of thousands who have already been converted under a cloud of halakhic doubt, not to speak of personal anxiety.

In an interview last spring, High Rabbinical Court Judge Rabbi Avraham Sherman questioned the validity of "all modern-era conversions in Israel and in the world since the start of the Jewish Enlightenment period," and affirmed that Israeli converts must "undergo examination by an authorized rabbinic court before they can enter the community of Jewish people. They are not Jews for certain." The requirement that all converts accept the commandments is, along with circumcision and ritual immersion in a *mikvah*, central to the halakhic definition of conversion. Nevertheless, the position that once such a conversion has taken place they are still "not Jews for certain" is surely an innovation. In fact, as Rabbi and Member of

Knesset (MK) Haim Amsalem has argued, there is great latitude within the tradition regarding how the requirement that the convert accept the commandments has been applied.

Last year, Amsalem published two massive and erudite volumes on conversion, *Zera Yisrael* (Seed of Israel) and *Mekor Yisrael* (Source of Israel). These books are *sefarim* (traditional rabbinic texts) in the best sense of that genre. The former work contains Amsalem's halakhic discussion of a host of conversion-related matters, while *Mekor Yisrael* is an invaluable anthology that reproduces (in full) the halakhic writings and responsa of the more than 120 rabbinic authorities upon whom Amsalem drew in writing *Zera Yisrael*.

What makes Rabbi Amsalem's position on these matters so important is his prominence on the Israeli political scene. He is the fifty-two-year-old Algerian-born Shas party rabbi/politician who has in the past couple of years outraged other ultra-Orthodox Jews, including the spiritual head of the party he represents, Rabbi Ovadia Yosef, with his heterodox views. He has, for instance, denounced the "shameful" state-subsidized studies of young adult Haredi (ultra-Orthodox) men who remain in Yeshiva despite having little talent for Torah study. And he has characterized Rabbi Sherman's position as halakhic grandstanding "at the expense of thousands of converts from the seed of Israel, whom he offends, particularly IDF soldiers who give their lives, even for him." For such heresies, Amsalem has been subjected to a torrent of abuse from the Haredi world. He was repudiated by Rabbi Yosef and expelled from the Shas party in November of 2010, but, as we shall see, he has by no means left the public stage.

As Amsalem emphasizes, the Russian immigrants with whom he is most concerned speak Hebrew and lead lives that are indistinguishable from secular, or even moderately traditional, Israeli Jews. What worries him is that marriages between these immigrants and those who are indisputably Jewish "multiply daily." He fears that this sociological fact will soon produce a distinction between what it is to be an Israeli and what it is to be a Jew within the state of Israel, forcing a potentially catastrophic split between the categories of nationality and religion in the country.

Focused as he is on an Israeli problem, Rabbi Amsalem confines his analysis and proposals of *Zera Yisrael* to the Israeli situation. He does not consider them to be applicable to the diaspora, nor to persons born of two Gentile parents anywhere, but only to persons born of non-Jewish mothers and Jewish fathers who live in Israel. He applauds those descended from Jewish fathers and non-Jewish mothers, who have come voluntarily from the diaspora to shape and share the destiny of the Jewish people. Describing them as *zera yisrael* (the seed of Israel), he argues that their act of *aliyah* (immigration to Israel) bespeaks their desire to "return to the rock from which they were cleft." Consequently, he argues that Jewish law holds that it is "fitting to love them and bring them near" when they come to convert, and this attitude "obligates us to be as lenient as possible within the parameters of Jewish law" in admitting them into the Jewish people. Moreover, he convincingly demonstrates that retroactive annulment of conversion is virtually unprecedented in the history of halakha.

Rabbi Amsalem believes that the present situation constitutes a halakhic "state of emergency." At such moments, many earlier authorities have relied upon Maimonides in applying more lenient legal standards *de jure* that might otherwise only be applied *de facto*. Amsalem cites the ruling of famed proto-Religious Zionist Rabbi Zevi Hirsch Kalischer who, in 1864, labeled children born of Jewish fathers and non-Jewish mothers as *zera kodesh* (holy seed) who should be converted to Judaism at the directive of the father. He also cites a responsum from the sixteenth-century sage Rabbi David ben Zimri, known as the Radbaz. In dealing with the descendants of *anusim*, or Marranos, who had been forcibly converted to Christianity but secretly retained an attachment to Judaism, Radbaz ruled that full "acceptance of the commandments" was not required.

Zera Yisrael also addresses the problems that arise when a conversion is sought "for the sake of marriage." While Jewish law seemingly forbids such conversions for an ulterior motive (see *Shulchan Arukh, Yoreh Deah* 268:12), Amsalem points out that a number of rabbis have permitted conversion in such cases. Those who do so rely in part upon the talmudic story told of R. Hiyya who allowed the conversion of a beautiful courtesan who admitted that she was converting to marry one of his students. As do others, Rabbi Amsalem couples this story from tractate Menachot with the tale in Berakhot 31a about Hillel permitting a man to convert though he had come with the outrageous (and impossible) motive of becoming the high priest. The Tosafot (medieval commentators on the Talmud) explain that both R. Hiyya and Hillel were able to overlook such nonspiritual motivations because they recognized that the converts in question would ultimately come to embrace Judaism wholeheartedly and selflessly. Consequently, a legal principle, "All depends upon the judgment of the rabbinic court," emerged that grants a rabbinic court broad discretion in matters of conversion, and Amsalem shows that this principle has been widely invoked by rabbinic authorities throughout history in cases of conversion.

Amsalem addresses the question of whether Jewish law can possibly rest content with a "partial acceptance" of the commandments on the part of the would-be convert. In a remarkable paragraph, he states that the requirement of "acceptance of the commandments" is actually "not a part of the conversion process in the same way that circumcision and immersion are." Rather, each rabbinic court convened for purposes of conversion must consider what the circumstances are that motivate each would-be proselyte to convert to Judaism. While there is surely no obligation on the part of the rabbinic court to perform a conversion in every instance, the case of Hillel cited above as well as decisions rendered by many rabbis, including nineteenth-century authorities Rabbi Eliyahu Guttmacher of Hungary and Rabbi David Zevi Hoffmann of Berlin, show that great rabbis have allowed conversions when they believed them to be in the best interests of the Jewish people even in instances where they knew that such converts were unlikely to become fully observant.

On this view, such a convert must certainly affirm the oneness and unity of God as well as reject idolatry and his former religion. Furthermore, in accord with the classic talmudic discussion of conversion in tractate Yevamot 47a–b, the convert must receive instruction in "some of the minor and some of the major commandments." However, he or she need not understand that this entails a commitment to observe all the commandments, nor is the convert obligated to make an explicit declaration to that effect during the conversion process. Amsalem does say that if it is understood that the aspiring proselyte has a principled intent not to observe the commandments *at all*, then he should not be converted. Nevertheless, even here he notes that if such a conversion is performed, then it is *de facto* valid and cannot be annulled. Here, along with the *Shulchan Arukh*, he cites Maimonides:

A convert whose motives were not investigated or was not informed about the commandments and their punishments, but was circumcised and immersed in the presence of three laymen, is a convert. Even if it becomes known that he became a convert for some ulterior motive, he has exited from the Gentile group once he was circumcised and immersed. However, he should be regarded with skepticism until his righteousness becomes apparent. Even if he returns to worshiping idols, he is an apostate Israelite, whose betrothal is valid. (Laws of Forbidden Intercourse 13:17).

Although it seems clear that Maimonides is categorically rejecting both the absolute necessity of accepting all of the commandments and the possibility of retroactive annulment, Rabbi Sherman and his rabbinic allies manage to read this passage as vindicating their position.

Rabbi Amsalem concludes that "in our time there are important and weighty reasons" for performing conversions for Israeli citizens who are the descendants of Jewish fathers alone—the unity of the entire Jewish nation depends upon the performance of such conversions. Therefore, rabbinic courts are now obligated to accept these converts "even when we know that they will not fulfill all of the commandments." This will facilitate the entry of Russian immigrants and their children into the Jewish people "under the wings of the Divine Presence." The courts, meanwhile, should "hope that the light that is in Torah will shine upon them" and ultimately bring these Jews to a full observance of the commandments.

As is the custom with works of traditional rabbinic scholarship, *Zera Yisrael* is prefaced by a large number of *haskamot* (approbations) testifying to Rabbi Amsalem's piety and erudition. These letters come from some of the most prominent rabbis in Israel, including his teacher Rabbi Meir Mazuz, Rabbi Shear Yashuv Cohen, Rabbi Dov Lior, Rabbi Nachum Rabinovitch, and Rabbi Yaakov Ariel, among many others. *Zera Yisrael* and *Mekor Yisrael* are serious works of breathtaking and well-researched scholarship that all scholars of rabbinic literature will want to consult. And while Rabbi Amsalem is very careful in his works to circumscribe the application of his research and rulings to converts born of a Jewish father and non-Jewish mother who live in Israel, the force and substance of his arguments and scholarship extend far beyond these limits, and could well allow other Orthodox rabbis in the diaspora as well as in Israel to follow the logic of his arguments to justify a more accommodating approach to conversion in general.

Whether that will in fact be the case surely remains to be seen. Rabbi Amsalem's opponents, however, have already made known their fierce disagreement with what he has written in *Zera Yisrael*. On May 20, 2010, *Yated Neeman*, the house organ of the United Torah Judaism party, ran on its front page a circular signed by the heads of the Ashkenazic Edah HaChareidis (ultra-Orthodox community) asserting that there was no halakhic justification whatsoever for Amsalem's positions. The authors contended that only a complete acceptance of the yoke of the commandments would permit inclusion into the Jewish people. A "convert," the circular maintained, who fails to make such an affirmation, regardless of any conversion ceremony performed under the aegis of any rabbi or rabbinic court, remains "a complete Gentile" (*goy gamur*) whether both parents are Gentile, or whether "the mother alone" is a non-Jew. Anyone who offers an opinion to the contrary is, by definition, incompetent (*eino bar hora'ah klal*). Indeed, such a man is "a complete heretic" (*apikoros gamur*). Although Rabbi Amsalem was not mentioned by name, an editorial, printed immediately under the declaration, reported that the *gedolei yisrael* (the great Torah Sages of our time) had expressed unalterable opposition to Amsalem's claim that Jewish law possesses sufficient latitude to sanction conversion based on a "partial acceptance of the commandments." Significantly, the newspaper refused to identify Amsalem as a rabbi, choosing instead to refer to him simply as "MK."

Although it might seem that the argument between Amsalem and his Haredi opponents can be reduced to a political struggle over the mechanisms of conversion in Israel, I think that it actually represents much deeper disagreements about Judaism, Jewish peoplehood, and the Zionist enterprise. From the perspective of Amsalem's Haredi opponents, we Jews are a people only by virtue of our Torah. Conversion to Judaism is, therefore, only possible when a Gentile embraces the duty thrust upon all Jews, forever, to observe all the 613 commandments that our tradition asserts were revealed by God. Anything less is unacceptable.

There is intellectual and historical precedence for this stance. As my teacher Jacob Katz pointed out in a brilliant chapter of his *Out of the Ghetto*, some of the nineteenth-century predecessors to contemporary Haredi authorities were tempted to rule that Jews who rejected the classical Jewish religious belief in revelation at Sinai along with halakhic practice were not Jews at all. They would have resolved their disputes with these heretics by defining them as beyond the borders of the Jewish people. However, the "quandary" these rabbis confronted was that Jewish law clearly states that one born of a Jewish mother is uncontrovertibly a Jew, and, as the Talmud states in tractate Sanhedrin, "A Jew, even when he sins, remains a Jew." Katz entitled the chapter "Conservatives in a Quandary." In the case of would-be converts, the same quandary does not exist, at least for present-day Haredi authorities.

His supposed heresy notwithstanding, Rabbi Amsalem, no less than the Haredim who savage him, affirms the belief that God revealed the Torah—both Written and Oral—to the Jewish people. Indeed, this is why Amsalem would never countenance the acceptance of conversions conducted under the supervision of Reform, Conservative, or Reconstructionist rabbis. But this should not obscure the fact that he has a substantively broader conception of Judaism than do his Haredi colleagues. For Amsalem, not only religion, but peoplehood is an indispensable component of Judaism. As the paradigmatic proselyte Ruth states to her mother-in-law, Naomi, when she embraces Judaism in the book of Ruth, "Your people will be my people, your God my God." This is what allows a traditionalist with Zionist commitments such as Amsalem to view the Russian immigrants, who have pledged their very lives and those of their children to share in Jewish fate and destiny as citizens of the Jewish state, as being of the seed of Israel.

In the course of his argument, Amsalem cites the lenient position that former chief Ashkenazic rabbi Isser Yehuda Unterman took in the 1970s on the conversion of Russian Israeli immigrants to Israel. Like Rabbi Unterman before him, he has a principled commitment to a Judaism that extends beyond religion alone. He encourages and tries to facilitate the conversion of non-Jews of Jewish ancestry to Judaism because his conception of the indivisibility of *leum* (nationality) and *dat* (religion) compels him to be inclusionary. His internalization of a Zionist ethos causes him to regard immigrants who constitute *zera yisrael* as part of the warp and woof of the Jewish people, and he therefore holds that the need to convert them under religious auspices to Judaism is a necessity fully in keeping with Jewish law.

On the very first pages of *Zera Yisrael*, prior to the rabbinic approbations that praise the book, Amsalem reproduces a *d'var Torah* by none other than Rabbi Ovadia Yosef, originally printed in the Shas party newspaper *Yom le-Yom* five years ago, which argues for leniency and empathy on the part of rabbis in matters of conversion. Yosef cites the talmudic legend that the patriarchs Abraham, Isaac, and Jacob refused to accept the princess Timna, "the sister of Lotan," as a Jew when she wanted to convert. This caused her to marry Eliphaz, and their union resulted in the birth of Amalek, the archetypal enemy of the Jewish people throughout history. To be sure, Yosef provided his own unique interpretation of this story. He claimed that Eliphaz actually performed a *giyur reformi* (Reform conversion), which was the cause of the calamitous birth of Amalek. Yosef prefaces this narrative with a rabbinic epigram that asserts, "The wise man wrote, 'He sees clearly.' What does this . . . mean?—That at the beginning of a matter, [a wise man] can foresee what will ultimately unfold."

In *Zera Yisrael* and *Mekor Yisrael*, Rabbi Amsalem leaves no doubt as to what a clear-sighted view of conversion in Israel requires or where the present disastrous policies are leading. Though expelled from Shas, he has not retreated from politics. Instead, he has become the founder of a new party, Am Shalem (The Whole People). When Amsalem established this party, he wrote:

> At a time like this, another type of leadership is required [in the Orthodox community]. . . . Reality requires us . . . to struggle with the challenges that stand at the threshold of the State of Israel. . . . The Am Shalem Movement promises to return sanity and moderation to the Haredi community.

Zera Yisrael and *Mekor Yisrael* surely provide the rabbinic basis for this aspiration. They are the intellectual fruits of his efforts to meet the challenges of our era while maintaining the heritage of religious Judaism. These *sefarim* should be welcomed, not least by those of us whose approbations would earn him no respect in the world he wants to change.

17

Moshe Zemer's *Halakhah Shefuyah*

An Israeli Vision of Reform and Halakhah

When the Hamburg Reform Temple was established in 1817, it became, in the words of Jakob Petuchowski, "the first congregation in the nineteenth century which was founded on a declared Reform basis."[1] A year later the Hamburg Temple was officially dedicated and in 1819 the first edition of the Hamburg Temple Prayer Book appeared. This *siddur* engendered considerable controversy, and contemporaneous champions of Orthodoxy savagely attacked it in *Eileh Divrei Habrit*, a collection of responsa compiled and edited by the Hamburg Rabbinical Court. The opinions contained within this volume marshaled talmudic and other halakhic sources against the innovations introduced by the Reformers into Jewish prayer.

M. J. Bresslau, an editor of the Hamburg Temple Prayer Book, responded to the Orthodox in a Hebrew volume, *Herev Nokemet Nekam Brit*, and contended that the authors of *Eileh Divrei Habrit* had misinterpreted some and ignored other classical rabbinical sources in making their case against the Hamburg Reformers' liturgy. Drawing upon earlier halakhic works (*Or Nogah* and *Nogah Hatzedek*) in defense of Reform, Bresslau did not confine his response to a critique of what he claimed was an Orthodox misuse of rabbinic literature. He also cited much rabbinic material to defend the deeds of the Hamburg Reformers. Nor was Bresslau alone among the Reformers in offering such a statement. David Caro, in his *Brit Emet* (1820), also condemned the Orthodox responsa as misinformed, and he too gathered together alternative halakhic sources to provide a traditional warrant for the deeds of the Reformers.[2]

While historians and partisans continue to debate the merits of each side's arguments in the dispute, "what remains of abiding interest [in this affair]," as Petuchowski observed, "is the fact that the early Reformers should have felt the need to defend themselves in that particular arena, and with these particular weapons. Nothing demonstrates more clearly than this that the farthest thing from their mind was the formation of a new Jewish sect, let alone the founding of a new religion. The Judaism to which they wanted to bring reform was a Judaism based on Bible, Talmud, and Codes; and it was by an appeal to these accepted bases of Jewish life that they sought to justify their place *within* Judaism."[3]

Gunther Plaut, commenting upon the same episode, analyzes it much as Petuchowski did and notes that the literature of the Reformers in this dispute "is couched in the same language which Orthodoxy had used." These initial proponents of Reform, Plaut asserts, "demanded that any change from the past be founded in genuine Jewish tradition." In so doing, these men, in Plaut's opinion, established a pattern for later generations of Reform leaders who "insisted that all of tradition was significant, that Reform had to grow organically from it, and that a renewal of Judaism could only come from a continuity of spiritual development."[4]

Of course, not all Reformers would affirm this sentiment. From Samuel Holdheim and David Einhorn in the nineteenth century to spokesmen such as Alvin Reines in the twentieth, the halakhic dimension of Jewish tradition has hardly been central to significant numbers of Reformers. Yet for others—ranging from the Hamburg Temple Reformers of the 1820s to scholars such as Jacob Lauterbach, Samuel Cohen, Solomon Freehof, Walter Jacob, Eugene Borowitz, Petuchowski, and Plaut in the 1900s—the Halakhah comprises too central and idiomatic a dimension of the Jewish Tradition for Reform Judaism to ignore. Reform Judaism, in the view of these men, is to be "predicated on organic growth and development, that is, on evolution." A Reform that would abrogate the halakhic elements of the Tradition "stands for revolution and [a] radical break with the Jewish past."[5] It would deny Reform Jews the continuity and wisdom this literature provides and would constitute an unwarranted break with the identity and community that have marked Jews and Judaism for millennia.

To be sure, these men have sought no communal mechanism to impose halakhic decisions upon the Reform Jewish world. Nor have they wished to supplant individual autonomy as a Reform principle.[6] As Rabbi Freehof felicitously put it, "Guidance not governance" should be the role halakhic sources play in Reform Jewish decision making.[7] In this sense, these proponents of a Reform halakhah have surely departed from a traditional approach to halakhah, which would regard halakhic decisions issued by the rabbinate as normative and binding for the Jewish community. Nevertheless, they still maintain that Reform, if it is to be authentic, must confront and at least express itself in part in terms taken from the halakhah.

In our day, no one has affirmed this approach to Reform with more integrity and tenacity than our colleague Rabbi Moshe Zemer of Tel Aviv. Zemer, currently *Av Bet Din* of the Israel Council of Progressive Rabbis and director of the Freehof Institute for Progressive Halakhah, recently published *Halakhah Shefuyah* (A sane halakhah) in Israel.[8] *Halakhah Shefuyah* constitutes, in its own right, an important link in the chain of liberal halakhah, and it is deserving of assessment and respect as a collection of responsa issued by an informed and concerned Reform rabbi eager to apply the precedents and ethos of Jewish law to the problems of the age. At the same time, Zemer's book can neither be understood nor judged apart from the religious-political reality of the Jewish state within which Zemer operates. Zemer's topics are often determined by events on the Israeli scene. Particular attention is paid to a whole host of issues ranging from the State of Israel's relationship to its own non-Jewish minorities and the Palestinians to the status of women within the state. These issues, and others, are treated within the context of an Israeli political situation where halakhah and state are frequently intertwined.

Halakhah Shefuyah is itself divided into eight sections and forty-two chapters that represent a distillation of thirty years of Zemer's scholarly and polemical writings on matters of Jewish faith and practice. It is a book reflecting Zemer's own commitment to the notion that Reform must speak in that most idiomatic of Jewish genres, the responsum, if Reform is to find its rightful place in the continuum of Jewish history. Consequently, Zemer's book and the efforts reflected in it must be viewed against the backdrop of his larger work in the area of Jewish law. This work has found its primary expression in the work of the Freehof Institute of Progressive Halakhah, which he and Rabbi Walter Jacob cofounded in 1988. In the publications issued by the Freehof Institute, Zemer, along with Jacob, has consistently argued that there exist progressive and pluralistic trends within normative Halakhah, and that these trends are consonant with the principles of Reform Judaism.

Jacob and Zemer contend that recognized *poskim*, from the tannaitic period to the present day, have always sought creative solutions within the halakhic system to all types of contemporary problems. Their legal decisions often pushed the boundaries of Halakhah in directions heretofore unrecognized, and they often reversed previous decisions and offered innovative interpretations of biblical texts in order to provide humane solutions to the dilemmas faced in past eras. All this, they contend, stands in sharp contrast to Orthodoxy today. As Jacob asserts:

> Orthodox Judaism has felt threatened and endangered for several generations. Therefore, it has been unwilling to make the kind of radical changes necessary for the times. It has overlooked the willingness and ability of the Tannaim, the Amoraim, the Geonim, the Rishonim, and the Aharonim to make changes. They always changed the outer forms in keeping with the inner spirit and adapted Judaism to radically different situations. Reform Judaism has followed this path, while traditional Judaism has lost its nerve.[9]

Zemer himself echoes Jacob on this point and throughout *Halakhah Shefuyah* argues that the way the current Orthodox rabbinical establishment renders halakhic decisions is stultified and all too often based on the narrowest and most stringent interpretations of Jewish law available.[10] He cites scores of stories in the Israeli press to make this point. His examples range from the rabbinate's failure to discover a solution to the plight of the *agunah* to the chief rabbinate's decision to have the body of a Christian exhumed from a Jewish cemetery, from an edict forbidding the conversion of a woman who is civilly married to a Jewish man to the Orthodox rabbinate's refusal to act on behalf of a widow whose brother-in-law refuses to perform the ceremony of *halitzah* unless she gives him her apartment, and from *haredim* who throw stones at tourists in order to preserve the sanctity of the Sabbath to the inability of Israeli citizens, declared *mamzerim*, to marry because their parents' marriage is declared invalid after twenty years of matrimony.

Zemer points to these cases and others to demonstrate the stridency and cruelty that marks much current Orthodox halakhic adjudication in Israel. The Israeli Orthodox rabbinic establishment has frequently created these dilemmas, Zemer argues, because it has chosen to interpret Jewish law in the most oppressive manner possible. These men have too often transformed the halakhah into a weapon that violates the very people whose lives it was designed to enhance and guide. Zemer excoriates the official rabbinate for this lack of sensitivity and decries its failure to employ the halakhah as a humane resource for the solution of many of life's quandaries. Their decisions dishonor the Jewish legal process they are purported to champion, and it is no wonder, in light of this, that Zemer contends that many Israelis feel that halakhah is callous and unresponsive to their lives.[11]

Halakhah Shefuyah seeks to reverse this trend in contemporary Jewish legal adjudication by reviving the creativity and humaneness evidenced and embodied in so much of the Jewish legal tradition. Zemer attempts to apply these qualities to a host of contemporary issues, and as he and Jacob have argued elsewhere, he contends that Halakhah, so viewed, is in accord with the tenets and ethos of Reform Judaism.[12] By demonstrating the evolutionary nature of the halakhic process and the ancients' willingness to make changes and reverse precedents in order to arrive at an appropriate solution to a current quandary, Zemer, as well as Jacob, asserts that Reform Jewish decision making today is an authentic inheritor of the halakhic process.[13]

The first section of *Halakhah Shefuyah* advances Zemer's own views on the nature of Halakhah, and subsequent sections indicate how Zemer applies these views to specific matters of illegitimacy, marriage, conversion, and burial, as well as medical ethics, within Jewish law. In offering his halakhic rulings on these matters, Zemer—not unsurprisingly—frequently contrasts a liberal halakhic position to those put forth by Orthodox rabbinic spokesmen in Israel and he consistently demonstrates that the Halakhah possesses broader resources than his Orthodox Israeli peers generally suggest. Indeed one of his goals, in most of his responsa, is to offer the Israeli public distinct liberal halakhic perspective on each topic he addresses.

At the outset of his book, Zemer puts forth the thesis that halakhah, as it has developed throughout the ages, has always been evolutionary and inherently ethical.[14] He makes the case for a "sane halakhah" by highlighting progressive and humane principles and rules that are the essential elements that inform and direct the entire halakhic system. Zemer points out that *Hazal* consistently "discovered" directives within the Halakhah that allowed them to circumvent rulings which offended their ethical sensibilities. He cites, for example, a story told of Hillel the Elder as illustrative of this halakhic tendency. The talmudic passage reads as follows:

Hillel the Elder used to interpret "common speech." For it has been taught: The men of Alexandria used to betroth their wives, and when they were about to take them for the huppah ceremony, strangers would come and tear them away. Thereupon the Sages wished to declare their children *mamzerim*. Said Hillel the Elder to them, "Bring me your mothers' ketubahs." When they brought them, he found therein, "When thou art taken for the *huppah*, be thou my wife." And on the strength of this they did not declare their children *mamzerim* (Baba Metzia 104a).[15]

Zemer selected this example because it demonstrates Hillel the Elder's willingness to change a halakhic ruling he deemed unjust. As Zemer explains it, the Halakhah, prior to Hillel's decision, held that a woman between the period of betrothal and *huppah* was considered an *eishet-ish*. This meant that the woman, after betrothal, was—in a legal sense—married to her husband. Should the relationship not be sanctified beneath the *huppah*, the woman still required a *get* in order to marry another man. If, during that period, she did not receive a divorce and conceived by a man other than her husband, she would be considered an adulteress and her children would be *mamzerim*, unable to marry another kosher Jew.[16] In the talmudic case under discussion, the women were captured and raped. Consequently, the children born from these rapes would have been consigned a legal status as *mamzerim*. Hillel, wishing to spare these children from such a fate, on the basis of the principle of "common speech," interpreted the relevant clause from their *ketubot*—"When thou art taken for the *huppah*, be thou my wife"—to mean that a woman is not a wife until she enters the *huppah*. This view enabled Hillel to release the children from the stigma of *mamzerut* even though their mothers received no *get*.

Zemer's reading of this passage is not without its problems. After all, if the ethical sensibilities of *Hazal* were so well honed, one could reasonably suppose that it would have been inconceivable for the rabbis to have ever even considered applying the category of *mamzerut* to these children. Furthermore, there is the morally disturbing recognition—at least to many moderns—that no attempt is made here to alleviate the status deprivation the women suffer as chattel in this incident. Nor is there any acknowledgment of the women's human plight. These points are not insignificant, and in light of Zemer's overarching argument about the nature of halakhah as compassionate and humane, the text's silences on these points need to be addressed. Nevertheless, while they pose a challenge to his thesis, they do not obviate it. As the beginning of the passage suggests, the Halakhah *ab initio* was clear regarding the status of these children. They were *mamzerim*. Hillel, responding to the injustice inherent in this application of the *din*, found an exegetical way to enable these children to marry within the Jewish community.

Zemer's argument here concerning the ethically sensitive nature of Jewish law is reinforced by other citations. Representative of them is a passage Zemer brings from the Mishnah concerning the fate of women who might have been consigned to the category of *agunah*, but were not, due to the boldness and empathy of a great tannaitic authority. The *agunah*, in Jewish law, is literally a "chained woman." It refers to a woman whose marriage has been terminated *de facto* (e.g., her husband is missing in war or has abandoned her for another reason), but not *de jure*. As husbands alone possess the right to initiate divorce in Jewish law, the *agunah* is prohibited from remarrying because she is still technically married to her previous husband.

In M. Yebamot 16:7, a story is told concerning some men who were killed at Tel Arza. The Written Law promulgates the rule that testimony is considered legally valid only when at least two witnesses can testify to an incident or an event (Deut. 19:15). Furthermore, those witnesses, according to halakhic precedent, cannot include women, slaves, or maidservants.[17] Despite these rules, the mishna reports that Rabban Gamliel the Elder performed wedding ceremonies for the widows of these men on the basis of testimony offered by one witness alone. These women were thus spared the fate of an *agunah*. In addition, a new rule was established, on the basis of this incident, to allow a widow to remarry in such cases on the strength of testimony delivered by only one witness. Furthermore, the rabbis, in this same mishnaic passage, held that this testimony could be given by a slave, a woman, or a maidservant—persons normally ineligible to serve as witnesses in such cases. For many of us with certain modernist liberal sensibilities, the entire mishna is not unproblematic. Nevertheless, Zemer's reading of the mishna does support his claim that it is well within the realm of halakhic adjudication for a decisor to alter a rule, or create a coherent exception to a rule, in order to render an ethical and humane remedy in an instance where the rabbi deems a particular halakhic rule or application unethical or inadequate to resolve a concrete situation. This suggests that a *posek* is empowered by the halakhic process itself to employ compassion, creativity, and logic, as well as his own moral intuitions, to extend the boundaries of halakhah so as to discover unprecedented solutions to contemporary problems.

Moreover, there are overarching principles, not simply isolated rules or stories within the tradition of Jewish law, that Zemer further cites to support his notion that the essential nature of the halakhah is one of sanity and ethical sensitivity.[18] There is, for example, *takanat hashavim*, a principle that allows a rabbinic authority to render a lenient ruling in order to encourage a "sinner" to repent. This is based on the assumption that a more stringent ruling might place insurmountable obstacles before the sinner and thereby discourage or prevent the individual's repentance altogether. Zemer quotes a passage from bt Gittin 55a as an illustration of this principle. The passage poses the following question: If a person steals a beam and builds a large house using this beam, must he destroy his home in order to return the beam to its rightful owner? Or may he make restitution of equal value? Shammai stated that the house must be destroyed and the original beam returned. Since the Torah in Leviticus 5:20 states, "A thief must return the object he stole," Shammai reasoned that the thief must destroy the entire building if necessary in order to return the original beam to its rightful owner. Hillel, ruling more leniently, asserted that the thief was only required to supply a beam of similar value, and he did so on the basis of the principle of *takanat hashavim*.[19]

As Zemer notes, Hillel's ruling makes it possible for the thief to rehabilitate himself without being compelled to offer a remedy he would be unable to endure. It demonstrates, in Zemer's view, Hillel's realistic willingness to be flexible and sensitive to the needs and the weaknesses of humanity.[20] As Zemer notes, quoting Maimonides, Shammai's determination, grounded as it is in Scripture, is itself a *din Torah*, a toraitic law. Yet Maimonides asserts that Hillel's ruling is authoritative.[21] The principle of encouraging repentance, in this case taken from the Talmud, took precedence over a *din Torah*.

For Zemer, this example of the self-corrective nature of Halakhah is not an isolated one. There are numerous other such principles which are frequently cited by halakhic authorities. Foremost among them is the notion of "human dignity." The talmudic statement "Great is human dignity, that it overrides negative precepts found in the Torah" (B. Berachot 19b), clearly grants a *posek* broad discretionary powers in circumstances where the authority deems its application appropriate. Zemer notes that no less a personage than the *Rema*, Moses Isserles, employed this principle in deciding to officiate at a wedding that actually occurred on the Sabbath.[22] The wedding was initially scheduled to take place on a Friday afternoon, at the eve of the Sabbath, when suddenly the groom refused to enter the huppah because the bride was an orphan without a dowry. Isserles implored the groom to fulfill his responsibilities and refrain from publicly humiliating the young woman by abandoning her over money. An hour and a half after the Sabbath had commenced, Isserles was finally able to convince the young man to marry the young woman. Isserles defended his decision by asserting, "In order not to embarrass a respectable daughter of Israel, I rose and arranged the Kiddushin at the above-mentioned time."[23] In justifying his decision, Isserles argued, "One can feel for the separation of this couple and the shame that this woman would endure. . . . The authorization to be lenient causes no damage, and will enhance the joy of Shabbat afterward. And, it will enable the groom to perform the mitzvah of atonement to God in peace."[24]

This is another example of the flexibility certain *poskim* are willing to employ to achieve a compassionate and ethical result. Isserles was especially concerned about the welfare of this couple and the reputation of the bride. This concern took precedence over the proscriptions against his officiating at the wedding on Shabbat. And so, in accordance with the principle enunciated in the passage from Talmud Berachot, Isserles was moved to violate a negative rule from the Torah in order to preserve the human dignity of this young woman. Should a *posek* demonstrate a halakhic ruling, even a law derived from the Torah, to be unreasonable or inhumane, it may—as in this instance—be invalidated in light of a principle derived from the halakhic system, and this can be done in order to achieve a more rational and humane solution to a vexing human problem.

Given an Israeli context where the Orthodox rabbinate discourages such perceptions of Jewish law's elasticity, Zemer, in offering these explications of talmudic passages and halakhic rules and principles, demonstrates to both the worldwide liberal Jewish community and the Israeli populace that there are ethical mechanisms operative within the halakhah and that these mechanisms inform and direct the ethos and ever-evolving character of the Jewish legal system. The desire to avoid undue pain, the determination to preserve human dignity, and the realization that new circumstances unknown to previous generations require contemporary *poskim* in every generation to exercise flexibility and compassion in rendering halakhic decisions are the criteria for a "sane halakhah." It is a halakhah that is not concerned with the rules of the Tradition alone or, as Zemer phrases it, with "the dry letter of the law." Rather, in the spirit of a theological anthropology, it seeks out the rules and principles of the Tradition so that it can address and guide "the human being qua human being and the Jew qua Jew."[25] In the end, Zemer argues quite persuasively that a "sane halakhah" embodies and treasures a set of core values that have always been at the heart of Judaism in general and Reform in particular. Like his Reform ancestors in the Hamburg Temple dispute in the early 1800s, Zemer maintains that this approach alone will maintain liberal Jewish continuity with the past. In addition, he argues that a failure to interpret Halakhah in an "enlightened and progressive spirit" will cause still other Jews to regard Jewish law as cruel and will lead them to consign not only halakhah but Judaism itself to the dustbin of irrelevance. *Halakhah Shefuyah* argues that the compassion, the ethical sensibilities, and the creative energy inherent in the halakhah must be resuscitated in our day for all Jews—liberal and Orthodox alike. It applies these features to a whole host of contemporary issues and problems in unique and bold, yet sensible, ways.

Our review-essay, by outlining the character of Zemer's approach to halakhah, has sought to provide a foundation and context for understanding both the concerns that animate Zemer and the normative judgments at which he arrives throughout his book. The Israeli venue of *Halakhah Shefuyah* marks Zemer's book as unique in the annals of Reform Jewish legal literature. As such, it commands the attention of all who are interested in liberal Judaism and its development in Zion today. At the same time, Zemer's articulation of the principles that undergird the halakhic process as well as the substantive matters he takes up in *Halakhah Shefuyah* commend his book to readers within and beyond the liberal Jewish camp in Israel. *Halakhah Shefuyah* constitutes a noteworthy achievement. It serves as a "bridge between the ways of our Sages and the needs of the present."[26] It is our hope that it will soon appear in English translation so that it will receive the broader readership it so richly deserves.

ACKNOWLEDGMENT

Michael White co-authored this article and I am grateful for his permission to include it in this volume.

NOTES

1. Jakob J. Petuchowski, *Prayerbook Reform in Europe* (New York: World Union for Progressive Judaism, 1968), 49.
2. For a summary of this controversy and its literature, see Petuchowski, *Prayerbook Reform in Europe*, 49–54, 84–98, as well as Michael Meyer, response to *Modernity: A History of the Reform Movement in Judaism* (New York: Oxford University Press, 1988), 53–61.
3. Petuchowski, *Prayerbook Reform in Europe*, 98.
4. Gunther Plaut, *The Rise of Reform Judaism* (New York: World Union for Progressive Judaism, 1963), xviii–xix, 37.
5. The wording here is taken from Petuchowski, "Abraham Geiger and Samuel Holdheim," *Leo Baeck Institute Yearbook* (1977): 159.
6. For a philosophical exposition and defense of the dialectical tension inherent in this stance, see two outstanding articles by Eugene Borowitz. The first is "The Autonomous Self and the Commanding Community," *Theological Studies* 45 (March 1984), while the second is entitled "The Autonomous Jewish Self," *Modern Judaism* 4, no. 1 (February 1984). For a representative internal Reform critique of this posture, see Dan Cohn-Sherbok, "Law and Freedom in Reform Judaism," *CCAR Journal* (Winter 1983): 90.
7. As cited in Meyer, *Response to Modernity*, 376.
8. Moshe Zemer, *Halakhah Shefuyah* (Tel Aviv: D'vir, 1993).
9. Walter Jacob, "The Source of Reform Halakhic Authority," in *Rabbinic Authority*, ed. Elliot Stevens (New York: CCAR Press, 1982), 36.
10. Zemer, *Halakhah Shefuyah*, 20.
11. Ibid.
12. Jacob and Zemer, *Dynamic Jewish Law* (Pittsburgh: Rodeph Shalom Press, 1991), 6.
13. For Jacob's views, see his article, "The Source of Reform Halachic Authority," 36.
14. Zemer, *Halakhah Shefuyah*, 20.
15. As translated in *The Soncino Talmud* (London: Soncino Press, 1935), *Seder Nezikim*, 1: 594–95.
16. Zemer, *Halakhah Shefuyah*, 21.
17. Ibid., 33.
18. In making this claim about the nature of Jewish law, Zemer is not alone. Leading Conservative rabbis such as Bradley Artson, Elliot Dorff, and Gordon Tucker describe the Halakhah in much the same terms that Zemer does. See

their many pieces during the last decade in journals such as *Judaism, Conservative Judaism, Sh'ma*, and *The Jewish Spectator*.

19. Zemer, *Halakhah Shefuyah*, 23.

20. Ibid., 22.

21. Ibid. Zemer quotes Rambam's *Hilchot Gezerah* 1:5.

22. Ibid., 30.

23. Ibid., 29, quoting Freehof, *Treasury of Responsa* (Philadelphia, 1962), 133.

24. Ibid.

25. Ibid., 42.

26. Ibid., 320.

18

Reform Zionism Today

A Consideration of First Principles

On July 17, 1810, in Seseen, Germany, Israel Jacobson, the father of Reform Judaism, dedicated the Temple of Jacob on the grounds of his school amidst great pomp and circumstance. A contemporary account of the dedication ceremony indicates that hundreds of "persons of distinguished rank, scholars, Jewish, Protestant, and Catholic clergymen, officials, businessmen of all kinds" were in attendance. The event displayed the universalistic aspirations of the dawning era and our commentator was visibly moved by the spirit of concord and "uniform tolerance" that marked the day and its participants. In a burst of unconcealed enthusiasm, he rapturously queried, at the end of his description, "Where would one have seen a similar day on which Jews and Christians celebrated together in a common service in the presence of more than forty clergymen of both religions, and then sat down to eat and rejoice together in intimate company?"[1]

Reform Judaism, as these words testify, was born in an Enlightenment crucible of messianic expectations. It embodied the universalistic hopes and commitments of the day and affirmed that the utopianism inherent in this enlightened vision of the world was capable of being transformed into reality. Jews would no longer view themselves or be regarded by others as part of a distinct ethnic-national-religious community. Rather, they would define themselves—and be seen by others—as individual citizens of a modern nation-state whose religion happened to be Jewish. The universalism inherent in this approach typifies a tendency that has characterized Reform Judaism to the present.

Contrast this to the political Zionism of Theodor Herzl. As Herzl himself phrased it in 1896, in his preface to *The Jewish State*, the source of the call for Jewish national revival and the restoration of our people to our ancestral homeland was the fact that "the world resounds with clamor against the Jews. . . . We have sincerely tried everywhere to merge with the national communities in which we live, seeking only to preserve the faith of our fathers. It is not permitted us."[2] Zionism thus burst onto the stage of modern history as a counteremancipatory movement, a counterweight to classical Reform. Emancipation and Enlightenment were deemed failures by Herzl. The universalism of Israel Jacobson, and Moses Mendelssohn before him, and of others such as Abraham Geiger and S. R. Hirsch after him, as well as their attempts to identify Judaism as a religious confession alone, were branded as naive and delusionary by Herzl and his followers. Jews would never be accepted as equals in the Christian world of Europe, they said, and the hopes of the universalists were dismissed as the aspirations of "amiable visionaries." The crowning ideal of the Enlightenment, "universal brotherhood, is not," Herzl thundered, "even a beautiful dream." The goal of creating a Jewish state was to allow Jews to "live at last as free men in our own soil, and in our own homes peacefully die."[3] The particularism that informed the nineteenth century Zionist visions and aims of Herzl could hardly stand in sharper opposition to the universalistic dreams and aspirations of Jacobson at the outset of that century.

Many years have passed since these movements—with their antithetical approaches to and attitudes toward the place of the Jew in the modern world—originated, and much has changed. Reform partisans of Zionism abound today and the Reform movement has, by any standard, moved from an extreme hostility toward the particularity of Jewish nationalism to a cordial, perhaps even warm, embrace of the Jewish state. The postures that marked each of these two movements at the turn of the century, and that often led to antagonisms between them, are for many no more than a page in history. Insights derived from the classical positions of each movement have come to permeate and inform the other. The boundaries that separated and distinguished them no longer appear so formidable.

Nevertheless, the ideological principles—the universalistic-religious sentiments—advanced by the architects of classical Reform have done more than historically inform our movement's attitudes (positive and negative) toward Zionism. They continue to shape our understandings and assessments of the State of Israel today. As we in the Reform movement prepare to draw up a statement of principles that will undergird our present-day position concerning the reality of the State of Israel, it is vital to remember that our Reform ancestors could and did confidently affirm that the prophetic spirit of Judaism and the universalistic ethos of an Enlightenment world were totally compatible. They asserted that Judaism was a religion alone and viewed discriminatory and prejudiced acts directed against Jews or other minority groups as atavistic remnants from a premodern past that were destined to wither away in a modern world where "superstition would no longer enslave the mind nor idolatry blind the eye."

This paper will question, in light of happenings in the twentieth century, whether the messianic optimism and unbridled faith in the goodness and moral progress of humanity that informed classical Reform and permitted those classical Reformers to define Judaism exclusively as a religion remain an appropriate Archimedean point for principled reflection on the meaning of the Jewish state in our era. Classical Reform understandings of religion may need to be reconsidered as Reform Jews seek to comprehend the meaning of Zionism and Israel in a post-Holocaust world. Our affirmation of a Reform Zionism may require a broader definition of religion than our ancestors would have offered, as well as a distinct ideological base more attuned to the events of our century and the reality of a Jewish state. This paper, therefore, will rehearse the ideological consistency that marked Reform Jewish approaches to Zionism in the past and will consider the possibility of a different type of ideology, a more nuanced and dialectical one, to frame our perspectives in the future.

The Approach of Classical Reform to Zionism

The Pittsburgh Platform of 1885 expressed the representative nineteenth century position of classical Reform toward Zionism. Judaism, the platform averred, was "a progressive religion, ever striving to be in accord with the postulates of reason." Its assessment of the contemporary world reflected the same messianic vision that had informed Jacobson and his followers in Seesen seventy-five years earlier. As the fifth principle of the platform proclaimed, "We recognize in the modern era of universal culture of heart and intellect the approach of the realization of Israel's great messianic hope for the establishment of the kingdom of truth, justice, and peace among all men." It is small wonder, given such sentiments, that the platform expressed an undisguised hostility and contempt for Jewish nationalism. As the platform's fifth principle continued, "We consider ourselves no longer a nation but a religious community, and therefore expect neither a return to Palestine, . . . nor the restoration of any of the laws concerning the Jewish state."[4]

Half a century later, as champions of Reform Zionism proudly note, this position was dramatically and officially altered. The Columbus Platform of 1937, in contradistinction to the Pittsburgh Platform, asserted as point number five, "In the rehabilitation of Palestine, the land hallowed by memories and hopes, we behold the promise of renewed life for many of our brethren. We affirm the obligation of all Jewry to aid in its up building as a Jewish homeland by endeavoring to make it not only a haven of refuge for the oppressed but also a center of Jewish culture and spiritual life."[5] Only the harshest critic could fail to appreciate the "Copernican revolution" this statement represents in the history of Reform's attitude toward Zionism. The distance from Pittsburgh to Columbus is considerable, and should not be cavalierly dismissed.

Nevertheless, this transformation in attitude does not represent a fundamental ideological break between the two platforms. For the authors of the Columbus Platform, upon concluding point number five, immediately proceeded to link the "rehabilitation of Palestine" to the messianic task of "repairing the world." The final paragraph of point number five declared, "We regard it as our historic task to cooperate with all men in the establishment of the kingdom of God, of universal brotherhood, justice, truth, and peace on earth. This is our messianic goal."[6] Again, my point here is not to claim that Reform's attitude toward Zionism in 1937 was akin to the attitude articulated in 1885. The change was substantial. However, despite this evolution in attitude, the principles that undergirded Columbus were in reality identical to those that supported Pittsburgh. Thus, even when Reform came to embrace Zionism, it did so in light of the universalistic-religious categories it had inherited from the nineteenth century.

This approach remains constant in the San Francisco Centenary Perspective of 1976. The State of Israel—the crowning political achievement of the Zionist movement—is hailed as the land to which Reform Jews are bound by "innumerable religious and ethnic ties." The admiration and love the framers of the Perspective have for the state is clear and unmistakable. Yet they, like their forebears, are careful to reject a view of the state that could be decried as "particularistic." Instead, they remain "true" to the universalism that has characterized Reform since its inception in 1810, and, in the section of the Centenary Perspective that deals with the state, they conclude with an affirmation of Jewish life in the Diaspora: "The State of Israel and the Diaspora, in fruitful dialogue, can show how a people transcends nationalism even as it affirms it, thereby setting an example for humanity which remains largely concerned with dangerously parochial goals."[7]

The sentiments expressed in these platforms have also been advanced by Reform ideologues throughout the twentieth century. Hermann Cohen opposed a Zionism that, in his view, rejected the messianic mission of the Jewish people and advocated in its stead this people Israel's "normalization." In the land of Israel itself, the ardent Zionist Judah L. Magnes paralleled something of Cohen's position when he insisted that a State of Israel could never be "like all the nations." Furthermore, Franz Rosenzweig, who saw the Jewish people as living *sub specie aeternitatis*, not only (in Eugene Borowitz's words) "distrusted Zionism, but looked askance at even its cultural aspirations."[8]

In more recent years, in the United States, our teacher Jakob Petuchowski, *z'l*, followed in the footsteps of these Reform luminaries in his *Zion Reconsidered*. There, he affirmed the traditional religious understanding that the people Israel is charged eternally with the task of serving as God's "kingdom of priests." The State of Israel could receive Jewish sanction only if the Jewish citizens of the state strove consciously to fulfill God's mandate to *k'nesset yisrael* to be a "holy people." Participation in the universal and messianic "mission" of the Jewish people alone could grant the ethnos of Jewish nationhood a modicum of legitimacy.

Even today, in the writings of our mentor Eugene Borowitz, *yibadel l'hayyim arukhim*, echoes of these attitudes abound. No one who reads Borowitz can doubt his devotion to and admiration for the State of Israel. No Jewish theology in our day can be complete, he writes, that does not recognize the central importance the Jewish state plays in the lives of Jews. Yet even he, in *The Masks Jews Wear*, expressed an attitude toward Hebrew that one would be hard-pressed to distinguish from that of Rosenzweig: "I doubt that using a language gives one any substantial identity."[9] In addition, his determination to define belief (as opposed to ethnicity) as the central element needed in a modern Judaism reflects a position that easily leads, as Richard Hirsch has pointed out, to a "non-Zionism."[10]

What emerges from all this is not just an understanding of why Zionism was rejected by classical Reform thought. Rather, this discussion indicates that those Reform thinkers who have affirmed and embraced the Zionist position have done so on the basis of principles and viewpoints supplied by the nineteenth century. Zionism remains countenanced within Reform only when the State of Israel is viewed from the perspective of universal categories. This position is congenial to the definition of Judaism offered by our Reform predecessors of the 1800s. It draws upon Rudolf Otto's vision of religion and the holy as being distinct from the secular and the profane, and sees Judaism's particularity as warranted only when it strives for the realization of Israel's universal mission to be "a light unto the nations."

Judaism, it is true, has often distinguished between the sacred and the profane. The universal and the particular have also always been present in Judaism. At times, they have complemented one another. More often, they have existed in some sort of creative tension. Yet, for Reform these two poles—truth be told—have not, from an ideological standpoint, been in conflict. The particular, as Ellen Umansky demonstrated and as Norman Patz confirmed, has always been subordinated to the universal in Reform thought and practice.[11]

This brief survey supports Umansky's contention. The nationalistic affirmations advanced by Zionism have remained suspect throughout the history of our movement, and they have not been granted religious status. Jewish nationalism has been accorded legitimacy by Reform only when it self-consciously acts in the service of some grander, more universal cause that "transcends nationalism" with its "dangerously parochial goals." The principled legacy and perspective of Jacobson have remained operative and dominant within Reform to the present.

Elements of this heritage certainly ought to be as cherished by us as they were by our ancestors. However, in a century in which our people have witnessed both the Holocaust and the birth of the Jewish state, other parts of that universalistic legacy must be reconsidered. We need not be held in slavish obeisance to the ideals of nineteenth century universalism. A new ideology, sensitive to but distinct from the patrimony of the past, must be contemplated, and other theological currents need to be explored as we seek to uncover and articulate a contemporary ideological basis for the Reform movement's approach to Zion.

Greenberg and Fackenheim—A Shift in Emphasis

This new basis has begun to be explored and articulated in the writings of the maverick Orthodox rabbi, Irving Greenberg, as well as in the work of our Liberal colleague, Emil Fackenheim. For both Greenberg and Fackenheim, the Holocaust requires a paradigm shift in Jewish thought. Their insights may prove instructive as we reassess our nineteenth century Jewish legacy and search for principles to guide our own Zionism today. Greenberg asserts that the Holocaust casts doubt upon the messianic optimism of our nineteenth century ancestors. "There is the shock of recognition," he writes, "that the humanistic revolt . . . is now revealed to sustain a capacity for death and demonic evil."[12] The Holocaust is a strong indictment of all inherited positions; it forces us, like others, to rethink our posture as we confront the post-Holocaust world.

For Jews, including liberal ones, this means the following: The confidence we formerly had in the goodness of humanity and the moral progress of civilization must be tempered by the recognition that the human capacity for evil, as for goodness, is virtually infinite. Reform Judaism can no longer completely identify and assert its compatibility with the tenets of Western or any other civilization. Contemporary civilization, to use Greenberg's words, "is not worthy of this transfer of our ultimate loyalty."[13] The very foundations and messianic optimism that formerly propelled Reform therefore must be reconsidered.

The Holocaust also demonstrates that the "easy dichotomy of atheist/theist," the secular and the holy, "is at an end." The secular is not the antithesis of the spiritual. The former is, if anything, the testing ground for the strength and expression of the latter. This indicates, for Jews, that the nationalism of our people can no longer be seen as distinct from our religion. We Reform Jews must understand, as our biblical ancestor Ruth did when she said, "Your people shall be my people, and your God my God," that religion and peoplehood are inseparable and intertwined. We must not warp our own expression of Judaism by condemning nationalistic manifestations of Judaism and Jewish identity as "anti-religious."

After the Holocaust, the religious enterprise must see itself as a desperate attempt to create and heal human life. For Jews, this accords theological significance to the birth and activities of the Jewish state. "The re-creation of the state is the strongest suggestion that God's promises are still valid and reliable," Greenberg writes. The State of Israel, a "secularist phenomenon, gives the central religious testimony of the Jewish people today."[14]

The Holocaust has empirically undercut the messianic confidence our ancestors had in Western civilization and the growing goodness and ethical progress of humanity. In so doing, it has led to an appreciation of the moral dimensions of power. For the Holocaust demonstrated that powerlessness is not necessarily a virtue. As Greenberg so insightfully puts it,

> Out of the Holocaust experience comes the demand for the redistribution of power. The principle is simple. No one should ever have to depend again on anyone else's goodwill or respect for their basic security and right to exist. . . . No one should ever be equipped with less power than is necessary to assure one's dignity. To argue dependence on law, or human goodness, or universal equality is to join the ranks of those who would like to repeat the Holocaust.[15]

Powerlessness, an absolute inability to assure the safety of one's children, can no longer be regarded as morally acceptable by the Jewish people. Reform Judaism must acknowledge this and recognize that the return of the Jewish people onto the stage of *machtpolitik* and history is a *bonum* at this point in time. The State of Israel embodies the Jewish people's thirst for and affirmation of life in a post-Holocaust world. This does not justify Jewish abuse of power. It is an assertion that power itself may be, and in this instance is, a religiously legitimated precondition for goodness to manifest itself. Power is morally required, if not totally sufficient, for the protection and maintenance of human dignity in our world.

The destruction of six million of our people by Hitler reaffirms life as a sacred value and causes Greenberg to attach theological significance to the State of Israel itself. The state, in a post-Holocaust situation, testifies to the continuity of the Jewish people and, in this way, to the faithfulness of God's covenantal promise. It is this emphasis on people, and the religious weight Greenberg ascribes to it, that is most crucial for Jews and others to appreciate. In the contemporary setting, can Yad Vashem be deemed less religiously important than the Western Wall? Is no religious weight to be assigned the Knesset as a symbol of our people's autonomy and return to our land in the twentieth century? Greenberg contends that contemporary Jews need to recognize that it is humanity, not God, which must be justified after the Holocaust. "In the silence of God and of theology," he concludes, "there is one fundamental testimony that can still be given—the testimony of human life itself. This was always the basic evidence, but after Auschwitz its importance is incredibly heightened. In fact, it is the only testimony that can still be heard."[16]

Greenberg's beliefs find parallel expression in the writings of the great Liberal theologian Emil Fackenheim. Fackenheim describes certain events in Jewish experience as "epoch-making." They make a "new claim upon Jewish faith," testing Judaism against these unprecedented historical happenings. For Fackenheim, as for Greenberg, the Holocaust is such an event. It demands that Jews abandon neither their people nor their faith because to do so is to hand Hitler "a posthumous victory." After the Holocaust, Jews "are left only one supreme value—existence."[17]

Fackenheim moves from this stance to an embrace and affirmation of the religious significance of the Jewish state. The State of Israel, for Fackenheim as for Greenberg, represents the Jewish people's response to the catastrophe of the Holocaust. Jewish survival is sacred in and of itself and the state is essential to that survival and to the continuity of Jewish existence in the world. Support of the state and Zionism become, for Fackenheim, the sacred obligation of every Jew. This leads Fackenheim, like Greenberg, to assert that an easy distinction between the secular and the religious can no longer be drawn. Indeed, secularity becomes a religious possibility in the contemporary world because even secular Israelis fulfill a religious obligation by helping to keep the state, and therefore the Jewish people, alive. Secular existence is thereby possessed of religious meaning.

The views of Greenberg and Fackenheim have been subjected to serious scrutiny and criticism. The most cogent and concise critique has been offered by Arnold Eisen who, in summarizing and assessing the thought of Fackenheim, observes that for Fackenheim "the significance of the state . . . lies on the mythic level of rebirth, rather than on the substantive level of what the state is or does, so crucial to [Israeli thinkers such as Gershom] Scholem and [Natan] Rotenstreich, [David] Hartman and [Eliezer] Schweid."[18] The force of Eisen's criticism cannot easily be gainsaid. Fackenheim himself is sensitive to it. For Reform Jews, weaned on concepts of universalism and mission, Eisen's attack on the positions of Greenberg and Fackenheim will surely strike a resonant chord. Our traditional emphases make it difficult to accept existence as a religious end in and of itself.

Eisen's critique is a significant one and we ought to heed elements of it. "What the state is or does" ought to be of great concern to all Jews, and for those of us who identify as Reform Zionists it ought to be doubly so. The legacy of our religious tradition's emphasis on justice as well as our Reform commitment to morality and ethics make Israel the ultimate testing ground for the truth of Jewish teachings and values. However, to accept this critique as decisive is, in my view, unwise and wrong in the current situation. For nothing should obscure or deny the religious significance the state possesses by virtue of the sheer fact of its existence. As Fackenheim asserts,

> After the Holocaust, Jews owe anti-Semites, as well as, of course, their own children, the duty of not encouraging murderous instincts by their own powerlessness. And after the absolute homelessness of the twelve Nazi years that were equal to a thousand, they owe the whole world, as well as, of course, their own children, the duty to say no to Jewish wandering, to return home, to rebuild a Jewish state. These aspects of Judaism in the making are moral and political. Their inner source is spiritual and religious. [Ours is] a time not for *kiddush ha-Shem* (martyrdom) but rather for *kiddush ha-hayyim* (the sanctification of life). . . . By any standard, secular or religious, Jewish life ranks higher than Jewish death. The Jewish people have experienced exile in a form more horrendous than ever dreamt of by the apocalyptic imagination; thereafter, to have ended exile bespeaks a fidelity and a will to live that, taken together, give a new dimension to piety. The product of this fidelity—the Jewish state—is fragile still, and embattled wherever the world is hostile or does not understand. Yet Jews both religious and secular know in their hearts that Israel—the renewed people, the reborn language, the replanted land, the rebuilt city, the state itself—is a new and unique celebration of life. . . . If a Jewish state had not arisen in the wake of the Holocaust, it would be a religious necessity . . . to create it now.[19]

A Reform Zionism for Our Time

I want to close on a personal note. Two decades ago I lived for a year at Mishmar Ha-emek, a kibbutz of Hashomer Ha-tza'ir located in the Jezreel Valley next to Meggido. On many afternoons, after the day's work had been completed, I would walk up into the hills of the kibbutz. There, I would gaze out onto the valley below. And each time, when I looked, I would see the orchards and the irrigation pools, the cotton fields and the trees, the factories and the roads—and most of all, the people. And I would think of the words with which the prophet Amos concluded his preachments to the people Israel:

A time is coming—declares the Lord . . .
I will restore my people Israel.
They shall rebuild ruined cities and inhabit them;
They shall plant vineyards and drink their wine;
They shall till gardens and eat their fruits.
And I will plant them upon their soil,
Nevermore to be uprooted
From the soil I have given them—said the Lord your God.[20]

And I would be deeply moved. However, no blessing would emerge. For I was never sure, despite the prophecy, if what I saw was the work of God or of persons. Perhaps, I now think, it does not matter. For how, in assessing the meaning of Israel, can one distinguish between the sacred and the profane, the religious and the secular? Furthermore, why should one try? This, I believe, is what Greenberg and Fackenheim have taught me.

After some time on the top of the hill, I would return to the kibbutz, and there I would see families sitting together and talking on the lawn. I would watch little children tumble and run after one another, screaming all the time in Hebrew. At this point, the words of the *sheheheyanu* would silently form in my heart and escape from my lips. Fackenheim, in numerous places throughout his work, has observed that Jewish action in our time has outpaced Jewish thought. My heart, even then, knew the truth of Fackenheim's observation, for in those moments my spirit moved me instinctively to thank God for the *kiddush ha-hayyim*, the sanctification of life that the Jewish state and Jewish existence embody.

Our people's return to our land is not simply mythic. It has taken on flesh and blood, and to celebrate that fact is to applaud much more than "mythic renewal." It is to acknowledge that the rebirth of Jewish life embodied in the State of Israel is fraught with religious import and significance. This does not mean, as we move to create a platform for Reform Zionism, that the daily conduct of life and the moral sensibilities evidenced in the political policies of the Jewish state are or ought to be matters of indifference to us. We cannot reject the universalism of our religion. To do so would constitute a betrayal of the best that marks us as a movement. These principles, and our Reform forebears' appreciation of and emphasis upon them, are as vital for us today as they were in the past. However, they are no longer sufficient.

Ours is a different time, and the sources of our nineteenth-century prede-cessors' thoughts and the distinctions they drew between the religious and the political dimensions, the spiritual and the national elements, of Juda-ism and Jewish life ought not to be made by us. Our ideological foundation must be fashioned in response to the realities of history in the twentieth century, and our responses to those realities must move us ideologically beyond our Reform ancestors' universalism. Max Weber, the brilliant Ger-man sociologist, writing in the second decade of this century, concluded his famous essay, "Science as a Vocation," with the following words. The position of the West, he wrote, "is the same as resounds in the beautiful Edomite watchman's song of the period of exile that has been included among Isaiah's oracles [21:11]: 'He calleth to me out of Seir. Watchman, what of the night?' The watchman said, The morning cometh and also the night: if ye will enquire, enquire ye: return, come." Weber, after cit-ing this prophecy, chillingly observed, "The people to whom this was said have enquired and tarried for more than two millennia, and we are shaken when we realize its fate. From this we want to draw the lesson that nothing is gained by yearning and tarrying alone, and we shall act differently."[21]

Our people, in building a state, have heeded Weber's imperative. We no longer "yearn" and "tarry," and we have "acted differently." The Jewish people have "returned to history" with a degree of power unknown for the previous two millennia. Reform Zionism needs to know and affirm the religious significance of this fact. The monism of universalism must be rejected. Our Zionism must be built upon the dialectical foundations of universalism and particularism and the interplay between them. Both poles must be accorded religious legitimacy by our movement, for only then can a platform be constructed in which each can inform and, at times, provide a corrective for the other. In so doing, a new ground for our Reform Zionism will be established, one in which, as Rav Kook put it, "*hayashan yithadesh, v'hehadash yitkadesh*"—"the old will be renewed, and the new will be made holy."

NOTES

1. Quoted in Gunther Plaut, *The Rise of Reform Judaism* (New York: World Union for Progressive Judaism, 1963), 27–30.
2. Herzl's words are found in Arthur Hertzberg, *The Zionist Idea* (New York: Harper, 1966), 204, 209.

3. Ibid., 223, 225.

4. These quotations from the Pittsburgh Platform are found in Gunther Plaut, *The Growth of Reform Judaism* (New York: World Union for Progressive Judaism, 1965), 34.

5. Ibid., 97.

6. Ibid., 97–98.

7. The Centenary Perspective is printed in Eugene B. Borowitz, *Reform Judaism Today: Reform in the Process of Change* (New York: Behrman House, 1978), xix–xxv. The quotations cited in this paragraph are found on xxiii–xxiv.

8. Eugene B. Borowitz, *Renewing the Covenant* (Philadelphia: Jewish Publication Society, 1991), 62.

9. Eugene B. Borowitz, *The Masks Jews Wear* (New York: Simon and Schuster, 1973), 164.

10. Hirsch's instructive essay is entitled "Toward a Theology of Reform Zionism," *CCAR Journal* (Fall 1991): 35–44. His comments on Borowitz are found on 35–36.

11. See Umansky's article and Patz's response in the inaugural issue of the *Journal of Reform Zionism*.

12. Irving Greenberg, "Cloud of Smoke, Pillar of Fire: Judaism, Christianity, and Modernity after the Holocaust," in *Auschwitz: Beginning of a New Era?* ed. Eva Fleischner (New York: Ktav, 1977), 15.

13. Ibid., 28.

14. Ibid., 50.

15. Ibid., 54.

16. Ibid., 41.

17. See Emil Fackenheim, *God's Presence in History* (New York: Harper, 1972).

18. Arnold Eisen, *Galut: Modern Jewish Reflections on Homelessness and Homecoming* (Bloomington: Indiana University Press, 1986), 174.

19. Emil Fackenheim, "Holocaust," in *Contemporary Jewish Religious Thought*, ed. Arthur A. Cohen and Paul Mendes-Flohr (New York: Charles Scribner's, 1987), 407–8.

20. Amos 9:13–15.

21. Max Weber, "Science as a Vocation," in *From Max Weber: Essays in Sociology*, ed. and trans. H. B. Gerth (New York: Oxford University Press, 1971), 156.

FOUR

Rabbis and the Rabbinate

Lezakot et Harabim

19

Wissenschaft des Judentums, Historical Consciousness, and Jewish Faith

The Diverse Paths of Frankel, Auerbach, and Halevy

In his 1965 book, *The Historian and the Believer*, Protestant scholar of religion Van Harvey observed that the commitment of the modern historian to "a sustained and critical attempt to recover the past" was motivated by a "Promethean will-to-truth" that was genuinely "revolutionary" when this approach first fully manifested itself during the nineteenth century. He observed that modern historical method was "based on [naturalistic] assumptions quite irreconcilable with traditional belief [based on supernatural metaphysics]," and went on to assert, "If the theologian believes on faith that certain events [as recorded in holy writ] occurred, the historian regards all historical claims as having only a greater or lesser degree of probability and he regards the attachment of faith to these claims as a corruption of historical judgment."[1]

The modern study of history, with its critical canons of scholarship and its dogmatic notion of change, is thus by definition seemingly antithetical to faith. As Soren Kierkegaard, the famed nineteenth-century Protestant theologian, stated, "One can 'know' nothing at all about 'Christ.' He is the paradox, the object of faith, existing only for faith. But all historical communication is communication of 'knowledge,' hence from history one can learn nothing at all about Christ. . . . He can only be believed."[2]

All this may seem an unusual place to begin this prestigious annual lecture held under the auspices of the Leo Baeck Institute. After all, our topic this evening is not Christianity. However, my citations of Professor Harvey and Soren Kierkegaard are meant to indicate that the topic tonight is not a parochial one confined to the Jewish community in the modern world. Rather, this question about the relationship between the modern study of history and the matter of religious faith, of how to reconcile adherence to sacred tradition with critical methods of historical research, has plagued many religious believers during the last two hundred years.

In this year, when we mark the 150th anniversary of the Jewish Theological Seminary of Breslau and consider the powerful heritage of academic scholarship that that seminary has bequeathed the modern Jewish world, no question could be more meaningful. Countless religious Jewish historians during the last two centuries have been occupied with this issue. It is one that has great meaning for me both as a personally committed religious Jew and as a head of a modern rabbinical seminary, Hebrew Union College–Jewish Institute of Religion, that has been marked since its inception in 1875 by a devotion—as have all major modern liberal Jewish religious seminaries—to *Wissenschaft des Judentums*. Indeed, a wrestling with this question of the relationship between faith and historical analysis has marked virtually all sectors of an acculturated and university-trained occidental Jewry since the rise of a modern critical historical consciousness during the last two hundred years.

No one has better addressed what this dilemma has meant from a Jewish standpoint and for the Jewish community and the modern professional Jewish historian nor what is so distinct about this mode of thought than Professor Yosef Hayim Yerushalmi of Columbia University. In his deservedly famous *Zachor: Jewish History and Jewish Memory*, Yerushalmi writes, "[The] discovery of history [by the Jewish historian] is not a mere interest in the past, which always existed, but a new awareness, a perception of a fluid temporal dimension from which nothing is exempt. The major consequence for Jewish historiography is that it cannot view Judaism as something absolutely given and subject to a priori definition. Judaism is inseparable from its evolution through time."[3]

In contrast, classical rabbinic thought, as Jacob Neusner has pointed out, is atemporal. Labeling such thought as "paradigmatic thinking," Neusner observes that for the rabbis, paradigms of different sorts dictate the organization of events, and these events are interpreted by appeal to these archetypical models. The patterns themselves impose meaning on the events that occur and in so doing they obliterate distinctions between past, present, and future, between here and now and then and there.[4]

This does not mean that the ancient or medieval rabbis, as Amos Funkenstein has argued, possessed no sense of "historical consciousness."[5] However, the sense of "collective memory" that marked classical Jewish culture and consciousness was far removed from the autonomous and secular historicism that burst forth among Jewish university-trained scholars during the nineteenth century. Of course, the historical method developed by these modern historians was itself a by-product of the process of secularization that ultimately came to dominate the modern West. This approach precluded sacred historical explanation. For the modern historian, every fact and event must be placed within its own singular context and an explanatory or analytical narrative appropriate to that context must be created.

"There is," Yerushalmi therefore observes, "an inherent tension in modern Jewish historiography. . . . To the degree that this historiography is indeed 'modern' . . . , it must stand in sharp opposition to its own subject matter, not on this or that detail, but concerning the vital core: the belief that divine providence is not only an ultimate but an active causal factor in Jewish history."[6]

It is therefore small wonder that many Jewish religious traditionalists have vehemently protested critical works of modern scholarship, for these works support, as Yerushalmi once more phrases it, "a Jewish historiography divorced from Jewish collective memory and, in crucial respects, thoroughly at odds with it."[7] The study of modern history would seem to be a subversive activity.

Yet modern historical scholarship has not always "been at odds" with the construction of Jewish memory and faith. While this mode of investigation clearly can be employed to "undermine" tradition, the method of *Wissenschaft des Judentums* has just as surely been utilized to construct new ways of approaching Jewish commitment and faith. In fact, during the nineteenth century in Germany, historical scholarship frequently played the role of handmaiden to religion, and its influence was pervasive in virtually every precinct of German-Jewish life.

As Ismar Schorsch has observed, "In nineteenth-century Germany the study of Jewish history functioned as both authority and medium. Construed as authority, a proper reading of Jewish history could yield the indispensable guidelines and validating principles to determine the future shape of Judaism. Invoked as medium, Jewish history could readily provide an interpretation of Judaism in terms of the idealistic idiom of the century. In the Middle Ages, these two functions were fulfilled by different disciplines: a rich and flexible legal tradition generally served as sole authority for changes within the Jewish community, while philosophy offered the common idiom in which Judaism could be expounded for Jew and non-Jew alike. In the wake of emancipation, . . . history assumed the role of both. It became the functional equivalent of halakhah and philosophy in the medieval world." *Wissenschaft des Judentums* was "the most potent intellectual force on the German Jewish scene," and Jewish scholars across the religious spectrum attempted to resolve "the dilemmas posed by the emancipation struggle through a proper reading of Jewish history. . . . *Wissenschaft* history was programmatic history."[8]

While a number of traditionally religious German Jews shunned *Wissenschaft des Judentums* and regarded critical historical study as an anathema, far more traditional Jewish believers did not. These traditional Jews embraced *Wissenschaft* and felt that modern study could actually enhance and deepen Jewish faith. As Schorsch notes, "By the 1840s a cluster of historians began to wield *Wissenschaft* in defense of traditional Judaism. *Wissenschaft* . . . could be wielded . . . conservatively to defend traditional Judaism and to resist Reform."[9]

By looking at selected parts from *Darkhei HaMishnah* of Zacharias Frankel and by considering the attacks and methods employed in two different and representative Orthodox critiques of his work, *Hatzofeh 'al Darkhei HaMishnah* by Zvi Benjamin Auerbach and *Dorot Harishonim* by Isaac Halevy, the different ways in which significant figures in traditional nineteenth-century German Judaism addressed and understood the nature of historical scholarship and its relationship to faith will be illuminated. In so doing, the diverse intellectual approaches that informed these men as well as the distinctive attitudes that different camps of Jewish religious traditionalists have taken toward critical scholarship will be elucidated. In this way, a concluding reflection can be offered on the implications that historical consciousness has for the maintenance of Jewish faith and life.

Frankel and Darkhei HaMishnah

A giant of Jewish scholarship and a completely observant traditional Jew, Zacharias Frankel (1801–1875) is famed for the leading role he played in the construction of modern Jewish scholarship and for his position as first head of the Breslau Seminary. His *Darkhei HaMishnah*, written in 1859, is a pioneering work in the field of critical rabbinic scholarship. In it, Frankel attempted to address the development of the Oral Law from the time of the Men of the Great Assembly (the *soferim*) through the editing and arrangement of the Mishnah (earliest major collections of Jewish law collated and codified by Judah the Prince around 220 CE).

At the very outset of his work, Frankel proclaimed, "God illuminated the spirit of Cynis, King of Persia, and he proclaimed freedom to all the people of the Children of Israel in his kingdom to go up to Jerusalem to build there the house of God." The introduction is hardly controversial from a traditional religious standpoint nor does it appear very "scientific." God is here depicted as an active agent in history, and the explanation offered as to the motives that informed Cyrus when he is reported to have ordered the return of the people Israel from Exile in Babylon to the Land of Israel hardly comports to the naturalistic criteria that a modern historian might provide in offering a description and analysis of this event. Clearly, his sense of the reliability and accuracy of the tradition hardly reflects the posture that a modern historian would adopt regarding classical religious texts.

However, Frankel was not particularly concerned with offering either a religious or social history of the Jewish people. Rather, his aim in *Darkhei HaMishnah* was to trace the development of the Oral Law from the era of Ezra and the *Soferim* to the end of the Mishnaic period. He therefore continued by asserting that the tasks of the *Soferim* were twofold: (1) to explain and clarify the laws of Torah in general and the application of other *mitzvoth* in particular to the people and (2) to establish new decrees and ordinances according to the needs of the hour and the time. Indeed, they established these decrees in accord with the political and social situation that obtained in their day (p. 2). They knew that with the passage of time, matters would arise that the earlier sages had not anticipated, whether in regard to the personal and familial needs of human beings or the conduct of the state. As a result, new customs and judgments were always required (p. 3) and the Men of the Great Assembly arose to fulfill these dual functions.

In speaking of the former explanatory function, Frankel illustrated his point by turning (p. 3) to *lex talionis*, the famed biblical passages found in Exodus 21:23–25 that deals with the law of retribution and speaks of "an eye for an eye." Frankel contended that the sages did not understand this passage literally and that they therefore fulfilled their interpretive task by explaining that this passage denoted monetary compensation for injury, not removal of a body part. Later in his argument (p. 12), in exemplifying the second legislative function, Frankel claimed that in the Mishnah there are "*halachot* that are of great antiquity whose authors we do not know, and they emerged from the mouths of the *zugot* (pairs of rabbis) and those who preceded them."

In concluding his introductory section to his book, Frankel also stated that there were other ways in which Jewish law developed (p. 20). He writes, "And besides those *halachot* which emerged from midrash on Scriptures and from the hermeneutical principles enunciated above, other *halachot* are found whose rationale is impossible to determine. They are received and classified by the term '*halachah l'moshe mi-sinai*.'" In the Mishnah, Frankel stated that this term is used twice—Peah 2:6 and Yadayim 4:3. In the Gemara, this term is sometimes applied to an anonymous *halachah* found in the Mishnah, Yebamot 8:3 and Nazir 7:4. Furthermore, the Talmud itself often employs this phrase without reference to the Mishnah whatsoever.

Frankel then went on to an account of the phrase "*halachah l'moshe mi-sinai*" itself. In what was destined to become the most famous and controversial part of the book, Frankel stated that the phrase could best be understood by looking at an explanation offered by Asher ben Yechiel (1250–1327), the famed medieval Talmudist widely known as the Rosh, in his *Hilchot Mikvaot* 1. There the medieval sage commented upon Yadayim 4:3 where the Mishnah states that granting "the poor man's tithe in the seventh year—*ma'aser 'ani ba-sh'vi'it*"— by the nations of Amon and Moav is a "law from Moses at Sinai." However, the law is actually not found in the Torah. Therefore, the Rosh says that this law is so "self-evident and well-known" (*davar barur*) that it is "*k'i'lu halachah l'moshe mi-sinai*—as if it were a law revealed to Moses at Sinai." On the basis of this account, Frankel concluded that the phrase "*halachah l'moshe mi-sinai*" referred to an "ancient law—*halachah y'shanah*" that should not be understood literally as coming from Moses at Sinai. Rather, the origins of such a law were lost in the mists of history and were of such great antiquity that it was as if it was a law revealed to Moses at Sinai. Frankel here acknowledged the developmental nature of Jewish law. At the same time, he employed a source taken from an authority with impeccable rabbinic lineage to justify this position.

Orthodox Reaction and the Response of Frankel

Though Frankel had produced a traditional warrant to support his position, the forceful reaction of Orthodox rabbis to his work was swift and

savage.[10] Foremost among these critics was Rabbi Tzvi Benjamin Auerbach (1808–1872) of Darmstadt and Halberstadt. In his 1861 *Hatzofeh 'al
Darkhei HaMishnah*, Auerbach constructed the following argument. He
asserted that "the foundation of our faith is the belief that the Oral Law
was revealed by God" (pp. 1–2). In contrast to this, the claims Frankel put
forth ascribe the *halachot* to human, not divine, authorship. This stands
in direct opposition to the teachings of the sages in Berachot 5b, which
asserts that all the commandments and teachings in Judaism—both Written
and Oral Torah—"*nitnu l'moshe mi'sinai*—were given to Moses at Sinai."
Furthermore, in the Sifra commentary on Leviticus, *Parashat Ba-har*, it
states, "All the commandments—both their general principles and their
detailed expositions—were stated to Moses at Sinai" (p. 3).

Auerbach continued by marshaling yet more sources to demonstrate
that the notion that God revealed both the Written Law and the Oral Torah
in their entirety to Moses was the cardinal foundation for the establishment of Jewish faith, and he cited Maimonides as the ultimate authority
for this view. As Auerbach wrote, in his introduction to *Seder Zeraim* in
his *Perush HaMishnah*, Maimonides states, "Moses our rabbi received the
Torah—its explanations and its laws, according to its general rules as well
as its details—and also the explanations of the written scripture, e.g., 'an eye
for an eye,' . . . from Moses who heard them [from God] and who passed
them on to Joshua (pp. 4–5). Indeed, "All of the [rabbis] received the Oral
Torah from the God of Israel" (pp. 8–9). Therefore, as Maimonides rules
in his *Mishneh Torah, Hilchot Teshuvah* 3, one who "denies that the Torah
comes from Heaven is a heretic" (p. 9). In Auerbach's opinion, Frankel
fell under this category, for his writings in *Darkhei HaMishnah* ran counter to this belief.

Auerbach went on to say that if Frankel were in fact genuinely pious,
he would have written that the "explanations of the commandments—
peirushei hamitzvot" came from "the mouth of the Almighty at Sinai—
mipi ha-gevurah ba-sinai" and were passed down in an unbroken chain
of tradition to the Men of the Great Assembly who taught them to the
people (p. 10). Frankel would then have said, "*Rabeinu Hakadosh* (Judah
HaNasi) gathered together all the laws, explanations, and commentaries that had come directly from the mouth of Moses and he wrote them
exactly in the book of the Mishnah," just as it says explicitly in Mishnah Avot 1:1.

However, Frankel did not do this. Instead, Frankel denied the "*shalshelet hakabalah*—the chain of tradition" that stands as the foundation of Jewish faith, in opposition to Sukkah 20b and Yoma 69a, where it states, "The men of the Great Assembly returned the crown to its original glory—*haheziru haatarah l 'yoshna*" (p. 10). In making his case, Auerbach obviously offered an argument derived from the tradition alone. For Auerbach, such an approach was self-sufficient. The authority of the tradition had no need of *Wissenschaft* to bolster traditional religious claims or understandings.

His traditionalism found climactic expression in the blistering attack Auerbach launched against the treatment Frankel had accorded the notion of "*halachah l'moshe mi-sinai*." Auerbach first cited the position Frankel had adopted in *Darkhei HaMishnah* regarding the term and repeated the argument that Frankel had put forth there through his citation of the Rosh that it is "self-evident and well-known" that the phrase "*halachah l'moshe mi-sinai*" refers to an "ancient law—*halachah y'shanah*" that should not be understood literally as coming from Moses at Sinai. Rather, such a law is so ancient that it is "*k'i'lu—as if*" it were a law revealed to Moses at Sinai.

As a result, Auerbach contended that the author of *Darkhei HaMishnah* attempted "to have it both ways." While Frankel feigned commitment to Talmud, his work placed Jewish law in a developmental context and therefore denied that the Oral Law comes "*mipi ha-gevurah*—from the mouth of the Almighty" (p. 11). In so doing, Auerbach charged that Frankel undermined the very authority of the tradition he professed to champion. Rather than asserting that God revealed the *halachot* categorized under the rubric "*halachah l'moshe mi-sinai*" to Moses at Sinai, Frankel maintained that they stemmed from "the *zugot*," or "the Men of the Great Assembly," or "those who preceded them" (p. 14). By claiming that these laws are simply "so called—*nikraot* laws from Moses at Sinai," Frankel destroyed the very foundation of the Jewish religion to which he professed devotion.

Auerbach also pointed out that Frankel was disingenuous in his citation of the Rosh on *Hilchot Mikvaot* 1. He argued that the citation there is unique and completely unrepresentative of the characterization that the Rosh elsewhere accorded the phrase "*halachah l'moshe mi-sinai*." Auerbach cited numerous examples from rabbinic literature on topics ranging from ritual slaughter to *tefillin* to defend his position, and cited the many more instances where the Rosh asserted, "*Halachah l'moshe mi-sinai* stems from the Torah—*meidoraita hi*" (pp. 15–16). Furthermore, Auerbach approvingly quoted Maimonides, who wrote, "*Halachah l'moshe mi-sinai* refers to a matter that emerges from the mouth of Moses as the Holy One, Blessed be He, commanded him" (p. 16). Auerbach asked why Frankel did not cite all these more numerous and more representative rabbinic passages and chided Frankel for citing the one single and exceptional instance. He contended that the sages of the Talmud transmitted an unchanging and timeless Torah "as an eternal inheritance—*moreshet 'olam*" to the Jewish people (p. 21). Auerbach concluded his indictment of Frankel by charging that the approach and content of *Darkhei HaMishnah* sabotaged a belief in "*Torah min hashamayim*—Torah revealed from the heavens" (p. 54).

Frankel was not insensitive to such critiques, and he reacted by posting an addendum to an edition of *Darkhei HaMishnah* published in 1867.[11] Entitled "The Apology of the Author—*hitnatzlut ha'mhaber*," Frankel wrote that critics attacked him mercilessly, and he stated that his own sense of honor would not allow him to compose a detailed response that would answer each of the charges hurled against him. However, he did claim, "The person who reads my book without preconceived notions and prejudices will not find anything in it" that would support the suspicions and charges that his opponents had put forth. "The searcher of men's hearts," he stated, "knows and is witness to the fact that any thought of undermining and diminishing either the Torah or the tradition was far removed from my thoughts when I wrote this book. The purpose of the book and my desired intention is apparent to every fair-minded reader."

Frankel wrote that the "scientific light—*hamaor hamada-i*" that *Darkhei HaMishnah* shed upon the Mishnah did nothing more than reveal the wisdom of the Mishnah and the "glory of its antiquity." He added that every page of his book testified to "my feelings of respect and honor" for the Oral Law, and he believed that his attempt to raise its esteem was palpable to every fair-minded reader. While his opponents spoke as if he attempted "to destroy the basis of this Torah and to cast doubts upon its foundations," Frankel asserted that his investigation of "the components and composition of the Mishnah" only reinforced respect for the "received tradition—*hakabbalah v'hamesorah*." As Frankel observed, "In a scientific study, it is enough to prove the antiquity of the Halachah from the earliest days of the nation." Indeed, "I attempted to demonstrate the existence of the law from the time that Israel became a nation." Furthermore, the term "*halachah l'moshe mi-sinai*" was itself indeterminate and subject to many viewpoints. His research did nothing more than protect this notion from the "scorn and derision" a number of historical critics had displayed in their efforts to debunk a literal understanding of this phrase. It was "to oppose those who" make such statements that "I spoke my words. God knows this is the truth, and it was in this context that I cited the Rosh. As for those who continue to critique me, I can only say in the words of Scripture, 'They curse and You bless.'"

In assessing this quarrel between Frankel and Auerbach, it is obvious that each man was informed by a radically different sensibility concerning the relationship between critical scholarship and religious faith. While Frankel was a religious traditionalist,[12] he had also come to embrace modern modes of critical study as a legitimate mode of approaching faith for the religious Jew. His assertion that academic study of the past could only "prove the antiquity of the Halachah from the earliest days of the nation" indicates that he sensed the limits of "history." Academic study could not provide complete empirical confirmation of religious belief. Such total confirmation was beyond the realm of "science." However, this did not mean history had no utility. Frankel would never have agreed with the Kierkegaardian assertion that "from history one can learn nothing at all about" faith. At the very least, history could provide a respectable cultural warrant to protect religious belief from its cultural despisers. More significantly, history could be employed to inform and deepen the nature of religious belief for the modern Jew and to fortify the modern Jew's quest for "truth."

Auerbach clearly disagreed. The case he advanced against Frankel in his *Hatzofeh 'al HaMishnah* displays no sense of modern critical historical consciousness. Auerbach simply marshaled significant numbers of prooftexts drawn from the tradition to condemn Frankel and his *Darkhei HaMishnah* as being profoundly opposed to what Auerbach regarded as a traditional notion of an unchanging Jewish law. While Auerbach did acknowledge that Frankel had found one traditional warrant for his position, the other citations he drew from the Rosh as well as the quotation from Maimonides where these authoritative rabbis defined "*halachah l'moshe mi-sinai*" as "a matter that emerges from the mouth of Moses as the Holy One, Blessed be He, commanded him," allowed Auerbach to charge that Frankel distorted the tradition through his selective mode of citation. Indeed, the Frankel reference to the Rosh on *Hilchot Mikvaot* only masked the heretical nature of the stance Frankel had put forth. Frankel had unjustifiably selected a lone precedent in keeping with his own modern historical sensibility to justify reformulating an established doctrine of revelation that Auerbach regarded as sacrosanct. What is noteworthy here is that as late as 1861, a major German Orthodox spokesman could still remain indifferent to the approach of *Wissenschaft*.

Isaac Halevy and Dorot Harishonim: *A Different Orthodox Approach*

Given the fully acculturated nature of all sectors of German Judaism, Orthodox Jews could not long remain unconcerned with the claims of academic research and method. By the 1870s, the Orthodox Hildesheimer Rabbinerseminar in Berlin could boast of scholars such as Jakob Barth, Abraham Berliner, and David Zevi Hoffmann, who were all prominent champions of *Wissenschaft*.[13] However, at this point in our narrative, I would turn beyond the "modern Orthodox" community to Isaac Halevy (1847–1914), the Lithuanian trained talmudic sage and scholar who journeyed to central and western Europe in the mid-1890s and ultimately settled in Hamburg in 1902, to illustrate and comprehend the type of historical consciousness that had come to inform even elements of the most highly traditional circles of Orthodox Judaism in the modern world. A leader and architect of Agudath Yisrael, Halevy is the author of the famed six-volume "magnum opus on Jewish history *Dorot Harishonim*," which "spans the biblical, talmudic, and Gaonic eras." As his biographer O. Asher Reichel states, "In that work—the first volume was published in 1897 and the sixth in 1964—the fundamentals of Jewish tradition were reaffirmed."[14]

Halevy possessed a distinct historical sensibility, and his work displays the all-pervasive influence that *Wissenschaft* enjoyed in Germany. At the same time, his allegiance to Orthodox Jewish faith and practice was fierce. The critiques he issued against Frankel and other members of the Positive-Historical school such as Heinrich Graetz and I. H. Weiss for the treatment they accorded the history of the Mishnah and its authors, as well as an exposition of his own analysis of the same topics, demonstrate a distinctive Orthodox approach to *Wissenschaft* and allow for another understanding of how a devoted religious believer can simultaneously be informed by and dissent from the phenomenon of modern historical consciousness.

Unlike Auerbach, the Orthodox Halevy did not abjure an academic approach to the Jewish past. In fact, he enthusiastically professed his devotion to such study. In his writings, Halevy praised the academic study of Judaism as heralding a "renaissance of Jewish literature" and spoke of the need for Orthodox Jews to "work together for the benefit of *Hochmat Yisrael*."[15] While he charged that the research conducted by non-Orthodox students of *Wissenschaft* did little more than "reduce the foundations of Judaism into chaos (*tohu va'vohu*),"[16] Halevy nevertheless asserted, "The foundation of Orthodoxy rests on a base of true *Hochmat Yisrael*."[17] Halevy therefore insisted that the Orthodox scholar adhere to the most stringent standards of scholarly research, and he maintained that internal Jewish sources alone were not enough to construct a serious Jewish history. Indeed, he explicitly called upon Orthodox authors to consult contemporaneous non-Jewish sources such as Josephus in writing a history of the Jewish community. Furthermore, these sources "had to be presented in the original language," and articles presenting the fruit or that research had to be written "in a scientific manner."[18]

Halevy felt that he himself achieved such a "scientific standard "in his own work and, in a 1900 letter to Salomon Breuer of Frankfurt after publication of the first volume of *Dorot Harishonim* and prior to the publication of the second, he stated that he was confident that Breuer would appreciate and rejoice in the forthcoming volume. He further boasted that his historical research had succeeded in strengthening the stature of traditional Judaism in the modern setting and that he had succeeded in responding to those modern academics who had distorted Jewish history. As he wrote, "Through my hand, God has fulfilled the desire of all pious Jews to establish *Hochmat Yisrael* and Jewish history properly and restore them to their rightful place." As a result, "All evil will vanish like smoke, and our Holy Torah will be rebuilt and reestablished as it was in earlier days."[19]

In describing his approach to Jewish history, Halevy wrote that history must not be based on "dreams—*halomot*." In a positivistic mode characteristic of his time, Halevy claimed, "History represents matters as they genuinely are from the depths of full research." The reader of a historical tome must be confident that the descriptions and representations of events and trends are fully reliable and accurate.[20]

Consequently, Halevy stated that the scholar must not depend upon "*aggadah*"—fanciful tales and interpretations for the writing of history.

Instead, he averred that the key to Jewish history for the modern student of the past lay in grasping an understanding of the halakhic sources of Jewish tradition. Halevy complained that many traditional historians of the talmudic era employed *aggadot* that had no connection to the historical time and place of the Amoraim, and this allowed for ahistorical flights of imagination that were no more than the expression of the subjective whims of each individual author. Halevy was genuinely committed to *Wissenschaft* as he understood it.[21]

In making this distinction between halakhic and aggadic sources for the writing of Jewish history, Halevy reflected traditional patterns of understanding that marked the eastern European yeshiva world from which he emerged, a world that granted primacy to the purported "objectivity" of halakhic sources over the presumed "subjectivity" inherent in aggadic ones.[22] However, in offering this assessment of *halachah* and *aggadah* for the construction of history, Halevy just as clearly did not take into account the types of considerations that modern historians would adopt regarding the use of these sources. After all, even if *aggadot* are "fanciful flights of imagination," the historian can nevertheless mine them, no less than the historian can analyze halakhic texts, to reveal a great deal about the intentions and attitudes of their authors. Furthermore, Halevy clearly presumed the historical accuracy of all legal sources. He completely ignored the types of issues that a critical historian today might raise as to whether particular sources are projections of a later era onto an earlier one, the subjective concerns of the author, the personal commitments of the writer, and the like. Indeed, questions of this type seemingly never entered his mind. In this way, his critical historical consciousness—like that of Frankel for that matter—appears rather "primitive."

In the first volume of *Dorot Harishonim*, Halevy treated the mishnaic period of Jewish history. Consequently, this volume provides the contemporary observer with a clear picture of his own historical sensibility as well as a useful point of comparison to see where his own approach and understanding were both akin to and distinct from that of a figure such as Frankel. Indeed, in this volume, Halevy stridently attacked not only Frankel but also Heinrich Graetz and I. H. Weiss, both leading members of the Positive-Historical camp of nineteenth-century German Jewish historians.

Halevy pointed out that all these leading Positive-Historical scholars regarded *Tannaim* such as Hillel and Akiba as the supreme architects of rabbinic Judaism, and they maintained that Jewish law was created and evolved during the first centuries of the modern era. For example, Halevy noted that Graetz asserted that "Hillel ushered in a new era" in the development of Torah. In so doing, "Hillel laid the cornerstone for the construction of the Talmud," and he established a foundation for Judaism that remains to this day (p. 157). Similarly, Frankel, in *Darkhei HaMishnah*, had written that while certain commandments from the time of Ezra were ancient ones—e.g., certain sacrificial offerings—others—e.g., relating to forbidden foods such as gentile oil—were new. In addition, Frankel declared, "Rabbi Akiba was the first to establish a certain *mishnah*." Therefore, averred Frankel, "Rabbi Akiba arose and he was the great man who began to construct the *mishnah* and lay its cornerstone" (p. 203). Finally, Weiss, in volume 1 of his *Dor Dor v'Dorshav*, stated that Hillel felt empowered "to employ logic (*sevara*) regarding every new matter that came before him to depart" from the established law (p. 203).

To all of this, Halevy queried, "Is there any end to these words of foolishness?" Indeed, all these academics were persons who were "shrouded in fog" and who "walked in chaos" (p. 203). In contrast to Frankel and the others, Halevy maintained that Hillel did not introduce a new era in the chain of tradition nor did any of the *Tannaim* establish a new foundation for the construction of the Mishnah. He asserted that Graetz was in error on this point, just as Weiss was when he contended that Hillel deviated from the Halachah. Similarly, Frankel was mistaken when he asserted that the first generations of the *Tannaim* laid the cornerstone of the Mishnah (p. 205). Rather, the Mishnah was already established before these rabbinic sages lived. Halevy referred to this original Mishnah as *Y'sod HaMishnah* and stated that all the arguments of the *Tannaim* were no more than expositions of and commentaries upon the earlier words and rulings they had received. As Halevy explicitly wrote, "All the Mishnah was arranged and its template sealed in its entirety, as it exists before us, and was transmitted during the days of the Men of the Great Assembly" (p. 204).

Halevy defended his stance in several ways. First, he argued that the language of the apocryphal work Ben Sira was akin in language and form to that of the Mishnah, thus demonstrating that the "Mishna was already familiar to all." Furthermore, he stated that the Mishnah was not connected homiletically to Scripture. Rather, the laws that the Mishnah contained were arranged systematically as they were received. Indeed, they were preserved despite the persecutions that obtained between the time of the Men of the Great Assembly and the *Tannaim*. Furthermore, all the general "enactments—*takkanot*" of the rabbis and all the foundations for these rabbinic *takkanot* emerged prior to the days of Simon the Just. Halevy conceded that "here and there" there were individual *takkanot* that were identified with the head of the generation in which they were enacted, e.g., those of Jose ben Yoezer, the *beit din* of the Hasmoneans, and Shimon ben Shetach. However, they were all circumscribed enactments. In contrast, all wide-ranging *takkanot* such as *safek d'oraita l'humra*, the concept of *shevut* in relation to Shabbat, the prohibition on carrying in a place defined as *karmalit*, and the foundations of the laws of mourning were from no later than the time of the Men of the Great Assembly.[23] Indeed, many of these laws preceded the Men of the Great Assembly. However, Halevy emphatically declared that none were later than this period. As Baruch Bokser, in a concise summary of his position, has observed, for Halevy *Y'sod HaMishnah* "consists of biblical based laws, other laws contemporary with the Sinaitic revelation of Torah, and later authoritative and collective enactments from the time of the prophets through the days of the scribes (*Soferim*). The Men of the Great Assembly received these laws, fixed their language and form, and thereby produced *Y'sod HaMishnah*." The *Tannaim* do no more than explain and clarify the rulings of *Y'sod HaMishnah*.[24]

While Halevy did concede that the *Tannaim* at times argued over the precise wording of the Mishnah, he was insistent that the literary formulation and redaction of the Mishnah stemmed from the time of the Men of the Great Assembly. He buttressed this position by offering numerous cases where the "original" Mishnah was followed by later rabbinic argumentation. One example will suffice to illustrate the mode of explanation he advanced. In Mishnah Hagigah 1:1, it states, "Everyone is obligated to see the Temple during the three pilgrimage festivals, except for the deaf-mute, the imbecile, and a minor . . . and he who is unable to go up by foot." After the list of persons who are exempt from seeing "the Temple during the three pilgrimage festivals" is completed, the Mishnah then asks, "Who is a minor?" An argument is then recorded between Bet Shammai and Bet Hillel. Bet Shammai contends that the phrase "Who is a minor?" refers to a child who cannot be carried on his father's shoulders. In contrast, Bet Hillel states that it refers to a child who cannot grasp his father's hand in going up to Jerusalem. A child who cannot walk on his own power is not obligated to be at the Temple Mount on these holidays. As Halevy would have it, the first sentence of the Mishnah is "the Foundation of the Mishna (*Y'sod HaMishnah*)." The arguments that follow are later additions and are restricted to a definition of what constitutes a "minor" for purposes of this law (p. 207).

Concluding Considerations and Thoughts

Halevy clearly strained to undermine the notions put forth by Frankel, Graetz, Weiss, and their Positive-Historical school. Yet there is a striking methodological similarity between Halevy and Frankel that easily distinguishes them from a man such as Auerbach. Though Halevy pushed the date of the composition of the Mishnah even further back into the mists of antiquity than did Frankel, Halevy did not abjure history. Indeed, Halevy parallels Frankel in that he also wields "history" as a weapon to posit the antiquity of the law. History becomes a category to grant religion cultural respectability and to instill a sense of self-confidence and self-respect in a contemporary generation of Jews.

However, history is more than a simple warrant to complement religious faith for men such as Halevy and Frankel. Their interpretations of Jewish legal texts are literary-historical, not halakhic. In the case of Halevy, his presentation of the Mishnah permitted him to argue that the rabbis were not complete innovators while simultaneously indicating as Frankel and others had that there were layers or strata in the Mishnah. It would therefore be a mistake not to distinguish Halevy from Auerbach and to dismiss Halevy as an Orthodox apologete who employed history only to defend traditional Jewish piety. His *Dorot Harishonim* no less than *Darkhei HaMishnah* displays a *Weltanschauung* that situates and understands its data within historical context. In so doing, history provides a sense of meaning for a current religious community.

There is therefore an unavoidable historicist mode of thought that brings us back to the position that Kierkegaard enunciated and that was cited at the outset of this presentation. The insistence of the historian that texts be placed in context seemingly dissolves, as David Myers has phrased it, "the veneer of transcendence in which sacred texts [are] wrapped."[25] Such a methodological approach not only aroused the ire of religious traditionalists such as Auerbach and Hirsch against Frankel. It also led Rav Kook to warn Halevy "that we need to be guarded against new ways." Kook protested the history that Halevy had penned and censured his description of strata in the Mishnah, his refusal to affirm the historicity of *aggadah*, and his use of Josephus and other non-Jewish sources in the writing of *Dorot Harishonim*. For a believer such as Rav Kook, this approach that Halevy adopted subverted the belief in Judaism as a timeless and sacred tradition.[26]

However, this lecture has sought to demonstrate that the relationship between historical consciousness and the scholarship such consciousness produces on the one hand and religious faith on the other can be more complex than men such as Kierkegaard and Kook suggest. The tensions between "history and faith" may never be completely resolved. The writings of men such as Halevy and Frankel indicate that historians who are religious are not confined to the response of Auerbach. The writings of Frankel and Halevy demonstrate that committed religious Jewish scholars can employ history in the service of religion and that Clio, the muse of history, often directs and informs the religious impulse by displaying the spiritual capacity and abiding inspiration that resides in the religious story. History seeks to serve and persuade the present as it recovers and presents the past. From this perspective, history can deepen faith and construct new modes of religious and communal memory and identity. The uses of history are many.

NOTES

1. Van A. Harvey, *The Historian and the Believer: The Morality of Historical Knowledge and Christian Belief* (Urbana: University of Illinois Press, 1996), 4–6.

2. Robert Bretall, ed., *A Kierkegaard Anthology* (Princeton: Princeton University Press, 1946), 388–89, as cited by David N. Myers, *Resisting History: Historicism and Its Discontents in German-Jewish Thought* (Princeton: Princeton University Press, 2003), 1.

3. Yosef Hayim Yerushalmi, *Zachor: Jewish History and Jewish Memory* (Seattle: University of Washington Press, 1982), 90–91.

4. See Jacob Neusner, "Paradigmatic versus Historical Thinking: The Case of Rabbinic Judaism," *History and Theory* 36, no. 3 (1997).

5. Amos Funkenstein, "Collective Memory and Historical Consciousness," *History & Memory* 1 (1989), 5–26.

6. Yerushalmi, *Zachor*, 89.

7. Ibid., 93.

8. Ismar Schorsch, *Heinrich Graetz: The Structure of Jewish History and Other Essays* (New York: JTS, 1975), 8–9, 11. Gerson Cohen, in his "German Jewry as a Mirror of Modernity," *LBIYB* 20 (1975): xxv, makes this point about the "programmatic nature" of nineteenth-century German Jewish history when he writes, "One of the singular features of German-Jewish scholarship was its ingenuousness: if anyone pretended about his real motives, it was not Zunz, Geiger, Frankel, Graetz, or David Hoffmann." Michael Meyer also reinforces the position Schorsch here puts forth when he demonstrates, in "Jewish Religious Reform and Wissenschaft des Judentums: The Positions of Zunz, Geiger, and Frankel," *LBIYB* 26 (1971): 19–41, that different nineteenth-century scholars employing the exact same *wissenschaftlich* methodology routinely drew diverse conclusions for practical Jewish religious faith and practice from their investigation. Finally, Jakob Petuchowski in his *Prayerbook Reform in Europe* (New York: World Union for Progressive Judaism, 1968), 84–104, demonstrates that the use of *Wissenschaft* was so ubiquitous during the 1800s in Germany that both Orthodox and Reform scholars defended their understanding of Judaism by an appeal to critical scholarship.

9. Schorsch, *Heinrich Graetz*, 1.

10. Rabbis Samson Raphael Hirsch and Gottlieb Fischer accused Frankel of heresy in a prominent series of articles published by Fischer in 1860–61 in *Jeschurun*, the Orthodox journal edited by Hirsch. These articles are printed in S. R. Hirsch, "Schriften betreffrend Dr. Z. Frankel's 'Darke hamischna,'" *Gesammelte Schriften* (Frankfurt: 1863), 4:322–434. See esp. 339ff.

11. This addendum is reprinted in *Darkhei HaMishnah* (Warsaw, 1923), 386.

12. Hermann Cohen, who studied with Frankel at the Breslau Seminary, offered striking testimony to the piety of his teacher in a letter Cohen wrote to *Jeschurun* 7 (1861): 297–98, after he read the savage criticisms that Hirsch and Fischer had lodged against Frankel (see note 10). Cohen, in what was probably his first published writing, described Frankel as an observant Jew who conducted himself in all respects in accord with a strict interpretation of rabbinic law, "standing in the synagogue with a prayer shawl over his head, singing *zemirot* on holiday evenings, and also, on occasion in his talmudic lectures, zealously commenting, 'A God-fearing Jew must be here stringent.'"

13. For an analysis of the approach the Hildesheimer camp of German Orthodox Judaism took on *Wissenschaft*, see David Ellenson, *Rabbi Esriel Hildesheimer and the Creation of a Modern Jewish Orthodoxy* (Tuscaloosa: University of Alabama Press, 1990), 148–65. Also see Mordecai Breuer, *Modernity within Tradition: The Social History of Orthodox Jewry in Imperial Germany,* trans. by Elizabeth Petuchowski (New York: Columbia University Press, 1992), 181–84.

14. O. Asher Reichel, *Isaac Halevy (1847–1914): Spokesman and Historian of Jewish Tradition* (New York: Yeshiva University Press, 1969), 9.

15. Asher Reichel, ed., *Iggerot Rabbi Yitzchak Isaac Halevy* (Jerusalem: Mossad Harav Kuk, 1972), Letter 27a.

16. Ibid., Letter 42b.

17. Ibid., Letter 134.

18. Ibid., Letter 27a.

19. Ibid., Letter 5.

20. Ibid., Letter 17.

21. Ibid., Letter 42a.

22. Note how different this viewpoint is from that of many contemporary Orthodox precincts where the Art Scroll series of Orthodox publications often ascribes historical accuracy to events and tales contained in classical aggadic writings. For an assessment of Halevy as a critical historian, see Breuer, *Modernity within Tradition*, 194ff.

23. *Safek d'oraita l'humra* is a principle that asserts that in a case where there is a doubt regarding a commandment that stems from the Torah, one leans toward stringency. *Shevut* is a category that refers to restrictions instituted by the sages of the Talmud in order to prevent violations of Torah prohibitions on or to enhance the holiness of the Sabbath and festivals. On the Sabbath, Jewish law prohibits carrying from a "private domain" into a "public domain." The rabbis of the Talmud extended this prohibition against carrying from the private domain into the public domain to include areas that resemble a public domain such as a field or an alley. They called such an area *karmalit*.

24. Baruch Bokser, "Y. I. Halevy," in *The Modern Study of the Mishnah*, ed. Jacob Neusner (Leiden: Brill, 1973), 137. Of course, as Jacob Lauterbach, in his *Rabbinic Essays* (Cincinnati: Hebrew Union College Press, 1951), 181, writes, "At the most, his arguments could only prove that there had been many *halakhot* and decisions in the days of the *Soferim*, and that the earliest *Tannaim* in our Mishnah in their discussion seek to define and explain these older *halakhot* and decisions. But it does not follow that these *halakhot* and decisions were already in the days of the *Soferim* composed in Mishnah-form."

25. Myers, *Resisting History*, 5.

26. *Iggerot Rabbi Yitzchak Isaac Halevy*, Letter 80.

20

"Creative Misreadings" in Representative Post-Emancipation Halakhic Writings on Conversion and Intermarriage

Introductory Considerations: Legal Process and the Antithetical Model

David Cole, in writing about American jurisprudence, notes that judges are expected "to adhere to established principles and rules." As Cole, professor of law at Georgetown University, states in his 1986 *Yale Law Journal* article "Agon at Agora: Creative Misreadings in the First Amendment," jurists are "not expected to create ideas out of thin air. . . . The rules of precedent . . . demand that justices follow past authority." Precedent, *stare decesis*, places constraints upon the judge, and judges are never permitted to break from the past, for their authority rests upon their fidelity to original texts and prior holdings. Cole therefore concludes, "The traditional account of legal adjudication emphasizes the faithful application of precedent to novel situations."[1]

However, in his article, Cole notes that this straightforward description of the legal process is overly constrained, and its borders are too narrow to capture or explain the full range of decisions that mark the adjudicatory process. This is because legal decision-making is analogical and always requires an interpretive performance on the part of those charged with rendering judgment. In order to follow precedent, judges must first articulate the meaning of the precedent, and such meaning—if not absolutely indeterminate—is always open to different understandings. Meaning in relation to a text is always produced by a socially situated reader with his or her own psychological proclivities. The text itself does not provide meaning without that intervention. While judicial legitimacy requires faithful adherence to precedent, even the most conventional reader engages in a hermeneutical act that is inherently contextual and therefore unavoidably subjective and oft-times creative.

In making this point, Cole echoes the work of David Hume, who in his *An Enquiry Concerning Human Understanding and Concerning the Principles of Morals*, noted that juridical reasoning—precisely because it is analogical and based on precedent as interpreted by a socially situated reader-judge—is optimally characterized by its dependence on imagination.[2] The rationale that determines whether and how the rule contained in the precedent can be applied does not lie exclusively in the merits of the rule or the case itself. Rather, the question is how the jurist understands the rule and how the judge then extends the rule and its logical entailments to the case at hand, and this determination depends on a host of logical, contextual, and personal factors. Consequently, case law is supple. Legal decision-making and the rationales and causes that support the holdings that emerge from the adjudicatory process are therefore best treated as more or less highly persuasive rather than absolutely incontestable.

As a result, Cole maintains that if a full account of the legal process is to be given, an "antithetical model" of analysis must supplement the "traditional account" of legal adjudication mentioned above. Cole borrows his notion of an "antithetical model of interpretation" from the work of the literary critic Harold Bloom, and he counterposes this antithetical model to the traditional account. Cole notes that Bloom maintains that "misreadings," novel and original readings of textual precedents and sources, are an unavoidably characteristic element of the interpretive act. In his schema, "misreadings" are not meant to be disparaging. Rather, Bloom insists that this term defines a necessary condition of interpretation. Indeed, he argues that all reading and writing involve "misreadings" as a necessary condition for creativity. Cole builds upon this approach and contends that this typology, while sharply opposed to the predominant understanding of how precedent operates, nevertheless captures the creative turns or misreadings that abound in the history of American constitutional law as judges understand and employ precedents in novel and at times "subversive" ways.[3]

Of course, the very nature of Anglo-American jurisprudence demands that judges insist that precedent always directs their decisions even when it is evident that their reading of the source is an inventive one. Judges, through such "misreadings," simultaneously revise and redirect the law while insisting that they are doing nothing more than applying precedent.[4]

Antithetical analysis focuses on these moments of tension. The antithetical model of analysis completes and "complicates the conventional account of legal development." This model claims that even as a notion of precedent guides the jurist, an undertow that allows for novel directions in policy emerges from misreadings of those precedents. Given the stability that the custom of precedent provides to a community, this understanding of precedent constitutes a way that allows for an acceptable break from the past as a community adapts to changed conditions and evolving sensibilities.[5]

The Anglo-American legal process Cole describes comports with *halakhic* notions of how authentic Jewish legal decisions are made. For more than a millennium, *poskim* have always sought to identify rules and principles drawn from Jewish "statutory texts" (i.e., Bible and Talmud), as well as holdings contained in Jewish case law (i.e., responsa), for guidance in arriving at decisions in an instant case. Rabbis, like jurists in the Anglo-American system of law, do so by following past precedents that are relevant to the present-day case before them. A rabbi would never admit that he "misreads." After all, decisions must always be grounded in the language of "precedential legitimacy," and the very authority of the *posek* rests on an assumed fidelity to an original text.

Nevertheless, rabbis themselves—like jurists in the American legal system—are sometimes strong, creative misreaders of prior texts. This paper will demonstrate that the phenomenon of "antithetical struggle" finds ample expression in Jewish legal tradition during the modern era as rabbis have struggled to adapt the Jewish community in "authentic and stable ways" to the social changes that the Jewish community confronted in the wake of Emancipation where marriage between Jews and Gentiles became common. Through examples drawn from the writings of three central European *poskim* on matters relating to intermarriage and conversion, this paper will demonstrate that rabbis themselves—like jurists in the American legal system—are sometimes strong and creative misreaders of prior texts. The three rabbis featured here—Tzvi Hirsch Kalischer (1795–1874) of Thorn, David Tzvi Hoffmann (1843–1921) of Berlin, and Menahem Mendel Kirschenbaum (1894–1942) of Frankfurt—all issued opinions that display ample evidence of "creative and original" departures from conventional understandings in their "bold misreadings" of the precedents they cited in justifying the rulings they delivered on matters of conversion and intermarriage. In so doing, they issued novel policy statements designed to guide a modern Jewish community confronted with the challenges of a novel post-Emancipation social setting in which Jews and non-Jews frequently socialized as equals and increasingly married one another.

Tzvi Hirsch Kalischer and Ezra 9:1–2

The considerations discussed above coalesce in a responsum written by Kalischer in 1864. Rabbi of Thorn on the border between Prussia and Poland, Kalischer was the famed author of the proto-Zionist pamphlet *D'rishat Tziyon* (1862) and one of the leading halakhic authorities of nineteenth-century Europe. An active messianist, he maintained an intense interest in Jewish communal and legal affairs and matters throughout his lifetime.[6]

On October 31, 1864, Rabbi Bernard Illowy of New Orleans had written a letter to *Der Israelit*, a leading Orthodox periodical in Germany, to elicit the opinions of the European Orthodox rabbinate as to whether boys born to a non-Jewish mother and Jewish father should be circumcised and converted to Judaism. Illowy addressed himself to Rabbi Marcus Lehmann of Frankfurt (1831–90), editor of the journal, and explained that questions surrounding this issue had been raised in the New Orleans community and that he had forbidden such circumcisions. He stated that the mothers had no intention of raising these boys as observant Jews, and he claimed that the fathers were flagrant violators of Jewish law. Illowy concluded his letter by asking Lehmann and the readers of *Der Israelit* whether his decision had been correct.[7]

Lehmann published the letter under the title "*Die Beschneidung der in Mischenhen van nichtjuedischen Muttern gebornen Kinder* (The Circumcision of Children Born to Non-Jewish Mothers in Mixed Marriages)," and replied by stating that when a similar situation had occurred in Hamburg that the rabbi there had likewise not permitted such children to be circumcised. Lehmann was of the opinion that this decision was the proper one, and he contended that if a blessing had been recited at the ceremony of such a boy, then God's Name would have been taken in vain.

Lehmann continued by stating that the real issue in these cases centered on the question of the child's status—that is, was the child a Jew or a non-Jew? The answer quite clearly was that the child was a non-Jew, and Lehmann therefore felt it desirable that such a child not be circumcised in a Jewish religious ceremony. The children of such unions—where the mothers were Christians and the fathers were nonobservant Jews—would never grow up to be loyal Jews. Lehmann stated that it was vital to remember that "Judaism has never sought to make proselytes," and he felt that the fact that their fathers were Jewish was of no consequence in rendering a decision on this matter. Indeed, such children, if they were to be converted, would only fulfill the Talmudic dictum, "Proselytes are as troublesome to Israel as a sore." Lehmann's article was followed several months later by opinions on the subject issued by Rabbi Dr. Feilchenfeld of Dusseldorf and Rabbi Dr. Esriel Hildesheimer, then of Eisenstadt in Hungary.[8] Both these rabbis agreed with Lehmann and Illowy.

However, Kalischer dissented from all of them. When he read the letters of Rabbi Illowy and the responses to it by other rabbis in *Der Israelit*, he decided to express his own views on the case by responding to Hildesheimer, whom he labeled the "greatest among them." He stated that he dissented from their opinion and claimed that "a Jewish sentiment struck root in the hearts of these fathers and they wanted their sons circumcised." Kalischer applauded this decision and said that it was a "*mitzvah* to circumcise such children."

Kalischer then offered a general excursus on conversion as a prelude to his discussion of the particular question regarding the status of the children in New Orleans. He stated that all humanity was "the work of God's hands" and that God had actually desired that all humankind receive Torah. Nevertheless, only Israel, at the time of the theophany at Sinai, was prepared to accept it. Yet God's purpose in granting Israel this precious gift was to enable Israel to conduct itself "as a nation of priests and a holy people" who would bring the truth of God's Torah to the entire world. In this way, any individual who desired "to convert and take refuge in the inheritance of the Lord like Onkelos, Shemaya, and Abtalyon" could enter into the community and partake of this gift of God. Kalischer clearly possessed a positive attitude concerning conversion, and he claimed that it was the hope of the rabbis that all would come to see the light of Jewish faith. Kalischer therefore stated that these youngsters in New Orleans should be circumcised in their infancy, as they would be reluctant to endure the pain of circumcision in adolescence and young adulthood.

In the part of the responsum most germane to our discussion, Kalischer contended that these particular children, born of a Jewish father and a gentile mother, were *zera kodesh*, holy seed, and the community should do everything in its power to facilitate their entry into the Jewish people. His identification of these children as *zera kodesh* was based on a biblical precedent found in Ezra 9:1–2. As Kalischer wrote, "Although Jewish law asserts that the status of a newborn child is determined by the status of the mother, we nevertheless find a child produced by a union between a non-Jewish mother and Jewish father is identified as *zera kodesh*, as Ezra proved to Israel when they married non-Jewish women. For after Ezra observed that these Israelite men had taken the daughters [of the seven Canaanite nations] as wives for themselves and their sons, he stated, 'And the *zera hakodesh* had become intermingled with the peoples of the land.'" Kalischer justified the identification of children born of gentile mothers and Jewish fathers as "holy offspring" and urged their inclusion in the community on the basis of this passage in Ezra.

Indeed, Kalischer added that if these children were not circumcised by a *mohel* in a *brit* ceremony when they were infants, then it would be more difficult for them to convert to Judaism as adults. Thus Kalischer wrote, "If we do not circumcise [them], we are pushing [them] away with both hands from the community of Israel." Kalischer also added that there was the possibility that "great leaders of Israel would sprout from among them." Thus Kalischer held, "how goodly and pleasant our portion will be" if, through our actions, such a child becomes fully Jewish. His reading of the Ezra precedent in this way provided legitimacy for the policy of inclusion he wanted to adopt for Jewish men and their non-Jewish wives and non-Jewish progeny in a modern setting where intermarriages between Jews and Gentiles were increasingly frequent despite the fact that the Ezra passage in the Bible was itself an exclusionary one. The interpretation Kalischer offered reversed the plain meaning of the biblical text.

Esriel Hildesheimer himself noted this and objected to the interpretation Kalischer had advanced on this passage. He therefore wrote, in response to Kalischer, "*Zera Kodesh* here does not refer to the children borne by these non-Jewish women. Rather, the Ezra prooftext only refers to the seed of Israel that was commingled, i.e., the men themselves were intermingled among the peoples of the land, i.e., among the foreign women. Regarding the children themselves—there is not even a hint about them in Scripture."

Hildesheimer refused to accord legitimacy to the "creative misreading" Kalischer offered of Ezra 9:1–2 and would not advocate the policy of inclusion in the Jewish community toward these children in the modern situation that Kalischer was able to justify on the basis of his reading of that text. Nevertheless, Kalischer remained adamant about the correctness of his posture, and later Orthodox rabbis have noted his labeling of these boys as *zera kodesh* and have employed this precedent in their own attempts to cope with the challenges that intermarriage poses to the Jewish people in the modern era. The power of "creative misreadings" and the influence of such readings on later generations of interpreters are thus apparent.[9]

David Tzvi Hoffmann on Yevamot 24b

David Tzvi Hoffmann, the head of the Orthodox Rabbinerseminar in Berlin and a giant of Jewish scholarship, was also the *posek 'elyon* (leading halakhic authority) of German Judaism. In his *Melammed Le 'Ho 'il, Even Ha-Ezer* #10, Hoffmann addressed "the matter of whether or not we should accept for conversion a non-Jewish woman who already married a Jew in the secular courts while she was non-Jewish."

Of course, the halakhic problem this case posed was that conversion for an ulterior motive is halakhically unacceptable. In order to make the claim that this conversion was permissible, Hoffmann felt constrained once again to "prove" that no ulterior motive existed. In this instance, Hoffmann did so by arguing that the civil marriage was effectively "marriage." Consequently, the couple had no vested interest in Jewish *kiddushin*. After all, they already lived together. As a result, it could not be said that the prospect of their ritual marriage after conversion constituted an ulterior motive for conversion. The argument he put forth to support this conclusion is fascinating. Hoffmann opened his responsum and justified this stance by citing a position from the responsa of the *Beit Yitzhak* that claimed it was absolutely forbidden to convert such a woman to Judaism. However, he immediately contrasted this position with one quoted by another rabbinic figure, Shalom Kutnah. In his *Ka-torah ya'aseh*, Kutnah had argued that since secular law also makes divorce difficult, and since formal dissolution of the relationship cannot take place without those very same courts, civil marriage in these circumstances should be considered *a posteriori* (*b'di'a'vad*) tantamount to "marriage."

Hoffmann himself supported this latter position and even extended it by quoting the famous *mishnah* from Yevamot 24b, which reads, in part, "If a man is suspected of intercourse with a slave who was later emancipated, or with a heathen who subsequently became a proselyte, he should surely not marry her. If, however, he did marry her, they need not be parted." In order to prove that no ulterior motive for conversion existed in this case, Hoffmann, as Daniel Gordis has observed, wished to demonstrate that a "marriage" was already in place.[10] Hoffmann therefore cited with approval the view that while the *mishnah* frowned upon such a marriage between a Jew and "an emancipated non-Jewish woman who subsequently converted," the rabbis nonetheless considered it marriage, i.e., *kiddushin.* Hoffmann then stated that the same could be said for the relationship that existed between this Jewish man and non-Jewish woman who desired to convert as a result of the civil ceremony that had already been performed.

As Gordis notes, Hoffmann's desire to permit the conversion was so powerful that he justified his decision by what can charitably be termed a "creative misinterpretation" of Yevamot 24b. Gordis writes, "When the *mishnah* states, 'if he did marry her,' it is obviously referring to some halakhically valid form of *kiddushin!*"[11] For the *mishnah*'s marriage involves a man who was Jewish by birth and a woman who was Jewish as a result of conversion.

In contrast, the case before Hoffmann involved a man who was Jewish by birth and his non-Jewish wife who now wanted to convert. *Kiddushin* between two such persons is simply impossible and unprecedented in Jewish law. In drawing an analogy between the case in the *mishnah* and the one before him, Hoffmann clearly took tremendous liberties with the legal precedent and read it in what can only be called a highly imaginative way. However, as Gordis shows in his insightful article, Hoffmann was so committed to an agenda of inclusiveness and constituency retention in a modern social situation where his laity frequently intermarried that he was willing to adopt this stance. Hoffmann was so concerned with the maintenance of the community for which he was responsible that he was prepared to read the *mishnah* eisegetically to make his case for leniency and inclusion. One can only conclude that Hoffmann pushed the "elasticity" inherent in Jewish law to "its limits" in order to adopt a lenient and inclusive stance on matters related to conversion and intermarriage.[12]

Menachem Mendel Kirschenbaum and Rashi on Yevamot 47b

In concluding this survey, it will be instructive to turn to a responsum issued by Rabbi Menachem Mendel Kirschenbaum (1894–1942) of Frankfurt in 1928. Rabbi Jakob Hoffmann (1881–1956), the Frankfurt *orthodoxer Gemeinderabbiner* from 1922 to 1937, had invited the Polish-born Kirschenbaum to leave his native Krakow and come to Frankfurt in 1927 to serve as *Av bet din* of the communal rabbinical court. Such an invitation from a German Orthodox rabbi to an eastern European one was not unusual as German Orthodox rabbis often recognized that their eastern European colleagues possessed greater halakhic expertise than they did. Rabbi Kirschenbaum himself was the product of a traditional yeshiva education, and his responsa are collected under the title *Menachem Meishiv*.[13]

In the responsum under consideration, Rabbi Kirschenbaum was asked whether the existence of a Liberal rabbinate should be a factor in determining whether Orthodox rabbis should receive gentiles as proselytes who desired to marry Jews. The rabbi who addressed his question to Kirschenbaum observed that there were "proselytes who have not been converted by Orthodox rabbis, but who have been converted by rabbis who are not scrupulous in requiring ritual immersion." The questioner then observed that these persons "now live together [with Jews] despite the fact that such unions are forbidden." He therefore asked, "Is it better that we accept converts such as these [under Orthodox auspices], for, after all, a posteriori (*b'di'a'vad*) such persons will be thought of as converts."

Kirschenbaum responded by citing Yevamot 47b. There the Talmud states, "If a man comes to become a proselyte at this time . . . he is taught some of the major and some of the minor commandments. What is the reason for this instruction—so that if he desires to withdraw, let him withdraw—*Mai tama? D'i peiresih, nifrosh.*" Kirschenbaum noted that Rashi, commenting upon the phrase "*D'i peiresih*—If he desires to withdraw," explained, "*She'lo yitgayer*—that he will not convert." Kirschenbaum then observed that Rashi, in explaining the word "*Nifrosh*—Let him withdraw," then stated, "and it does not trouble us—*v'lo ichpat lan*."

Kirschenbaum cited this Rashi for what would be his own lenient and inclusive reading in this case. However, he did so by turning the plain meaning of this Rashi on its head and utilized this passage of Rashi as a textual warrant to advise his questioner and other Orthodox rabbis to perform conversions in instances where a non-Orthodox rabbinate would usher these gentiles into the Jewish community if Orthodox rabbis refused to do so. Whereas Rashi wrote that "it does not trouble us— *lo ichpat lan*" if a non-Jew does not convert to Judaism, the social reality of early twentieth-century Frankfurt caused Kirschenbaum to write, "In the event that it does trouble us that the gentile will dwell with a Jewish woman—and here it does trouble us (*a'val 'al kol panim 'ichpat lan*) [we should conduct such conversions]. For in our case, they [Jews and gentiles] will certainly continue to dwell together, and if those non-Orthodox rabbis mentioned above accept them as Jews, then, according to the Holy Torah, they are not genuine converts. Yet they will be registered as proselytes in the community registry and after many years they will eventually marry other Jews. And this troubles and troubles us over and over again—*shuv ichpat v'ichpat lan.* Therefore, it is better to receive them and not ask whether they are converting for an ulterior motive."[14]

In short, Kirschenbaum feared that if the Orthodox rabbinate did not conduct such conversions, then these people would mistakenly be considered a part of the Jewish community by Jew and non-Jew alike. Moreover, the error would be compounded because these persons, converted by Liberal rabbis, would have offspring who would be identified as Jews and who might subsequently marry other Jews. As a result, Kirschenbaum felt the matter was of grave concern to the community and he reasoned that an Orthodox rabbi was not only permitted to receive such persons as proselytes. Because these people would be accepted by a Liberal rabbi if the Orthodox one should reject them, Kirschenbaum urged the Orthodox rabbi to accept them. His recognition of a social situation where Jews and non-Jews mixed freely as equals in an open society and where the presence of a non-Orthodox rabbinate meant that Liberal Jewish clergy were prepared to sanction the entry of these non-Jews into the community as proselytes led Kirschenbaum to adopt a "creative halakhic posture" that allowed for the entry of gentiles who had married Jews into the community as Orthodox proselytes. Here the reality of a post-Enlightenment Jewish world led an Orthodox authority to read precedent in a novel way.

Conclusion and Summary

To be sure, none of the rabbis discussed in this paper would have acknowledged that the departures or turns from precedent that I have described could be found in their decisions precisely because their own claims to authority rested on their insistence that their fidelity to precedent was absolute. The requirements and conventions of the Jewish legal process require an allegiance to precedent that is no less complete than it is in the Anglo-American system of law. However, we have seen that while the decisions these rabbis issued cited foundational Jewish legal texts, these rabbis did not hesitate to provide these texts with new meanings or offer novel readings of them. This approach allowed each rabbi to maintain the appearance of following precedent even as each one subtly altered these precedents though the new meanings their redefinitions conferred. In so doing, they strove to display fidelity to a flexible Jewish legal tradition while guiding the response of the Jewish community to the social and cultural challenges and transformations that Emancipation had fashioned in Jewish life. An analysis of these responsa demonstrates that these rabbis reinterpreted precedent so as to admit people who came for purposes of intermarriage into the Jewish fold, and they reread precedent to encourage the acceptance of children born to Jewish fathers and Gentile mothers.

A key to understanding Jewish law on this "antithetical model" is not whether there turns out to be a precedent for the decision that is rendered, as a traditional model of legal positivism would suggest. That account turns out to be—as examination and discussion of these decisions shows—too simple. Rather, the antithetical model alerts the student of these decisions to be mindful of what factors cause the *posek* to reformulate precedent in novel ways. All these rabbis—in response to the reality of a modern world where intermarriage between Jew and Gentile was rife—reconfigured the legal tradition by interpreting the precedents upon which they drew in fresh ways. In so doing, they recontextualized the past in light of what they perceived as the needs of the present. The use of precedent—upon such examination—turns out to be quite supple, and the notion of "creative misreadings" provides for a more complete account of the dynamics that often mark the Jewish legal process in the modern setting than the traditional model alone.

NOTES

1. David Cole, "Agon at Agora: Creative Misreadings in the First Amendment," *Yale Law Journal* 95 (1986): 858, 860.
2. David Hume, *An Enquiry Concerning Human Understanding and Concerning the Principles of Morals*, 3rd ed., ed. L. A. Selby-Bigge (Oxford: Clarendon Press, 1975), 195–96, 210, and 308–9.
3. Cole, "Agon at Agora," 860ff.
4. Ibid., 868.
5. Ibid., 869.
6. For the definitive biography on Kalischer, see Jody Myers, *Seeking Zion: Modernity and Messianic Activism in the Writings of Tsevi Hirsch Kalischer* (Portland OR: Littman Library of Jewish Civilization, 2003).

7. Illowy wrote his letter on October 31, 1864. It appears in *Sefer Milhamot Elokim*, "The Controversial Letters and the Casuistic Decisions of the Late Rabbi Dr. Bernard Illowy" (Berlin, 1914). See a full discussion and analysis of this entire episode in David Ellenson, "A Jewish Legal Decision by Rabbi Bernard Illowy of New Orleans and Its Discussion in Nineteenth-Century Europe," in *American Jewish History* 69, no. 2 (1979): 174–95.

8. Feilchenfeld's article appeared in *Der Israelit* 2 (1865), while Hildesheimer's appeared in *Der Israelit* 5 (1865).

9. See Jack Cohen, *Intermarriage and Conversion: A Halakhic Solution* (Hoboken NJ: Ktav, 1987).

10. Daniel Gordis, "David Zevi Hoffmann on Civil Marriage: Evidence of a Traditional Community under Siege," *Modern Judaism* 10 (1990): 94.

11. Ibid.

12. Professor Mark Washofsky, in a personal communication to me after my oral presentation of this paper at the Freehof Institute, pointed out that the Talmud itself, in Yevamot 24b, focused on whether the prohibition against marrying the woman after her conversion (M. Yevamot 2:8) applied only to one who was suspected of having previous sexual relations with the woman, while excluding one who was unquestionably known to have had relations with her. Those rabbis who raised this question in the Talmud did so because Jewish law holds that marriage between a Jew and a convert is valid even if it is known that the conversion was undertaken initially for the sake of the marriage. Since that is so, it would appear unfounded that the former master would be prohibited from marrying a former slave who had been converted. The Gemara, based on the verse in Proverbs 4:24, "Put crooked speech away from you, and keep devious talk far from you," thus explains that the prohibition is based on the concern that no credence be given to the original rumor that the master had been behaving immorally by having sexual relations with this slave woman. Rabbi Benzion Meir Hai Ouziel (*Mishpetei Ouziel, Yoreh De'ah* 1:14, paragraph 2), takes note of this argument. However, he explicitly rejects this line of reasoning and asserts that the prohibition applies even if it is conclusively known that these people had cohabited while the husband was the master and the woman his slave. While R. Ouziel does in fact permit the conversion and marriage out of pragmatic concerns, he explicitly—in contrast to Hoffmann—rejects the suggestion, made by others, that the fact that these people were married under civil law alleviates the prohibition against their relationship. This leads to the possibility that the only reason the man should not marry the woman is because this would confirm the suspicion. However, in a case where it was known that they had lived together, there would be no prohibition. In the case of a Jew and a gentile married under civil law, in other words, the conversion is permitted not because the *halakhah* invests civil marriage and intermarriage with any validity but because there is no "suspicion" involved in such a public case. Profes-

sor Washofsky's points are well taken, and I am grateful for his explication of this passage in the Talmud and later Jewish law. However, it seems to me that this exposition does not count against the reading I offer in this paper precisely because Hoffmann does not make this argument. That is, Rabbi Hoffmann makes no mention of the issue of *hashad* (suspicion), but instead discusses *kanas* (marriage) alone. Consequently, the notion that Hoffmann here engages in a "creative misreading" of *halakhah* by assigning civil marriage some degree of substance as "marriage" appears justified.

13. Biographical information on both Jakob Hoffmann and Menachem Mendel Kirschenbaum is found in Ya'akov Zur, *Jakob Hoffmann: The Man and His Era* (Jerusalem, 1999).

14. Menachem Mendel Kirschenbaum, *Menachem Meishiv*, no. 42.

21

A Portrait of the *Poseq* as Modern Religious Leader

An Analysis of Selected Writings of
Rabbi Hayim David Halevi

Rabbi Hayim David Halevi (1925–98), *talmid muvhak* of the famed Sephardic chief rabbi of Israel Ben Zion Meir Hai Ouziel at the prestigious Yeshivat Porat Yosef, served for many years in the post of Sephardic chief rabbi of Tel Aviv-Jaffa. His nine volumes of responsa, published under the title of *'Aseh lekha rav*, made him one of the most prolific and famous rabbinic authorities in Israel during the latter part of the twentieth century.[1]

This article will explore the attitude Rabbi Halevi assumed concerning the issue of religious leadership in the modem setting by analyzing samples of his *halakhic* writings that illustrate his attitudes and opinions on the matter of leadership. These texts provide ideal sources for investigating his approach to the topic, for as a traditional rabbinic authority he remained absolutely committed throughout his life to Jewish law and its processes as the rightful foundations for the exercise of legitimate Jewish religious leadership. An examination of representative responsa of his therefore yields insight into and understanding of the substance and application of his approach to the question of religious leadership.

The first section of this essay provides a brief outline of the historical and theoretical considerations that will frame the discussion and analysis of the sources examined. This first part places the writings of R. Halevi within a broader Occidental context that has established specific parameters for and constraints on the exercise of religious authority and leadership in the modern setting. At the same time, the Sephardic heritage internalized and championed by this rabbi, as well as the distinct concerns the Israeli venue presented to him, are highlighted to yield a more detailed and accurate appreciation of how this man confronted the challenge of exercising religious leadership in the contemporary era. The paper then turns to an essay written by his teacher Rabbi Ouziel on the topic "The *poseq* in Israel."² This writing by the *Rishon letsiyon* illuminates R. Ouziel's theoretical approach to matters of religious authority and leadership, and there is no doubt that the attitudes championed by his teacher had a seminal impact on R. Halevi's position on this issue. He clearly internalized his teacher's viewpoints and attitudes on Jewish law, and he applied the perspective he drew from his teacher in his own halakhic writings. The next section of this essay presents specific representative examples drawn from his halakhic corpus to show precisely how R. Halevi did this. Finally, the article concludes with a brief observation on how this approach reflects the manner in which R. Halevi believed authentic Jewish religious leadership ought to be exercised in the modern era.

Historical Contexts and Theoretical Considerations

At the outset, it is crucial to note that religious leaders in the modern West can no longer exercise what sociologists frequently label "performatory authority over society." In the present-day Occident, religion is largely confined to the private realm, and it is civil government that generally enjoys a monopoly over coercive legal authority. For the traditional rabbi living in the modern setting, this means that he must confront a situation where he has been stripped of imperative power. Simply put, this rabbi can no longer employ legal sanctions to compel others to follow his lead.

Of course, this reality does not imply that the rabbi has no authority whatsoever. After all, the failure of the government to invest political control in the hands of the rabbinate does not, in one sense, involve a direct challenge to the validity of religious authority whatsoever. Indeed, such authority continues to exist, and the rabbi may well claim—by virtue of his knowledge and learning and through his adherence to halakhic method and norms—to speak authoritatively. Furthermore, a constituency may recognize this claim as legitimate. Thus a rabbi can often exert considerable religious authority over individuals as well as a community. The rabbi can issue a decree or ruling and an individual or a community will obey it, that is, act on the command issued by the rabbi.

However, the exercise of such authority is best understood as "influential." The rabbi has no recourse to the state for the imposition of his will. As noted above, the political configurations of the modern state delimit the exercise of such authority in the public arena. Instead, these political arrangements confine the exercise of religious authority to the voluntary sphere. Religious authority is therefore operative only among those who willingly accept it. The modern rabbi must depend on the voluntary compliance of those who would be his adherents if he is to exercise leadership among them, for his constituents are able to determine whether they regard the authority of the rabbi as legitimate. They alone have the right to decide whether they will let the directives issued by the rabbi direct their own conduct.

The contemporary rabbi must be mindful of such considerations in issuing his own rulings, and while he may resist or resent the reality imposed by the modern situation, he cannot completely ignore this reality if he is to exercise religious leadership in his community. His authority and leadership may well be effective, and his followers may well have internalized norms that assert the legitimacy of his rule. However, his sanctions are informal. They bear no civil implications. The modern situation, therefore, does not call for the rabbi to surrender his claims to authority. Rather, the modern setting requires the rabbi to understand that his authority is not "legal," but "influential."[3]

The task of the traditional rabbi in the modern West is thus twofold. The rabbi is called upon to recognize that it is the halakhic tradition that vests him with authority and allows him to assert his leadership. Simultaneously, he must grapple with a modern state that no longer legally enforces such authority. Such recognition is no less demanded of contemporary Sephardic and Ashkenazic rabbis in Israel than it has been of all rabbis living in Central and Western Europe and North America during the past two centuries. An analysis of how R. Halevi sought to effectuate religious leadership during his lifetime places him within the broader context of how the modern rabbi as a religious specialist has had to cope with the loss of coercive legal authority.

Of course, it must be acknowledged that the Israeli setting in which R. Halevi operated was not identical with the setting that existed for rabbis in nations like the United States. As an Israeli government official, there were discrete areas of life where R. Halevi was empowered by the state. His was not a world of complete religious voluntarism. Yet even here such empowerment was limited, and R. Halevi was surely aware that his authority was influential in most of the spheres of life that he would address.

The language and style adopted in the responsa by R. Halevi only underscore this point. In contrast to a classical rabbinic language and style that would have been far more esoteric and impenetrable to the less scholarly Jewish reader, R. Halevi wrote virtually all of his responsa in a modern Hebrew idiom and manner that was accessible to a modern Israeli Jewish audience. While knowledge of classical rabbinic sources is certainly necessary to comprehend his legal opinions, there is no doubt that R. Halevi purposefully chose to write in a "popular style" that was accessible to a broad Israeli public. In this sense, the "rhetorical language and performance" that marked his responsa can be seen as crucial elements in his program to achieve religious authority and provide religious guidance and leadership for his community as well as the broader Israeli public. What R. Halevi shares in common with other Orthodox rabbis in the modern West—who also strive to achieve influential authority in a world where they are denied political power—as opposed to what distinguishes him from them, is therefore properly underscored in the analysis offered in this essay.

While these commonalities between Rabbi Halevi and Orthodox Ashkenazic rabbis will be emphasized, other factors that distinguish him from them will not be neglected. After all, R. Halevi still engaged with a more traditional constituency than did rabbis in the West. The primary people among whom he exercised his leadership were Sephardic Jews embedded in the culture and ethos of traditional Judaism. His constituents did not question the legitimacy of his religious authority, even if they failed—for a host of reasons—to emulate his strictly halakhic lifestyle. Allied closely to this was another factor. Simply put, R. Halevi did not operate in a world where Jewish religious pluralism was a present or pressing reality. While he was well aware of secular Jewish nationalism, R. Halevi did not have to confront the specter of a Reform or Conservative movement that challenged the hegemony of traditional Judaism. He thus had no need to combat these denominations, nor did he subsequently feel constrained—as did many Orthodox authorities in the West—to erect boundaries over against these movements and their spokespeople in order to defend traditional Judaism.[4] As a result, his consciousness as to how religious leadership could be exercised in the modern setting and how authority could be maintained was played out in an arena that was distinct from that of most Orthodox rabbis in the West. This point must also not be neglected in an analysis of his work.

Finally, R. Ouziel transmitted a specific tradition of halakhic discourse to him, and R. Halevi internalized the approach that his teacher had taught him. As the heir to the halakhic mantle bestowed on him by R. Ouziel, R. Halevi utilized the ethos that marked this method as a guide in his own efforts to realize authority and provide authentic Jewish religious leadership in the modern setting. Consequently, we now turn to an examination of a key essay by his teacher, R. Ouziel, on the subject of Jewish legal decision-making, an essay that had a seminal impact on R. Halevi's own views.

The Poseq in Israel: Rabbi Ben Zion Meier Hai Ouziel

R. Ouziel, in his essay "The Poseq in Israel," puts forth his own thoughts concerning the nature of Jewish legal adjudication and the role that the decisor was required to play in arriving at a decision. He roots his views in the history of Jewish jurisprudence and measures the role and qualifications of the poseq against the backdrop of the ancient Sanhedrin and the attributes that characterized its members. R. Ouziel notes that the judges who sat on the Sanhedrin were required to possess three sets of qualifications: personal, intellectual, and legal. On the personal level, he asserts that they were to be wise, pious, humble, logical, and well-liked by their fellow human beings, as well as personally righteous. Second, members of the Sanhedrin had to possess experience as lower court judges before they could serve on the High Court. Such legal experience constituted the sine qua non for service as a poseq. Finally, there were intellectual requirements that had to be met. The judge was to be knowledgeable in both the Written and Oral Laws and well versed in secular subjects.

In the course of his discussion of the last point, R. Ouziel turns to the area of the Oral Law and delineates the expertise demanded of the poseq as well as the nature of Jewish law as he saw it. R. Ouziel likens the Oral Law and the halakhic process to an "ever-growing fountain" and states that Jewish law is dynamic, not static. He asserts that halakha is supple, and he claims that Jewish law constantly adapts to new conditions. Most important for purposes of this discussion, R. Ouziel believes that the halakha granted broad discretionary powers to the poseq, for he asserts that "the poseq is not bound by the precedent provided by earlier halakhic rulings." Indeed, he fears that if a legal decisor displays an overly rigid fidelity to precedent and does not pay appropriate attention to novel contexts and situations, then he might well issue rulings that would be in "great error" (qilqulah merubbah). In fact, R. Ouziel maintains that blind conformity to earlier precedent "diminishes" the broad-based flexibility inherent in Jewish law. Precedent, while vital, should not prevent later courts or rabbis from exercising their own independent judgment.

R. Ouziel then turns to the Rambam, the great giant of Jewish jurisprudence, to provide a warrant for this approach to the nature of Jewish law and the role the *poseq* is called upon to play in it. In a lengthy discussion of Maimonidean jurisprudence, R. Ouziel argues that Maimonides maintained that contemporaneous rabbinic leaders were required to display an independent attitude toward the past, and he asserts that great rabbis throughout the ages did in fact display this streak of independence. He acknowledges that the rabbi must master "the general principles and precise details" contained in the Torah. However, R. Ouziel insists, "The desire of the Torah is that the Jewish authority will himself be a *sefer Torah*." If a Jewish legal authority attains this rank, then he, no less than Maimonides, will be empowered—on the basis of his logic and intellect (*sevara*) to innovate novel Jewish legal rulings, for they will be consonant with the spirit of Torah. As R. Ouziel puts it, the *poseq* possesses the privilege of "establishing law through halakhic instruction that is in accord with justice. He may make the halakha more consonant with logic, and logic more consonant with halakha."

This methodology that R. Ouziel put forth had a profound impact on R. Halevi. The younger Sephardic rabbi internalized his teacher's views and championed this approach and embodied these attitudes in his own halakhic writings. They dovetailed nicely with the sociopolitical realities of the world that R. Halevi and his constituency inhabited, and they permitted him to respond in a flexible manner to the issues of the day. A presentation of pertinent selections drawn from selected responsa will demonstrate how R. Halevi strove faithfully to apply the ethos of Jewish law to present-day challenges confronting the Jewish people so that he could exercise authentic Jewish religious leadership as a *poseq* in the modern setting of *Medinat yisrael*.

The Writings of Rabbi Hayim David Halevi

The approach to religious leadership that R. Halevi adopted can be seen in numerous responsa he issued on a whole host of matters. Practical rulings he issued in three representative areas will display his attitude and approach to the question of how to achieve effective and authentic Jewish religious leadership in the modern era. The first subsection below focuses on decisions he issued concerning non-observant Jews, while the second analyzes a remarkable responsum R. Halevi wrote on Christians and Christianity. The last subsection relates to questions of Jewish sovereignty in the State of Israel. In all three areas, we will see how R. Halevi drew creatively on the classical sources of Jewish tradition and relied on his own intellect to arrive at supple positions that were both pragmatic and halakhically authentic.

Non-Observant Jews

In a series of responsa dealing with the issue of nonobservant Jews being included in a prayer quorum (*minyan*), R. Halevi displays an awareness of the secular nature of the Jewish community in the modern world. In the premodern setting, Jewish religious and civic life were virtually undifferentiated. In such a world, the rabbis were able to assert that "one who violates the Sabbath in public, even if he violates only a prohibition of the rabbis, is reckoned a gentile" (*Orah Hayyim* 385:3). With the advent of the modern world, Jewish stirrings toward cultural and social integration into the larger world meant that most Jews soon no longer observed the strictures of traditional Jewish laws. Furthermore, the rabbis no longer possessed the political power essential to command conformity to the Law among those Jews who remained within the bounds of the community. Consequently, the demands of the modern situation compelled the rabbi to recognize these facts if he was to exercise authority and leadership in an effective way. Caught between the demands of a traditional legal system he regarded as divine and the realities of the nonobservant Jewish population, R. Halevi had to navigate between these twin concerns in providing religious leadership for his community.

In a brief responsum found in *Aseh lekha rav* 4:28, R. Halevi empathizes with a building supplier who sold materials to Jewish workers who the supplier knew would use them to work on the Sabbath. While R. Halevi understand the distress (*'agmat nefesh*) that marked the soul of his questioner over the contemporary state of nonobservance that marks Jewish life, he does not prohibit the sale of these materials to these men and states emphatically that the supplier was not guilty of the sin of "aiding and abetting sinners" (*mesayeia yedei 'ovrei 'aveirah*). Such interactions and business transactions are unavoidable in the modern setting.

In *Aseh lekha rav* 5:1–3, R. Halevi deals first with the dilemma of a young yeshiva student who elected to stay at home rather than pray in a synagogue where the members of the *minyan* were nonobservant Jews. The young man told R. Halevi that his presence was required if the necessary ten men for a prayer quorum were to be gathered, and he also stated that his father had asked him to participate in the *minyan*. After a lengthy discussion of the sources, R. Halevi states that the rule of Torah is clear: "Anyone who commits even a single sin intentionally (*'over 'aveirah afilu ahat le-hahis*) cannot be counted in a *minyan*." And "if one is a transgressor for appetite (*'avaryan leteiavon*), or a public violator of the Sabbath, . . . or denies the words of our sages (*she-kofer be-divrei rabboteinu*), then they too cannot be counted in the *minyan*." R. Halevi therefore asserts that it would at first glance appear that it is forbidden to pray with persons "who are neither religious nor Sabbath observers."

However, he states that there are other considerations that have to be borne in mind before a final ruling can be issued on this matter. Indeed, R. Halevi points out to his interrogator that "if you do not join them [in this instance], then the synagogue will be closed and those who do observe Torah will not be able to pray." R. Halevi regards this as an unacceptable outcome and therefore states quite boldly that "it is incumbent on us to search for a way to be lenient." As R. Halevi saw it, the question here was not primarily one of deciding whether it was permissible to pray with nonobservant Jews. As a legal authority and leader, he felt he had the right and duty to redefine what was at stake in this question. Nothing less than the maintenance of a local Jewish community hung in the balance. If the young man refused to attend the synagogue on Jewish legal grounds, then a vital communal-religious institution would be removed from a specific locale. R. Halevi wanted to avoid this at all costs, and he therefore concludes that the rules forbidding a pious Jew to pray in a *minyan* composed of nonobservant Jews have to be circumscribed, for a strict application of these regulations would result in a synagogue being closed. His sense of communal good demanded that he maintain a communal institution such as the synagogue even if the behavior of its members did not conform to his own notion of what would be ideal conduct.

R. Halevi also takes conscious note of the contemporary context and state of Jewish life, and he identifies them as vital factors in rendering his decision. In premodern times, the Jewish community was overwhelmingly observant. Therefore, he writes, failure to observe the Sabbath was surely a mark of communal deviance and rebellion. However, such nonobservance cannot be considered an act of revolt "in our time." He states that Sabbath violators (*hillulei shabbat*) increased daily in the contemporary Jewish world, and "most Jews neither know nor understand the severity of the prohibition." R. Halevi notes that it is not uncommon for Israeli Sephardic Jews to attend synagogue on Saturday mornings and then violate the Sabbath in the afternoon. Like many other Orthodox rabbis, R. Halevi therefore holds that such Jews should not be regarded as openly rebelling against the tradition. Rather, they would be better regarded as falling under the legal category of "a captured babe" (*tinok she-nishbah*) who knows no better. Such Jews should not be held completely culpable for their actions, and it is possible to join with them for prayer and other activities. On this additional ground, R. Halevi urges the young man to join the *minyan*.[5]

R. Halevi then adds two more considerations to justify this stance. First, he observes that if the son attends this *minyan*, he will be acceding to the request of his father. This would grant his father great satisfaction, and it would constitute an act of filial piety. In this way, the son would fulfill the commandment of *kibbtud av* (honoring father). Second, the young man, by participating in the *minyan*, would also observe the commandment of "granting merit to the public" (*lizkot et ha-rabbim*). Indeed, it is R. Halevi's hope that the "holy and pure spirit" of the synagogue would cause some of those who prayed there to return in repentance (*teshuvah*) to God.

This consideration was far from a minor one to R. Halevi. In an ancillary question that came before him in 5:1–3, he expresses precisely the same sentiment. Here a young "*talmid hacham*" asked to serve as a cantor for the High Holidays in a community where most of the members were nonobservant. R. Halevi regarded his young interrogator's question as most difficult. As he phrases it, "Woe if we permit him to travel there, woe if we forbid it, and woe to us that our generation has reached a situation like this." However, as he did in the previous responsum, R. Halevi rules leniently and feels the student should serve the congregation. He states, "The matter of granting merit (*zikui ha-rabbim*) to the community is one of great and vital import." The religious leader must be concerned with the maintenance and welfare of the community, and it is the duty of the *poseq* to employ the precedents and flexibility available in Jewish law to attain these ends. Indeed, this consideration caused R. Halevi to observe that he himself had delivered a sermon at a comparable congregation years earlier when he was serving as a *shaliach* (Israeli emissary) in the United States, and he feels that such an act had allowed him to address a community that would otherwise not have been exposed to his words of Torah. In this way, "my reward exceeded my loss." While he was uncomfortable with elements of his decision, the social reality of the modern world compelled him to make a utilitarian calculus as to which decision would better promote Judaism in the present situation, and the nature of the halakhic process as he understood it and as it had been transmitted to him by his teacher R. Ouziel granted him the discretionary power to do so.

Christianity

In a remarkable responsum (9:30) that focuses on the question of relationships between Jews and Christians,[6] the boldness of R. Halevi as a *poseq* and his determination to employ the resources of Jewish law in an aggressive and flexible manner in order to exercise effective leadership in a modern setting are readily apparent. Here we see how R. Halevi was resolute in his resolve to point out that the elasticity inherent in the Jewish legal process permits Judaism to adapt to reality and therefore guide the lives of Jews in the contemporary world.

At the outset of his responsum, R. Halevi expresses his misgivings concerning the talmudic dictum, "on account of the ways of peace," (*mippenei darkhei shalom*) as a resource for guiding Jewish-Christian relations in our day. The Babylonian Talmud, Gittin 61a, states, "We support the non-Jewish poor along with the Jewish poor and visit the non-Jewish sick along with the Jewish sick and bury the non-Jewish dead with the Jewish dead, *mippenei darkhei shalom*." Maimonides, in *Hilkhot Melakhim* (Laws of kings) 10:12, codifies this statement as law, when he writes, "With regard to non-Jews, the Sages enjoined that we visit their sick and bury their dead with Jewish dead and support their poor with Jewish poor, *mippenei darkhei shalom*." This concept has regularly been employed in Jewish law to establish peace among peoples, and its aim has been to minimize disputes between Jews and non-Jews.

Nevertheless, R. Halevi regards the concept of *mippenei darkhei shalom* as one of limited utility for Jews in the modern State of Israel in particular and for all modern Jews in general. He argues that this concept is essentially prudential, and he feels that it was designed by the rabbis to protect a minority Jewish population from the wrath of the gentile majority that consistently surrounded them throughout more than a millennium of Exile. In his opinion, this concept is sadly deficient as a basis for Jewish relations with the non-Jewish world as it does not champion a universalistic ethos that recognizes the equal worth of non-Jews as human beings created in the image of God. Rather, this notion promotes Jewish kindness and concern toward non-Jews on pragmatic grounds alone. R. Halevi therefore voices a principled objection to its employment as a contemporary warrant for Jewish action toward gentiles in the modern era, and he regards this concept as inappropriate for Jews who now live in a world informed by democratic values and ideals. He argues that Western political and religious culture was established on the principle of "equal rights for every person," and R. Halevi therefore contends that Judaism must promote an ethic in relationship to other religions that is consonant with this modern notion. As he observes, Israel is a democratic society and "there is no place in a democratic nation for discrimination on the basis of religion."

At this juncture in his responsum, the impact of the contemporary setting on the thought and leadership style of R. Halevi could not be more pronounced. He clearly feels that it is incumbent on the religious leader to motivate his community to act in accord with the noblest elements present in Jewish and secular political traditions. By "reconfiguring" the teachings of the tradition in this way, R. Halevi indicates that the modern Jewish religious leader ought not hesitate to "assimilate" elements found in non-Jewish thought into the body of Judaism so as to move the community in proper directions.[7]

In continuing his responsum, R. Halevi acknowledges that the historical record of Christianity vis-à-vis Jews and Judaism is rife with episodes of persecution and discrimination. Indeed, Christian priests often incited their congregants to riot against Jews, and the anti-Jewish sentiments expressed in certain passages of the New Testament cannot be denied. Furthermore, Rabbi Halevi has difficulties with Christianity on theological as well as historical grounds. He sees the Christian belief in the Trinity as theologically problematic from a Jewish perspective, as Judaism affirms an absolute monotheism that is compromised by a Trinitarian conception of the deity. While no less a personage than Maimonides had defined Christianity for this reason as a form of idolatry, R. Halevi notes that other rabbinic authorities took an opposing stance on this question.

These authorities would not consign Christianity to the category of idolatry, nor would they accept a definition of Christians as idol worshippers. In a comment on Sanhedrin 63b, Rabbi Isaac of late twelfth-century France, the nephew of Rabbenu Tam, spoke of Christians and Christianity in the following terms:

> Although they [Christians] mention the name of Heaven, meaning thereby Jesus of Nazareth, they do not at all events mention a strange deity, and moreover, they mean thereby the Maker of Heaven and Earth too; and despite the fact that they associate the name of Heaven with an alien deity, we do not find that it is forbidden to cause gentiles to make such an association . . . since such an association (*shittuf*) is not forbidden to the sons of Noah [i.e., gentiles].

In adopting this position, Rabbi Isaac adopted a perspective that removed Christians from the category of idol worshippers. While Trinitarianism remained a forbidden theological posture for Jews, adherence to this notion by Christians was deemed an acceptable form of monotheism, as this doctrine fell under the rabbinic category of Associationism *(shittuf)*. Indeed, Rabbi Menachem Ha-Meiri of early fourteenth-century Provence expanded on this doctrine and stated explicitly that contemporary Christians "recognize the God-head" and "believe in God's existence, His unity and power, although they misconceive some points according to our belief." He further declared that his Christian peers did not fall under the category of "idol worshippers" and stated, "Now idolatry has disappeared from most places." This trajectory found later expression in Jewish legal writings, and Rabbi Yehuda Ashkenazi, writing about Christians and Christianity in his commentary on the *Shulhan Arukh, Yoreh De'ah* 151:2, asserted, "In our era, when the gentiles in whose midst we dwell . . . [speak of God], their intention is directed toward the One Who made Heaven and Earth, albeit that they associate another personality with God. However, this does not constitute a violation of Lev. 19:14, 'You shall not place a stumbling block before the blind,' for non-Jews are not warned against such Associationism."

As a result of these rulings and others, R. Halevi feels that he can confidently and legitimately distinguish between the historical record of Christianity and Christians vis-à-vis Judaism and Jews, as well as talmudic condemnations of Christianity as a form of idolatry, and the attitudes and positions that Judaism and Jews ought to adopt toward Christianity and Christians today. R. Halevi points out in lengthy detail that numerous authorities throughout the past five hundred years followed the Meiri and his school of legal exegesis on the question of Christianity, and he demonstrates that these rabbis issued lenient rulings on discrete episodes and matters—such as use of wine produced by gentiles, business transactions with non-Jews before holidays, offering greetings to gentiles—that indicated that these *posqim* did not place present-day Christians in the category of "idol worshippers." He therefore concludes that the category of "idolater" is today inoperative as Christianity constitutes—at worst—*shituf*.[8]

In a postscript appended to his responsum, R. Halevi notes that Professor Menachem Elan, the prominent Israeli jurist and great authority on *Mishpat 'Ivri* (Jewish law), commented on his responsum and conceded that it was true that the Meiri did not view Christianity as idolatry. However, Elon also maintained that the Meiri was virtually alone in the history of Jewish jurisprudence in putting forth such an overarching stance, and he further noted that most rabbinic authorities did not agree with the Meiri. Even when these rabbis did not apply rabbinic categories of idolatry to present-day Christians, they were careful to circumscribe their rulings, and they explicitly applied these lenient rulings only to specific situations. In Elon's view, the thrust of Jewish legal tradition maintained the position that Christianity was a form of idolatry, and the privileged position R. Halevi had granted to only one strand of Jewish jurisprudence on this matter did not warrant the expansive posture that he had adopted. Therefore, Elon challenged R. Halevi and wanted to know on what grounds he dared to remove contemporary Christians from the category of idolaters.

R. Halevi responded by admitting that it was perhaps accurate to assert that the Meiri was the only major authority to advance an unrestricted reading that excluded Christians and Christianity altogether from the category of idolatry. Nevertheless, the Meiri alone was hardly a minor figure in the history of Jewish law, and as a later jurist, he himself can surely rely on the Meiri as a warrant for the stance he has taken. Furthermore, R. Halevi also maintains that the other authorities he cited on specific issues employed the same logic that the Meiri did in offering their rulings, and the permissions they issued in each instance did not stem from any desire for political advantage or financial gain. Rather, these holdings on the particular matters enumerated above emerged from the theological judgment that Christians were "not idolaters." R. Halevi feels these rulings provided him with ample warrant for his own position, and he does not hesitate to transform and expand circumscribed individual applications into a general rule.

In concluding his response to Justice Elon, R. Halevi boldly affirms his prerogative as a *poseq* and reiterates his claim that the category of idolatry is irrelevant today in dealing with modern-day Christians and Christianity. Indeed, he consigns this category to the past and argues that such a stance in the contemporary world is contrary to the overarching spirit of the tradition itself. Its adoption in the modern era could lead to an immoral xenophobia discordant with the moral sensibility that ought to mark modern-day Jewish behaviors. As a *poseq* and religious leader, R. Halevi feels that it is his right as well as his obligation to expand the application of Jewish law in this matter so as to provide new guidelines and directions that can inspire and lead modern-day Jews in positive directions. In adopting this position and "expanding this permission" that other rabbis had adopted "into other areas of life," R. Halevi demonstrates once more in this ruling that he had no hesitancy in affirming the authority he possessed as *poseq* to move in novel directions. In so doing, he once more reveals that he had internalized the ethos that he learned from his teacher R. Ouziel and displays his own view that authentic religious leadership has to be prepared to expand the parameters of the tradition so that guidelines from the past can be transformed into rulings that will lead the community in the present and direct the Jewish people toward the future.

The Israeli Setting as a Novel Context for the Application of Jewish Law

In *'Aseh lekha rav* 7:52, R. Halevi strikingly expresses his attitude toward the manner in which religious leadership has to be exercised on painful political-military choices confronting the State of Israel. In this 1986 decision, R. Halevi addresses the question of whether 1,150 Arab terrorists incarcerated in Israeli jails can be released in exchange for three Israeli soldiers who have been captured in Lebanon. On the basis of a rule contained in Gittin 45a, "Captives should not be redeemed for more than their value, to prevent abuses" (*mippenei tiqqun 'olam*), R. Shlomo Goren had stated that such an exchange was impermissible. R. Halevi disagrees. In fact, R. Halevi holds that it was possible to provide an innovative reading of Jewish law in this instance that would countenance such a decision.

R. Halevi notes that the Gemara, in explicating the Gittin passage, offers two possible justifications for the stricture. One explanation maintains that the aim of this judgment was to prevent captors from extorting the public for exorbitant sums of money. In this way, no undue burden that would financially imperil the community could be imposed. The other ground suggested for this decree by later rabbis was that a communal policy that refused to redeem these prisoners would ward off "the possibility that the activities [of the bandits] would be stimulated." It would likely deter these gentiles from seizing even more Jews, for such seizure would be pointless inasmuch as these gentiles could not now extort excessive amounts of money from the Jewish people. As the Talmud states (Gittin 45a), the rule "Captives should not be redeemed for more than their value" was advanced so "that robbers should not be tempted to kidnap persons and then offer them for ransom."

R. Halevi points out that several later rabbinic authorities concluded that the second explanation provided the foundation for this ruling, as this would prevent gentiles "from risking their own lives in order to capture more Jews." Thus Maimonides, in *Hilkhot mattanot 'aniyim* 8:12, writes, "'Captives should not be redeemed for more than their value, to prevent abuses (*mippenei tiqqun 'olam*),' for then enemies will not pursue [Jews]." R. Halevi extends this logic and reasons that a decision to return Palestinian terrorists in exchange for Israeli soldiers cannot be regarded as an enticement that would lead to the abduction of more Jews.

He argues in this way on several grounds. After all, in the changed setting of the modern world, Jews are no longer a hapless, politically impotent minority. Jews living in the State of Israel, unlike past generations of Jews in the Diaspora, enjoy political and military power, and "due to the kindnesses of God upon us," the kidnapping of Jews by Palestinians seldom occurs. Several recent attempts to kidnap "soldiers and others Jewish citizens have not succeeded," for the Israel Defense Forces have proven able to defend and protect the citizens of Israel. "In my humble opinion," R. Halevi writes, "this is a crucial factor that must inform our discussion concerning the matter of ransoming our captive soldiers." He therefore disagrees with R. Goren as to the applicability of the Gittin precedent in the instant case. Unlike R. Goren, he maintains that the rule it contained is unrelated to the present situation, as the current circumstances for all the reasons cited above are unprecedented. The original considerations that gave rise to the rule no longer obtain.

The current situation therefore demands halakhic boldness and creativity. As R. Halevi phrases it, "At the outset, we must acknowledge that there are difficult problems that arise in our lives for which there is no clear and decisive halakhic precedent and solution." He continues by asserting that there is no real parallel "to the situation that we find ourselves in today. We therefore need halakhic innovation (*hiddush hilkhati*) in this instance, one that is consistent with the spirit of earlier halakhic sources and suitable to them—that is, a new halakhic decision" (*hakhra'ah hilkhatit hadashah*). In staking out this position, R. Halevi feels that he is only highlighting that quality of innovation that stands at the heart of the Jewish legal system, for in summarizing this point he writes, "This was the power of our sages," for whenever a novel situation arose, "they were not satisfied with those *halakhot* that had been transmitted to them up to that point. Rather, they struggled to offer innovative halakhic rulings." In making this point, R. Halevi is once again both echoing the words of his teacher R. Ouziel and arguing that the halakhic system allows for and even demands such innovation.

Indeed, a clear example of how the rabbis engaged in such innovation can be found in rabbinic discussions concerning the *sugya* in Gittin 45a itself. For example, the *Tosafot*, commenting on the phrase "in order that activities of the robbers not be stimulated," offer the following thoughts. They note that in Gittin 58a the Talmud relates a story concerning Rabbi Joshua ben Haninah. This tannaitic authority, in seeming opposition to the rule that it is forbidden to redeem a captive for more than his worth, had in fact redeemed a child from his captors in Rome for an excessive sum of money. The *Tosafists* reason that R. Joshua did this because this child possessed exceptional intellectual talents. According to the talmudic narrative, R. Joshua, in explaining his decision, said, "I feel sure that this one will be a teacher in Israel." R. Joshua was correct, and this boy grew up to be R. Ishmael ben Elisha, a great tannaitic authority.

In this instance, R. Halevi praises R. Joshua for his courage and holds him up as a model decisor. He states that R. Joshua circumscribed the applicability of the law "on the strength of his own logic and authority" (*sevarato ve-samkhuto*). In so doing, R. Joshua was only exercising his rightful prerogative as a *poseq*. As R. Halevi phrases it, "This was the might and courage of the early sages, who would innovate *halakhot* in response to contemporaneous events in the national life of the Jewish people." These rabbis refused to confine their applications of the law "to well-known and familiar sources of the law." In so doing, authorities like R. Joshua served as exemplars for all *posqim*, and he once more declares that the right to exercise such halakhic creativity and courage is not limited to the sages of the Talmud alone. Indeed, he repeats his claim that Jewish law grants broad discretionary powers to the *poseq*. Later authorities, no less than the *Tannaim* and *Amoraim* of old, are called upon to "offer novel legal rulings by relying on their own logic and wisdom." In "new and changing situations, one cannot construct a legal ruling on the authority of the sources alone." Rather, R. Halevi contends, "There is a clear need to search for [new or novel] solutions that are consistent with the spirit of the sources and absolutely faithful to them in constructing novel rulings." The right of the *poseq* to exercise leadership is grounded in a mastery of the sources of Jewish tradition. However, the ability to exercise that leadership effectively and wisely is contingent on the courage the *poseq* possesses to exercise the right accorded him by Jewish law in flexible and novel ways.

R. Halevi therefore concludes—hardly surprisingly—that the Jewish legal tradition grants him as much right as any past rabbinic authority to determine how or whether a precedent should be applied. His prerogatives as a *poseq* are not inferior to theirs. He can judge whether conditions have sufficiently changed to warrant the setting aside of the rule in this instance. Indeed, in this matter he does so, and R. Halevi disagrees with R. Goren and concludes that the rule is not actionable. He reiterates his earlier observation that the terrorists "are unable to kidnap Israeli captives. Those prisoners who fell into their hands were at war in Lebanon." The rule enunciated in Gittin should not be employed as a precedent that would prohibit the government from engaging in the proposed exchange, as the purpose for which the rule was originally designed has been rendered obsolete by contemporary conditions. In making this assertion, R. Halevi employs the readings offered by one school of Jewish legal exegesis on this passage and relies on his own authority as a *poseq*.

R. Halevi feels that the modern State of Israel embodies a novel reality for the Jewish people. He feels that nothing in the vast halakhic literature on this passage is directly analogous to the issue at hand. The rule has to be applied and a decision has to be made against a novel backdrop where changed political conditions demand a fresh response. In his view, the genius of the halakhic system is that it allows for and encourages such innovation. Consequently, R. Halevi is able to conclude his responsum with the following overarching observation. Of the halakhic process in such cases, he writes:

> I am certain that if a question of this type had stood before our early sages, they would have found a solution for it through their efforts to discover novel halakhic application consistent with the spirit of the previous halakhic sources.
>
> Therefore, it cannot be said that the government of Israel acted here in opposition to Jewish law. Indeed, it seems that her deliberations in this matter were consistent with the type of halakhic innovation that Torah sages might have introduced in such an event.

In offering these final thoughts, R. Halevi once again reveals his view of the Jewish legal system as open and supple. In this instance, R. Halevi displays his conviction that the state represents a *novum* in Jewish history that demands "novel halakhic application," and he once more demonstrates his own willingness to interpret the sources of Jewish tradition in a creative way that will allow secular as well as religious Jewish leadership to move in innovative and independent directions.

Concluding Observation

This article has demonstrated that Rabbi Hayim David Halevi consistently emphasized that the contemporary traditional Jewish religious leader ought to be flexible in meeting the challenges of the modern age. The rabbi should not hesitate to avail himself of the broad range of precedents that the Tradition provides him, nor should he vacillate in exercising the authority that the halakhic tradition vests in him. In setting forth this position, R. Halevi championed a stance he had received from his teacher R. Ouziel and displayed a strong sense of self-assurance regarding his own knowledge and ability. Indeed, R. Halevi felt that such self-confidence and elasticity had to inform every *poseq* if effective religious leadership and guidance was to be provided to the Jewish community, and he boldly made this point in *'Aseh lekha rav* 7:54. There he states:

I do not agree that . . . innovations in the spirit of the halacha, as written and received, and in utter faithfulness to it, constitute deviation—even if these innovations change, in a particular instance, the halakha as written. . . . [This is so because] permission was granted to the sages of Israel in every generation to introduce halakhic innovations in accordance with changes of time and circumstance. Only thus was it made possible for Torah to persist in Israel. . . . [Indeed,] such innovation is part of the halakha given to Moses, our Master. Whoever thinks that the halakha is frozen, and that we may not deviate from it right or left, errs greatly. On the contrary, there is no flexibility like that inherent in the halacha. . . . If the sages of our own generation will have the courage to introduce halakhic innovations true to Torah, with utter faithfulness to the body of Torah as written and received, then the halakha will continue to be the path of the Jewish people until the last generation.

The capacity of the Jewish legal system and its decisors to respond to novel challenges in authentic Jewish voices had been evidenced in the past. R. Halevi was therefore certain that Jewish law in the hands of competent and courageous decisors possesses the resources and spirit to meet such demands in the present. Confident and capable contemporary *posqim* can mine the resources of Jewish law in ways that will prove worthy as these rabbis attempt to lead the people Israel through the demanding challenges of the modern era. His own responsa testify to the way in which he felt contemporary Jewish leaders can meet the test of effectuating creative religious leadership in an authentic Jewish spirit for a modern Jewish community. An analysis of his thought and his decisions provides an instructive model that can surely inspire and direct Jewish religious leadership today as it struggles to meet the demands of the hour.

NOTES

1. Two significant English-language articles on R. Halevi are Marc Angel, "Rabbi Hayyim David Halevy: A Leading Contemporary Rabbinic Thinker," *Jewish Book Annual* 52 (1994): 99–109; and Zvi Zohar. "Sephardic Religious Thought in Israel: Aspects of the Theology of Rabbi Haim David HaLevi," in *Critical Essays on Israeli Society, Religion, and Government*, ed. Kevin Avruch and Walter Zenner (Albany: SUNY Press, 1997), 115–16. In addition, I have written two recent essays on his thought. See David Ellenson, "Interpretive Fluidity and *P'sak* in a Case of

Pidyon Sh'vuyim: An Analysis of a Modern Israeli Responsum as Illuminated by the Thought of David Hartman," in *Judaism and Modernity: The Religious Philosophy of David Hartman*, ed. Jonathan Malino (Jerusalem: Shalom Hartman Institute, 2001), 341–67, and "Jewish Legal Interpretation and Moral Values: Two Responsa by Rabbi Hayyim David Halevi on the Obligations of the Israeli Government towards Its Minority Population," *CCAR Journal* (Summer 2001): 5–20.

2. This Hebrew writing of Rabbi Ouziel, entitled "Ha-poseq beyisrael," is found in his responsa collection, *Pisqei Ouziel be-she'elot hazman* (Jerusalem: Mossad Ha-Rav Kook, n.d.), 470–84.

3. This nomenclature is taken from Jerome E. Carlin and Saul H. Mendlovitz, "The American Rabbi: A Religious Specialist Responds to Loss of Authority," in *Understanding American Judaism*, ed. Jacob Neusner (New York: Ktav, 1975), 1:165–214.

4. Ira Robinson, in his insightful article "Because of Our Many Sins: The Contemporary Jewish World as Reflected in the Responsa of Moses Feinstein," *Judaism* (Winter 1986): 35–46, points out how the existence of Conservative and Reform movements in the United States consciously informed the legal decisions issued by Rabbi Feinstein. His determination to defend traditional Judaism and its authority led the Ashkenazic rabbi to erect boundaries over against what he regarded as non-Orthodox encroachments on traditional rabbinic authority and practices and caused him to issue stringent rulings in a variety of areas. None of these considerations are present in the writings of Rabbi Halevi.

5. For a thorough and insightful study of how this category of "captured babe" was employed in the legal literature of modern Central European Orthodox rabbinic authorities, see Adam Ferziger, "Orthodox Judaism in Central Europe and the Development of Its Attitude towards Non-Observant Jews in the Modern Era" (PhD diss., Bar Ilan University, 2001). This comparative perspective indicates that similar states of nonobservance among the Jewish populations of late nineteenth- and early twentieth-century Central Europe and late twentieth-century America and Israel prompted many Ashkenazic rabbinic authorities and the Israeli Sephardic sage to select the same halakhic category as appropriate for dealing with the challenges of the modern era from a Jewish legal perspective.

6. Another article in this volume describes this responsum at great length.

7. Here one is reminded of the point made by Gerson Cohen, "The Blessing of Assimilation in Jewish History," Commencement Address, Hebrew Teachers' College, Brookline MA, 1966, in his *Jewish History and Jewish Destiny* (New York: JTS, 1997), 145–56.

8. For a contrary view that opposes any generalization that would remove Christianity altogether from the category of idolatry in Jewish jurisprudence, see David Berger, "Jacob Katz on Jews and Christians in the Middle Ages," in *The Pride of Jacob: Essays on Jacob Katz and His Work*, ed. Jay Harris (Cambridge: Harvard University Press, 2002), 61, where Berger writes, "Christian worship remains *avodah zarah* even for gentiles."

22

Rabbi Eliezer Berkovits on Conversion

An Inclusive Orthodox Approach

Eliezer Berkovits devoted a great deal of his efforts in the field of Jewish law to the issue of conversion. He was well aware that this issue was one of serious practical consequence. His sense of solidarity with the entire Jewish people as well as his conviction that Jewish legal interpretation had to be sufficiently flexible to accommodate the entire people of Israel and not just its Orthodox and halakhically observant segment led him to play a seminal role in the 1970s in the establishment of a communal *beit din* in Denver marked by joint Reform, Reconstructionist, Conservative, and Orthodox rabbinic participation. His writings and actions on conversion catapulted him into a position of prominence in the larger Jewish world even as they provoked a great deal of debate and controversy within the precincts of Orthodox Judaism.

This article will examine the position Berkovits adopted on the issue of conversion by first focusing on the application of his thought to the Denver *beit din* project. This will indicate that for him this matter was not one of theoretical speculation alone. The essay will then discuss his views regarding the social and moral dimensions of Jewish law itself. Berkovits was convinced that rabbis had to take account of social context in rendering their legal decisions, and he was equally certain that renderings of Jewish law had to be in accord with the highest moral and ethical standards. These views informed and framed his writings in every area of *halakhah*, and his stance on conversion was informed by these considerations. This article will conclude with a detailed explication of how he characterized what Jewish law demanded in this area and how the Jewish law of conversion was to be applied in a religiously pluralistic Jewish world.

In *Jew vs. Jew*, journalist Sam Freedman wrote, "In 1977, two Orthodox rabbis, both known as mavericks, appeared in Denver as speakers in adult education programs."[1] One was Eliezer Berkovits, professor emeritus at the Hebrew Theological College in Chicago, ordained at the Hildesheimer Rabbinical Seminary in Berlin, and the *talmid muvhak* of Yehiel Yaakov Weinberg.[2] Berkovits warned the Denver community that the issue "Who is a Jew?" was destroying Jewish unity. The second speaker was Steven Riskin, then rabbi of the Lincoln Square Synagogue in New York. (He was later known as Shlomo Riskin, chief rabbi of Efrat, south of Jerusalem.) Berkovits and Riskin argued that passages from the Talmud and Maimonides that deal with conversion allowed for a lenient attitude concerning the applicant's commitment to observance of the commandments. Orthodox rabbi Stanley Wagner of Denver thought that "Berkovits and Riskin offered theological justification for conversion as an ongoing process, not a contract signed as a condition of admission,"[3] and their lectures prompted him to initiate a bold and flexible experiment regarding conversion in Denver. Within a few weeks, seven Denver rabbis of all denominations met, determined to find a way to provide for a single, citywide conversion apparatus.

Ultimately, these rabbis worked out a system whereby prospective converts would take classes on the fundamentals of Judaism, to be taught by rabbis across the denominational spectrum of the Jewish community. Upon completion, a panel of rabbis representing different movements would examine the candidate. If the panel found the candidate fit for conversion, a formal rabbinic court (*beit din*) of traditional rabbis would perform the conversion. Needless to say, if a male candidate was not already circumcised, he would undergo circumcision or, in the more likely event that he were already circumcised, *hatafat dam brit* (symbolic ritual circumcision). Men as well as women would be immersed in a *mikvah*. Participants who converted through this program would agree to basic Jewish observances (such as fasting on Yom Kippur, joining a synagogue, and lighting candles for the Sabbath and holidays). Dietary laws were mentioned, as was "keeping a Jewish household," but both practices were left vague. This not only made it possible for Reform applicants to accept the *beit din*'s stipulations, but also protected Orthodox rabbis from the accusation that they had not required converts to commit to a Jewish life of observance.

This chapter in American Jewish religious history, initiated in no small measure by Eliezer Berkovits, came to an end in 1983, but not before 750 people had been converted to Judaism under this transdenominational arrangement. On June 17, 1983, six years after the initial agreement, the Orthodox rabbis of Denver formally announced that they were withdrawing. The *Intermountain Jewish News* published an article discussing the withdrawal, shining a spotlight on a program that had been content to operate in the shadows away from public scrutiny. Harold Jacobs, president of Orthodoxy's American Council of Young Israel, responded:

> We have no choice but to draw the line, clearly, as to who is a Jew and who is not, as to what limits and basic standards of elementary Jewish identity and personal conduct we must insist upon. . . . It is time that Orthodoxy put the rest of the Jewish community on notice: no longer will 'Jewish unity' be bought at the expense of Jewish identity. For Klal Yisrael today, that is too high a price.[4]

These sentiments were more strongly put forth by the *Jewish Observer*, an American journal associated with the Agudath Israel:

> While compromise for the sake of unity can often make good sense, when dealing with basic principles of faith, 'compromise' is actually a sell-out. . . . It is time that all Orthodox rabbis recognize that Reform and Conservative Judaism are far, far removed from Torah, and Klal Yisroel is betrayed—not served—when Orthodoxy enters in religious association with them.

As far as the experiment being tried elsewhere, the *Observer* warned that "other communities contemplating this type of interdenominational cooperation [ought to] take note of the awesome pitfalls involved and step back from the abyss."[5]

I begin with this episode for two reasons. One is obvious—the critical role Berkovits played in triggering this experiment in interdenominational Jewish cooperation. Second, the episode itself indicates that for Berkovits, his lectures and writings on these matters were not *devarim b'alma*, theoretical speculations unrelated to the actual life of the Jewish people. His concerns and commitments to the Jewish people and their unity, as well as to the service of God, were quite real, and his being was devoted to the practical application of his thought in shaping the life and community of the Jewish people. With that as our starting point, I will now turn to his writings on Jewish law in general and the issue of conversion in particular that serve as the foundation for the applied stance on this matter that found real-life expression in Denver.

In his 1974 article, "Conversion and Decline of the Oral Law," Berkovits stated that he wished to discuss the issue of conversion as a means of addressing the overarching problem of Jewish law in our day. Thus he pondered the meaning of the common phrase 'al pi halacha (according to halakha), which plays such a central role in considerations surrounding geirut (conversion) in both Israel and the Diaspora.[6]

Berkovits asserted that the laws regarding conversion were actually quite simple, involving three requirements: (1) acceptance of the commandments of the Torah, (2) circumcision in the case of a male convert, and (3) immersion in a ritual bath. The problem, he noted, was "that there are a great many Jews who either do not accept the Talmud as the ultimate authority for their own religious conscience, or give to the law regarding conversion an interpretation which differs widely from the one given it by Orthodox Judaism." He stated that it "makes little sense to argue that since the unity of the Jewish people is at stake, all Jews must accept the Orthodox viewpoint." This is not because it is difficult to comprehend why the Orthodox would make such a demand. Rather, it is because a position that insists upon complete Orthodox hegemony in this area "shall not safeguard the unity of the Jewish people" as "the essential nature of being a Jew becomes more and more diluted for more and more Jews." He noted that many Orthodox Jews might retort, "We are not concerned with the practical consequences. Here is the law. We insist that it be adhered to." However, Berkowits countered, "But would this still be a halachic position? Is it indeed so that authentic halakha is free of meaningful practical considerations?"[7]

Berkowits also maintained that there was a moral question involved here and that Jewish law should address it. He observed that by insisting that an Orthodox view alone prevail in this area, "we have stated that our numerous non-Orthodox brothers and sisters have to be excluded from having any say in such a vital issue as what it means to be a Jew. Do we have the moral right to make such demands?" Of course, he, like all Orthodox Jews, believed in the divinity of Jewish law. Nevertheless, there is an inescapable personal element in the act of textual interpretation, for there is always a human reader of the text. As Berkovits observed,

The Torah is from heaven, but my faith that it is, is not so, neither is my interpretation of the meaning and consequences of that faith from heaven. If so, how can we deny Conservative and Reform rabbis and scholars the right to their interpretation? Of course, we Orthodox Jews are the only Jews faithful to the demands of Torah. But no matter how much we insist on this, it will, nevertheless, remain our own subjective insistence.[8]

There is no epistemology that can absolutely and irrefutably demonstrate the truth of that claim—it remains subjective on some level, and that subjectivity means that it would be "immoral" for an Orthodox Jew to demand that his interpretation be the only one on this topic of Jewish law.

Berkowits continued by asserting once again that "an Orthodox Jew might say . . . I have my own convictions and I shall not depart from the letter in the *Shulchan Aruch* regarding conversion, even by a hair's breadth." However, if an Orthodox Jew does adopt this stance, "one should have a proper understanding of the meaning of such a decision. In its consequences, this would be a decision of seceding from community with non-Orthodox Jews or excluding them from community with us."[9] The Orthodox Jew should fully grasp this implication, for an Orthodox insistence upon a monopoly on conversion means that "this is no longer a question purely of conversion," but of Jewish unity itself. Indeed, he believed that "the importance of the unity of the Jewish people, the idea of the community of Israel, *klal yisrael*, in relationship to the laws of conversion" should lead the Orthodox community to consider compromise in this area.[10]

Once again, Berkovits contended that the problem was not that of specifying how one should convert to Judaism. That was clear. Rather, the problem was one in which "the prescribed laws on conversion are in conflict with another important principle of Judaism, that of preserving the unity of Israel, the idea of *knesset yisrael*, through the obligation of *ahavat yisrael*, the love for the people Israel." This is the genuine halakhic problem: "Strict adherence to one law is in conflict with the strict adherence to another obligatory principle of Judaism."[11]

How can one decide between these two claims when the "rules" of Judaism in regard to conversion are seemingly in conflict with the overarching Jewish value of "love for the people Israel"? The authoritative basis for such a decision cannot be found in the *Shulchan Aruch* or any other book or code of Jewish law. While the Orthodox Jew has the right to grant priority to the laws of conversion over the principle of *ahavat Yisrael*, Berkovits insisted that there is an element of decision-making here that the Orthodox Jew cannot avoid—"he must make this decision by himself, in his own Jewish conscience. But how so?"[12] How can the Orthodox Jew accept the authority of Jewish law on conversion, at the same time acknowledging "the importance of the unity and love of Israel?" Is there a way beyond the inescapable subjectivity involved in resolving this conundrum?

Berkovits argued that there was. The Orthodox Jew can avoid the seemingly absolute subjectivity inherent in this dilemma through a "resolution of the conflict from within the comprehensive ethos of Judaism, from what Judaism is about in its totality, according to his understanding and commitment. Moreover, this understanding has grown into a measure of maturity as the result of the dedicated study of the classical sources of Judaism and of adherence to a way of life inseparable from it. This is not a purely subjective decision but just because of the subjective element involved in it, it will be a truly halakhic solution to a genuinely halakhic problem."[13]

In another essay, "The Role of Halakha: Authentic Judaism and Halakha," Berkowitz explicates more fully what he means in asserting that while there is a "subjective element" involved in halakhic decision-making, the decision is nevertheless not "purely subjective." He writes, "Halakha is the bridge over which Torah enters reality. . . . Halakha is the technique of Torah-application to a concrete contemporary situation. While the Torah is eternal, the concrete historic situation is ever-changing. Halakha, therefore, as the application of Torah in a given situation, will forever uncover new levels of Torah-depth and Torah-meaning."[14] Each *posek* puts forth a single application of Torah to a specific constellation of conditions. In short, the halakhic decisor applies the spirit of the rules, principles, and policies found in a Torah that is eternal and prescribes them in concrete situations in a world that is in constant flux. Clearly, personal judgment on the part of the decisor cannot be avoided. Indeed, such judgment is an unavoidable and integral part of the halakhic process. At the same time, Berkovits claims that such judgment is not "purely subjective," as it is guided by the overarching ethos of Jewish law that the student of halakha internalizes as a result of his immersion in the Jewish textual tradition.

Having placed the problem of how to approach conversion from a Jewish legal perspective in this wider context, Berkovits feels that he and his readers are now required to ask, "What is *halakha*?" Of course, he observed, it is principally the Oral Law, for the *Tora sheb'al peh* (Oral Law) determines how the *Tora shebikhtav* (Written Law) is to be understood and applied. He then describes a number of cases that display how Jewish law functions when conflicts arise among rules and principles found in the halakha.

While all the cases Berkovits cited in his article are well known to students of Jewish law, this essay will present only his discussion of the *prosbul* of Hillel. This famous case in talmudic jurisprudence and his analysis of it will illuminate the thrust of the overarching argument Berkovits put forth. He explains that according to the Bible, private debts are cancelled with the coming of the sabbatical year. The obligation dictated by the Torah was that the interests of the poor must be protected. However noble the intention of the scriptural commandment, the impact, as the sabbatical year approached, was the opposite of what was intended. The wealthy, knowing that their loans would not be repaid, refused to extend money on loan to the poor. This law created hardship for the poor. It also imposed hardship on the wealthy as the inability to provide loans caused commerce to grind to a halt. Consequently, Hillel created the legal fiction of a *prosbul* to transform private debts into public ones (Gittin 36b–37a). Rabbi Hisda comments on this innovation in the Talmud and, in the words of Berkovits, provides an "etymologically monstrous yet essentially correct interpretation [of this enactment]: *Pros buli ubuti*, an ordinance in the interests of the rich and poor." Berkovits further observes,

> Where did Hillel find the authority for his innovation? Where was it written in the Torah? It was, of course, not found in any text or code. He found it within himself. There was [here] a clash between equally valid laws, principles, and concerns of the Torah. He had to find a resolution to the conflict. There was no text to tell him which course to follow. He could find the solution to the problem within his own understanding of the comprehensive ethos of Judaism, as he was able to gather it in his own heart and in his own conscience from the totality of the teaching and way of life of Torah.[15]

Berkovits thus concludes that the written Torah, the rules of the tradition, must always be completed by an ongoing process of interpretation. He contends,

Every written law is somewhat 'inhuman.' It must express a general idea and an abstract principle of what is right. But every situation is specific, . . . unique. No written code can provide the resolution. Only the Oral Torah, alive in the conscience of the contemporary masters and teachers, can fully evaluate the significance of the confrontation between one word of God and another in a given situation and resolve the conflict with the creative boldness of application of the comprehensive ethos of the Torah to the case. Thus, the Oral Torah as halakha redeems the written Torah from the prison of its generality and 'humanizes' it. The Written Law longs for this, its redemption, by the Oral Torah.[16]

The Covenant that stands at the heart of Jewish faith, Berkovits goes on, marks a relationship of "mutuality" between God and Israel. God and the covenantal relationship that exists between the Divine and Israel demand human responsibility. The *posek* (rabbinic legal decisor) therefore cannot evade his duty to rule according to his conscience, a conscience formed by the teachings of Torah. As he writes,

Halakha is not subjective, but it has a subjectively creative element to it. The halakhist is wholly committed to the law and to the teaching of the Torah. But in the mutuality of covenant, the responsibility has fallen upon him to take upon himself the risk of determining, in light of the totality of Torah as teaching and living, the manner in which the will of the other party to the covenant (God) is to be realized in a specific situation. Ultimately, he has to do that in the independence of his conscience, which is imbued with Torah. Loyalty to the Torah, to the divine partner to the covenant, demands that we accept the responsibility, notwithstanding the risk involved in the subjective aspect of our participation. Only in this way may the generality and abstractness of the Written Torah be transformed into *torat hayim*, a Torah of life.[17]

The depiction Berkovits offers of the halakhic process regarding the obligations God and Jewish law impose upon the halakhist is surely not incontestable within the Orthodox world. After all, no less an authority than Rabbi Moshe Feinstein (1895–1986) would have disagreed with Berkovits. Indeed, it is difficult to imagine that Feinstein would have asserted that "creative boldness" marked the task of the *posek*. After all, in his *Iggerot Moshe*, Feinstein, wrote, "First, it is necessary to know that all the Torah, whether Written or Oral, was given by the Holy One Blessed be He to Moses, peace be upon him, at Mt. Sinai. It is impossible to change even a single jot or tittle, neither to be lenient nor stringent."[18]

At the same time, Berkovits is not alone among modern Orthodox authorities in describing the process of halakhic decision-making as he does. Other voices in the Orthodox world have spoken in a similar cadence. For example, Haim David Halevi (1924–98), chief Sephardic rabbi of Tel Aviv–Yaffo, in one responsum, wrote the following:

> And the strength of the early Sages of Israel was that they would innovate *halachot* in keeping with events that arose during the course of national life, and they were not content [to rely upon] well-known and famous halakhic sources. And this was not the case with the Sages of the Talmud alone, but characterized both the early medieval and later early modern rabbinic authorities, who acted thus and innovated [Jewish law] in accord with their own logic and wisdom.[19]

In a later responsum, Halevi further contended,

> Anyone who thinks that the halakha is frozen and that one cannot deviate from it either to the right or the left errs greatly. On the contrary, there is nothing as flexible as the flexibility inherent in Jewish law. For every legal decisor in Jewish history was able to rule on the same question asked at the same time to two questioners, and state to one questioner that it was *treif* while responding to the other questioner that it was kosher. . . . And it is only by the merit of the flexibility that is inherent in halakha, through the strength of the many beneficial innovations that the Sages of Israel have legislated throughout the generations, that the people Israel has been able to walk in the pathways of Torah and *mitzvot* for thousands of years. And if the Sages of our generation resolve to display similar courage through innovations constructed in accord with the *genuine* essence of Torah, in absolute faithfulness to the halakha as it has been written and transmitted, the halakha will continue to be the path of the people Israel until the end of time.[20]

Indeed, no less an American Jewish legal authority than J. David Bleich (b. 1936) of Yeshiva University, in his magisterial work *Contemporary Halakhic Problems*, takes a position akin to Berkovits and Halevi when he observes,

> Although the Torah is immutable, the Sages teach that the interpretation of its many laws and regulations is entirely within the province of the human intellect.... Definitive *psak halakha* (Jewish legal decision-making) is a matter of practical necessity, but not a reflection upon transcendental validity.[21]

Berkovits, in his essay on "Conversion and the Decline of the Oral Law," thus reveals an Orthodox attitude toward Jewish law and a discretion that Jewish law affords the *posek* that surely frames and informs the substantive position he puts forth on the issue of conversion. It is to a description of that position that this essay now turns.

Having placed the subject of conversion within a larger meta-framework, Berkovits is now prepared to analyze the issue itself. He begins his discussion on the topic with the following observation: "This is not just a matter of conversion, but, rather, the problem of how to decide in the case of a conflict between the laws of conversion and one's obligation, according to the Torah, of preserving the unity of Israel and having love for all Israel."[22] To be sure, Berkovits indicates that there is a flexibility inherent in the laws of conversion, *dinei geirut*, themselves. If a person is circumcised and immersed in a *mikvah*, even if religious responsibilities have not been explained to him or her, even if they convert *l'shem ishut* (for purposes of marriage),[23] and even if the conversion takes place in the presence of three laymen ignorant of Judaism and its laws of conversion, then *bedi'avad* (a posteriori), the conversion is still valid. While this would not be true *l'chatchilah* (a priori), there "exists a general principle of halakha that all cases of severe need or urgency (*sha'at hadehak* or *eit la'asot*) are to be treated as if they are *bedi'avad*.... Now I do not hesitate to say that the preservation of the unity of Israel and the practice of love of Israel are matters of utmost urgency. With this understanding of the problem, I might well imagine that a compromise with our non-Orthodox brethren is possible."[24]

Thus, in his typescript "A Suggested Platform of Unity on Conversion According to Halakha," Berkovits states that it is his "intention to create a platform on the basis of which rabbis of differing ideologies, notwithstanding their theological or religious differences, may be able to recognize conversions done by each of them, to consider the creation of such a platform of unity an essential demand of the hour." At all times, regardless of the demands of the hour, "it is a basic requirement of the Torah that Jews should foster *achdut yisrael* (Jewish unity) in a spirit of *ahavat yisrael* (love of the people Israel) in the interest of *klal yisrael* (the people Israel). This is incumbent on every Jew insofar as he is a Jew." The recognition "of the paramount importance of *achdut* (unity), imbued with *ahavat yisrael*, for the sake of *klal yisrael*, is the basis of the platform of unity suggested here." Indeed, Berkovits here repeats his belief that this stance is halakhically required, "especially if one bears in mind the well-established halakhic principle that *shaat hadehak* (a time of emergency) and *eit hatzorekh* (a time of need) is considered a *bediavad* situation and whatever is acceptable *bediavad* may be acted upon even initially."[25]

Conversion, he specifies, must be undertaken out of conviction, though "sincerity and conviction should not and need not be adjudged dogmatically on their actual strength at the time of conversion," but can "bear in mind the likelihood that the adherence to Judaism on the part of the would-be convert may, in the course of time, deepen and gain in commitment and dedication, or, possibly, weaken and dissolve."[26] Berkovits maintains that Jewish law is clear in granting discretion to the rabbinic court in cases of would-be proselytes. He cites two talmudic precedents in support of this position. The first involves the story of the gentile "who came to Hillel to be converted on the condition that he would be appointed a high priest" (*Shabbat* 31a) while the second concerns the "case of the woman who asked Rabbi Hiya to be converted in order to be able to marry one of his disciples" (*Menachot* 44b). As a result of these narratives, medieval rabbinic commentators on the Talmud articulated the principle "*hakol lefi rut einei habeit din*—everything depends upon the judgment of the rabbinic court" to justify rabbinic discretion in these matters.[27]

To be sure, Berkovits insists that there are several conditions that the prospective convert is required to fulfill. He states that the convert needs to be "sincere" and come "out of conviction." In addition, there has to be an acceptance of *kabbalat mitzvot*, and he defines this as meaning a rejection of previous faith and religion and the affirmation of belief in one God.

The convert also has to agree to identify completely with the people Israel and to undergo the rites of circumcision and ritual immersion.[28]

As for *hoda'at hamitzvot* (communication and delineation of the commandments that the convert is expected to observe) required as part of the conversion process, Berkovits observes, "This is an extremely vague concept." After all, the *locus classicus* for the Jewish legal stance on conversion, found in Yevamot 47a, states that the would-be proselyte is only to be taught "*miktzat mitzvot kalot v'hamurot*—some of the minor and some of the major commandments." As a result, a rabbi need only insist upon the minimum requirements stipulated above to allow a conversion. Of course, every rabbi is free to teach far beyond the minimum requirements. Furthermore, no rabbi should ever tell a convert that any *mitzvah* need not be observed. The principle taken from the story concerning Hillel in Shabbat 31a, who instructed the would-be proselyte, "The rest is commentary, *zil g'mor*, now go and study," should guide every rabbi who oversees the process of conversion.[29]

Berkovits then turns directly to the issue of whether Orthodox rabbis can allow non-Orthodox rabbis to constitute a *beit din* that the Orthodox would recognize as legitimate for purposes of conversion. Authorities such as Moshe Feinstein and J. David Bleich assert an emphatic "no" to this question. In his *Iggerot Moshe, Yoreh Deah* I:160, Feinstein states, in regard to a woman converted to Judaism by a Conservative *beit din*, "It is self-evident that the conversion performed by Conservative rabbis is meaningless." Similarly, in the *Journal of Halacha and Contemporary Society*, Bleich writes that however well meaning attempts are at establishing communal rabbinic courts that would include Conservative and Reform rabbis for purposes of conversion, it is nevertheless forbidden to do so. Reform and Conservative rabbis, by dint of their religious viewpoints, cannot possibly affirm the divinity of all the *mitzvot*, a prerequisite for sitting on a *beit din* for these purposes.[30]

In adopting this position, R. Moshe Feinstein and R. J. David Bleich were completely in accord with all their Orthodox colleagues. Berkovits's own teacher, Yechiel Yaakov Weinberg, when asked whether individuals converted to Judaism by Liberal rabbis should be permitted burial in a Jewish cemetery, ruled that such conversions were not legally viable. Therefore, he held that, if possible, the Orthodox rabbi in a given community should publicly protest the burial of such "Jews" in a Jewish communal cemetery. However, if the Orthodox rabbi, because of public pressure, could not prevent such a burial, he was not obligated to initiate a public controversy over the matter. Rather, the rabbi should simply warn the Orthodox members of the community to be buried at least "eight *amot* [cubits] from the graves of such false converts."[31]

Most significant for our purposes are Weinberg's closing comments in this responsum, in which he went beyond the specific question posed to him to a consideration of the entire issue of conversion and intermarriage. Weinberg was alarmed that so many gentiles were converting to Judaism for purposes of marriage under the auspices of non-Orthodox rabbis. Significantly, this did not lead him to urge Orthodox rabbis to perform these conversions. Instead, Weinberg stated that "in our generation, it is impossible to maintain Judaism except through war and strength of spirit. There are boundaries one cannot cross with indifference." Such conversions, performed by Liberal rabbis for the purpose of marriage, were "meaningless exercises and appear ridiculous to the best of Christians as well. A Jew who marries a convert of this type knows that he is throwing dirt in the face of his fellow creatures."[32]

In yet another responsum regarding the issue of whether it was permissible for an Orthodox *mohel* to circumcise sons of mothers who had been converted to Judaism by a Liberal rabbi, Weinberg wrote:

> If they circumcise him, people will assume that he is Jewish, and [the fact of his non-Jewishness] will be forgotten. . . . Woe to us if we allow this to happen. We should do nothing to cast in a positive light those who marry non-Jewish women. On the contrary, we must distance ourselves from them and separate ourselves from them, declaring that their sons and daughters are absolute gentiles and that it is forbidden to marry them.[33]

In light of the uniformly negative attitudes that Weinberg, Feinstein, and Bleich adopted on the question of whether a Reform or Conservative rabbi could sit on a *beit din* for purposes of conversion, the distinctiveness of Berkovits's position and his quest for transdenominational unity on this matter is both striking and remarkable. Berkovits acknowledges that this element of his proposal for the creation of communal rabbinic courts that would unite the Jewish community for purposes of conversion is surely "the most difficult" dimension of his proposed unity platform. He then observes, "It is probably here that the highest measure of holiness in the exercise of *ahavat yisrael* is demanded." Of course, every rabbi, regardless of denomination, who sits on such a rabbinic court must affirm faith in *hashem elokei yisrael*, the Lord God of Israel, believe in *Torah min hashamayim* (the heavenly origin of Torah), and accept the notion that God established a covenant between the Divine and the people Israel.[34]

Berkovits then puts forth his belief—remarkable in its singularity for an Orthodox rabbi and scholar—that Reform and Conservative colleagues could fulfill these conditions, and he maintains that they could possess sufficient *yirat shamayim* (fear of Heaven) to act as *dayanim* (judges) on rabbinic courts overseeing conversions.[35] Surely sensitive to the criticism he would receive from so many in the Orthodox world for adopting this position, Berkovits attempts to anticipate this criticism and provides an halakhic rationale for his stance by first arguing that the Orthodox rabbi who accepts a non-Orthodox colleague for these purposes does not thereby imply that he accepts the authenticity or legitimacy of the *semikhah* (rabbinical ordination) of his non-Orthodox colleague. Rather, to support his position, Berkovits cites a passage from the commentary of the *Ba'er Heitev* (Rabbi Zechariah Mendel of Belz): "However, ordination in our day is nonexistent. Rather, it is the granting of license in general, and for that function for which the person is authorized, he is authorized" (*Aval semicha shel zman hazeh eino klum, ela netilat reshut b'alma u'l'mah she'ra'ui, ra'ui* [*Shulchan Aruch, Yoreh De'ah*, 242:15]). One could therefore grant limited "authorization (*reshut*)" to a Reform or Conservative rabbi for such purposes.[36]

Having disposed of the objection to a non-Orthodox rabbi sitting on a rabbinic court with an Orthodox colleague for purposes of conversion, Berkovits then asserts explicitly that Orthodox colleagues are wrong who disqualify all Reform and Conservative rabbis from serving on a *beit din* for conversion. He states his belief in this matter boldly and forthrightly.

It is just not true that rabbis who believe in *torah min hashamayim*, as we have defined the concept, are, because of their Conservative or Reform interpretation, incapable of *yirat shamayim* (fear of heaven). To insist on that is to insist on an untruth. It represents a violation of important *mitzvot* of Torah. There are quite a few among them who are sincere *yirei shamayim* (God-fearers). . . . To become a *y'rei shamayim* (a God-fearing person) is a lifelong test and struggle for all Jews. Since they do not violate with the knowledge or the intention of violating, but, on the contrary with the conviction—however mistaken from the Orthodox point of view—of practicing a valid form of Judaism, they are not to be considered as *mumarim lehach'is* (principled rebels against the tradition), nor even as *mumarim letei'avon* (violators of the tradition on account of appetite or convenience). They are not to be identified with the category of *resha'im* (evil ones), but as *to'im* (those in error). What is the halakhic status of *to'eh* (one in error)? He is *kasher le'eidut* (fit to provide testimony). Since such a *to'eh* is *kasher le'eidut*, he may be acknowledged as a *dayan* for the purpose of conversion, for *l'mah shera'ui, ra'ui* (for that for which he is authorized, he is authorized).

On the basis of this reasoning, Berkovits maintains that a Reform or Conservative rabbi could sit as a member of a rabbinic court called to admit proselytes into the community of Israel. Or, to phrase it even more exactly, he argues that identification as a Reform or Conservative rabbi does not automatically disqualify such a rabbi from serving on such a court.[37]

In a remarkable display of sensitivity, Berkovits then goes on to consider the negative feelings that his arguments might conjure up for his non-Orthodox colleagues. He recognizes that they might judge these arguments, allowing them to be included in the *beit din* as "condescending." However, he maintains that this is not so. He states that he is doing nothing more than attempting to delineate the status of Reform and Conservative rabbis for purposes of conversion from the viewpoint of halakha. Berkovits even acknowledges that non-Orthodox rabbis might well view him as being a *to'eh*. For Berkovits, the mutual respect that sincere and principled colleagues across denominational lines owe one another demands candor and honesty. Pluralism does not entail relativism, nor does it require the surrender of one's convictions. He writes, "Ideological differences should not be watered down, but neither should they destroy the respect that we owe each other, nor should they erode our sense of responsibility to work for *shalom yisrael* (peace in the household of Israel) to the ultimate limits that our ideological position permits."[38]

Berkovits regretfully concedes that there is little likelihood that his suggestion for this platform of unity will "be acceptable. . . . to the denominations among us." However, he insists that "what I consider to be halakhically possible and necessary . . . becomes an inescapable halakhic responsibility."[39] He keenly believes that the halakhic approach to conversion he proposes and the Jewish communal unity he espouses is a demand required by God of his generation.

> Now the hour has come when the need to act for God places upon us the responsibility to free the Oral Torah from its shackles, in obedience to God's original commandment. There are risks involved in such an undertaking. Because of it we need not less but more fear of Heaven. But possibly most of all, we need more love of all Israel, to illuminate our love of Torah. And to pray to God for His guidance.[40]

With these words, *siftotav dovevot*, Berkovits's words speak from the place of his eternal rest, offering instruction and insight even today. May his much-needed judicious, learned, inclusive, and embracing spirit guide our community and our people now and for generations.

NOTES

1. Samuel Freedman, *Jew vs. Jew: The Struggle for the Soul of American Jewry* (New York: Simon and Schuster, 2000), 91–92.
2. Yehiel Yaakov Weinberg, *Seridei Eish I*, 1. There, in a highly moving account, Rabbi Weinberg describes how his student Rabbi Berkovits saved his legal writings from destruction during the Holocaust and made their publication possible.
3. Freedman, *Jew vs. Jew*, 92. See also "Rabbinical Council Institutes New Programs to Equalize All Conversions," *Intermountain Jewish News*, February 10, 1978, 10.
4. Freedman, *Jew vs. Jew*, 110.
5. Quoted in Jack Wertheimer, *A People Divided: Judaism in Contemporary America* (Waltham MA: Brandeis University Press, 1997), 173.
6. Eliezer Berkovits, "Conversion and the Decline of the Oral Law," in *Eliezer Berkovits: Essential Essays on Judaism*, ed. David Hazony (Jerusalem: Shalem Press, 2002), 89. This article originally appeared as "Conversion 'According to Halacha': What Is It?" *Judaism* 23, no. 4 (Fall 1974): 467–78.
7. Berkovits, "Conversion," 89, 90.
8 Ibid., 90–91.
9. In taking this stance, Rabbi Berkovits displays a viewpoint regarding non-Orthodox Jews that is highly unusual among Orthodox rabbis. Compare, for

example, the position adopted by Rabbi Samson Raphael Hirsch (1808–88), the architect of Modern Orthodox Judaism, who maintained that it was non-Orthodox Jews, through their failure to observe the commandments of Torah, who were guilty of "seceding" from the community of Israel. As Rabbi Hirsch wrote, "All who turn from Torah have revolted from the Jewish people, and all who return to Torah become once again a part of the body of Israel." This quotation from Rabbi Hirsch, as well as a fuller discussion of his views on non-Orthodox "secession" from the Jewish people, can be found in David Ellenson, *Rabbi Esriel Hildesheimer and the Creation of a Modern Jewish Orthodoxy* (Tuscaloosa: University of Alabama Press, 1990), 92–93.

10. Berkovits, "Conversion," 91.

11. Ibid.

12. Ibid., 92.

13. Ibid.

14. Eliezer Berkovits, "The Role of Halakha: Authentic Judaism and Halakha," *Judaism* 19, no. 1 (1970): 72.

15. Ibid., 83.

16. Ibid., 96–97.

17. Ibid., 97–98.

18. Moshe Feinstein, *Iggerot Moshe, Orah Hayim* 4:49.

19. Rabbi Hayim David Halevi, *'Aseh l'kha rav,* 7:53.

20. Ibid., 7:54.

21. J. David Bleich, *Contemporary Halakhic Problems* (New York: Ktav Publishing House, Yeshiva University Press, 1977), xiv–xv.

22. "Conversion and the Decline of the Oral Law," 98.

23. The *Shulchan Aruch, Yoreh Deah* 268:12, forbids conversion for purposes of marriage.

24. The stance of Rabbi Berkovits on the possibility of compromise with the non-Orthodox on the issue of conversion is found in "Conversion and the Decline of the Oral Law," 98. For a full exposition of all the halakhic points cited in this paragraph that Rabbi Berkovits advanced, see his Hebrew article *"Beirurim b'dinei geirut—On the Laws of Conversion,"* *Sinai* 77, nos. 1–2 (1975): 28–36.

25. Eliezer Berkovits, "A Suggested Platform of Unity on Conversion According to Halakha" (typescript), 9–10. I am grateful to Professor Josef Stern for providing me with this text, which clearly served as the basis for the Denver *beit din* program. A later version of this paper, quite close to the original, appeared in Eliezer Berkovits, *Not in Heaven: The Nature and Function of Halakha* (New York: Ktav, 1983), 106-12. I will cite from each of these versions in this article, as together they provide a complete sense of the evolution and substance of the thought of Rabbi Berkovits on the topic of conversion.

26. Berkovits, "A Suggested Platform," 10.

27. Berkovits, *Not In Heaven,* 109.

28. Berkovits, "A Suggested Platform," 10.

29. Ibid., 11.

30. J. David Bleich, "Parameters and Limits of Communal Unity from the Perspectives of Jewish Law," *Journal of Halakha and Contemporary Society* 6 (Fall 1983): 13–14.

31. Yehiel Yaakov Weinberg, *Seridei Eish* 3:100.

32. Ibid.

33. Ibid., 2:96.

34. Berkovits, "A Suggested Platform," 11–12.

35. Again I would emphasize the extraordinary nature of the position Rabbi Berkovits took on this matter by contrasting his willingness to view Reform and Conservative rabbis in this way in complete opposition to the stance adopted by contemporary Orthodox teachers and colleagues like Rabbis Weinberg, Feinstein, and Bleich. His opinion stands out even more when one considers that nineteenth-century Orthodox stalwarts and luminaries such as Rabbi S. R. Hirsch and Esriel Hildesheimer said that Orthodox Jews should secede from a community rather than tolerate the appointment of a rabbi who was a graduate of the Positive-Historical Jewish Theological Seminary in Breslau. On this episode in modern Jewish history, see Ellenson, *Rabbi Esriel Hildesheimer*, 81ff.

36. Berkovits knew that Jewish law does not require ordained rabbis to form a *beit din* for this purpose. This is based on Maimonides, *Mishneh Torah, Hilchot Issurei Bi'ah* 13:17, who states that "*Shalosh hedyotot* (three non-ordained persons)" can sit on a rabbinic court that oversees a conversion, Consequently, the question of whether Reform or Conservative rabbis possess an authentic or authoritative *semikhah* could be avoided altogether.

37. Berkovits, "A Suggested Platform," 12–14.

38. Ibid., 14.

39. Ibid., 16.

40. Berkovits, *Not in Heaven*, 112.

23

Transformation of the Rabbinate

Future Directions and Prospects

Jewish tradition is replete with legends and tales. Each generation receives, creates, and transmits still more stories and, in providing such narratives, helps to forge meaning, identity, and linkages for generations past, present, and future. Community emerges out of stories, as do moral and religious visions. We now celebrate a new chapter in the ongoing history of Judaism—twenty years of women being ordained as rabbis among and for the people Israel. It is appropriate, as we ponder the meaning and significance of this novel development in our people's history, and as we reflect upon what the meaning of this story will be for a future generation, to return to an ancient and puzzling legend of our people, one that I believe can instruct us in our deliberations today.

"*Tanu rabbanan*—our rabbis taught" are the familiar words with which this talmudic tale from Shabbat 53b begins. The story continues: "It once happened that a man's wife died and left a child to be suckled, and he could not afford to pay a wet nurse, whereupon a miracle was performed for him and his nipples opened like the two nipples of a woman and he suckled his son. Rabbi Joseph observed, 'Come and see how great this man was that a miracle was performed on his account.' Said Abaye to him, 'How despicable [*garu-a*] this man was that the order of creation was changed on his account.'" Rashi, the exegete par excellence of the Jewish tradition, in commenting upon this passage, observes that *garu-a*, as employed by Abaye in his description of the miracle wrought for this man and his son, should be translated as "lowly," for the man's impoverished state prevented him from hiring a wet nurse to suckle his motherless child. However, as with all stories and legends, other interpretations are surely plausible and, as my own translation indicates, perhaps more appropriate for deriving meaning from the text that is relevant to our purposes.

Unlike Rashi, I would suggest that Abaye's perspective on this father and the miracle performed on his behalf must be viewed as more than a simple commentary on the man's financial state. After all, as Rashi himself observes, elsewhere in the Talmud Abaye looks upon the performance of a miracle on an individual's behalf as a sign of divine grace. Why, we may ask, does this act in our story not adduce similar approbation on Abaye's part? The answer, it seems to me, lies in rabbinic tradition's strict definitions of gender roles. Abaye, in labeling this man *garu-a*, is driven to such anger because the strict sense of order and the boundaries that mark his world are dependent upon the routinization of sex functions and gender roles. The comprehensibility and predictability of the social order have been violated through this act of grace bestowed upon the father. The father's being miraculously blessed and empowered with the ability to sustain and nurture his son in this way has violated sexual demarcations that Abaye regards as essential for the world to be intelligible. Abaye has internalized these demarcations as not just appropriate but inviolate in defining the universe. This particular alteration in the natural order of sexual function, unlike other miracles, appears to enrage him precisely because it threatens to plunge the world of daily living, everyday life, into chaos. As such, it must be deplored.

Echoes of this attitude about sexual roles abound in the writings of rabbinic tradition. A modern example can be found in a responsum of the late Rabbi Moshe Feinstein. Rabbi Feinstein, when queried in 1976 about the inroads feminism was making in the Orthodox community, noted that some groups of Orthodox women (*shomrot torah*) desired to carry into the realm of Jewish law the "war" that feminists in the outside world were waging against traditionally assigned gender roles. Such intrusions and attempts at transformation and change, Rabbi Feinstein felt, were totally inappropriate and illegitimate. Judaism, he wrote, was based upon the principle that all of the Torah, both written and oral, was given by God to Moses at Sinai. Later generations of Jews therefore possessed no right to change even a single element in God's eternal and revealed law. While the rationale for some precepts of Torah are unknown, the reasons for the domestic role assigned by Jewish tradition to women are "clear to everyone—*g'iluyim lakol*." It is obvious, according to Rabbi Feinstein, that in the very act of creating the world, God assigned specific roles to each sex in the animal kingdom. The task God designated for the female sex was that of raising children, and humankind is no exception to this law of nature. Women are more suited than men for the performance of this domestic task.

The rabbis, aware of this truth, legislated a domestic role for women. Social conventions and domestic arrangements may be transformed in the larger world. Men may desire domestic roles and women public ones. Nevertheless, the Torah of God is eternal (*nitzhit*), and one who would transform gender roles is engaged in a struggle against God and the order of nature as God ordained it. From Abaye through Rabbi Feinstein, one Jewish attitude toward the role women properly ought to render in society is maintained.[1] For women to suggest or engage in a role that questions traditional boundaries placed around the sacred is to challenge more than the social construction of gender. It is, as Abaye put it, to alter the "order of creation."

Furthermore, we would be naive and mistaken to assume that it has been only the world of traditional rabbinic Judaism that has insisted upon the maintenance of these gender roles and boundaries. Traditional Judaism has not been alone in defending the public prerogative of the male sex. Every patriarchal society and institution has socialized its members into accepting this sexual division of labor as correct and proper. As Riv-Ellen Prell has demonstrated, the Reform movement, despite its proclamation of the religious equality of men and women as early as the 1840s, rendered women "invisible in the public realm" and over 125 years lapsed between the declaration of the religious equality of men and women and the ordination of Sally Priesand in 1972.[2]

The decision to ordain women as rabbis, to have them engage in public roles of religious leadership within the Jewish community, must thus be considered revolutionary. The ordination of women as rabbis has brought into focus the dynamics of a gendered religious life that has both silenced women's voices and muted feminist values of cooperation, mutuality, and equality. It has spoken directly to the reality of how power is gendered as well as conceptualized within our community and its traditions. As Paula Hyman has observed: "Gender is not merely about social and culturally defined differences between the sexes. It is also a primary way of signifying relationships of power."[3] In electing to ordain Sally Priesand as rabbi, the Reform movement broke with the past. The significance of this act should not be underestimated, and the novel presence of women in the rabbinate, like other transformative moments in the history of Judaism, grants us ample reason to celebrate today. The reasons for celebration are many.

Causes for Celebration

"*Dibrah Torah kilshon b'nei adam.* The Torah," our tradition asserts, "speaks in human language." The variegated languages employed to express the truths of Torah, as well as the institutional patterns that are established to express those truths, are internalized in the minds and hearts of Jews in every generation who adhere to and identify with tradition. These religious truths, superimposed as they are on life, shape the deepest ways we envision and experience the reality of the world. The ordination of women as rabbis is potentially so transformative precisely because it breaks the gendered patterns of image, power, and role bequeathed from the past. The emergence of women in the rabbinate has provided and continues to provide new paradigms for how the present and future may be experienced and understood by Jews. By establishing an ideal of gender equality in the public roles and private lives of Jews, this decision has altered the character of our community in ways that would have been unthinkable twenty years ago.

An anecdote illustrating the nature of this change concerns an incident involving my wife, Jackie, nearly a decade ago, when she served as a rabbi in a suburban Los Angeles congregation. One day a mother of one of the kindergarten children showed Jackie a picture that her daughter had drawn in school. It was a drawing, the little girl had told the mother, of God. What made such a pictorial representation of the deity unusual was that, in this instance, God was not depicted as an elderly gentleman with a beard. Instead, God was wearing a skirt. When the mother asked her child why she envisaged God in this manner, the little girl replied, "This is how the rabbi looks."

Such a story is significant precisely because it is not unique to my wife. Other women rabbis relate similar, if not identical, incidents. The childhood images children in such stories possess of God as female undoubtedly open up the possibility that in their adult years many Jews will envision the divine, to use Judith Plaskow's felicitous phrase, as something besides "Dominating Other." The very theological foundation of God's maleness upon which so much of Judaism is established is challenged by the appearance of women in the pulpit. The story testifies to the ineffability of God and the mystery and infinity of all religious symbols and how penultimate they are in their plausibility. Most important, the presence of women in the pulpit instructs all Jews that God is beyond all words and cannot be contained by insisting upon the masculinity of the divine.

Furthermore, the ordination of women as rabbis has granted some women access to other positions of religious authority in the community that had been denied them in the past. Dr. Deborah Cohen, a physician in Los Angeles, reports that despite her upbringing as a Reform Jew in Long Island in the 1960s, it never occurred to her that women could serve as religious functionaries. However, after listening to a speech delivered by Rabbi Laura Geller, she recognized that it was possible for women to serve in such a capacity. As a result, she approached the Reform movement to initiate a program that would train both female and male physicians as *mohalim* and *mohalot*. Due to her persistence—and the scholarly and organizational leadership provided by Rabbi Lewis Barth—there are now dozens of Reform women and men throughout the United States who have been educated and certified by the Reform movement as *mohalim* and *mohalot*. The decision to ordain women as rabbis, and the appearance of women in other roles of religious leadership as a result of this decision, have contributed directly to a more inclusionary style of leadership in Jewish life for both men and women than would have been possible had women not been ordained as rabbis.

Moreover, the decision to ordain women as rabbis has meant that the ritual and liturgical life of the Jewish community has been opened to the possibilities of change unprecedented in the contemporary era. The authorship of gender-inclusive prayer books informed by the tenets of feminist Judaism is a challenge large sectors of the non-Orthodox community now uncontestably regard as a legitimate enterprise. Surely the next twenty years will see many more efforts in this direction. The bat mitzvah ceremony is universally observed now in liberal Jewish congregations, and the simhat bat ceremony is well on its way to similar inclusion. Rituals marking moments in the life cycle that were formerly ignored—from miscarriage through birth, from weaning to the onset of menstruation and menopause—are now in the process of creation.[4] Other changes of this type that affect the lives of both Jewish men and Jewish women could readily be cited. Furthermore, these changes are witnessed both in noninstitutionalized and traditional denominational settings. The appearance of women in the pulpit has surely promoted, and will certainly continue to stimulate, these innovations.

All the achievements enumerated thus far are real. They bespeak the impact of women's entry into the rabbinate and are indicative of a direction the community is more and more likely to take as children mature who have been reared on the ideal of gender equality and provided with the example of strong women in public roles. In this sense, there is no question that the appearance of women in the rabbinate is revolutionary and subversive of traditional Judaism. It constitutes, as have other innovative moments in the Jewish past, an act, in Gershon Shaked's words, of "creative betrayal," a moment when ideals and cultural forms present within the larger host culture are incorporated into the religious and national life of the Jewish people.

The changes I have described and celebrated up to this point were and are based upon a liberal ideal that affirms that women and men share a common human nature that endows both sexes with identical social and natural rights. From such premises the conclusion follows that equal rights and opportunities ought to be granted to all members of society. Simple justice demands that equal opportunity be extended to all members of society regardless of gender. These liberal assumptions have unquestionably succeeded in opening up the rabbinate to women and in raising the realities and possibilities for transformation enumerated above. In short, this liberal ideal and model has secured for women the right to ordination. It has simultaneously made us aware of the "glass ceiling" that marks virtually every area of our institutional lives. Much remains to be done. While recent years have seen the addition of women to the faculty of Hebrew Union College–Jewish Institute of Religion, more women—particularly ordained women—need to be hired. The curriculum should be formally expanded to include women's studies or feminist concerns. Issues such as sexual harassment or female rabbinic placement should be more sufficiently addressed. Lack of salary parity for women who perform the same tasks as their male counterparts in the congregational rabbinate is an egregious wrong that cries out for remedy. Our affirmation of the truth of the liberal ideals enumerated above and our belief that these ideals are at the heart of and are accommodated within the best of Jewish religious tradition demand that we examine and act upon all these matters as we confront the next twenty years.

These commitments and affirmations also compel us to face other questions that transcend the liberal commitments that have brought us to this moment. They force us to ask how the presence of women in the rabbinate will transform, as other comparably novel moments have, the nature of the rabbinate, the synagogue, and Judaism itself. Will the appearance of women in the rabbinate simply indicate that traditional Judaism has extended itself so as to provide "equal access" to women in the variegated arenas of Jewish life? If the latter alone is true, and if, in view of the tasks I have enumerated above, this dream of equal access can be realized, it is surely no mean feat, and we, schooled in the canons of Western liberalism, should applaud these accomplishments. However, in considering the future impact of women in the rabbinate, the prospects of what more this decision might mean should also be considered.

Revolutionary Prospects

Rabbi Tracy Guren Klirs, in speaking of the ritual transformations that have marked contemporary Jewish life as a result of the appearance of women's voices and concerns in the public life of Judaism, has written:

> Steps [such as the ones I have described] are merely ameliorative. They do not begin to affect what many see as the fundamentally patriarchal nature of the classic rabbinic tradition, of Jewish theology, of Torah itself. Women did not have a hand in forming these traditions, and so women's experiences have been left out of them. For women to be fully included in normative Jewish liturgy and practice and to be truly valued by the entire Jewish community, it will be necessary for them to create new traditions which reflect their experiences and include their unique spiritual insights.[5]

Rabbi Klirs reminds us that the religious and cultural forms, the patriarchal assumptions that have supported and defined traditional Judaism, including the rabbinate, are to be questioned, amended, supplemented, and possibly redefined in light of feminist concerns and consciousness. This is the issue that most seriously and radically confronts us as we deal with the question of how the presence of women rabbis will challenge and possibly change the future of the rabbinate, congregational life, and the Jewish community itself twenty years from now. It is an issue that few male leaders foresaw when the decision was made to grant women equal access to the rabbinate two decades ago.

Prophecy, as the Talmud informs us, is no longer a Jewish gift. The enterprise of offering predictions is clearly a hazardous one. The directions the Jewish story will take as a result of women in the rabbinate cannot yet be fully appreciated or defined, precisely because we have not yet seen what the parameters and contours of this new chapter will be. It is impossible to give a definitive answer to the questions and musings in this essay. Thus I offer some final thoughts as prescriptions, hopes that reflect the directions in which I believe the Jewish community and the Reform movement ought to move as a result of women in the rabbinate. In order to offer such prescriptions, we must ask what a feminist orientation in the world might be. Such an orientation will help us envision how a Judaism, a synagogue, and a community informed by these principles might appear. In so doing, we must also ponder how, in light of the feminist principles of transformation, the integrity of the Jewish story might be maintained.

The myth of Persephone is well known to all of us. Persephone, the beautiful daughter of Demeter, the goddess of agriculture and fertility, was kidnapped by Hades, god of the underworld, who desired Persephone on account of her beauty. Demeter was heartbroken by this loss, and she wandered the earth looking for her daughter. When Demeter discovered the fate that had befallen Persephone, she was furious and demanded that Zeus retrieve her daughter from the clutches of Hades. Persephone, heartsick at her absence from her mother, was anxious to return. Tragically, she had eaten six seeds from a pomegranate while living in the underworld and was thus, according to the tale, unable to return permanently to her mother Demeter. Zeus arranged a compromise. For six months each year, Persephone would depart the underworld and dwell with her mother; the remaining months of the year would be spent in the underworld with Hades. During the period that Persephone dwelt with Demeter, Demeter was overjoyed and warmth and fertility marked the earth. However, when Persephone returned to Hades, Demeter was beside herself with grief and winter ensued, the earth becoming cold and barren.

This tale, commonly cited as an explanation for the changes in season, is much more than that. It is, as many have pointed out, the archetypical feminist myth. Primacy is accorded in this story to the relationship that exists between Demeter and her daughter Persephone. It is a myth that sees the worth of the individual as expressed most fully only in response to another. The notion of the autonomous individual as the highest expression of the moral self—an ideal that has long dominated both classical and modern trends in Western philosophy—is here dislodged in favor of a moral vision that sees reciprocity and responsiveness in relationships as the most appropriate and ethically compelling vision of what it means to be human. Attachment is preferred to detachment, connection to separation. Mutual dependence is seen as possessing a greater moral valence than an atomizing individuality. The myth of Persephone provides an alternative moral vision, an ethical corrective, to the excessive individualism that has heretofore so dominated our Western vision of a mature and appropriate morality.

The vision of Persephone promotes an image of self in relationship that views community, the self standing in relationship to and engaged in dialogue with others, as the central fact of moral life. The self comes to be defined in interactions with others and, in so doing, is open to the possibility of transformation that responsiveness in human engagement offers. The individual stands in a state of mutual interdependence with others, and relationships are sustained and nurtured through attention and response. As one person, commenting upon such a vision, has observed, moral responsibility does not signify a Kantian notion of "an internalized conscience enacted by will and guided by duty or obligation." Instead, it means being "aware of others and . . . of their feelings. . . . Responsibility is taking charge of yourself by looking at others around you and seeing what they need and what you need . . . and taking the initiative." The traditional concept of autonomy, as Carol Gilligan has pointed out, is not wholly abandoned in such a vision. It is, however, unmistakably altered. The individual is not separate, nor are relationships essentially either hierarchical or contractual. The self stands in connection with others and is "defined by gaining voice and perspective known in the experience of engagement with others." Being dependent in such a vision "no longer means being helpless, powerless, and without control; it signifies a conviction that one is able to have an effect on others, as well as the recognition that the interdependence of attachment empowers both the self and the other, not one person at the other's expense."[6]

Dialogue and response replace reflection and abstract commitment to principle. Such a potentially communitarian ethic is a compelling one at a time when tribalization, conflict, and isolation have so dominated and diminished national, religious, and ethnic life in the world and the nation as well as among our own people. A consciousness of that ethic is among the great gifts that feminism and feminist theory have bestowed upon us. The ordination of women as rabbis has helped grant this vision an audience among contemporary Jews that will ultimately enrich the entire community and allow us self-consciously to direct our energies into the creation of a Jewish community that is marked as much by care and compassion as it is by an abstract and impersonal commitment to duties and rules. Such an orientation is, in a very real sense, critical of certain aspects of traditional Judaism. It indicates that those elements within the tradition that have been employed to subordinate others—particularly women—in the name of abstract and putatively divine laws must be attacked as inauthentic and oppressive. Few liberal Jews would, I presume, dissent from this stance. After all, much of Reform Judaism can be construed as offering a comparable critique of elements of rabbinic tradition.

The crucial issue is whether a call for a feminist approach to Judaism that emphasizes the relational dimensions of the tradition in a nonhierarchical way is one that can be harmonized with the past. Or, to use the language employed earlier in this presentation, can the integrity of the Jewish story be maintained if personal elements of the tradition are assigned a weight and authority they seemingly did not possess in earlier times? These questions, from my own perspective, are largely rhetorical, for the feminist ethic I have described is one that is thoroughly consistent with the primary thrust of biblical and rabbinic tradition. The book of Ruth provides a classical warrant for this type of thought within biblical Judaism and assures us that an affirmation of a relational model of ethics is at the core of Jewish tradition.

As my friend Rabbi Patricia Karlin-Neumann pointed out to me in a recent conversation, the first chapter of Ruth is a story of relationship. Viewed from a feminist perspective, one sees that Naomi, after the death of her husband and her sons, feels bereft and isolated, alone in the world. It is the devotion and care shown to her by Ruth, Ruth's insistence on the bond of relationship that links Naomi to her, that brings Naomi from the realm of solitude and mourning back into life. When Ruth, despite the insistent pleadings of her mother-in-law that she return to Moab, asserts, "Entreat me not to leave you, or to return from following after you, for where you go, I will go; and where you lodge, I will lodge, your people shall be my people, and your God my God. Where you die, I will die, and there I will be buried," she displays a feminist sensibility that acknowledges that attachments are irreplaceable. Ruth's attachment to her husband and her love for Naomi cannot be forgotten, and they find expression in the present affirmations she offers her mother-in-law.

Furthermore, the obligations that Ruth then takes upon herself are not abstract constructs imposed upon her in a vacuum. They are duties that emerge out of the transformative capacities of human relationship. If one looks to the Bible and the writings of the rabbis as "historical prototypes" that provide us "with a sense of [our] ongoing history as well as [our] theological identity,"[7] this interpretation of Ruth indicates that the feminist ethic of which we have spoken is embedded in the historical narratives of our people. It reminds us that all the abstract duties imposed upon us by our tradition are ultimately embedded in a story that speaks of our people's relationship with the divine, and it reminds us that the rules imposed by that tradition are ultimately expressions of and thus subservient to a broader ideal of covenantal partnership that bestows ultimate meaning upon our actions and upon our attempts to forge community. The feminist ethos I have described, far from being a break with the tradition, ultimately embodies the tradition's most noble sentiments—albeit with some different emphases. In this sense, the feminist ethos described in these closing remarks is akin to the sentiments expressed about Jewish religiosity in our century by Martin Buber, the great philosopher of dialogue whose influence upon contemporary liberal Judaism has been immense.

The challenge that remains is whether this ethic of compassion, care, and relationship will ultimately find the expression it deserves in our institutions. Much needs to be done to see that the agenda of egalitarianism is fully realized and achieved over the next twenty years. Even more challenging, however, is the degree to which we will be able to forge community in our institutions and congregations and transform these entities as well as ourselves and our families into caring persons, places, and units that provide the support and nurturance heralded by a feminist and Jewish ethos.

This transformation can only be done if we have the courage to go beyond the rhetoric of this ethos and implant it in the lives of rabbis, the rabbinate, and the institutions we serve. The lifestyle of the rabbinate and the work ethic that has traditionally accompanied it must be transformed. How can we, who are supposed to provide care and nurturance for others and model compassion for our communities, do so if the professional demands of a seemingly endless work week preclude us from spending time with our families? How can we provide the responsiveness our vocation legitimately requires if we are too exhausted by the demands of work? How can we speak of the integrity, beauty, and warmth of the Jewish home and family, the importance of community that the synagogue and the Jewish federations provide, if we do not understand that the personal dimension of our lives is foremost and must be the anchor from which we draw our strength and the integrity of our institutional direction? The "personal is political" is by now a time-worn slogan of the feminist movement. Yet it remains vital. It reminds us that these two realms of life are not separate from one another but are distinct parts of an overarching whole.

The feminization of the rabbinate introduced by the Hebrew Union College–Jewish Institute of Religion twenty years ago when Rabbi Alfred Gottschalk ordained Sally Priesand a rabbi among the people Israel means more than the appearance of women in the pulpit, alterations in the liturgy, creations of new rituals, and the discovery and expression of women's voices in both the history and the ongoing public life of our people. Of course, it means all those things. However, it points to much more. It asks us to create the wholeness promised by the ethic of relationship in both our personal and our communal lives. It points to the possibility that rabbinical positions in the Jewish community will be shared so that rabbis can practice the family and communal ethos about which they so eloquently preach. It points to the possibility that a laity will be educated to understand and appreciate that their rabbis are not their servants who are at their beck and call at every moment for any reason nor are their rabbis their superiors who dictate the essence and practice of Judaism to and for them. Instead, the feminization of the rabbinate points to rabbis who are their partners, persons knowledgeable of and trained in the Jewish tradition who are prepared and delighted to grant their congregants access to the wisdom, insights, ethics, rituals, and spirituality inherent in Judaism. This transformation does not mean the demise of large congregations. Nor does it signal the necessity of small ones. Instead, it calls for the restructuring of our institutions so that intimacy and support can be provided through a myriad of programs and by a variety of persons for the care and nurturance of our beleaguered and tired, yet ever hopeful and optimistic, people. This is the revolutionary potential that the ordination of the women has released.

In the beginning of this essay, I cited the famous passage from Shabbat 53b and Abaye's outrage at the miracle that allowed the anonymous man to nurse his motherless child. I also recognize that many women, commenting upon this passage, have viewed it as just one more instance in which the male authors of the text claim for men biological functions of which they are normally deprived and, in so doing, rob women of their uniqueness. Undoubtedly there is more than a modicum of fairness in this critique. However, in light of the analysis I have presented, I would like to offer yet one more commentary—this one focusing upon the remarks of Rabbi Joseph and the contrast they present to the words of Abaye.

When Rabbi Joseph asserts, "How great is this man," I like to think he is proclaiming that divinity is ultimately found in the ability to nurture and sustain, in the loving bonds that result from the intimacy of relationship and compassion that is literally embodied in the act of nursing. Abaye's outrage about this miracle stemmed, in part, from the fear he felt because of the unknown meaning and outcome of this act. Today, too, others are outraged, and perhaps fearful, of the portraits of transformation and potential for change outlined at this conference that celebrates twenty years of women as rabbis. Yet Rabbi Joseph, unlike Abaye, understood and had the courage to affirm the ultimate truth—the Jewish truth—this story expresses. The future, of course, is unknown, and many Jews, like Abaye, are afraid of what it holds. That fear may well prevent the promises I have discussed here from becoming reality.

As we look forward to the next two decades, may we have the courage to dissent from Abaye and affirm the wisdom of Rabbi Joseph. May the presence of women in the rabbinate mean that all Jews—men as well as women—strive to create intimate moments and settings within both our private lives and our institutions where an ethic of care within a framework of relationships will find increasing expression. This would represent the promise of transformation already heralded by the appearance of women in the rabbinate. It would mean the increasing fulfillment of the messianic promise that lies at the heart of our religion.

1. *Iggerot Moshe, Orah Hayyim* 4:49.
2. Riv-Ellen Prell, "The Dilemma of Women's Equality in Reform Judaism," *Judaism 30* (Fall 1981): 418–26.
3. Paula Hyman, "Gender and Identity in Modern Jewish History," *Masoret 2, no. 1* (Fall 1992): 9. (*Masoret* is a publication of the Jewish Theological Seminary.)
4. Elana Zaiman, then a fifth-year rabbinical student at the Jewish Theological Seminary of America, and now a rabbi at Park Avenue Synagogue in New York, has testified to this development in her article, "Grappling with 'Tradition and Change,'" in *Masoret 2, no. 1* (Fall 1992): 8.
5. Tracy Guren Klirs, *The Merit of Our Mothers* (Cincinnati: Hebrew Union College Press, 1992), 10.
6. Carol Gilligan, "Remapping the Moral Domain: New Images of Self in Relationship," in *Mapping the Moral Domain*, ed. Carol Gilligan, Janie Victoria Ward, and Jill McLean Taylor, with Betty Bardige (Cambridge: Harvard University Press, 1988), 3–19; quotes from 6, 7, 17, 16.
7. The language here is taken from Elizabeth Shussler-Fiorenza, *In Memory of Her* (New York: Crossroad, 1984), 33–34.

Source Acknowledgments

I am grateful to these publishers for granting permission to reprint the following articles, which originally appeared in their publications.

1. "A Response by Modern Orthodoxy to Jewish Religious Pluralism: The Case of Esriel Hildesheimer." Originally published in *Tradition* 17, no. 4 (Spring 1979).
2. "German Orthodox Rabbinical Writings on the Jewish Textual Education of Women: The Views of Rabbi Samson Raphael Hirsch and Rabbi Esriel Hildesheimer." Originally published in *Gender and Jewish History*, ed. Marion A. Kaplan and Deborah Dash Moore (Bloomington: Indiana University Press, 2011).
3. "Rabbi Samson Raphael Hirsch to Liepman Phillip Prins of Amsterdam: An 1873 Responsum on Education." Originally published in the *Edah Journal* 3, no. 2 (2003).
4. "An Ideology for the Liberal Jewish Day School: A Philosophical-Sociological Investigation." Originally published in *Journal of Jewish Education* 74, no. 3 (2008). Reprinted by permission of Taylor & Francis (www.tandfonline.com).
5. "Denominationalism: History and Hopes." Originally published in *Jewish Megatrends: Charting the Course of the American Jewish Future*, ed. Sidney Schwarz (Woodstock VT: Jewish Lights, 2013).
6. "The Integrity of Reform within *Kelal Yisra-el.*" Originally published in *Yearbook of the Central Conference of American Rabbis* © 1986 by the Central Conference of American Rabbis. Reprinted with permission of the CCAR; all rights reserved.
7. "A Theology of Fear: The Search for a Liberal Jewish Paradigm." Originally published in *Confronting Omnicide: Jewish Reflections on Weapons of Mass Destruction*, ed. Daniel Landes (Northvale NJ: Jason Aronson, 1991).
8. "Eugene B. Borowitz: A Tribute on the Occasion of His 70th Birthday." Originally published in *Jewish Book Annual* 51 (1994): 125–36.
9. "Laws and Judgments as a 'Bridge to a Better World': *Parashat Mishpatim.*" Originally published in *Torah Queeries: Weekly Commentaries on the Hebrew Bible*, ed. Gregg Drinkwater, David Shneer, and Joshua Lesser (New York: New York University Press, 2009).
10. "Heschel and the Roots of *Kavanah.*" Originally published in *New Essays in American Jewish History Commemorating the Sixtieth Anniversary of the Found-*

ing of the American Jewish Archives, ed. Pamela S. Nadell, Jonathan D. Sarna, and Lance J. Sussman (Cincinnati: American Jewish Archives of Hebrew Union College–Jewish Institute of Religion, 2010). Co-authored with Michael Marmur.

11. "Rabbi Hayim David Halevi on Christians and Christianity: An Analysis of Selected Legal Writings of an Israeli Authority." Originally published in *Transforming Relations: Essays on Jews and Christians throughout History in Honor of Michael A. Signer,* ed. Franklin Harkins (Notre Dame IN: University of Notre Dame Press, 2010).

12. "Interreligious Learning and the Formation of Jewish Religious Identity." Originally published in *Religious Education* 91, no. 4 (Fall 1996). Reprinted by permission of Taylor & Francis (http://www.tandfonline.com).

13. "A Zionist Reading of Abraham Geiger and His Biblical Scholarship." Originally published in *Making a Difference: Essays on the Bible and Judaism in Honor of Tamara Cohn Eskenazi,* ed. David J. A. Clines, Kent Harold Richards, and Jacob L. Wright (Sheffield: Sheffield Phoenix Press, 2012).

14. "National Sovereignty, Jewish Identity, and the 'Sake of Heaven': The Impact of Residence in Israel on Halakhic Rulings on Conversion." Originally published in *Zionist Halacha,* ed.Yair Sheleg and Yedidya Stern (Israel Democracy Institute, 2014). Co-authored with Daniel Gordis.

15. "The Talmudic Principle, 'If One Comes Forth to Slay You, Forestall by Slaying Him,' in Israeli Public Policy: A Responsum by Rabbi Hayyim David Halevi." Originally published in *Studies in Mediaeval Halakhah in Honor of Stephen M. Passamaneck,* ed. Alyssa Gray and Bernard Jackson, vol. 17 of the *Jewish Law Association Studies* (2007).

16. "The Rock from Which They Were Cleft: A Review-Essay of Haim Amsalem's *Zera Yisrael* and *Mekor Yisrael.*" Originally published in *Jewish Review of Books* 8 (Winter 2012).

17. "Moshe Zemer's *Halakhah Shefuyah*: An Israeli Vision of Reform and Halakhah." Originally published in CCAR *Journal: The Reform Jewish Quarterly* 43, no. 2 (Spring/Summer 1996) © 1996 by the Central Conference of American Rabbis. Reprinted with permission of the CCAR; all rights reserved. Co-authored with Michael White.

18. "Reform Zionism Today: A Consideration of First Principles." Originally published in the *Rabbi Stanley M. Davids Journal of Reform Zionism* 2 (March 1995), ed. Naomi Steinlight Patz. A publication of ARZA: the Association of Reform Zionists of America.

19. "Wissenschaft des Judentums, Historical Consciousness, and Jewish Faith: The Diverse Paths of Frankel, Auerbach, and Halevy." *Leo Baeck Memorial Lecture* 48 (2004).

20. "'Creative Misreadings' in Representative Post-Emancipation Halakhic Writings on Conversion and Intermarriage." Originally published in *Napoleon's Influence on Jewish Law: The Sanhedrin of 1807 and Its Modern Consequences,* ed. Walter

Jacob and Moshe Zemer (Pittsburgh: Solomon B. Freehof Institute of Progressive Halakha, 2007).

21. "A Portrait of the *Poseq* as Modern Religious Leader: An Analysis of Selected Writings of Rabbi Hayyim David Halevi." Originally published in *Jewish Religious Leadership: Image and Reality*, vol. 2, ed. Jack Wertheimer (New York: Jewish Theological Seminary, 2004).

22. "Rabbi Eliezer Berkovits on Conversion: An Inclusive Orthodox Approach." Originally published in *Shofar: An Interdisciplinary Journal of Jewish Studies* 31, no. 4 (Summer 2013).

23. "Transformation of the Rabbinate: Future Directions and Prospects." Originally published in *Women Rabbis: Exploration & Celebration Papers Delivered at an Academic Conference Honoring Twenty Years of Women in the Rabbinate, 1972–1992*, ed. Gary Zola (Cincinnati: HUC-JIR Rabbinic Alumni Association Press, 1996).

Bibliography of the Published Writings of David Ellenson

"Ellis Rivkin and the Problems of Pharisaic History." *Journal of the American Academy of Religion* 43, no. 4 (December 1975): 787–802.

"Emil Fackenheim and the Revealed Morality of Judaism." *Judaism* 25, no. 4 (Fall 1976): 402–13.

"Modern Orthodoxy and the Problem of Religious Pluralism: The Case of Rabbi Esriel Hildesheimer." *Tradition* 17, no. 4 (Spring 1979): 74–89.

"The New Ethnicity, Religious Survival, and Jewish Identity: The 'Judaisms' of Our Newest Members." *Journal of Reform Judaism* 26, no. 2 (Spring 1979): 47–60.

"A Jewish Legal Decision by Rabbi Bernard Illowy of New Orleans and Its Discussion in Nineteenth-Century Europe." *American Jewish History* 69, no. 2 (December 1979): 174–95.

"Rabbi Zvi Hirsch Kalischer and a Halachic Approach to Conversion." *Journal of Reform Judaism* 28, no. 3 (Summer 1981): 50–57. Co-authored with Robert Levine.

"Accommodation, Resistance, and the Halakhic Process: A Study of Two Responsa by Rabbi Marcus Horovitz of Frankfurt." In *Jewish Civilization: Essays and Studies Honoring the One Hundredth Birthday of Rabbi Mordecai Kaplan*, edited by Ronald Brauner, 83–100. Wyncote PA: Reconstructionist Rabbinical College, 1981.

"Rabbi Esriel Hildesheimer and the Quest for Religious Authority: The Earliest Years." *Modern Judaism* 1, no. 3 (December 1981): 279–97.

"American Courts and the Enforceability of the Ketubah as a Private Contract: An Investigation of Some Recent U.S. Court Decisions." *Conservative Judaism* 35, no. 3 (Spring 1982): 35–42. Co-authored with James S. Ellenson.

"The Role of Reform in Selected German-Jewish Orthodox Responsa: A Sociological Analysis." *Hebrew Union College Annual* 53 (1982): 357–80.

"Jewish Religious Leadership in Germany: Its Spiritual and Cultural Legacy." In *Genocide: Critical Issues of the Holocaust, A Companion Volume to the Film "Genocide*," edited by Alex Grobman and Daniel Landes, 72–81. Los Angeles: Simon Wiesenthal Center, 1983.

"Church-Sect Theory, Religious Authority, and Modern Jewish Orthodoxy: A Case Study." In *Approaches to the Study of Modern Judaism*, edited by Marc Raphael, 63–83. Atlanta: Scholars Press, 1983.

"Jewish Tradition, Contemporary Sensibilities, and Halakha: A Responsum by Rabbi David Zvi Hoffmann." *Journal of Reform Judaism* 30, no. 1 (Winter 1983): 49–56. Co-authored with Robert Levine.

"The Evolution of Orthodox Attitudes towards Conversion in the Modern Period." *Conservative Judaism* 36, no. 4 (Summer 1983): 57–73.

"The Holocaust, Covenant, and Revelation." *Encounter* 45, no. 1 (Winter 1984): 53–59.

"Liberal Judaism in Israel: Problems and Prospects." *Journal of Reform Judaism* 31, no. 1 (Winter 1984): 60–70.

"The Dilemma of Jewish Education: To Learn and to Do." *Judaism* 33, no. 2 (Spring 1984): 212–20. Co-authored with Isa Aron.

"Jewish Covenant and Christian Trinitarianism: An Analysis of a Responsum on Jewish-Christian Relations in the Modern World." In *Jewish Civilization: Essays and Studies*, edited by Ronald Brauner, 3:88–103. Philadelphia: Reconstructionist Rabbinical College, 1985.

"Jewish Legal Interpretation: Literary, Social, and Ethical Contexts." *Semeia* 34 (1985): 93–114.

"Representative Orthodox Responsa on Conversion and Intermarriage in the Contemporary Era." *Jewish Social Studies* 47, nos. 3–4 (Summer–Fall 1985): 209–20.

"Mordecai Kaplan." In *Biographical Dictionary of Social Welfare in America*, edited by Walter Trattner, 432–34. New York: Greenwood, 1986.

"'Our Brothers and Our Flesh': Rabbi Esriel Hildesheimer and the Jews of Ethiopia." *Judaism* 35, no. 1 (Winter 1986): 63–65.

"Eternity and Time." In *Contemporary Jewish Religious Thought*, edited by Arthur A. Cohen and Paul Mendes-Flohr, 189–94. New York: Charles Scribner & Sons, 1986.

"Abraham Geiger," "Esriel Hildesheimer," "Samson Raphael Hirsch," "David Hoffmann," "Samuel Holdheim," and "Isaac Eichanan Spektor." In the *Encyclopedia of Religion*. New York: Macmillan, 1986.

"The Integrity of Reform within *Kelal Yisra-el*." *Yearbook of the Central Conference of American Rabbis* 96 (1986): 19–32.

"The Orthodox Rabbinate and Apostasy in Nineteenth-Century Germany and Hungary." In *Jewish Apostasy in the Modern World: Converts and Missionaries in Historical Perspective*, edited by Todd Endelman, 165–88. New York: Holmes and Meier, 1987.

"Scholarship and Faith: David Zvi Hoffmann and His Relationship to *Wissenschaft des Judentums*." *Modern Judaism* 8, no. 1 (February 1988): 27–40. Co-authored with Richard Jacobs.

"Halakhah for Liberal Jews." *Reconstructionist* 53, no. 5 (March 1988): 28–30, 32.

"Modernization and the Jews of Nineteenth-Century Frankfurt and Berlin: A Portrait of Communities in Transition." Dworsky Center for Jewish Studies, University of Minnesota, Paper no. 2 (1988): 1–23.

"The Validity of Liturgical Pluralism." *Reconstructionist* 53, no. 7 (June 1988): 16–19.

Tradition in Transition: Orthodoxy, Halakhah, and the Boundaries of Modern Jewish Identity. Lanham: University Press of America, 1989.

"The Challenges of Halakhah." *Judaism* 38, no. 3 (1989): 358–65.

"A Jewish Response to Jack Verheyden: On the Christian Doctrine of God." In *Three Faiths—One God*, edited by John Hick and Edmund S. Meltzer, 58–62. London: Macmillan, 1989.

Rabbi Esriel Hildesheimer and the Creation of a Modern Jewish Orthodoxy. Tuscaloosa: University of Alabama Press, 1990.

"'Who Is a Jew?' Issues of Jewish Status and Identity and Their Relationship to the Nature of Judaism in the Modern World." In *Berit Mila in the Reform Context*, edited by Lewis M. Barth, 69–81. Secaucus NJ: Carol, 1990.

"Sacrifice and Atonement in the Literature of German Orthodoxy: Defense of a Discarded Institution." In *Versöhnung in der jüdischen und christlichen Liturgie*, edited by Hanspeter Heinz, Klaus Kienzler, and Jakob Petuchowski, 27–40. Freiburg: Herder, 1990.

"Jewish Identity in the Changing World of American Religion: A Response to Jonathan Sarna." In *Jewish Identity in America*, edited by David Gordis and Yoav Ben-Horin, 105–10. Los Angeles: Susan and David Wilstein Institute of Jewish Policy Studies, 1991.

"The Continued Renewal of North American Jewish Theology: Some Recent Works." *Journal of Reform Judaism* 38, no. 1 (Winter 1991): 1–16.

"A Theology of Fear: Liberal Jewish Thought and the Nuclear Arms Race." In *Confronting Omnicide: Jewish Reflections on Weapons of Mass Destruction*, edited by Daniel Landes, 142–63. Northvale NJ: Jason Aronson, 1991.

"Reform Judaism in Present-Day America: The Evidence of the Gates of Prayer." In *Threescore and Ten: Essays in Honor of Rabbi Seymour J. Cohen*, edited by Abraham Karp, 377–85. Jersey City: Ktav, 1991.

Translation from the Hebrew of Jacob Katz's "Towards a Biography of the Hatam Sofer." In *From East and West: Jews in a Changing Europe, 1750–1870*, edited by Frances Malino and David Sorkin, 223-66. Oxford: Basil Blackwell, 1991.

"How to Draw Guidance from a Heritage: Jewish Approaches to Mortal Choices." In *The Ethics of Choice: A Time to Be Born and a Time to Die*, edited by Barry Kogan, 219–32. Hawthorne NY: Aldine de Groyter, 1991.

"German Orthodoxy, Jewish Law, and the Uses of Kant." In *The Jewish Legacy and the German Conscience: Essays in Memory of Rabbi Joseph Asher*, edited by Raphael Asher and Moses Rischin, 73–84. Berkeley: Judah L. Magnes Museum, 1991.

"The Other Side of S'vara." *S'vara: A Journal of Jewish Law and Philosophy* 2, no. 2 (1991): 8–10.

"Religious Pluralism in Israel: American Jewish Perspectives and Policy Options." *American Jewish Committee* (1992): 1–27.

"Sociology and Halakha: A Response." *Tradition* (1993): 5–22.

"German Jewish Orthodoxy: Tradition in the Context of Culture." In *The Uses of Tradition: Jewish Continuity in the Modern Era*, edited by Jack Wertheimer. New York: Jewish Theological Seminary and Harvard, 1993.

"Conservative Halakha in Israel: A Review Essay." *Modern Judaism* 13, no. 2 (May 1993): 191–204.

Bits of Honey: Essays for Samson H. Levey. Atlanta: Scholars Press, 1993. Co-edited with Stanley Chyet.

"A Note on Peter Berger's 'Charisma and the Social Location of Israelite Prophecy.'" In *Bits of Honey: Essays for Samson H. Levey*, edited by Stanley Chyet and David Ellenson, 229–32. Atlanta: Scholars Press, 1993.

"American Values and Jewish Tradition: Synthesis or Conflict." *Judaism* 42, no. 2 (Spring 1993): 243–49.

"Eugene Borowitz." In *Interpreters of Judaism in the Late Twentieth Century*, edited by Steven Katz, 17–39. Washington DC: B'nai B'rith Books, 1993. Co-authored with Lori Krafte-Jacobs.

Between Tradition and Culture: The Dialectics of Jewish Religion and Identity in the Modern World. Atlanta: Scholars Press, 1994.

"Retroactive Annulment of Conversion: A Survey of Halakhic Sources." In *Conversion to Judaism in Jewish Law*, edited by Walter Jacob and Moshe Zemer, 49–66. Tel Aviv: Rodef Shalom, 1994.

"Zion in the Mind of the American Rabbinate: A Survey of Sermons and Pamphlets of the 1940s." In *The Americanization of the Jews*, edited by Naomi Cohen, Norman Cohen, and Robert Seltzer, 193–212. New York: New York University Press, 1994.

"Eugene Borowitz: A Tribute on the Occasion of His 70th Birthday." *Jewish Book Annual* 51 (1994): 125–36.

"Wissenschaft des Judenthums" and "Samson Raphael Hirsch." In *HarperCollins Dictionary of Religion*. New York: HarperCollins, 1995.

"Artificial Fertilization and Procreative Autonomy: Thoughts Occasioned by Two Israeli Responsa." In *The Fetus and Fertility in Jewish Law*, edited by Walter Jacob and Moshe Zemer, 19–38. Tel Aviv: Rodef Shalom, 1995.

"A Disputed Precedent: The Prague Organ in 19th-Century Central European Legal Literature and Polemics." *Leo Baeck Institute Yearbook* 40, no. 1 (1995): 251–64.

"A Sociologist's View of Contemporary Jewish Orthodoxy: The Work of Samuel Heilman." *Religious Studies Review* 21, no. 1 (January 1995): 14–18.

"Reform Zionism Today: A Consideration of First Principles." *(Rabbi Stanley M. Davids) Journal of Reform Zionism* 2 (March 1995): 13–19.

"Transformation of the Rabbinate: Future Directions and Prospects." In *Women Rabbis: Exploration & Celebration Papers Delivered at an Academic Conference Honoring Twenty Years of Women in the Rabbinate, 1972–1992*, edited by Gary Zola, 93–108. Cincinnati: HUC-JIR Rabbinic Alumni Press, 1996.

"Emancipation and the Directions of Modern Judaism: The Lessons of *Melitz Yosher*." Edited by Emile Schrijver. *Studia Rosenthaliana* 30, no. 1 (1996): 118–36.

"Symposium on Jewish Belief." *Commentary* (August 1996): 12–13.

"Orthodox Reactions to Modern Jewish Reform: The Paradigm of Germany." In *The Routledge History of Jewish Philosophy*, edited by Daniel H. Frank and Oliver Leaman, 732–58. London: Routledge, 1996.

"Envisioning Israel in the Liturgies of North American Liberal Judaism." *Envisioning Israel: The Changing Ideals and Images of North American Jews*, edited by Allon Gal, 117–48. Jerusalem: Magnes, 1996.

"Interreligious Learning and the Formation of Jewish Religious Identity." *Religious Education* 91, no. 4 (Fall 1996): 80–88.

"A Responsum on Fundraising." *Judaism* 45, no. 4 (Fall 1996): 490–96.

"A Separate Life." In *Jewish Spiritual Journeys: 20 Essays Written to Honor the Occasion of the 70th Birthday of Eugene B. Borowitz*, edited by Lawrence A. Hoffman and Arnold J. Wolf, 93–101. West Orange NJ: Behrman, 1996.

"Moshe Zemer's *Halakhah Shefuyah*: An Israeli Vision of Reform and Halakhah," *CCAR Journal* 43, no. 2 (Spring/Summer 1996): 31–41. Co-authored with Michael White.

"Zionism." In *Jewish Women in America: An Historical Encyclopedia*, vol. 2, edited by Paula Hyman and Deborah Dash Moore, 1544–48. New York: Routledge, 1997.

"Modern Liturgies." In *Minhag Ami/My People's Prayer Book*, edited by Lawrence A. Hoffman. Woodstock VT: Jewish Lights. 1: The *Sh'ma* and Its Blessings (1997); 2: The *Amidah* (1998); 3: *P'sukei D'zimrah* (Morning Psalms) (1999); 4: *Seder K'riat HaTorah* (The Torah Service) (2000); 5: *Birkhot Hashachar* (Morning Blessings) (2001); 6: *Tachanun* and Concluding Prayers (2002); 7: Shabbat at Home (2003); 8: *Kabbalat Shabbat* (Welcoming Shabbat in the Synagogue) (2004); 9: Experiencing Nightfall: *Minhah* and *Ma'ariv* for Shabbat and Weekdays (2005); and 10: Shabbat Morning: *Shacharit* and *Musaf* (Morning and Additional Services) (2007).

"Some Reflections on Max Weber on Judaism and the Jews in the Modern Era." In *What Is Modern about Modern Jewish History?* edited by Marc Raphael, 78–88. Williamsburg VA: College of William and Mary, 1997.

"'A Seminary of Sacred Learning': The JTS Rabbinical Curriculum in Historical Perspective." In *A History of the Jewish Theological Seminary of America*, edited by Jack Wertheimer, 527–91. New York: Jewish Theological Seminary, 1997. Co-authored with Lee Bycel.

"Preface." In *Engendering Judaism*, by Rachel Adler, viii–xi. Philadelphia: Jewish Publication Society, 1997.

"Jakob Petuchowski: The Man and His Thought." In *Studies in Modern Theology and Prayer*, edited by Jakob Petuchowski, xi–xvii. Philadelphia: Jewish Publication Society, 1998.

"The Rabbiner-Seminar Codicil: An Instrument of Boundary Maintenance." In *Through Those Near to Me: Essays in Honor of Jerome R. Malino*, edited by Glen Lebetkin and Jerome R. Malino, 200–207. Danbury CT: United Jewish Center, 1998.

"The Direction of Modern Jewish Thought: A Comment." In *Contemporary Jewish Theology*, edited by Elliot N. Dorff and Louis E. Newman, 498–501. Oxford: Oxford University Press, 1999.

"Visions of *Gemeindeorthodoxie* in Weimar Germany: The Positions of N. A. Nobel and I. Unna." In *In Search of Jewish Community: Jewish Identities in Germany and Austria. 1918–1933*, edited by Michael Brenner and Derek Penslar, 36–55. Bloomington: Indiana University Press, 1999.

"Samuel Cohon." In *American National Biography*, edited by John A. Garraty. Oxford: Oxford University Press, 1999.

"Autonomy and Norms in Reform Judaism." *CCAR Journal* 46, no. 2 (Spring 1999): 21–28.

"A New Rite from Israel: Reflections on Siddur Va'ani Tefillati of the Israeli Masorati (Conservative) Movement." *Studies in Contemporary Jewry* 15 (1999): 151–68.

"Samuel Holdheim on the Legal Character of Jewish Marriage: A Contemporary Comment on His Position." In *Marriage and Impediments to Marriage in Jewish Tradition*, edited by Walter Jacob and Moshe Zemer, 1–26. Tel Aviv: Freehof Institute, 1999.

"The *Israelitischer Gebetbücher* of Abraham Geiger and Manuel Joel: A Study in Nineteenth-Century German-Jewish Communal Liturgy." *Leo Baeck Institute Yearbook* 44, no. 1 (1999): 143–64.

"Mordecai Kaplan." In *The Routledge Encyclopedia of Philosophy*, 433. London: Routledge, 1999.

"Commentary on Einhorn and Hirsch." In *The Jewish Political Tradition*, edited by Michael Walzer, Menachem Lorberbaum, and Noam Zohar, 373–78. New Haven: Yale University Press, 2000.

"A Jewish View of the Christian God." In *Christianity in Jewish Terms*, edited by Tikva Frymer-Kensky et al., 69–76. Boulder: Westview, 2000.

"Marcia Falk's *The Book of Blessings*: The Issue Is Theological." *CCAR Journal* 47, no. 2 (Spring 2000): 18–23.

"Women and the Study of Torah: A Responsum by Rabbi Zalman Sorotzkin of Jerusalem." *Nashim: A Journal of Women's Studies and Gender Issues* 4 (2000): 119–39. Co-authored with Elissa Ben-Naim.

"A Jewish Legal Authority Addresses Jewish-Christian Dialogue: Two Responsa of Rabbi Moshe Feinstein." *American Jewish Archives* 52, nos. 1–2 (2000): 112–28.

"History, Memory, and Relationship." In *Memory and History in Christianity and Judaism*, edited by Michael Signer, 170–81. Notre Dame: University of Notre Dame Press, 2000.

"Gender, Halakhah, and Women's Suffrage: Responsa of the First Three Chief Rabbis on the Public Role of Women in the Jewish State." In *Gender Issues in Jewish Law*, edited by Walter Jacob and Moshe Zemer, 58–81. New York: Berghahn Books, 2001. Co-authored with Michael Rosen.

"A Vindication of Judaism: The Polemics of the Hertz Pentateuch: A Review Essay." *Modern Judaism* 21, no. 1 (February 2001): 67–77.

"Jewish Legal Interpretation and Moral Values: Two Responsa by Rabbi Hayyim David Halevi on the Obligations of the Israeli Government towards Its Minority Populations." *CCAR Journal* 48, no. 3 (Summer 2001): 5–20.

"Judaism Resurgent? American Jews and the Evolving Expression of Jewish Values and Jewish Identity in Modern American Life." *Studies in Contemporary Jewry* 17 (2001): 156–71.

"David Hartman on the Modern Jewish Condition: A Review Essay." *Modern Judaism* 21, no. 3 (2001): 256–81.

"Interpretive Fluidity and *P'sak* in a Case of *Pidyon Sh'vuyim*: An Analysis of a Modern Israeli Responsum as Illuminated by the Thought of David Hartman." In *Judaism and Modernity: The Religious Philosophy of David Hartman*, edited by Jonathan Malino, 341–67. Burlington VT: Ashgate, 2001.

"Jacob Katz on the Origins and Dimensions of Jewish Modernity: The Centrality of the German Experience." In *The Pride of Jacob: Essays on Jacob Katz and His Work*, edited by Jay Harris, 97–123. Cambridge: Harvard, 2002.

"Parallel Worlds: *Wissenschaft* and *Pesaq* in the *Seridei Eish*." In *History and Literature: New Readings of Jewish Texts in Honor of Arnold J. Band*, edited by William Cutter and David Jacobson, 55–74. Providence: Brown Judaic Studies, 2002.

"Rabbi Samson Raphael Hirsch to Liepman Phillip Prins of Amsterdam: An 1873 Responsum on Education." *Edah Journal* 3, no. 2 (2003): 2–5.

After Emancipation: Jewish Religious Responses to Modernity. Cincinnati: Hebrew Union College Press, 2004.

"A Portrait of the *Poseq* as Modern Religious Leader: An Analysis of Selected Writings of Rabbi Hayyim David Halevi." In *Jewish Religious Leadership: Image and Reality*, edited by Jack Wertheimer, 2:673–93. New York: Jewish Theological Seminary Press, 2004.

"Wissenschaft des Judentums, Historical Consciousness, and Jewish Faith: The Diverse Paths of Frankel, Auerbach, and Halevy." *Leo Baeck Memorial Lecture* 48 (2004): 1–15.

"On Conversion and Intermarriage: The Evidence of Nineteenth-Century Hungarian Orthodox Rabbinic Writings." In *Text and Context: Essays in Modern Jewish History and Historiography in Honor of Ismar Schorsch*, edited by Eli Lederhendler and Jack Wertheimer, 321–46. New York: Jewish Theological Seminary Press, 2005.

"Rabbi Leo Baeck: A Personal Appraisal and Appreciation." *European Judaism* 39, no. 2 (2006): 58–64.

"American Rabbinic Training," *Encyclopaedia Judaica*, 2nd ed. (2006): 17:23–31.

"The Talmudic Principle, 'If One Comes Forth to Slay You, Forestall by Slaying Him,' in Israeli Public Policy: A Responsum by Rabbi Hayyim David Halevi." In *Studies in Mediaeval Halakhah in Honor of Stephen M. Passamaneck*, edited by Alyssa Gray and Bernard Jackson, 73–79. *Jewish Law Association Studies* 17 (2007).

"American Jewish Denominationalism: Yesterday, Today, and Tomorrow." *Reconstructionist* 71, no. 2 (Spring 2007): 5–15.

"'Creative Misreadings' in Representative Post-Emancipation Halakhic Writings on Conversion and Intermarriage." In *Napoleon's Influence on Jewish Law: The Sanhedrin of 1807 and Its Modern Consequences*, edited by Walter Jacob and Moshe Zemer, 79–93. Pittsburgh: Solomon B. Freehof Institute of Progressive Halakha, 2007.

"An Ideology for the Liberal Jewish Day School: A Philosophical-Sociological Investigation." *Journal of Jewish Education* 74, no. 3 (2008): 245–63.

"Michael A. Meyer and His Vision of Reform Judaism and the Reform Rabbinate: A Lifetime of Devotion and Concern." In *Mediating Modernity: Challenges and Trends in the Jewish Encounter with the Modern World, Essays in Honor of Michael A. Meyer*, edited by Lauren B. Strauss and Michael Brenner, 17–24. Detroit: Wayne State University Press, 2008.

"Laws and Judgments as a 'Bridge to a Better World': *Parashat Mishpatim*." In *Torah Queeries: Weekly Commentaries on the Hebrew Bible*, edited by Gregg Drinkwater, David Shneer, and Joshua Lesser, 98–101. New York: New York University Press, 2009.

"Rabbi Hayim David Halevi on Christians and Christianity: An Analysis of Selected Legal Writings of an Israeli Authority." In *Transforming Relations: Essays on Jews and Christians throughout History in Honor of Michael A. Signer*, edited by Franklin Harkins, 340–61. Notre Dame: Notre Dame Press, 2010.

"Heschel and the Roots of *Kavanah*." In *New Essays in American Jewish History: Commemorating the Sixtieth Anniversary of the Founding of the American Jewish Archives*, edited by Pamela S. Nadell, Jonathan D. Sarna, and Lance J. Sussman, 345–66. Cincinnati: American Jewish Archives of Hebrew Union College–Jewish Institute of Religion, 2010. Co-authored with Michael Marmur.

"Colleagues and Friends: Letters between Rabbi Samuel Belkin and Rabbi William G. Braude." In *Continuity and Change: A Festschrift in Honor of Irving Greenberg's 75th Birthday*, edited by Steven Bayme and Steven Katz, 63–79. Lanham MD: University Press of America, 2011.

"German Orthodox Rabbinical Writings on the Jewish Textual Education of Women: The Views of Rabbi Samson Raphael Hirsch and Rabbi Esriel Hildesheimer." In *Gender and Jewish History*, edited by Marion A. Kaplan and Deborah Dash Moore, 158–69. Bloomington: Indiana University Press, 2011.

"The Rock from Which They Were Cleft: An Review-Essay of Haim Amsalem's *Zera Yisrael* and *Mekor Yisrael*." *Jewish Review of Books* (Winter 2012): 41–43.

"A Zionist Reading of Abraham Geiger and His Biblical Scholarship." In *Making a Difference: Essays on the Bible and Judaism in Honor of Tamara Cohn Eskenazi*, edited by David J. A. Clines, Kent Harold Richards, and Jacob L. Wright, 121–31. Sheffield: Sheffield Phoenix Press, 2012.

Pledges of Jewish Allegiance: Conversion, Law, and Policymaking in Nineteenth- and Twentieth-Century Orthodox Responsa. Stanford: Stanford University Press, 2012. Co-authored with Daniel Gordis.

"Rabbi Eliezer Berkovits on Conversion: An Inclusive Orthodox Approach." *Shofar: An Interdisciplinary Journal of Jewish Studies* 31, no. 4 (Summer 2013): 37–53.

"Mothers and Sons, Sisters and Brothers: The Women of Reform Judaism and Hebrew Union College–Jewish Institute of Religion." In *Sisterhood: A Centennial History of Women of Reform Judaism*, edited by Carole Balin, Dana Herman, Jonathan D. Sarna, and Gary P. Zola, 72–85. Cincinnati: HUC Press, 2013. Co-authored with Jane Karlin.

"The Responsa of Rabbi Solomon Judah Rapoport and Rabbi Samson Raphael Hirsch on the Proposed Judah Touro Monument: A Translation of Two Texts." In *As a Perennial Spring: A Festschrift Honoring Rabbi Dr. Norman Lamm*, edited by Bentsi Cohen, 163–71. New York: Downhill, 2013.

"Denominationalism: History and Hopes." In *Jewish Megatrends: Charting the Course of the American Jewish Future,* edied by Sidney Schwarz. Woodstock VT: Jewish Lights, 2013.

IN THE JPS SCHOLAR OF DISTINCTION SERIES

To order or obtain more information on these or
other Jewish Publication Society titles, visit jps.org.